HARRIET MARTINEAU
IN THE LONDON
DAILY NEWS

GARLAND REFERENCE LIBRARY
OF THE HUMANITIES
(VOL. 1600)

HARRIET MARTINEAU IN THE LONDON *DAILY NEWS*

Selected Contributions, 1852–1866

Edited by

Elisabeth Sanders Arbuckle

GARLAND PUBLISHING, INC.
New York & London / 1994

© 1994 Elisabeth Sanders Arbuckle
All rights reserved

Library of Congress Cataloging-in-Publication Data

Martineau, Harriet, 1802–1876.
   Harriet Martineau in the London Daily News : selected contributions, 1852–1866 / edited by Elisabeth Sanders Arbuckle.
     p. cm. — (Garland reference library of the humanities ; vol. 1600)
   Includes index.
   ISBN 0-8153-0835-3
   1. Arbuckle, Elisabeth Sanders. II. Title. III. Series.
PR4984.M5A6 1993
824'8—dc20   93-22864

Printed on acid-free, 250-year-life paper
Manufactured in the United States of America

Contents

Introduction ix

I. Women
1. Australia: 8 June 1852 — 3
2. Harriet Beecher Stowe/Cotton Supply: 22 April 1853 — 11
3. Married Women's Property Laws: 21 October 1856 — 19
4. Women's Fashions: 15 October 1861 — 31
5. Nurses: 23 February 1865 — 39
6. Education of Middle Class Girls: 30 March 1865 — 47

II. Reviews of Essays, Social and Economic Issues, and Education
7. William Rathbone Greg: Essays: 27 January 1853 — 57
8. Cholera at Newcastle: 24 September 1853 — 63
9. Sydney Smith: Essays: 24 July 1854 — 69
10. Temperance: 7 August 1855 — 75
11. Railroads: The United States, England, and Russia: 10 February 1857 — 83
12. The National Association for the Promotion of Social Science: 25 October 1858 — 91
13. Cotton Supply: India, U.S.A./Slavery: 18 February 1859 — 99
14. Sheffield Outrages: 26 March 1862 — 107
15. Drainage: 27 May 1862 — 113

16. Factory Act: 4 August 1863 — 121
17. Education: Rural Laborers: 11 November 1864 — 129

III. The Crimean War
18. Czars: 15 June 1853 — 141
19. Cromwell vs. Aberdeen: 26 December 1853 — 149
20. Circassians: 18 January 1854 — 155
21. Allies: 2 March 1854 — 161
22. The Baltic Sea: 16 May 1854 — 169
23. Russian History: 25 August 1854 — 177
24. Sebastopol: 7 November 1854 — 185
25. Raglan's Successor: 3 July 1855 — 191
26. The Czar and Scandinavia: 19 November 1856 — 199
27. Sidney Herbert: 2 December 1861 — 207

IV. Politics and Foreign Affairs
28. Gervinus: 14 February 1853 — 217
29. Robert Burns: 25 January 1859 — 225
30. War of Opinion: Italy: 26 May 1859 — 233
31. Syria: 25 September 1860 — 239

V. The United States: Antislavery
32. *The Times*: Kansas and *Dred*: 24 September 1856 — 247
33. Presidential Election: 15 November 1856 — 255
34. Slave Trade/U. S. Newspapers: 25 November 1856 — 263
35. Turgenev vs. Everett: 4 June 1858 — 271
36. The Isthmus of Panama: 27 July 1858 — 279
37. The Isthmus of Panama: 15 October 1858 — 287
38. Sale of Pierce Butler's Slaves: 4 April 1859 — 295
39. Emerson: The *Atlantic Monthly*: 11 November 1862 — 301
40. William Lloyd Garrison: 9 January 1866 — 307

Contents

Appendix
  Harriet Martineau's Contributions to the
    London *Daily News*   317

Index of Names, Topics, and Titles of Works by
  Harriet Martineau   431

Introduction

The productive life and work of Harriet Martineau (1802–1876) show what a determined Victorian woman could achieve. Martineau came to London from a provincial non-conformist background, prefiguring her intellectually more forceful successor George Eliot. While she lived in London, Martineau enjoyed the *éclat* of literary celebrity. As did her friends Elizabeth Barrett Browning and Florence Nightingale, Martineau also spent long periods of her life as an invalid.

Martineau grew up in Norwich, where her Unitarian parents encouraged her studies but failed to support the feelings of emotional deprivation that came partly from her progressive deafness. In early childhood, Martineau began to take refuge in serious reading. She survived a turbulent adolescence and, when the family lost its money during the financial panic of the 1820s, set herself to an apprenticeship in writing. Martineau's success seemed a phenomenon but, in fact, came from calculation and hard work. In the early 1830s, she moved with her mother to London and thereafter lived on her earnings.

Martineau's writing career may be briefly summarized. In 1821, she began to send essays and tales to the Unitarian *Monthly Repository*. From 1832 to 1834, she managed a publishing coup with two series of didactic tales that illustrate workings of the new science of "political economy." Prudently investing her earnings, she sailed off for a two-year tour of the United States. Back again in London, 1836 to 1839, she published two books on America and *Deerbrook*, an original novel of domestic realism. Then, owing partly to family tension, Martineau fell ill. A tumor kept her bedridden for five years until friends urged her to try mesmerism. She recovered and soon set out to travel and to write more books and articles. In 1848, publisher Charles Knight asked her to take over his chronicle history of nineteenth-century England. After the history, Martineau translated Comte and, in a joint edition of "letters" to and from her friend Henry Atkinson, declared she had become an agnostic. Through this period and after, her articles appeared in journals such as the *Westminster*, *Edinburgh*, and *Quarterly Reviews* and *Macmillan's*, *Household Words*, and *Once a Week*. Finally, from 1852 to 1866, Martineau took on the task of "leader" [editorial] writer for the London *Daily News*.

When she began to write for the *Daily News*, Martineau enjoyed vigorous health and high professional respect. As a journalist, writer on political economy (and what we now define as sociology and psychology), travel writer, novelist, and compiler of a history, Martineau competed in the predominantly male world of Victorian publishing. During the spring of 1852, for example, she wrote articles for Dickens's *Household Words* and a review of the German historian Niebuhr for the *Westminster Review*. She was also working on her translation of Comte's *Cours de philosophie positive*. In her free time, she gave talks to her Ambleside neighbors on emigration to Australia. In April, she was surprised by a request from Frederick Knight Hunt of the London *Daily News*: Hunt wanted her to send him occasional leaders—a demanding genre she had not yet tried. Martineau and Hunt corresponded (they were to meet in July), and Hunt then printed six leaders on emigrating to Australia plus others Martineau sent. At Hunt's suggestion, Martineau made a journey through parts of Ireland, from where she wrote twenty-seven "Letters from Ireland" (printed in the *Daily News* 13 August to 14 October 1852) that combine travel narrative with social, economic, and political commentary—in the manner of her books on the United States and the Near East. Martineau was now embarked on the last and arguably most significant phase of her career.

The *Daily News* had been launched in 1846 as an organ of liberal reform. Most of its financial support came from the printing firm of Bradbury and Evans, with Charles Dickens as first editor. Aimed at middle-class readers, the new publication advocated "progress and improvement, of education, civil and religious liberty, and equal legislation." By the mid-1850s, editor William Weir told Martineau he hoped "to stir up the more or less instructed class to self-exertion." Implicitly too, the newspaper strove to secure the "loyalty of the working class to the social order." Martineau's sympathy with these aims sealed her close personal relationship with three successive *Daily News* editors.

Dickens lasted only briefly as editor of the *Daily News*, to be followed by John Forster, his future biographer, then Frederick Knight Hunt (1814–1854). Hunt had begun in a newspaper printing office at sixteen, working days as a barrister's clerk. He later studied medicine, edited a medical journal, and qualified as a surgeon—but writing and newspaper editing were his real vocation. When Dickens chose Hunt as subeditor for the *Daily News* in 1846, he had served on the *Illustrated London News* and had edited the *Pictorial Times*. (His book *The Fourth Estate: Contributions towards a History of Newspapers* came out in 1850.) As editor of the *Daily News*, 1851 to 1854, Hunt by his energy and judgment made the paper a commercial success. In July 1852, he called on Martineau at Portobello, Scotland, to confirm their new partnership. "For two half days he poured out so rich a stream of conversation," she records, "I felt a bright new career was indeed opened to me." In September 1854, Hunt met and took Martineau to his home in London, where they agreed on a "glorious programme of work" to Christmas. Two months later Hunt died of cholera. "One of the most upright and rational of men," a saddened Martineau calls him in her *Autobiography*.[1]

William Weir (1802–1858), a widely read Scot, succeeded Hunt as *Daily News* editor. Weir had studied at the University of Göttingen and was a member of the Scottish bar. He had worked as an editor and occasional writer in Scotland and England and in 1846 became a financial writer on the *Daily News*. Like Hunt, Weir relied heavily on Martineau as a leader writer. During the Crimean War, he trusted her to formulate the newspaper's anti-French, pro-hostilities stand. In 1857, following the Indian mutiny, he instigated her *British Rule in India: A Historical Sketch*, followed by *Suggestions towards the Future Government of India*

(1858). Like Martineau, Weir suffered from deafness. He died unexpectedly, after a short illness, in September 1858.

Thomas Walker (1822–1898), a young member of the *Daily News* staff, next took over as editor. He quickly assured Martineau he "could not get on without" her. Like Hunt, Walker came of humble parents and through Hunt got work on the *Daily News* editorial staff in 1846. (Walker later contributed numerous entries to *The Men of the Time*—a publication finally merged with *Who's Who*.) The growing tension in the United States, with the threat to Britain's cotton supply, gave Martineau's writing on American affairs decisive importance. British fear over cotton and defiant posturing by the North, once the Civil War started, brought on a public backlash in favor of the Confederacy. The proprietors of the *Daily News* divided over the American issue. Walker, relying on Martineau's American expertise, held firm for the North. Later, managing editor of the *Daily News* Sir John Robinson eulogized Martineau as a newspaperwoman and quoted W. E. Forster, that it was "Harriet Martineau alone who kept public opinion on the right [i. e., pro-North] side."[2]

Three years after Martineau joined its staff, in 1855, the *Daily News* competed with nine London dailies. *The Times*—with enormous advertising revenues and access to international news—dominated the market. Though outspoken in its views and sometimes (its enemies *and* friends complained) perverse, *The Times* derived much of its political clout from the settled custom of editorial anonymity. MPs and cabinet ministers are known to have passed confidential information to *The Times'* editor and to have written crucial leaders, but they also trembled at its "thunder." In favor of free trade and social justice, the *Daily News* aspired to provide a liberal counterpoise to the powerful, usually conservative voice of *The Times*.

Ironically, Martineau, like readers all over the country, looked to *The Times* for her news. Though it had opposed repeal of the stamp duty on newspapers—reduced from 4d to 1d in 1836 and abolished in October 1855—*The Times* kept the lead among all new competitors. By the time she began work for the *Daily News*, Martineau had moved to Ambleside in the Lake District. Hunt arranged for her to get her copy of *The Times* by teatime, so in the evening she could scan the day's events to decide on a

Introduction

topic. Next morning, she wrote up the leader in two or three hours and sent it to London by rail in time for that evening's wrap-up of the newspaper. In December 1853, Martineau successfully pressured Sir Rowland Hill (responsible for the penny post) to add a morning mail pick-up from Ambleside.[3]

Besides furnishing her with a source of news, *The Times* served Martineau's writing strategies. As a whipping boy, a purveyor of misinformation and ignorance, *The Times*—especially on American affairs—prompted Martineau to attack vested interests that in her view were retarding progress and human understanding. When *The Times*, for example, sent its famed Crimean War correspondent William Howard Russell to Washington in 1861, Martineau sputtered to a friend:

> I'm afraid Mr. Russell won't do us much good this time. How poor his letters are! He went ignorant; and now he must find himself in a false position.

Eight months later, she assaulted the "ruffianism" of *The Times* and "the captious contempt" of Russell, who had forgotten he could see "nothing of genuine American life at Washington [and] has never seen the life of the North at all."[4] A reference to *The Times*, in Martineau's writing, signaled sarcasm or rebuke.

Martineau based her interpretation of events in the United States on the experiences of her tour of 1834 to 1836. An unusual and distinguished visitor, she was able to meet dignitaries in both the North and the South to study the country's laws and customs and to make friends with such later informants as Maria Weston Chapman. At home in England, she began to receive a steady stream of American newspapers and other (mostly antislavery) publications. Over the years, well-known Americans like Ralph Waldo Emerson and Margaret Fuller came to Ambleside to stay with her.

Virtually all Martineau's *Daily News* writing on the United States attacks slavery directly or indirectly. In July 1852, for example, she notes the illegal detention of colored British seamen in Southern ports. As events lead towards a confrontation of North and South, she points to the slavery-related European/American aggression in Central America, to filibustering (by American freebooters) in Central America and Cuba, to western expansionism and fighting in Kansas, to

French/American revival of the slave trade, to American presidential elections dominated by the slavery issue, to the new freesoil movement, to final development of the North/South crisis, and to the slave system's waste of men and resources, according to irrefutable economic law.

Clearly, utilitarian and reform principles underlie Martineau's writing for the *Daily News*. We have noted her early leaders on Australia, her "letters" from Ireland and some specific issues of the American antislavery struggle. In fact, Martineau's contributions range through the spectrum of *Daily News* concerns. She writes about responsible (utilitarian) government of India. She speaks as an expert on political, military, and trade relations with countries of the Near and Far East and of Europe. She acts as an authority on agriculture, discusses technical problems of manufacturing, lectures capital and labor on their duties and mutual reliance, explores ways to insure a cotton supply, argues in favor of more accessible and practical education for both boys and girls, supports health measures like vaccination and learning to swim, publicizes government sanitary efforts such as inspection and quarantine, backs military and government reorganization and reform and seriously treats a number of problems peculiar to working and middle-class women. She produces obituaries, special reports, and letters to the editor. She reviews books and journals and compiles yearly summaries of events.

In her *Autobiography*, Martineau records that in 1853 *Daily News* editor Hunt advised her to buy books and to visit London often, "to keep up with the times." Hunt originally asked her to write for the *Daily News*, she claims, because of her *History of the Peace*.[5] "[A]nd now that [the Crimean] war was beginning, my recent study of the politics of the last half-century *was* a fair qualification." The political beliefs Martineau shared with Hunt would shape her facts:

> We were precisely agreed as to the principle of the war, as to the character of the Aberdeen Ministry, as to the fallaciousness and mischievousness of the negotiations for the Austrian alliance, and as to the vicious absurdity of Prussia, and the mode and degree in which Louis

Introduction xv

Napoleon was to be regarded as the representative of the French nation.

Though Martineau's editors seem to credit her success in the *Daily News* to her grasp of facts, she clearly draws on her considerable skills at organizing data. Besides her reading, moreover, she has a store of vivid travel memories. As she claims in her *Autobiography*, she can visualize

> the magnificent coast of Massachusetts in autumn, or the flowery swamps of Louisiana, or the forests of Georgia in spring, or the Illinois prairie in summer; or the blue Nile, or the brown Sinai, or the gorgeous Petra, or the view of Damascus from the Salahiey; or the Grand Canal under a Venetian sunset, or the Black Forest in twilight, or Malta in the glare of noon, or the broad desert stretching away under the stars, or the Red Sea tossing its superb shells on shore, in the pale dawn.

Martineau exults that she has now also learned of a world "only beginning to be explored," of Comte's "mass of glorious facts, and the hierarchy of the sciences."[6]

The secret of Martineau's success, in her fourteen-year association with the *Daily News*, may have been the imaginative quality of her writing. In her earlier *History of the Peace*, pointedly taken from published sources, Martineau dramatically illustrates events by piquant biographical detail. The amount of material to be covered had at first daunted her, she tells in her *Autobiography*, but she became "really interested" when she reached a section on her hero, statesman George Canning, vis-à-vis European reactionaries after the Napoleonic Wars. "Never," she begins the passage in her *History of the Peace*,

> did the fires of western forests run through the wilderness more gloriously than the speeches of Canning through the political wilds of Europe, under the deep night of the Holy Alliance. (1: 293)

In the *Daily News* leaders, Martineau utilizes powerful (usually male) figures to focus on the continuing struggle between progress and reactionism. Cromwell, Aberdeen, Palmerston, the Czar, Schamyl (leader of the Russian Circassians), Napoleon III, Lincoln, Emerson, and William Lloyd

Garrison take the stage like actors in an epic drama. Using Plutarchian comparative biography, Martineau also pits heroes (or heroines) against villains or commanding figures against each other. With barely concealed scorn, she compares foot-dragging prime minister Lord Aberdeen to Oliver Cromwell, vacillating American patriot Edward Everett to the idealistic Russian exile Nikolai Turgenev, sensible Queen Victoria to a mad Czar Nicholas, and unsuccessful Crimean commander-in-chief Lord Raglan to past heroes like Cortés, Washington, and Wellington.

In the months before the Crimean War, Martineau set out to educate the British public on the history of Eastern European geo-politics. In *History of the Peace*, she several times reiterates her view that Russia is a barbaric, essentially Asiatic, state, not to be trusted by western nations. The present Czar Nicholas, she claims in her *Daily News* leader of 15 June 1853, is simply a reincarnation of Peter the Great, builder of St. Petersburg, and of Peter's unscrupulous successors. In *Daily News*, 25 August 1854, Martineau accuses Nicholas of sending out "secret tentacles," and she urges Britain to see that his military ambition is "strangled in the cradle." In comparing Nicholas to Peter the Great, Martineau sends a veiled warning to British readers by her use of potent kinesthetic and visual imagery. She first notes an ominous "trembling [of the scales] to a decision between war or peace." Long ago, she continues, Peter the Great launched "the spectacle in the Finnish marshes [when] the stagnant lakes began to dimple and drain off." Later from behind his "granite embankments," Peter saw "his growth as an European Power would be accelerated [by his owning] the whole of the Eastern length of Europe from sea to sea." Through the narrative, Martineau creates the effect of a seething land mass waiting in ambush along the eastern border of Europe. Peter, she goes on, "[b]y his will enjoined his successors to obtain Turkey, and to foment such quarrels among the western nations as would give time and opportunity for Russian enterprises." Peter's intransigence ends with a favorite apocalyptic notion: a future "War of Opinion." His acts, Martineau charges, mark "the real beginning of the conflict, which has yet little more than begun, between the principles of Oriental Despotism and Representative

Introduction   xvii

Government in Europe; the conflict, which must come at one time or another, and on the issue of which the fate of Europe hangs."

Martineau's leaders and letters to the editor on social issues, especially those devoted to women, offer original, no-nonsense solutions to problems. In *Daily News*, 8 June 1852, on emigration to Australia (urged by utilitarian reformers as a way to relieve overpopulation among the working classes), she advises single, middle-class governesses to go out for the sake of a future Australian "aristocracy." To clinch her argument, Martineau reports that governesses in Australia are bound to collect tidy nest eggs and will likely find husbands.

When she agitates for women's causes, Martineau's strategy leans to blunt example. To support reform of the unjust married women's property law, in *Daily News*, 21 October 1856, she moves from a scathing put-down of male sexist reviewers to citation of high-earning women artists and writers, a female social reformer and the first modern woman doctor. Martineau does not hesitate to censure female failings (including, on occasion, the Queen's). In *Daily News*, 15 October 1861, Martineau lashes out at women for following silly fashions that include the wearing of dangerous crinolines. In *Daily News*, 23 February 1865, Martineau pleads for applicants to Florence Nightingale's foundering nurses' training program. To reassure parents of the middle-class young women sought by Nightingale, she keeps her appeal low-key, emphasizing the respectability of such nursing. When she turns to the reform of female education, in *Daily News*, 30 March 1865, Martineau patiently argues girls' equal mental capacity and the advantage of women advisors to the parliamentary committee—without success, as it turned out. Three years after her retirement from the *Daily News*, on 28, 29, 30 and [31] December 1869, Martineau returned to contribute forceful pieces on the heated drive to repeal the Contagious Diseases Acts.

Other examples of writing strategies Martineau uses for social issues are to evoke disgust at filth and immorality (as for the slum dwellers in *Daily News*, 24 September 1853, who are given a reprieve in a pastoral tent city) or the use of heroic imagery at unsolved problems. Before she began at the *Daily*

News, Martineau had abandoned her religious faith for reliance on the power of human reason and on science. After she scolds the National Association for the Promotion of Social Science for its lack of direction, in *Daily News*, 25 October 1858, Martineau moves to an extended metaphor of climbing a snowy mountain. The literary device provides a soothing "closure" to anxiety over the inconclusive papers read at the meeting. Noticeably in antislavery leaders, Martineau uses gerundive forms like "sinking," "crumbling," and "degenerating" to signal Southern decadence. To underscore the chaos in Central America over control of the isthmus, related to the spread of slavery, in *Daily News*, 27 July and 15 October 1858, she fires rhetorical questions at her readers. A leader on the pre-Civil War secession of Southern states, *Daily News*, 24 January 1861, contains a long passage of plain invective. "It is bad enough," she raves,

> to witness the madness of rebellion and treason from afar. We cannot have it here; and the proposition that a barbaric slave-holding community has a prospect of splendor and wealth, in virtue of its barbarism, while a free and thriving people will become a mere rump of the Republic, because it is free, is treason to political principle in any civilized country in the world.

At the diamond jubilee celebration of the *Daily News* in 1906, Martineau was commended long after her death as "the first and greatest of women journalists."[7] Yet the contents of her remarkable stream of contributions to the *Daily News* remain to be fully studied. In her many writings on social, economic, and political subjects, Martineau claims to see passing events as part of Necessarian/Positivist design. By means of the imaginative qualities of her writing, including that for the *Daily News*, she brings events and issues to life. Thus most of Martineau's topics seem to be plots unfolding over time, and all her plots form part of a Necessarian/Positivist scheme of social progress.

Recent scholars have noted nineteenth-century historians' preference for a theoretical reading of historical events. Yet literary giants like Scott and Carlyle—admired by Martineau— triumphed in expounding history through narrative. In "The Value of Narrativity in the Representation of Reality,"[8] Hayden White concludes that narrative takes precedence over theory as a

Introduction xix

vehicle for moral teaching. Although committed to reform principles based on utilitarian theory, Martineau succeeds as a journalist partly by her use of literary and narrative techniques. She was not (and did not claim to be) an original thinker. But she was an acclaimed proponent of theory. We must conclude that Martineau's literary and narrative skills help to explain her high reputation as a theorist and moral teacher.

This selection of *Daily News* contributions is meant to illustrate Martineau's range of topics and stylistic virtues. As nearly as possible, *Daily News* contributions already reprinted have been avoided. Because the list of Martineau's leaders on the American Civil War is surely incomplete, I have included a number on the Crimean War—Martineau's response to the first military/political crisis to become a media event.

For summaries of Martineau's *Daily News* contributions, see particularly Robert Kiefer Webb, *Harriet Martineau: A Radical Victorian* [9] and Valerie Kossew Pichanick, *Harriet Martineau: The Woman and Her Work*.[10] Professor Webb compiled the first handlist of Martineau's known *Daily News* contributions (about 1,500 of the 1,642 she claims) and has given his permission to include that list here. In the text, references to the *Daily News* in quotation marks are to those included in the selection. Other references to the *Daily News* without page or column numbers are also by Martineau and appear in Appendix A.

Notes

1. *Harriet Martineau's Autobiography, with Memorials by Maria Weston Chapman.* (London: Smith, Elder, 1877); henceforth *Autobiography* 2: 406, 405.
2. *In Fifty Years of Fleet Street, Being the Life and Recollections of Sir John R. Robinson*, ed. Frederick Moy Thomas (London: Macmillan, 1904).
3. Martineau to Rowland Hill, 17 December 1853 and 11 January 1854 (MS British Library 31,978: 290 and 296).
4. *Harriet Martineau's Letters to Fanny Wedgwood*, ed. Elisabeth Sanders Arbuckle (Stanford: Stanford U P, 1983), 206, 215.
5. Martineau, Harriet. *The History of England During the Thirty Years' Peace, 1816–46*, 2 vols. (London: Charles Knight, 1849); henceforth *History of the Peace.*
6. *Autobiography* 2: 412–13, 415–16.

7. See Stephen Koss, *Fleet Street Radical: A. G. Gardiner and the "Daily News"* (London: Allen Lane, 1973), 91.
8. Hayden White, *The Content of the Form* (Baltimore: Johns Hopkins U P, 1987).
9. London: Heinemann, 1960.
10. Ann Arbor: U of Michigan P, 1986.

I. Women

1. Australia

Introduction

Nineteenth-century British reformers, aware of Malthus's 1798 prediction of a population explosion, supported laboring-class emigration to British North America (Canada), the United States, Australia, and the other colonies. Finding a solution to overpopulation became more pressing in the 1840s and during the cotton famine of the 1860s. Australia, opened for settlement in 1827 after serving as a penal colony for nearly forty years, attracted only 9,000 of the 250,000 emigrants from Great Britain and Ireland in the decade 1821–1830. The proportion of emigrants going to Australia grew slowly over the next two decades, but when gold was discovered in 1851, numbers rose to 109,000 out of a total of 705,000 emigrants for the two-year period 1851–1852.

Among schemes to help emigrants to Australia were those of the Colonial Office, whose emigration commissioners at times set requirements such as for "labourers and domestic servants" who would be given free passage to Australia in government vessels. Various private plans rivaled those of the government: for example, *How to Emigrate to the Gold Regions for Ten Shillings* (London: John King, n. d.) proposes a cooperative scheme, and in 1850 Mrs. Caroline Chisholm founded the Family Colonization Loan Society. For general advice, prospective emigrants could turn to booklets like Mrs. Anne James' *The Australian Emigrant's Companion, Containing Practical Advice to Intending Emigrants, Especially Those of the Working Class* (London: H. Green, 1852). Mrs. James pays particular attention to women, advising them on details such as the need to take cloth and nails for bed curtains on shipboard and to beware on their arrival of men who come on the ship looking for wives—they might already be married. She labels most societies to aid emigrants "humbug" except Mrs. Chisholm's, which was temporarily out of funds, and one or two others, including the government scheme.

In a leader of 23 September 1851, *The Times* declared the gold discovery a benefit to the settlement of Australia and—in an exchange with her in January 1852—drew attention to Mrs. Chisholm's scheme. On 18 February 1852, the Earl of Shaftesbury chaired a grand meeting at the Royal British Institution in support of Mrs. Chisholm's Family Colonization Loan Society.

Martineau records in her *Autobiography* that in spring 1852 she gave "two or three lectures on Australia" to her neighbors. (Her talks to "worky" neighbors began in 1848. One of her most successful series, on sanitation, led to the formation of a Building Society meant to use small investments to provide cottages for local families.) In April 1852, she received a letter from a London friend "asking . . . by desire of the Editor of 'Daily News,' whether I would send him a 'leader' occasionally." Martineau then sent seven leaders on emigration to Australia.

In this leader, the sixth in the series, she expands on topics she came to favor: the innovative use of capital and education and careers for women, especially of the middle class. Her use of a recent letter or article from the *Daily News* (or *The Times*) was to become a favorite rhetorical strategy. She has not quite, however, gained control of the usual 1,500–word (1 1/3 columns) leader length, and she pads the subject with far-fetched examples (cut and summarized here). At times, she seems to forget the mostly male audience toward whom she consciously aimed the great bulk of her later leaders.

* * * *

Daily News
8 June 1852

A VERY practical letter recently appeared in our columns, advising the people to take into their own hands their own great

Australia

affair of emigration to Australia. The writer points out that the people are possessors of millions in the savings banks, and that thousands can always be raised for the ruinous investment of strikes.[1] He asks why the mechanics in every town should not form co-operative emigration societies, by which a continuous course of advantageous settlement in the colonies might be sustained. If such an organization were to be prudently formed, and maintained and guarded with the care natural to earnest men in transacting their own vital affairs, we believe that the needs of both countries would be better met by this than by any of the means now in operation; while these other means would be invigorated and improved, rather than driven out of the field. Nobody wishes to destroy any existing method. All are wanted, and some may effect what a far superior organisation cannot achieve. Admitting that unions, well founded, well led, and communicating with a variety of ports all round our islands, appear to be amongst the best organisation yet proposed, we must not lose sight of classes of would-be emigrants who must remain outside of such societies.

The government commissioners lose no opportunity of declaring their growing sense of the importance of sending out women. Everybody else says the same; even, at last, the stock-owners on the Australian plains, whose cry was all for bachelors, till the gold began to draw their bachelors from the sordid homes to which they were connected by no domestic ties. But when all parties talk of sending out women, what classes of women are they thinking of? Single women, of course; as the married go with their husbands. But of what rank and order? There is no need to make more than a passing reference to the tremendous mistake committed a few years ago in providing the first female emigration for Sydney.[2] That mistake was abundantly repented of and mourned over long ago, and there is no fear of its being repeated. But now, when people urge female emigration, they are thinking, if not actually of paupers from the workhouses, of poor needlewomen, of servant-maids, of shopwomen, and of mechanics' daughters. This is all very well. Let them go, by all means, in numbers as large as those of the working men, departing and already there, who will be wanting wives. But what, we cannot but ask, are the prospects of the colony, if the mothers of the next generation are to be all uneducated women? This question, serious as it is, appears to be almost a novelty here. We have reason to know that it is very much otherwise in Australia. We know that, years before the gold was discovered, the heaviest care that lay at the hearts of anxious parents, in the most flourishing settlements as well as the least, was that they could neither educate their children themselves, nor procure education for them. Such parents were they who sent for the governess who went out, and, ere long, married with a dower of 1,000 £. of her own earning.[3] There are more and more such parents; and, if their virtuous desire be not gratified, what is the prospect of the colony?

[*As a warning against sending ignorant women to Australia, Martineau cites the better educated daughters of New England farmers who marry, move west and fall prey to religious cranks.*] And, if Australia is to become a great country in any sense, it will doubtless have some sort of aristocracy. What is to be expected of any aristocracy (whatever may be its basis), issuing from the rearing and training of uneducated mothers? An aristocracy of birth there can hardly be, under the circumstances; nor of wealth, where wealth is, as at present, the most vulgar incident of all. An aristocracy of intelligence appears to be the most natural; and, as far as the men are concerned, the most probable. If we intercept such a privilege by sending out only women who cannot give birth to an intellectual nobility, we may expect to reap the curses, instead of the blessings, of the nation to come.

No one can pretend that there is any difficulty. No one supposes that there are not hundreds and thousands of poor ladies who would heave a long sigh of relief if they found themselves where they might work to some purpose, and be valued in some proportion to their qualifications. The time was when every gentlewoman was supposed to be provided for by her father, her brother, or her husband. That time is no longer. Such is the fact, whether it be welcomed or lamented; and it may as easily be the one as the other. As times are now, we see governesses supporting their parents, and, too often, their brothers, while a very small proportion of them become wives. We see the programme of the Governesses' Institution crowded with cases which sicken the heart, and make us turn away our eyes from contemplating wretchedness which we cannot relieve.[4] We read in newspapers of ladies offering five shillings per week, and dinner, for the instruction of a family by a daily governess; and in the best cases, where a governess is well-treated, and—as times go—liberally paid, she has scarcely a chance of a home of her own, and none of independence in old age. Her life is dreary enough in youth; and it is weary and irksome in advancing years; and as for old age, it is a dark horror in the prospect. And all this while, in Australia there are parents who would give almost her weight in gold for her educational services; there is an elastic air of hope over there, under which her heart might beat lightly once more; there is a voice of appreciation over there, calling to her, if only she could find means to come; there is a home over there, which sooner or later she might find to be meant for her, if only she could get near enough to the threshold. In a little while she would be entering it, with her dower of 1,000 £. of her own earning.[5]

It strikes us how rare a thing it is in England for any woman, not on the stage, to earn a thousand pounds. Less rare is the other fortune—of bitter dependence on the earnings of others. At the very time that one governess was laying by her thousand pounds at Adelaide there was another, in England,—no matter where-abouts,—who, disabled for the piano and for fancywork, by an accident to her right hand, silently went to the workhouse. Nobody knew it for long. A suppressed sobbing was heard in the night by casual wakers, and in the morning it was seen that her pillow was wet through, and the truth was discovered at last. She was a woman who now, in Australia, might have been one of the founders of the aristocracy of intelligence, which we ought to be prophecying for that country. This is enough. That country wants educators and cultivated women. Our educators and cultivated women want a country.[6] The inference is too clear not to assume a practical form ere long. But it must be remembered that men—almost every order of men—can help themselves and one another; whereas there are very few women who can. They cannot go into and through the enterprise alone, though, once launched, they would, in their relief from helplessness, find themselves stronger than they thought. And combination seems scarcely possible for them.

They have not the funds, nor any other of the requisites. If we do but open our eyes, we may chance to see that here is a great honour lying close to our hands;—that of furnishing a noble intellectual and moral element to our magnificent dependency, while converting a crowd of the pining daughters of England into rejoicing Australian matrons, the mothers of a new race.

Notes

1. See letters from "Sam" Sidney (*Daily News*, 31 May 1852: 2, col. 4) and from "Peregrinus" (*Daily News*, 1 June 1852: 5, col. 5). Sidney was a frequent contributor to *Household Words* (see next note). Two more letters in support of emigration to Australia also appeared in *Daily News*, 1 June 1852. Savings banks, which accepted small deposits and invested them at compound interest, originated in the late eighteenth century. Other institutions open to small investors were Friendly Societies and the railways. For Martineau's later attacks on the use of union funds for strikes, see *Daily News*, 6, 19, 26, 30 September, and 3 October 1859 (on the London builders' strike).
2. Martineau reflects a statement by Samuel Sidney in "Better Ties than Red Tape Ties" (*Household Words*, 28 February 1852: 529–34— on the work of Mrs. Chisholm) that the first "bounty" system females taken to Sydney were the "refuse of our seaport towns." Margaret Kiddle notes, in *Caroline Chisholm* (Melbourne: Melbourne U P, 1969), that the government first sent women and girls from orphanages and workhouses to New South Wales (9–10). See also, Mary Hoban, *Fifty-one Pieces of Wedding Cake. A Biography of Caroline Chisholm* (Kilmore, Victoria: Lowden, 1973).
3. A pamphlet published in 1839 urges every family to bring a governess but to expect her to marry within three months (*The Land of Promise . . . South Australia* [London: Smith, Elder]). By 1863, however, the [Catholic] Reverend P. Dunne specifies those who ought *not* to emigrate, including "governesses, and single females who have not been in service at home." He quotes wages—needlewomen and dressmakers, 2s to 6s a day ("employment difficult"), "nurse girls," £15 to £25 a year, and female cooks, £26 to £36 a year, the latter two with board and lodging. (*The Emigrant's Guide to Queensland and Other Australian Colonies* [Dublin: James Duffy, 1863].)
4. Founded in 1841 and supported by donations and public subscriptions, the Governesses' Benevolent Institution aimed to give temporary financial help to governesses for illness and other difficulties,

Australia

to provide annuities for needy aged governesses, and to oversee individual annuities bought through the institution. Among its activities in 1851, the institution also maintained an Asylum for nineteen aged governesses, a London home for governesses temporarily disengaged, and a registration service. For details of individual cases and yearly lists of subscribers, see *Governesses' Benevolent Institution* [reports for 1843 to 1853] (London: Edward Brewster, 1844–1854). Martineau was not a subscriber, as a Norwich cousin was. See also, *Daily News*, 29 November 1858.

5. To Martineau's surprise, her enthusiasm for Australia convinced her servant Jane, originally from Tynemouth, to emigrate to Australia: see *Autobiography* 2: 407.

6. For education for middle-class girls, cf. "*Daily News*, 30 March 1865," below; for education for girls in India and Egypt, cf. *Daily News*, 23 April 1862 and 27 January 1863.

2. Harriet Beecher Stowe/Cotton Supply

Introduction

Harriet Beecher Stowe's long-running serial, *Uncle Tom's Cabin*, came out as a book in March 1852 and soon became a runaway best-seller in both America and Europe (within a few years it had been translated into forty different languages). Stowe's hopes for the abolition of slavery prompted her to send copies of the novel to Prince Albert and to aristocratic British reformers, as well as to writers like Dickens and Macaulay. She also began to correspond with British supporters of the American antislavery movement. In spring 1853, she accepted the invitation of the Ladies' New Anti-Slavery Society of Glasgow as well as other invitations to visit Scotland, England, and the continent.

Stowe's welcome at Liverpool, Glasgow, Edinburgh, Aberdeen, and Dundee included invitations to her husband, Calvin Ellis Stowe (1802–1886), and her brother Charles Beecher to preach abolitionist (and temperance) sermons. Later in Birmingham, she was entertained by the Quaker philanthropist Joseph Sturge and in London by such dignitaries as the Duchess of Sutherland, the Earl of Carlisle, Lord Shaftesbury, and Lord John Russell, prime minister.

In *Daily News*, 9 May 1853, Martineau points to Stowe's healthy effect on Englishmen of all ranks. Though "no wonderful new novelist," Stowe has "plenty of ability, a sound head, a keen sagacity, accurate intuitions if not always sober judgment, and charming . . . humour." She is "unintentionally and even unconsciously, the apostle of the greatest cause now existing in the world." In 1856, Martineau invited Stowe to stay with her during her second trip to Europe.[1]

Martineau wrote over fifty leaders on cotton, beginning 2 August 1852 and increasing in number through 1862 (after which fewer are identified), urging the need for a reliable supply of free-grown cotton. In *History of the Peace*, she notes efforts to stimulate the growing of cotton in India and describes the ill-fated Niger expedition to set up a model farm to teach Africans to grow cotton rather than export slaves (2: 446–47).

Martineau's unsentimental view of the Stowes, owing to their church-inspired "benevolent" abolitionism here allows her to use their visit mainly to promote her long-term antislavery cause.

Notes

1. Harriet Martineau to Harriet Beecher Stowe, 1 June 1856. Charles Edward Stowe, *Life of Harriet Beecher Stowe* (Boston: Houghton, Mifflin, 1889), 307–11.

* * * *

Daily News
22 April 1853

MANY people will observe with regret that Mrs. STOWE'S stay in this country will be very short. The crowds that awaited her at every station on her journey from Liverpool to Glasgow show how great is the desire to obtain a mere sight of her.[1] This is natural enough; but we had hoped that when the staring was over and the first eagerness of welcome past, we should be able to obtain, in peace and quiet, from one who knows so much, some information which may be useful for practical guidance. The occasion of a service like hers is too great and too serious to be disposed of with compliments and empty enthusiasm on the one hand, and recrimination and vituperation on the other. A book written for the relief of an oppressed heart, and going out to stir the hearts of whole nations, is no theme for flattery, or occasion for such spiritual pastime as the most ordinary of our May meetings are expected to yield; and it is worse still to fall into taunting and bickering about national faults and misfortunes.[2] Having got Mrs. STOWE among us, we hoped to keep her and her husband long enough to learn a great deal from them of what must be under the surface, and all round about the subject-matter of "Uncle Tom's Cabin." But they say they must make haste home, and be hard at work again in the United States by the 1st of June. This is an instance of American rapidity which we would gladly have spared; but we must be all the more diligent to learn what we can during the month of their stay, which will afford, no doubt, a series of public addresses, more or less like that of Glasgow.[3] From this first address we derive one fact, which it is of the highest importance that we should consider. Professor STOWE agrees with all other authorities in saying that sugar and rice would not support American slavery; and that if it depended on those products, it would die in a year. No British traveller in the United States can have any doubt of this. He could almost count the estates on the low-lying lands which grow rice; and he observes that, cruel as is the aspect of slavery in the sugar-growing districts, they are narrowly circumscribed: so that the United States have to import sugar largely for their own consumption. And tobacco is no great grievance. Besides that the toil is light, in comparison with that of sugar and cotton-growing, the consumption of tobacco, vast as it is, can never support slaves by millions. It is the cotton that is the vantage ground of slavery. So Professor STOWE tells us; and so we have been often told before; and we always like to hear it, because we think, if this be true, that we see a way out of the evil. Professor STOWE was reminded of cotton from the hour when he landed in Liverpool to that in which he addressed the citizens of Glasgow. "In this country," said he, "is the great market for American cotton; and it is cotton which sustains American slavery. I do not say you can do without it. I wish I could do without it myself. I have a large family to clothe; I am a poor man; and I must use cotton; but I wish I could do without it. But the thing is, can we live without supporting American slavery?"

That is a question to which thousands now feel no hesitation in answering—Yes, we can live without supporting American slavery, and without depriving ourselves of cotton either. If that were the alternative, we should not say a word; because we certainly could not wish to deprive millions of our people of the healthful, cheap, and convenient clothing that our cotton manufacture affords, or the millions of the maintenance they derive from our manufacture and commerce in that article. In short, it would be nonsense to think of it, and mere cant to talk of it, as the American planters and British manufacturers know perfectly well. But we know something else which may be less familiar to Professor STOWE than to his anti-slavery friends in this country; that cotton may be had, whenever we exert ourselves properly to get it, from many other parts of the world than the United States. When we began seriously to see what was doing in India in the way of cotton-growing, the Carolina planters grew uneasy; but when they saw what the difficulties were of bringing the product down the ghâts—how many bullocks were lost, and how many bales were spoiled by mud and dust, they laughed. But the effect of railroads in India has yet to be tried, together with that of a good many more ameliorations which we may hope for, from our strengthening determination to obtain better government for India.[4] Then there is Australia. Before the gold was discovered, there seemed some reason to believe that our Australian colonies might become a chief cotton field of Great Britain; and we do not see that the discovery of the gold need spoil the prospect altogether, though it may cause some delay in the realisation. If labourers flock into Australia in sufficient numbers we may have the bulk of Australian cotton yet.[5] One of the oldest cotton brokers in Liverpool, since dead—a man who had grown cotton himself in the United States in his early days—declared, in 1848, after examining divers specimens of Australian cotton, that that product would make a great country hereafter of that distant dependency of ours. So lately as last summer, Mr. BAZLEY, the President of the Manchester Chamber of Commerce,[6] declared "his opinion that such superior and excellent attributes of perfect cotton have been rarely seen in Manchester; and that the samples offered indisputably prove the capability of Australia to produce most useful and beautiful cotton, adapted to the English markets." Then, again, there are the West Indies. In Jamaica, specimens of very fine cotton are seen, in the midst of the desolation and dreary waste of that island, where there are millions of acres of fertile land, of which only half a million have ever been appropriated, and where there is no regular traffic, or means of conveyance by land or water, except fifteen miles of railroad. There may be a fine commerce in sugar between Jamaica and this country yet, after all that has come and gone, and we hope there will be; but there will still be hundreds of thousands of acres to spare for cotton; and cotton is a product which it may suit the convenience of the coloured people extremely well to give their attention to when they increase in numbers.[7] This is proved by the success of whatever experiments have been made in Africa; and experiments have been tried there of a very important kind. As long as it was merely a suggestion of the missionaries, in their eagerness to divert the natives from slave trading, and to furnish them with resources which might raise their condition, men of business might be excused from attending seriously to proposals of a cotton trade. They might be expected to smile and shake their heads, and say that a vast deal depends on the ginning, packing, &c., of cotton, if the soil and the plant were ever so good. But Manchester itself now avows that great results may be anticipated from the humble efforts of the missionaries and their friends. The quality of the samples sent home would be excellent if the cleaning were well managed; and the increase of the quantity grown is so encouraging, that the cleaning is to be well managed. [*Martineau claims that "machinery and men" are being sent to Africa, proved to be a viable place for cotton production by the (slightly sinister) presence of Americans already on the spot.*] There are many inducements to an independence which we have not yet contemplated with a sufficient seriousness. It is not for our dignity, it is not for our safety, it is not for our moral welfare, to be absolutely dependent on any one country, in any one respect, for a supply of a necessary of life, when that necessary may be had from so many different places. It is not pleasant to know that the old Liverpool broker avowed that he dared not say publicly what he thought of Australian cotton, lest he should lose all his American business. It is not pleasant to hear from Professor STOWE that the price of a slave, who was formerly worth 400 dollars, has risen, through our demand for cotton, to 300£. It is not pleasant to think that the moral sense and judgment of any portion of our countrymen are under coercion by commercial interests. The one pleasant thing about the whole affair is the certainty that, if cotton be all, we can get out of the difficulty. We can penetrate Western Africa for geographical purposes: we can ascend the Nile for antiquarian recreation: we can go to India to make war, and to Australia for gold, and to China for tea and silk, and to the Pacific Islands to Christianise the people:—therefore we can go to these same places for cotton, whenever we so will. And we shall *will it* when we see fully, clearly, and universally, that this is the one way in which, without offence or mischief, we can bear our share in the extinction of remaining negro slavery, and save our national peace and commercial independence from a certain degree of peril.

Notes

1. Stowe's party arrived at Liverpool on 10 April 1853. Men, women and children pressed against her cab windows wherever she stopped. Two thousand people came to drink tea with her at the Glasgow Anti-Slavery Association *soiree* on 15 April 1853.

2. Stowe began *Uncle Tom's Cabin; or, Life Among the Lowly* (Boston: John P. Jewett, 1852) after suffering various misfortunes, including the death of her youngest child in July 1849. Martineau also refers to the notion that England was to blame for American slavery, noted by Stowe in her account of the European visit: *Sunny Memories of Foreign Lands* (Boston: Phillips, Sampson, 1854) 1: 19, 29.

3. From what follows, Martineau must refer partly to the remarks of Stowe's husband, Professor of Sacred Literature in the Theological Seminary at Andover (Massachusetts), at Liverpool: see *Sunny Memories* 1: 37. At the Glasgow *soiree* on 15 April, Professor Stowe answered the address to his wife, saying that slave holders tyrannized over the nation by force of politics and economics: see *The Times*, 18 April 1853: 8, cols. 2–3. Professor Stowe also spoke at Edinburgh on 20 April and at Aberdeen on 21 April: see *Harriet Beecher Stowe in Europe. The Journal of Charles Beecher*, eds. Joseph S. Van Why and Earl French (Hartford, Connecticut: The Stowe-Day Foundation, 1986).

4. For cotton growing in India, cf. "*Daily News*, 18 February 1859," below. In addition to *British Rule in India* (London: Smith, Elder, 1857), *Suggestions towards the Future Government of India* (London: Smith, Elder, 1858), and articles like "Old and New Things for the Hindoo"

(*Once a Week*, 27 June 1863: 8–12) and "Death or Life in India" (*Macmillan's* 8 [August 1863]: 332–40), Martineau wrote over 100 *Daily News* leaders on India, reacting to events such as the mutiny in 1857 but also urging agrarian, economic and monetary reforms.

5. For the discovery of gold and the settlement of Australia, cf. "*Daily News*, 8 June 1852," above.

6. (Later) Sir Thomas Bazley (1797–1885), MP for Manchester 1858–1880. For Martineau's connection to Manchester cotton manufacturers, cf. "18 February 1959."

7. In *Daily News*, 20 December 1852; 5 January, 3 February, 11 August 1853; 7 September 1858; 31 January, 25 October 1859; and 22 February 1866, Martineau focuses on labor problems of Jamaican sugar planters vis-à-vis the government and the emancipated blacks. On 11 August 1853, for example, she praises the richness of the land and decries wasteful estate management.

3. Married Women's Property Laws

Introduction

In the Benthamite era after 1832, reform of the laws concerning women lagged owing to conservatism over law that affected family life.[1] Eventually reform came in two related areas: the Divorce Act of 1857 moved jurisdiction from an ecclesiastical to a civil court (making divorce possible—if still difficult—for women of ordinary means), and the Married Women's Property Acts of 1870–1893 gave recognition to the new earning capacity of women in the middle and lower ranks of society. Before 1870 under common law, husband and wife were legally "one person." The husband controlled all his wife's property, inherited or earned, not protected by a costly "marriage settlement." (The latter fell under equity law, a distinct body of laws eventually made to supersede the common law on married women's property.) Blackstone's famous *Commentaries* of 1765 had in fact strengthened the sway of common law over married women's limited rights.[2]

Agitation to reform married women's property laws began early in the 1850s: Barbara Leigh Smith's pamphlet, *A Brief Summary, in Plain Language, of the Most Important Laws Concerning Women, Together with a Few Observations Thereon* (1854), clearly set out the few instances where English law referred specifically to women. Though the laws of property were not the only unjust ones concerning women, she concluded, they formed a "simple, tangible, and not offensive point of attack." Smith's pamphlet caught the attention of the Society for Promoting the Amendment of the Law, which published a report on it in 1856. Meanwhile, petitions to Parliament were circulated, and in 1857 a Married Women's Property Bill to give married women equal status with their husbands in owning and disposing of property was introduced. The contentious Divorce Bill, however, took center stage and agitation for the former bill fell off.

Martineau treats a variety of women's concerns in the *Daily News*, applying principles to specific issues and using a male point of view. For this particular leader, however, she had special motivation. An article in the *Westminster Review* for October 1856 mentions her as a principal signer of a petition to reform the married women's property laws.[3] A recent letter in the *Daily News* names her in protesting antifeminist views expressed in the *National Review* (a journal watched over by her brother James, with whom she had quarrelled).[4] Finally, in 1855 Martineau had disagreed strongly with Charles Dickens on factory legislation and must have his sentimental portraits of wives and sisters in mind when she cites evidence of women working.

Martineau draws on the current national mood of ambivalence towards France under Napoleon III to heighten the contrast of liberal French and American attitudes to women's work in comparison to English backwardness. She balances an exciting new notion, women in the medical profession, against other women's obsession with frivolous fashions. Martineau generally concerned herself for professional rather than political rights for women, and this leader can be considered a succinct statement of her feminism.

Notes

1. See A. V. Dicey, *Lectures on the Relation Between Law and Public Opinion in England During the Nineteenth Century* (London: Macmillan, 1924), 385.

2. See Mary R. Beard, *Women as Force in History* (New York: Macmillan, 1946), 78–95.

3. See Martineau to Eliza Fox, 5 January 1856. *Harriet Martineau: Selected Letters*, ed. Valerie Sanders (Oxford: Clarendon, 1990), 133.

4. In *Daily News*, 15 December 1856, Martineau urges readers to send more petitions to Parliament in support of the anticipated bill on married women's property.

* * * *

Daily News
21 October 1856

A LETTER appeared in our columns last Thursday on a subject which occupies much attention at present, and will do so for some time to come, on account of its connexion with a proposed amendment of a law which nobody justifies.[1] The proposal urged by the Law Amendment Association, seconded by a large proportion of society, and supported by a great strength of public sentiment, to make the laws which affect the property of Married Women more just and practicable than they are, has brought up the subject of the capacities and character of the female mind, causing in some quarters a repetition of the old cant about the charms of woman in the function of a plaything or a slave, and in others a rational recognition of the sober and serious duties and claims of this half of the human race in our own country and time.[2] We find, accordingly, in the *National Review* an article on the Female Character, which called forth the commentary of our correspondent of Thursday last, and in the *Westminster Review* of the same date an article on the Report of the Law Amendment Society on the Property of Married Women.[3] Our correspondent has done all that is needed in the way of exposure of the low tone, intellectual and moral, of the first of these articles; and the latter will commend itself, by its good sense, strong facts, and excellent temper, to the approbation of all readers. It is a very old trick that is now attempted once more by the writer in the *National Review*—to assume that clever bad women are illustrations of the consequences of giving liberty of thought and action to women, and that all who desire such liberty and the means of using it do so because they are bad. It is altogether trite to represent the question, in its educational and legal sense, as a controversy about "the equality of the sexes;" yet the writer in the *National Review* goes back to these exploded notions, and to the language which has long been banished from good society as silly and offensive, as if he were really unaware of the magnitude and the bearings of the actual question.[4] We have heard nothing, for our part, for these twenty years past, of the equality of the sexes—it being clear to all sensible people that argument on that matter is mere waste of words. What sensible people of both sexes desire is, that all human beings should be as good as they are capable of being—that their powers, small or great, and of every kind, should be made the most of. A claim like this obviates all objection, as there is no sane and upright person who will contend that any natural powers and endowments can be extinguished by neglect or violence without guilt—the guilt of blasphemous levity on the one hand, and of injustice and cruelty on the other. Not only have sensible people arrived at a clear perception of the point to be aimed at—the development and use of human powers, instead of useless *a priori* argument about those powers in the case of women; but events are daily revealing, under the influence of the time, the true position of women in the most civilised countries in the world. A sound, solid, indisputable fact is worth more than any amount of one-sided argument and loose rhodomontade; and facts are showing with increasing rapidity what women can do and ought to do.[5] When the Women's Petition of last session was circulated, presented to Parliament, and discussed, many persons expressed surprise at the importance that female industry has assumed—at the amount of earnings that was in question.[6] The property and incomes earned by women having been proved so considerable as to require legislative interference to protect them from spoilation, there are people living in London in the middle of the 19th century who profess amazement at so solid a proof of the powers of women. Sentimentalists, like the reviewer in the *National*, may still be talking about fine manners as the first requisite and choicest characteristic of women: selfish egotists would have their wives and sisters aim at sitting in a drawing-room, elegantly dressed, and at leisure for the recreation of man the bread-winner. Others are apt to scold all women of the labouring class who are not at work for hire in one way or another; and all these, and all other persons know very well what sums of money are earned by JENNY LIND, and RACHEL, and Mrs. STOWE, and ROSA BONHEUR, and by several literary women in England; yet the fact that the women of England now need protection from the law for an amount of earnings that can no longer be made light of, causes an exclamation of wonder all round at the proportions the question has assumed.[7] This surprise could not exist if the phenomena of our time had been duly noted.

In France the wars of NAPOLEON I. caused a great social change, and opened new prospects to women. The tremendous sacrifice of soldiers during the Emperor's reign and the close pressure of the conscription placed a whole generation of women in a position of responsibility and dignified industry from which their descendants could not recede. The women of France became "men of business" to an extent which drew the attention of all who had eyes and minds. The women of the labouring class worked before that, as a matter of course; but it was new to see widow ladies conduct the manufactory, the shop, the farm and vineyard, and manage house property and landed estates, as their husbands had done. From that point the process has gone forward naturally and advantageously, till it is now too late to argue whether women can work, and whether they ought; and it remains only for their industry to be placed under the protection of the law, like that of men. Fifty years ago there seemed to be but two methods by which women above the labouring class could earn a maintenance—by teaching and by sewing. Into the governess or the milliner class every woman must go who must earn her support and would not be a maid-servant. By degrees, and in spite of sturdy opposition, one department of industry after another has opened to the admission of women. In every department of the arts, and in many of manufactures, a great number of women are employed, and some few are eminent.[8] Within a very short time, new employments, neither superficial nor sentimental, have been created by the advance of social amelioration. There is an urgent need of more female assistance in the care of the insane. FLORENCE NIGHTINGALE has naturalised in England an occupation which demands many more women than are at present qualified; and so has MARY CARPENTER.[9] And American example seems likely to accomplish the desire of many generations of British wives and mothers—the opening of the medical profession to female practitioners.[10]

[*A Boston newspaper reports a $10,000 grant, by the Massachusetts Legislature, to found a "NEW ENGLAND FEMALE MEDICAL COLLEGE."*] It is nothing new and surprising now in the most enlightened parts of the United States, that the practice of medicine and surgery should be shared by women, though at first opposition was made by vulgar-minded persons there as elsewhere. When a few ladies sought a regular professional education, and made their way into class-rooms and hospitals by courage, patience, and devotion to their object, it was presently found that the manners of the student-class of young men underwent a favourable change. The next discovery was of the eager desire (which might have been anticipated) of more than half society for female physicians. Not only did wives and mothers desire the attendance of qualified ladies in their own cases and those of their children, but husbands and fathers sanctioned the natural preference. There are already eight female physicians practicing under a diploma in Boston, some of whom have a large and lucrative practice. There were 38 students in the Female Medical College last year, and eight have already graduated from this young institution. The legislative grant of 10,000 dollars was bestowed on condition of an equal sum being raised from other resources; a stipulation which is now nearly fulfilled, while it is known that divers legacies will accrue in course of time. Of the graduates who have entered upon practice, one can exhibit a register of nearly 700 births, which have been accomplished with a singular safety and success. Another has attended between 900 and 1,000, with like results. Whenever there are sufficient data to establish the fact (now little, if at all, disputed in America) that childbirth is freed from its worst difficulties and dangers when the unnatural presence of men is dispensed with, the medical and surgical care of women and children will pass into the hands for which nature designed it. Nor, indeed, is this idea quite unknown in this country. For in the Universities both of Edinburgh and Glasgow the Professors are in the habit of giving courses of lectures to females on midwifery.[11] As a necessary consequence of this opening of the curative profession to women, a project is on foot for the establishment of a Practical School of Medicine in New York—a Hospital for Women and Children, where students may study and also nurses be trained.[12] All ridicule of lady-physicians has for some time ceased in the presence of genuine learning, ability, and success; and there seems to be a clear prospect of a fair division of the professional field. It is not in the medical profession alone that women are finding scope for their industry. The press of the United States employs women as regularly as the factory;[13] and in a youthful and imitative country, which copies with exaggeration the sentimentalities of the Old World, "the chivalry of man" is at length permitting woman to be wise, useful, and happy. Not only art and literature, but science, commerce, and the useful arts are now thrown open to all who can work at them. In connexion with these new opportunities the dress reform of the United States is thoroughly respectable, however it may be hindered and ridiculed by bigots and small wits. While too many of the women of Europe are ruining their husbands' fortunes, and their own reputation for sense and modesty, by a mode of dress which is as unhealthy and barbarous as it is unnatural and ugly, hundreds of the respectable matrons of the United States are endeavouring to supplant modes of dress which are injurious to health and convenience, by one or more which may have the advantage in these respects, and in grace also.[14] It appears that the gentlemen of the family are as well pleased with a rational costume for their wives and sisters as the husbands of Paris and London are incommoded by the barbarous female fashions of the time. Whatever may be the result of any one effort in connexion with the general move, it is pretty clear that there is no use arguing any longer for women being made dolls or slaves. Considering that nine-tenths of the women of England earn their bread in one way or another, and that it is naturally impossible to exclude them from any new department of science, art, or industry, it is evidently high time to leave off discussing or protesting against a hypothetical "equality of the sexes" in regard to powers, and to ensure a better equality for their industry before the law.

Notes

1. A letter from "B"—possibly Bessie Raynor Parkes, later Mme. Belloc (1829–1925)—entitled "The 'National Review' on the Female

Character" (*Daily News*, 16 October 1856: 2, cols. 4–5) protests as insulting to Englishwomen a review of Victor Cousin on seventeenth-century noblewomen who intrigued at the court of Louis XIII and after (see notes 3 and 4, below). "B" compares the frivolity of Cousin's subjects to crusaders like Martineau, and she points to the current struggle for juster laws on women's property (see note 6, below, and *Daily News*, 26 March 1856). See also, Lee Holcombe, *Wives and Property. Reform of the Married Women's Property Law in Nineteenth-Century England* (Toronto: U of Toronto P, 1983); Mary Lyndon Shanley, "'One Must Ride Behind' Married Women's Rights and the Divorce Act of 1857," *Victorian Studies* 25 (1982): 355–76; and for other works on Victorian marriage, A. James Hammerton, "Victorian Marriage and the Law of Matrimonial Cruelty," *Victorian Studies* 33 (1990): 269–92. For earlier legal ideas of married women's property, see Susan Staves, *Married Women's Separate Property in England, 1660–1833* (Cambridge, MA: Harvard U P, 1990).

2. For the proposal, see *Report of the Personal Laws Committee (of the Law Amendment Society) on the Laws Relating to the Property of Married Women* (1856). The Report summarizes the conflict between common law and equity on married women's rights and recommends that Parliament legislate "one uniform rule, based on general principles, which shall keep in view all the relations of the married state, be applicable to all classes, and be administered by all courts of justice, whether of law or equity" (quoted in the *Westminster Review* 347: see next note). The Society for Promoting the Amendment of the Law had been formed by Lord Brougham in 1844 and was currently made up of more than three hundred MPs, lawyers, and public officials. For the "old cant" about women's capacities, see *Autobiography* 2: 419 (on Dickens' view of women) and Elisabeth Sanders Arbuckle, "Dickens and Harriet Martineau: Some New Letters and a Note on *Bleak House*," *Dickensian* 81 (1985): 157–62.

3. The article by Coventry Patmore was: "Victor Cousin on Madame de Hautefort and Her Contemporaries" (*National Review* 3 [October 1856]: 317–42). Two years later Martineau was to comment, "the disgust with the 'National' seems to be general and very intense. Who can wonder?—of those at least who know the vile spirit and notions entertained by the clique about Women's interests of all sorts?" (*Harriet Martineau's Letters to Fanny Wedgwood*, ed. Elisabeth Sanders Arbuckle [Stanford: Stanford U P, 1983], 170) The other article was: Caroline Frances Cornwallis, "The Property of Married Women," *Westminster Review* 66 (October 1856): 331–60.

4. The writer of the letter to the *Daily News*, "B," partly excuses the reviewer because he is reported to be a poet and seems to feel he

Married Women's Property Laws 27

honors women when he says, "there is nothing comparable for moral force to the charm of truly noble manners." But his review is not "family reading" (for example, Patmore echoes praise for one Frenchwoman who made politics subservient to her *liaisons*, and not vice-versa). Patmore further commends women's "docile and self-adaptive natures," their enjoyment of the "privilege of subordination," and obedience to the "near and comprehensible," i. e., the men they love. He finally pronounces as "monstrous . . . the doctrine of the equality of man and woman."

5. In Martineau's more than thirty leaders dedicated to women's issues, 1853 to 1865, she treats wife-beating, marriage and profession, the divorce bill, married-women's property rights, equal job opportunities, equal pay, heroic women, homes for single women, governesses, needlewomen, nurses, women's education—including domestic training, health practices, and dress (for the last, see *"Daily News*, 15 October 1861," below). Organizations that helped women diversify their skills particularly intrigued her. See, for example, *Daily News*, 9 July 1863, 18 February and 5 May 1864 on the Society for Promoting the Employment of Women; "*Daily News*, 4 August 1864," below, on workingwomen's colleges; and *Daily News*, 2 April, 2 December 1856, 25 March 1859, and 9 January, 2 November 1860 on various occupations suitable for women. In "Female Industry" (*Edinburgh Review* 222 [April 1859]: 293–336), she comprehensively surveys past, present, and future women's work.

6. Martineau probably means the first petition (of many) from 3,015 "Women of Great Britain, Married and Single" presented to both Houses of Parliament on 14 March 1856, which she signed (reprinted in the *Westminster Review* article, 336–38nn). The petition asked for a remedy to unjust married women's property laws and noted the "absolute power" [under common law] of the husband over all his wife's property and earnings, now of particular interest because "married women of education [were] entering on every side the fields of literature and art." By the end of July 1856, seventy-four petitions with 23,477 signatories had been received: *Reports of the Select Committee of the House of Commons on Public Petitions. Session 1856*, 1303.

7. Martineau makes the same points about women's earning capacity when she earlier reports Parliament's probable openness to reform of the married women's property laws (*Daily News*, 29 February 1856). She picks examples of successful women popular with feminists (articles on Florence Nightingale, Elizabeth Blackwell [see below, note 10], Rachel and Rosa Bonheur were to appear in *English Woman's Journal* (1 [April, May, June 1858]: 73–79, 80–100, 158–63 and 227–43). Jenny Lind (1820–1887), the "Swedish nightingale," earned vast sums (£68,000

in thirty-eight nights) when she toured the United States in 1850–1852; she had just earned £80,000 from her tour of England, Scotland, and Wales in April to May 1856. The French tragedienne Elisa Félix, "Rachel" (1821–1858)—vividly described by Charlotte Brontë in *Villette* (1853)—earned £12,000 performing in Russia in 1854 and sent home £6,000 from her interrupted tour of the United States in autumn 1856. Harriet Beecher Stowe (1811–1896) earned $10,000 in the first three months from *Uncle Tom's Cabin* (1852), but got nothing for dramatizations or pirated editions; from *Dred: A Tale of the Great Dismal Swamp*, published in England in August 1856, she eventually earned $10,000 in England and the United States. Rosa Bonheur (1822–1899), French painter of animals and later of American cowboys and Indians, sold her huge painting *The Horse Fair* (taken to Windsor Castle for a private viewing by Queen Victoria) for 40,000 francs ($8,000) in 1855. (Bonheur dressed eccentrically in men's clothing and lived with a devoted female companion.) She came to Britain for a visit in July 1856, when Martineau praises her courage and satisfaction in her work (*Daily News*, 26 July 1856). Among English literary women who earned large sums, Martineau may be thinking of the religious writer Hannah More (1746–1833), who left more than £30,000 she had earned to charity and for religious purposes (see *Daily News*, 29 February 1856), Mary Russell Mitford (1786–1855), or Mrs. Anna Jameson (1794–1860)—see *Biographical Sketches* (London: Macmillan, 1869, 1876). Martineau reported her own earnings in 1859 at £620/year (*Harriet Martineau's Letters to Fanny Wedgwood*, 187) and in a later year earned £802 (*Autobiography* 3: 282).

8. According to the census of 1851, 71,966 women were employed as school mistresses, governesses, general teachers, and music mistresses (the only subgroup for women in the arts) vs. 34,378 men teachers and professors; in the class of "artizans, mechanists and handcraftsmen," only 16,905 women and girls vs. 746,431 men and boys were employed (P.P. 1852–1853 LXXXVIII.I: lxxxvii–viii and xcii–iii). Martineau quotes slightly different figures in "Female Industry" and more than 385,000 women employed in manufacturing (see note 5, above). Women filled many positions in rural areas, like the postmistress in Martineau's village of Ambleside.

9. Florence Nightingale (1820–1910) was felt to have raised the status of nurses and to wish to found a nursing school (cf. "*Daily News*, 23 February 1865," below). Between 1855 and 1857 public admiration for her care of soldiers in the Crimean War brought donations of £45,000 to the Nightingale Fund. She had returned from Scutari in July 1856, and newspapers followed her movements (including meetings with the Queen at Balmoral in September to October 1856). For an alternate

assessment of Nightingale, see Francis Barrymore Smith, *Florence Nightingale, Reputation and Power* (London: Croom Helm, 1982). Mary Carpenter (1807–1877), daughter of Martineau's early religious mentor Lant Carpenter, opened a ragged school in Bristol in 1846 and the first reformatory for girls, run mostly on non-retributive principles, in 1854. She also worked for the causes of industrial schools, prison reform, and Indian women's education.

10. Martineau repeatedly points to the example of Elizabeth Blackwell (1821–1910), the first modern woman doctor of medicine, who received her M. D. at Geneva, New York, in 1849 and then studied at Paris and at St. Bartholomew's Hospital, London, in 1850. See note 12, below.

11. For a dramatic account of the difficulties of the first women medical students at Edinburgh, however, see Enid Moberly Bell, *Storming the Citadel* (London: Constable, 1953), 62–83.

12. In May 1857, Elizabeth Blackwell and two other women doctors established the New York Infirmary for Women and Children, entirely conducted by women. For a follow-up on Blackwell, see *Daily News*, 25 March 1859.

13. For women telegraphers and compositors, see "Female Industry," 313–14.

14. For Martineau's attacks on crinolines and support for the efforts of women like Amelia Jenks Bloomer to reform women's dress, see "*Daily News*, 15 October 1861," below.

4. Women's Fashions

Introduction

Taking their cue from the French, stylish women in the mid-1850s favored dresses made from eighteen to twenty yards of cloth, with elaborate undersupports to provide fullness. A new kind of hoop then came into fashion, replacing horsehair petticoats or "crinolines" in use since about 1840. As described by Cecil Willett Cunnington in *Feminine Attitudes in the Nineteenth Century*,[1] the new hoop or "Artificial Crinoline" evolved from "a hooped skeleton skirt, then a wired petticoat" and finally in 1857, "the perfected article, the Watch-Spring Crinoline," costing 15–30s (163). Though worn with greater ease than several heavy petticoats, the new crinolines hampered women's movements and often caught fire. Even so, by 1859 Sheffield steel-makers were producing wire for a half-million crinolines a week.[2]

Martineau turns easily from major national and international events to social issues, including ones that pointedly concern women. In earlier works, for example, she advises women on sensible dress for travel. For a sea voyage, she urges taking dresses, "too bad to be spoiled" but also a "well wadded" black silk cap, which "no lady should go to sea without" and a quantity of "cloaks, furs, and woollen overshoes" (see "A Month At Sea" [rpt. *Autobiography* 2] and *Retrospect of Western Travel* [London: Saunders & Otley, 1838]). In *Eastern Life, Present and Past* (London: Moxon, 1848), she advises women making the hazardous trip through Egypt and the Holy Lands to take white cotton and linen clothing, a large floppy hat (rather than a bonnet), and wire-mesh sun goggles. (She and her woman friend also took flatirons to iron dry their own and the men in their party's clothes as they sailed down the Nile.)

Finally, Martineau warns women against unhealthful fashions like tight lacing and crinolines: see, for example, "A New Kind of Wilful Murder" (*Once a Week*, 3 January 1863: 36–39). In this leader, she is responding to recent reports on crinolines in the *Daily News*.

Notes

    1. London: William Heinemann, 1935.
    2. See Cunnington, *English Women's Clothing in the Nineteenth Century* (London: Faber & Faber, 1937), 205.

* * * *

Daily News
15 October 1861

A REAL SOCIAL EVIL

Last week we had to report of an inquest at Holloway on the body of a young lady who met her death, as many other women have within the last five years, from the absurd and mischievous fashion of wearing enormous and distended skirts. From Wakefield we had an account of a female servant burnt nearly to death from the same cause, and yesterday a London physician walking in the public streets had his leg caught by a steel skirt and received very serious injuries. The remark seems to be a just one—that no fashion of dress on record has probably caused so many deaths. In the fatal case of last week the jury added to their verdict of Accidental Death "a strong recommendation that, from the numerous fatalities which have occurred in all classes of female society, the present fashion should be immediately abandoned." The deputy-coroner agreed with the jury.

A wish has been more than once expressed that somebody would publish the number of victims to accidents from the use of crinoline and hoops since this present mania set in. In the last century there was a fashion of hoops, which we all, in our young days, considered so foolish and ugly that it sensibly affected our impression of female character in that generation.[1] The idea that our countrywomen could ever again adopt such an absurdity was scouted, when propounded by some philosophers who understood the laws of the human mind in regard to the authority of fashion. But the hoop of the eighteenth century was far less troublesome and mischievous than that of the nineteenth. Readers of "Sir Charles Grandison" remember that Harriet Byron and her friends were wont to "slip their hoops over the left shoulder" in order to get into a sedan chair, and also to make room for the gentlemen in the coach.[2] The roomy family coach of those days would not have accommodated the gentlemen if the ladies' hoops had hung down. But the ladies were more considerate then than now, and had their dress so made as that the hoop would slip out of the way. The grates then stood higher and further into the fireplace; there were no railway platforms, and no narrow steamboats from which victims could be swept to destruction by the ladies' petticoats. Bad as the fashion was, it did not compel the appeal to the conscience and humanity of the sex which our very juries now find themselves called upon to make.

Nothing can be more distasteful to us, and to many others who will say "Amen!" to the comment of this jury than the petty tyranny which overbears the will and pleasure of women in regard to their dress, or which annoys them in their proper work and amusement of arranging themselves according to their own taste and convenience. True gentlemen were as heartily disgusted as any ladies when, some years ago, a dirty trick was resorted to to discredit the Bloomer dress, which was supposed to have some recommendations in regard to health, cleanliness, and convenience, as well as grace. Instead of leaving women free to decide this for themselves, their judgment was overborne in a singularly disgraceful way.[3] This was not the only occasion on which Englishwomen have had reason to complain of molestation by masculine opinion in a province which is professedly their own. They have also, on the other hand, met with great and long-continued indulgence in regard to fashions pernicious to themselves and others. The bonnets of the last two or three years are declared by our physicians to be the cause of the great increase of maladies of the head and eyes; the rheumatism, the neuralgic pains, the decaying teeth, the inflamed eyes: yet the bonnets which Mr. Spurgeon would have preached against, but that looking round him he "could not see any"[4] have not been interfered with by coroners' juries, or by patriarchal domestic authority, any more than the tight lacing which has tortured to death many a poor martyr to a conventional idea. This very evil of crinoline and hoop we have borne with now for above five years, with more or less discontent, but without interfering. The date is fixed, and will be remembered in history, by its being a trifle older than the Prince Imperial of France.[5] It suited his mother's convenience to adopt the fashion when his birth was expected; and "all ladies in all lands" in which French fashions bear sway have senselessly followed the lead of the Empress till they have become responsible for more deaths, as we before observed, than any other fashion ever caused. During these five years we have done our best to be patient under an evil which we hoped would be short-lived. We have had no comfort in social meetings, because no dinner-table and no ball-room, no box or stall at the theatres, no carriage, and no boat could accommodate both our families and ourselves.[6] We have found it difficult and disagreeable to walk with our wives and daughters on pavements and in lanes and country footpaths made for people more naturally dressed. We have seen the choicest flowers in our gardens, and the most cherished plants in our greenhouses cut off by the hoop. We have paid a fare and a half each for wife and daughters in travelling by coach in rural districts, and have lost all our pleasure on board steamboats from the anxiety of watching lest any of our party should sweep a child over into the lake or river. Our wardrobes afford no room for our clothes, because the women of the family want more space than they can get. For five years we have not had room to turn ourselves round in our own homes. The cost of female dress in a household when every gown and petticoat, from the wife's to the cook's, is twice as large as it ought to be, is no small consideration to the breadwinner of the establishment; and a graver one still is the effect on the morals, sense, and taste of the maid servants. In the recent report of the Education Commissioners there is an anecdote of a school filled by 150 girls, nearly all of whom would afterwards be domestic servants. Of those 150 scarcely one had a pocket-handkerchief, and scarcely one had *not* a hoop—a thick, hard, heavy, unyielding hoop. After an address by a lady who remonstrated against the folly, and cited Miss Nightingale's excellent remarks on crinoline petticoats in her "Notes on Nursing," many hoops disappeared, and pocket-handkerchiefs became more common.[7] The girls who did not yield had the example of ladies and their maids to plead for continuing to require yards of space apiece wherever they went. But what a prospect was before them! The cook could not pursue her business without incessant personal danger; the housemaid may meet the fate of other housemaids, and be burnt to death upon the hearth; and the nursemaid is more likely than not to push some one of the children off a footbridge, or a river side path, or from the causeway into the road. Such things as these we have borne for five years without further resistance than a declaration of our distaste to the fashion, and an occasional hint of its inconveniences and of the effect produced by this folly on the general estimate of female sense and delicacy in our day and generation.

The matter has now become more serious. It is a question whether we can be justified in permitting a practice which we were anxious to keep our tempers with as a nuisance, but which is now recognized as dangerous to life. It would be a public service if somebody would publish a list of the known casualties from this cause. Besides the deaths by fire there have been many by crushing under carriage wheels and in machinery, and in narrow spaces where a woman reasonably dressed would be in no danger. There have been cases of actual disembowelling from the gashes inflicted by broken steel springs and hoops. There have been drownings, wounds, crushings, burnings,—many torturing modes of death; and it is no wonder that juries and coroners now appeal to the sex to cease their subornation of murder.

How is it to be done? some ask. Our countrywomen are apt to follow a fashion abjectly, we are told, because they have a horror of appearing independent in their judgment about external appearances, and of earning the name of being "strong-minded women." Has it never occurred to them what dreadful strength of mind it must require to uphold a fashion which will inevitably cause the death by torture of a certain number of persons before the end of the year? We are told that the imaginations of women are too strong for their judgment; and that they are carried away by an idea. We should rather say that it is from defect of imagination that they err in this case. If they could once see a girl in the agonies of burning, and hear her shrieks; if they could once encounter the little procession carrying a child to the hospital, his back broken by a lady's petticoat having swept him under the wheel of a dray; if they could see a factory worker caught by the skirt, and crushed before the shaft could be stopped, they would gladly wear any shape of gown for the rest of their days rather than be responsible, in the millionth degree, for any more such intolerable spectacles. But who is to move? There are ladies, and not a very few, who have throughout declined making themselves foolish and mischievous; there are millowners who have interdicted crinolines in their factories, and hospital authorities who insist on a rational and inoffensive dress in the wards. But who will introduce a change in places of less grave occupation—at home, and in scenes of public resort?

Surely we may look for this to the first lady in the land. She has never exhibited the extreme of that or any other fashion, and it must naturally be a consideration with her that whatever mode she adopts will be exaggerated by others. When her daughter was on fire, some years since, from her hanging sleeve catching the flame as she was sealing a letter, the Queen adopted in the royal laundry the mode of starching muslins which prevents their burning dangerously, and in multitudes of private houses the example has been followed.[8] If it had been as well known in America the house of the poet Longfellow would not now have been desolate, and the six ballet-dancers at Philadelphia, whose fate has shocked us all, would have been living still.[9] If the Queen were known to discountenance, practically and expressly, the fashion of hoops which renders it but too easy to set women and children on fire, and impossible to put it out, the evil would immediately disappear from our drawing-rooms—presently after from the farmhouse, the shop, and the school-room—and ere long from the kitchen and the workhouse. Meantime, a coroner's jury has pointed out to our countrywomen a responsibility which we trust they will, of their own free will, take to heart, so as to be ready to follow the royal example which we anticipate; or, if that should be wanting, to act without it in that sphere of home in which every English matron is a queen.[10]

Notes

1. Hoop skirts had begun to disappear in the last decades of the eighteenth century. By the beginning of the nineteenth, classic "Grecian" gowns with high waists and simple clinging skirts had come into fashion. This style persisted, with modifications, to about 1820; then skirts gradually became fuller and more complex as the century progressed. See Phillis and Cecil Willett Cunnington, *Handbook of English Costume in the Nineteenth Century* (London: Faber & Faber, 1959).

2. Samuel Richardson's *Sir Charles Grandison* (1753) was long seen as a point of reference for real-life situations: see Jocelyn Harris, introduction to *The History of Sir Charles Grandison* (London: Oxford U P, 1972).

3. The Bloomer dress, named after the American journalist and lecturer Amelia Jenks Bloomer (1818–1894), consisted of Turkish pantaloons worn under a calf-length skirt. Though the costume appeared in Britain in 1851, Cunnington notes that English women of the middle classes objected to Mrs. Bloomer as a plebeian American and champion of women's rights (*Feminine Attitudes in the Nineteenth Century*, 154). Martineau's mention of a "dirty trick" may refer to insults received by women advocates of female dress reform who wore Bloomers. On 30 September 1851, *The Times* reported that Mrs. Caroline H. Dexter, "the apostle of Bloomerism," had been unable to speak in Finsbury owing to a noisy and unruly lecture audience and to a mob of curious spectators locked outside. On 5 January 1852, *The Times* published a letter from Mrs. Dexter protesting an impersonation of her as Thais, wearing bloomers, in a satire performed at Westminster School.

4. Martineau earlier inveighs against the new small hats or caps that exposed "the heads as well as the face" (*Daily News*, 17 June 1856); Charles Haddon Spurgeon (1834–1892) was a Baptist preacher who drew enormous crowds by the power of his oratory—enhanced by a homely sense of humor.

5. The Empress Eugénie of France, wife of Emperor Louis Napoleon and trend-setter for women's fashions, had her first child on 16 March 1856. Martineau claims the world had smiled at the young empress for hiding her pregnancy with hoops and other devices (*Daily News*, 4 August 1856). Martineau also attacks Eugénie for extravagance and frivolity in dress, for lacking "hereditary quality" as potential regent for her son, and for trying to introduce bull-fighting into France (*Daily News*, 17, 23 June; 29 September 1856).

6. From here on Martineau's point of view is doubly fictional because after 1855 she did not leave her Ambleside home.

7. The report was *Commissioners Appointed to Inquire into the State of Popular Education in England* (P. P. 1861 XXI.I). In *Notes on Nursing: What It Is, and What It Is Not* (London: Harrison, 1859) under "Noise," Nightingale contends: "The fidget of silk and crinoline . . . the creaking of stays and of shoes, will do a patient more harm than all the medicines in the world will do him good." Putting alum in the starch, she notes, helps keep crinolines from blazing up, should they catch fire. Yet a respectable elderly nurse, wearing crinolines, is exposed when she bends over like "any opera dancer" (27).

8. The occasion of a princess's dress sleeve catching fire has not been traced.

9. Henry Wadsworth Longfellow's second wife, née Frances Elizabeth Appleton, was burned to death on 10 July 1861 from spilling hot wax on her starched dress. The burning of ballet-dancers at Philadelphia has not been traced and may be apocryphal.

10. Martineau usually praises the Queen's good sense but does not hesitate to point out her errors in judgment. In fact, Queen Victoria had been charmed with the Empress Eugénie, dressed in Parisian crinolines, when they met in 1855.

5. Nurses

Introduction

Late in 1858, Florence Nightingale approached Martineau to help publicize the cause of army sanitary reform, enclosing "extremely 'Confidential' recent Reports" to the war minister (*Harriet Martineau's Letters to Fanny Wedgwood*, 178). Nightingale also asked Martineau's help in her campaign for sanitary reform in India (starting with the Army) and for her nurses training program.[1] In the Crimean War, Martineau had followed Nightingale's efforts at Scutari by way of Nightingale family members she knew. She reports on the Nightingale Fund and on Nightingale's special schemes to help soldiers in *Daily News*, 4 September and 18 December 1855.

In 1860, Nightingale sent Martineau her *Notes on Nursing: What It Is and What It is Not* (London: Harrison), written for the layperson. Martineau reviewed the small book for the April *Quarterly Review* (107: 392–422), calling it a "work of genius."

In 1861, when Martineau told Nightingale that *England and Her Soldiers* (London: Smith, Elder, 1859), based on Nightingale's materials, was "much taken to heart in America," Nightingale offered additional "War-Office Regulations . . . statistical forms &c" for the "War-office at Washington."[2] Martineau sent the materials to American Secretary of War Simon Cameron (who delayed several months in thanking the two women). Martineau also wrote two articles based on Nightingale's work for the *Atlantic Monthly*: "Health in the Camp" (November 1861: 571–80) and "Health in the Hospital" (December 1861: 718–30).

Meanwhile, in June 1860, the Nightingale School of Nursing had opened at St. Thomas Hospital, London.[3] At first restricted to fifteen pupils a year, the Nightingale program held to high standards of neatness, dependability, obedience, and qualities such as self-esteem. Probationers often dropped out or were expelled for failing to satisfy the matron, Mrs. S. E. Wardroper. In fact, Nightingale thought of her future nurses as "ladies" whose high character would enforce adoption of their superior nursing skills. The midwife-nurses, by contrast, were "persons selected by county parishes" who would pursue their calling as a business.[4]

On 12 February 1865, Nightingale wrote to Martineau about introducing "Trained Nursing into London Workhouse Infirmaries"; and she notes a recent "death from the Holborn Union" (MS British Library Add 45788: f 280, and see note 4, below). Martineau proposed an article, and Nightingale replied on 20 February 1865, saying "workers" were desperately wanted, workhouse nurses as well as matrons and nurses for India. Though twenty-three nurses were in training at St. Thomas Hospital, not many "of the right sort" or "*any* sort" applied. (MS British Library Add 45788: ff 284–90[5])

Nightingale's letter reveals two sides to the difficulty with her nurses training program. Standards were too high for working or lower middle-class women who might have applied, and the program was failing to attract middle or higher-class women, i. e., "ladies."

Martineau then displays her skill at responsive journalism. Her tone here is unusually low-key, almost circumspect. She aims to convince parents and relatives of respectable young women that nursing is an exalted vocation for women. She is also acting quickly. There was just time for her to get Nightingale's letter of Monday, 20 February, write her leader that night or next morning, and send it back to London in time for it to appear in the *Daily News* of Thursday, 23 February.

Notes

1. Cf. "*Daily News*, 2 December 1861," below.
2. *Harriet Martineau's Letters to Fanny Wedgwood*, 211.

3. In September 1861, a Training School for Midwife-Nurses also supported by the Nightingale Fund opened at King's College Hospital, London.
4. Nightingale to Martineau, 24 September 1861 (MS British Library Add 45788: ff 131–32).
5. Quoted in Martha Vicinus and Bea Nergaard, ed., *Ever Yours, Florence Nightingale: Selected Letters* (London: Virago, 1989), 259–61.

* * * *

Daily News
23 February 1865

THERE are two unhappy features in our social condition which apparently ought not to coexist: and so absurd is it that they should present themselves at the same time, that it can only be supposed that the facts of the case are not understood. We are at our wits' end to save the starving women who, with every desire to earn their bread, cannot obtain remunerative employment; and the most remunerative employment ever offered to an unlimited number of women is at the same time going a-begging through society. Social Science Associations and sensible and benevolent persons in private life are striving, in increasing numbers and with ever-growing zeal, to open new occupations to educated women,[1] as well as to the poor needlewomen who may be yet capable of doing something else than bad sewing; and all the while there is an occupation, more indispensable than any thus proposed, and far better paid than any of them, which seems to be seldom or never recommended by the patrons or sought by their clients. While the preachers of woman's mission are enforcing their own views, or denouncing the existing conditions of female life in society,[2] there is a mission for women, a vocation for them, honoured, undisputed, and well rewarded, which is left so nearly unnoticed that one would suppose the champions of the sex had never heard of it. While we have an unmanageable crowd of hungry and disappointed women, poor and idle, on the one hand, we have on the other an absolute destitution of nurses of all classes—sick nurses for the household, hospital nurses, midwifery nurses, and nurses for our civil and military stations in India and elsewhere.

We are all in the habit of hearing of the private demand for trained nurses, and of the inability of such institutions (homes and schools for nursing) as there are to meet a twentieth part of the demand for the services of the members. Once having had the opportunity of knowing what the comfort is of a trained nurse in a sick house, we cannot wonder at the consideration which attends that inestimable person, nor at the terms which she can command. If this demand were all, there would be a good prospect open before not only hundreds but thousands of women, more or less educated, who can otherwise only turn to dressmaking or teaching, affording only low pay, and involving many hardships and mortifications. But this private demand is but one feature of the case. Hospital reform is proceeding, both at home and wherever we have settlements abroad; and the want most difficult to supply is that of trustworthy and capable nurses. The Sanitary Commissions in India, at the outset of their prodigious task, see before them an alarming difficulty in the demand they have to make on this country for qualified nurses.[3] For the female regimental hospitals alone, midwifery nurses and assistants are wanted in hundreds: and this is but one item in the demand created by that sanitary reform in India which is to save life and health incalculably, and obliterate the worst features of life, civil, military, and native, in our Eastern Empire. It needs no gift of prophecy to forsee that we must have trained nurses in our workhouse in infirmaries—and that immediately. We shall hear of TIMOTHY DALY till this is accomplished—and of every other pauper death in which there is any room for suspicion of the quality of the nursing in the workhouse; and there will be such a peremptory demand of a system of paid nursing, skilled and effective, as will show the authorities very plainly what they must do.[4] But, it they were ready and willing at this hour—as they probably are, after recent exposures—what could they do, so long as the nurses are actually not to be had? Let the patrons and friends of working women of all degrees consider for a moment what a body of honourable and well-paid workers we should have among us if every workhouse in the country contained its proportion. Again, there is that admirable institution of Village Hospitals stopped in its development by the difficulty which meets us everywhere. Wherever the Village Hospital has been tried it has been found such a blessing, that our rural districts generally would soon be provided with them if the indispensable presiding nurse could be had for the asking and the pay. A small house can be got, and a few beds put into it, and the kitchen be well arranged and furnished. The doctors are always favourable to the scheme, not only because it saves them great fatigue to have their surgical and fever cases at hand, and under their own eye, but because their patients have the chances all in their favour instead of against them, as they have in their own poor homes. As agricultural machinery comes more into use, accidents become commoner, and a hospital for their treatment is almost indispensable, wherever the county infirmary is some miles off. The theory is that a trained nurse is resident in the house, and that she is qualified to act as a midwifery nurse in the village when the hospital is empty. But this prime element is deficient, and while it is so we shall have to wait for our Village Hospitals, which ought already to be scattered over all our rural districts.[5] Meantime, let the promoters of women's work consider what a body of useful, independent, well-provided women would be supported by Village Hospitals alone. The fact is they are wanted by thousands in half-a-dozen different departments of society at this hour.

What can be the reason? How can there be so plain a case of too much on the one hand and too little on the other, while the employment of women is really an interesting object to wise and good people among us? The only conceivable reason is that the women of England (and we may add their parents) do not know anything about the matter. The whole thing is perhaps still rather new; and even the high pay and the social regard may need time to operate. But still, everybody has heard of the Nightingale Fund, and multitudes must have heard how it is applied in the training of nurses.[6] If not, the particulars cannot be made known too widely. That fund provides lodging, board, washing, and some outer clothing for young women of good character, who should be from twenty-five to thirty-five years old, and who learn their business while serving as assistant nurses in St. Thomas Hospital. They receive regular instruction, and some pay at the end of each quarter, for a year, when they are considered qualified to act as hospital nurses. The demand for them is so urgent as to be perplexing to the managers, and most encouraging to themselves, and to anybody who may be disposed to follow their choice of an occupation. The mischief is that so few know anything of the matter, or, knowing, venture to propose for themselves any plan that may be called new and strange.

Perhaps the circumstances of female life may account for the slowness that women show in such cases as this. If ladies, or clergymen, or the prosperous branch of the family will lead and persuade them, and a few companions will join in the pursuit, young women will sometimes venture to propose to become nurses; but we shall have to wait long if we wait for them to stir of their own accord. We appeal, then, to their countrywomen, to sensible and benevolent mothers, neighbours, and friends, to look out for the nursing element wherever they live, in town or country, and to do what they can to give society the benefit of it, as well as the young women themselves the respect, profit, and blessing of such an occupation. As for those champions of the sex who have most to say about a mission, we hope they will tell us what woman's mission is if it be not nursing the sick. Those who are gifted with the high female quality—the capacity for domestic administration—may find full use for it in the same department of enterprise. The lack of matrons for hospitals of all kinds is as perplexing as that of nurses. Let this fact become known to the hundreds of women who are eating the bitter bread of dependence, and we shall soon see whether some of them have not sense and spirit enough to emancipate themselves in a practical way which shall command unmingled respect, and authorise warm congratulations from their friends, and gratitude from the society in which they live.

Notes

1. At the eighth meeting of the National Association for the Promotion of Social Science (cf. "*Daily News*, 25 October 1858," below), held at York, 22–29 September 1864, Mary Carpenter urged "ladies" to

establish refuges for discharged female prisoners (*The Times*, 28 September 1864: 6, col. 1). For other societies to help women find work, cf. "*Daily News*, 21 October 1856," note 5. In "Nurses Wanted" (*Cornhill Magazine* 11 [April 1865]: 409–25), a follow-up to this leader, Martineau comments on "circulars of Societies for the benefit of women" (412).

2. In the *Cornhill* article, Martineau hits at "treatises on Women's Mission, and the like" which ignore nursing and nurses. Nightingale speaks of "the cant of Women's Missions" (MS British Library Add 47714: ff 89–91).

3. Sanitary commissions in the three Indian presidencies had begun work under Nightingale's friend, Viceroy Sir John Lawrence. By early 1865, Nightingale had hopes of placing nurses in military hospitals in India. Her letter of 20 February 1865 specifies "a small staff of Trained Nurses & a *Trained Training* Matron" to be sent out. Martineau comments on the Indian sanitary commissions in *Daily News*, 17 June and 2 December 1864, in "Death or Life in India" and in "Florence Nightingale's Latest Charity" (*Once a Week*, 15 August 1863: 205–9).

4. Nightingale also promoted training for pauper nurses to serve in workhouse infirmaries, "with our Trained Nurses as heads—& Pupil Nurses from the larger [workhouse] Union Schools" (letter of 20 February 1865). The case of Timothy Daly, an Irish laborer who died after six weeks of neglect in the Holborn (London) workhouse infirmary, led to an inquiry reported in *The Times* (24 December 1864—16 February 1865), at which poor law officials defended the "system."

5. Martineau was attracted to homely self-help schemes. In the *Cornhill*, she notes the comfort of village hospitals, to be financed by taking "a small payment out of the [men's] weekly wages, "where patients will feel a "right" to the care they enjoy. Nightingale had begun to advise Liverpool philanthropist William Rathbone on district nursing in 1861, turned her attention to London in 1866, and continued a strong interest in training and in individual district nurses (but see Smith, *Florence Nightingale, Reputation and Power*, 168).

6. For the Nightingale Fund, cf. "21 October 1856," note 9. Martineau reports details of the Nightingale School of Nursing, started at St. Thomas Hospital in June 1860, in *Daily News*, 25 June 1860. In "Women's Battlefield" (*Once a Week*, 3 December 1859: 474–79), Martineau outlines the need and duty of nurses and in "The Training of Nurses" (*Once a Week*, 30 June 1863: 7–9), she gives details of the Nightingale scheme.

6. Education of Middle Class Girls

Introduction

With passage of the Corn Law repeal in 1848, the newly empowered British middle class determined to remodel the private education system to smooth its own access to schools and universities and to keep the poor firmly out.[1] The three parliamentary commissions that resulted were the Royal commission of 1850 to inquire into Oxford and Cambridge, the Clarendon commission of 1861 to investigate nine main public schools, and the Taunton commission of 1864 to investigate all other endowed schools including schools for girls. All three brought about reforms of benefit to education.

From early in the century, parents in the manufacturing and commercial classes hoped for reform of the old secondary (grammar) schools, but most such schools held to a traditional classics-based curriculum. By the time the 1864 Schools Inquiry Commission or Taunton commission reported in 1868, it had investigated nearly eight hundred endowed schools, "making outspoken criticisms and assessments [and] radical proposals for reform" (319). Secondary education for middle-class Victorian girls was usually conducted by their mothers, by untrained gentlewomen governesses, or in (often silly and unmonitored) boarding schools.[2] Almost passed over in the inquiry, these schools came under the scrutiny of a new group of women working for feminist causes like middle-class women's employment, married women's property rights (see "*Daily News*, 21 October 1856," above), and women's suffrage.

Unlike most girls in middle-class families, from age 11 to 13 Martineau went to a co-educational school. As was common, she was also taught by her elder siblings and by a visiting music master. At 16, she went to stay for fifteen months with an aunt who conducted a girls' boarding school. Partly owing to her deafness, she spent much of her free time in serious reading and study. In her adult life, Martineau was close to several women educators: her sister Rachel opened a girls' school at Liverpool, her friend Elisabeth Jesser Reid became the main founder of Bedford College for Women[3] and her Ambleside neighbor Anne Jemima Clough (later first principal of Newham College, Cambridge) ran a school for the daughters of artisans and tradesmen.[4] Other friends served on the council and as "Lady Visitors" at Bedford College.

From her early article, "On Female Education" (*Monthly Repository* 18 [February 1823]: 77–81), Martineau argues that the "natural powers" of women are equal to those of men and must be developed. Her writing for the *Daily News* on middle-class education deals with the problems of providing secondary education for both sexes. She insists on private over state control in spite of great disparity in standards. In 1864 at the behest of Matthew Arnold, she wrote two long articles for the *Cornhill Magazine*: "Middle-Class Education in England: Boys" (10 [October 1864]: 409–26) and "Middle-Class Education in England: Girls" (10 [November 1864]: 549–68). In the first, she notes the problem of where to send boys (partly caused by Church affiliation vs. dissent) and the vexed question of studies (i.e., the classics) that served to maintain class distinctions but failed to prepare boys for careers in commerce. In the second, she surveys the history of English girls' education vis-à-vis French and American education for girls. She approves of girls taking the Cambridge examination "framed for boys" and recommends that endowments, originally meant to include girls but now mostly taken over to educate boys, be used to support training schools. Privately in 1857, Martineau attacked her neighbor Mrs. Mary Arnold for failing to educate Matthew Arnold's sisters, who then passed their lives in "one scene of busy idleness, pursued with the most astonishing complacency."[5]

Notes

1. Cf. Brian Simon, *Studies in the History of Education, 1780–1870* (London: Lawrence & Wishart, 1960).
2. See George Malcolm Young, *Victorian England: Portrait of an Age.* Annotated edition by George Kitson Clark (London: Oxford U P, 1977), 99–101.
3. See Margaret J. Tuke, *A History of Bedford College for Women 1849–1937* (London: Oxford U P, 1939).
4. In "Hints on the Organization of Girls' Schools" (*Macmillan's* 14 [May–October 1866]: 435–39), Clough outlines a plan for large central town schools for girls with some participation by girls from smaller schools or taught at home.
5. Martineau to George Combe, 5 December 1857 (*Harriet Martineau: Selected Letters*, 150–51).

* * * *

Daily News
30 March 1865

THE Schools Inquiry Commissioners are justifying the hopes of the middle classes in regard to the interests of female education. They have intimated their readiness to comprehend girls' schools and colleges into their inquiry. It may be remembered that in January last a Memorial was in preparation on behalf of such an extension of the inquiry; and probably some of our readers may have felt a certain interest in the action of the Memorialists, and anxiety about its result. The Memorial, presented on the 23rd of January, was signed by a remarkable group of the friends of female education—from some of the most eminent churchmen and lay professors of our time to unassuming country school-mistresses.[1] To all, throughout the range of signatures, it was plain that girls' schools needed, as much as boys' schools, to be inquired into; and the good reason for an investigation was pointed out that some of the old endowments, proposed to be turned to educational uses, were expressly devised to recipients of both sexes.[2] It is indeed time that a stop should be put to the licence with which bequests for the benefit of men and women are appropriated to schools for boys only; and it appears, by the Commissioners' reply to the Memorial, that no such perversion will be countenanced by them. It is not their business to occupy themselves with the appropriation of endowments; but, where endowments for educational purposes exist, they will look into their operation in the case of girls as well as of boys. They freely recognize the examination of girls' schools as coming within the terms of their commission; and they will go to work upon them accordingly. They anxiously explain that circumstances narrow the inquiry very much in the case of the existing generation of girls, and that the endowments in which these have an interest are far inferior in number and value to those enjoyed by the other sex; and thus, the Commissioners cannot give anything like an equal amount of time and attention to the two classes of schools.[3] It is hardly likely that any fault will be found with this honest warning by middle class people at least, for none know so well as they how many girls never go to school at all, or only for a short time. But the large proportion of children educated at home, by parents, governesses or masters, have as real an interest as anybody in the Commissioners' dealings with schools and colleges, because their own governesses or other instructors must receive their training in the institutions to be now examined. The object is not that as many of the one set of schools as of the other should be investigated; but that the quality of existing schools should be carefully ascertained, and that the sufficiency or insufficiency of, the actual means of education for girls should be broadly represented at the close of the inquiry. The important questions are—first, how far the education provided in schools is what it ought to be, and professes to be; and next, how much of deficiency, in quantity and quality, remains which should be supplied by existing or by feasible means. Subject to the limitations inherent in the case, the Commissioners say they will endeavour to embrace in their inquiry the education of both sexes alike.

Their method is to send Assistant Commissioners into selected districts, to report on the girls' as well as the boys' schools in those districts. This looks fair enough; but the first idea that will occur to everybody will be that the whole value and success of the inquiry will depend on, not only the general quality, but the special fitness of these Assistant Commissioners. We are not aware that they have yet been named; so that there can be nothing invidious in saying that much depends on whether these gentlemen are young and unpracticed in the study of female education, or so far experienced as to know what to look for in the process of developing the intellect of girls, and how to understand many things that they will see, differing from the mental training of boys.[4] If these gentlemen were sent out merely as examiners, they would have simply to apply the same tests to the classical or mathematical or other attainments of the pupils of both sexes. But the present task is very different from this. It is to ascertain what is taught to middle class girls in England—whether it is properly taught; whether more might not be put within reach of the actual pupils; and whether there is any deficiency of means for girls to obtain what they ought to have the opportunity of learning. In brief, the business of these gentlemen will be to ascertain among them the proportion which a sound and thorough education bears in England to the girls who ought to be profiting by it. It is clear that the doubt about the sufficiency of the Assistants of the Commission has occurred to the Principals who are going to send them forth; for their reply contains a virtual appeal to the Memorialists to indicate the persons, throughout the country, whose opinions and whose evidence will be likely to throw light upon the case. From such persons the Commissioners "expect to derive much important information." Again, they express gratitude to the Memorialists, who are all persons practically experienced, or at least interested, in female education, for their offer of assistance. Such being the position of affairs, the question presses on all reasonable minds—why do not the Commissioners join some experienced women in the inquiry? There are many ladies among us who have for years sanctioned and aided by their countenance and their efforts the very highest kind of education given to women in this country; and there are others—signers of the Memorial—who have themselves been educators, and who understand, as none but a very few schoolmasters can, the whole case of the education of middle class girls. The Assistant Commissioners could not but be thankful for the guidance and co-operation of ladies so qualified. The plan would relieve the members of the Commission of their chief embarrassments and difficulties in this department of their duties; and no doubt there are duly qualified ladies public-spirited enough to accept the task. They will have, at all events, to give evidence; and the Commissioners avow their sense of the value of what will be learned in that way; but these ladies could do, in addition to that service, far more good as a part of the organization of the inquiry. Such an opportunity seems precisely what is needed to make their experience and their views available to their countrywomen (we may say to their country); while the standards of attainment and the tests of knowledge which professional inspectors of schools carry about with them for application in their inquiry will supply in the best manner the most essential requisite of all. Is it not true, in short, that the duly qualified gentlemen and ladies would do their work better by uniting their forces? May it not be true that neither, and certainly not the gentlemen, can do the work in the most sound and effectual way by any other means than such an union of forces?[5]

The proposal will probably be more welcome than surprising to the Commissioners; and it certainly appears to outside observers that there are many reasons why they should, and none why they should not, relieve themselves in this way of a part of the embarrassment and of the difficulty which must be pressing on their minds and hands.

Notes

1. The memorial was organized by [Sarah] Emily Davies (later co-founder of Girton College, Cambridge) and Elizabeth Ann Bostock (active in Bedford College affairs): see Barbara Stephen, *Emily Davies and Girton College* (London: Constable, 1927), 128–32. The eighty-eight signatories included A. P. Stanley, Dean of Westminster, Henry Alford, Dean of Canterbury, and F. D. Maurice (all associated with Queen's College); most of the others were principals, head mistresses, managers and superintendents of girls' schools (P. P. 1867–68 XXVIII.II: 192–93). In a paper read at the NAPSS in 1864, Davies had pointed out that girls of the poorer classes received an education equal to that of boys but that middle-class girls were purposely kept ignorant and forced to live unhappy, idle lives: *On Secondary Instruction Relating to Girls* (London:

William Ridgway, 1864); cf. *Daily News*, 16 August 1864, on exceptional women.

2. The memorial begins by noting that endowments available for education of the middle classes had been applied "almost exclusively" to the education of boys. Cf. Davies, *The Application of Funds to the Education of Girls* (London: Longman, Green, 1865) [paper read at the NAPSS in 1865].

3. P. P. 1867–68 XXVIII.II: 193–94. Davies denies that the education of girls is a narrower field than that of boys and says that funds are needed to build school houses, to found new schools with endowments for head mistresses and teachers, to endow professorships to teach special subjects and for scholarships: *The Application of Funds to the Education of Girls*.

4. Martineau echoes popular sentiment on a distinct education for girls. A recent *Times* article, "Examination of Girls" (4 March 1865: 5, col. 4), reports a Liverpool committee's statement that girls had no need or desire to take the [Cambridge] local university examinations; the testing of girls would be hard to supervise and would weaken the influence of the universities, the committee said. George Kitson Clark claims that admission to the junior and senior local examinations and the report of the Taunton commission were "turning points in the modernization of girls' schools" (Young, 322, n22).

5. No women served as assistant commissioners. Davies gave evidence before the commissioners in November 1865, probably the first woman to do so before a Royal commission; seven other women also gave evidence (Stephen, 135–39).

II. Reviews of Essays, Social and Economic Issues, and Education

7. William Rathbone Greg: Essays

Introduction

Samuel Greg, William Rathbone Greg's father, was a paternalistic cotton mill owner from Cheshire. As dissenters and political radicals, the Gregs shared Unitarian friends with the Martineau family at Norwich. William Greg attended the school at Bristol run by Lant Carpenter, Martineau's early mentor. He went into business and wrote on liberal topics. In 1844, his interest in mesmerism led him to call on Martineau at Tynemouth, during her recovery from her tumor. Greg and his wife then invited Martineau to stay with them in their new home near Ambleside. From that stay, Martineau determined to settle permanently in the Lake District.[1]

Greg believed that Utilitarian reform should be carried out by the enlightened few. Martineau, he knew, came to scoff at his Whiggish ideas. And when Martineau broke off relations with her younger brother, James Martineau, Greg kept up his close friendship with James. After Martineau's death, Greg reviewed her *Autobiography*, praising her good intentions but pointing to her frequent lack of good judgment.[2]

In assessing the first of several editions of Greg's collected essays, Martineau here makes her debut as a book reviewer for the *Daily News*. Two more of her reviews appeared the following week: of a work by Richard Cobden and of Charlotte Brontë's novel *Villette*. Between 1853 and 1865 Martineau contributed a total of forty-seven review articles (on thirty-seven books and journals) to the *Daily News*, about fifteen of which appear as leaders.

Martineau's reservations about Greg contrast with her praise of Sydney Smith a year and a half later (see "*Daily News,* 24 July 1854," below). For Martineau, Smith's Augustan good sense far outweighs Greg's agonizing over complex social and economic problems. Although she tars Greg with the later Whiggish *Edinburgh Review* brush, only nine of Greg's twenty-three essays included in this edition were published there. Others came from the *Westminster Review,* the *North British Review,* the *Economist,* and elsewhere.

Notes

1. Cf. Martineau to Henry Crabb Robinson, 24 June 1845 (MS Dr. Williams's Library).
2. *Nineteenth Century* 2 (August 1877): 97–112.

* * * *

Daily News
27 January 1853

LITERATURE.
Essays on Political and Social Science. Contributed chiefly to the "Edinburgh Review." By WM. R. GREG. 2 vols. Longmans.

The second part of this title will tacitly describe the character of the greater part of this work. Political essays contributed to the *Edinburgh Review* during recent years are, of course, conservative-whig—less whig than conservative. Under the editor who succeeded Jeffrey the politics were anything that might be contributed by anybody in any way connected with the existing government, or who had ever been connected with it—(which included Lord Brougham)—the existing government being whig.[1] So we were presented with a curious medley—papers by Lord Brougham or his *attachés,* and by Lord Monteagle, and Mr. Senior,[2] and others, as likely as not

William Rathbone Greg: Essays 59

contradicting each other in divers particulars of doctrine or fact, and pretty sure to be more or less incompatible. When the *Review* came into the hands of Mr. Empson it somewhat improved in consistency, if not in ability: and it has evidently improved in both since Mr. W. R. Greg joined the corps, while growing continually more conservative.[3] It has been the common remark for some time that the *Quarterly* is now the more liberal of the two reviews;[4] and it appears from these volumes that the fact may be ascribed, in a large degree, to Mr. Greg's participation in the political portion of the *Edinburgh*. He has brought an accession of qualities to the old whig action which must have been very acceptable to the somewhat *effete* cause and literature, while exciting no alarm by any troublesome liberalism, or novelty of any sort. We find in the political portions of these volumes the ordinary whig traits of condescending explanations of trite matters, promulgation of what is past, proposals of what is too late, and a curious obtuse complacency; but, added to these, or pervading them, an earnestness which is new in whig political writing, a benevolence which, however haughty, is sincere; and, what is infinitely valuable, an absence of all effort to propriate, or flatter, or attack the "lower orders." Mr. Greg, not feeling that the upper classes have, politically, anything in common with the lower, does not pretend that they have; and this is honest, and in every way serviceable. In his essay on the expected Reform Bill, published a year ago,[5] he says, "However it be got together, it cannot be denied that the House of Commons is now, on the whole, a faithful representative and servant of the intelligence and influence of the country;" and he afterwards proceeds to set forth the leading idea of the essay, which is repeated in a great variety of forms and connexions; that our parliament, which is so very faithful a representation, "professes to be a representation, not of numbers, nor yet of property, but of classes." "The English idea," he says, is the representation of classes; the House of Lords, to represent the peerage; the Knights of the Shire to represent the landed gentry and the agricultural interests; the burgesses to represent the commercial and industrial interests; and the members for the University (but a poor allowance) to represent the interests of literature and learning." Then must occur the question—what of the working "classes"? They form rather a considerable portion, not only of the numbers and property, but of the intelligence and virtue, of the nation. They come in as an after-thought, after the establishment of the fairness of our representation on the whole. "Some plan" must be added to the system which shall harmonise with it; and so on—a postscript in which some of us see something as important as anything in the letter. This way of regarding the matter is quite sincere on the part of the author; for, regarding the position of the industrial classes from his own point of view, and not theirs, he does not see why they want the franchise, nor believe that they could or would use it if they had it. It does not occur to him that this is their affair. He sets down the aims that reformers have in view,—the particular reforms that they want to carry; and he does not remember that there may be others, outlying and future, which may be of vast consequence to the excluded, and of which we are kept in ignorance by the restriction of our representation. As for the measures which organic reformers have in view,

"Are they not," he says, "a frugal expenditure of the public money, equitable taxation, cheap and prompt justice, unfettered freedom of industry, the abolition of unjust and barbarous laws, the protection of the rural population against the abusive temptations of the game laws, and gratuitous, or at least easily accessible education?" And all beyond these things, he thus characterises: "If they have any other aims more sinister and less fair than these, they do not avow them, and we therefore need not discuss or insinuate them." He asks whether the objects set down by him may not be obtained more speedily and easily from the existing House of Commons than any change in that house. Reformers think not, of course. They think now, as they did twenty years ago, that the shortest and easiest method of obtaining their objects in parliament is to get represented there; and as for ulterior or new objects, we shall learn what they are when those who entertain them get a hearing for them. Meantime, there is no occasion to conclude them to be sinister and unfair. These sayings of the essayist appeared rather more than a year ago, when an extension of the franchise was talked about, but was not the required and promised thing that it is now.[6] The essayist perceives that some time or other, some little postscript must be put to the document of our constitutional programme, but is not aware that there is any hurry. Bearing dates in mind, we look with some curiosity to his resumption of the subject, three-quarters of a year later—in last October.[7]

And here we find what we so much relish, after some of our political and party experiences—the honesty which eschews all false pretences. By October, it had become settled that we are to have a new Reform Bill, and, instead of rushing to the head of the column, with valorous flourishings, when the battle is half done by being begun,—instead of taking credit for reforming, when all chance of retarding reform is over, Mr. Greg lets it be seen that he dislikes and dreads what he admits to be a necessity. He assigns the grounds of the necessity, submits, and proceeds to propose his scheme, which, originating from such a position, is not likely to find acceptance with the promoters of the movement. We need not repeat our comments on the proposed reforms, some of which were, on their publication, discussed in our columns. At some future time, they may be regarded as a curious record of the conflicts of Conservative Whiggism with necessity, when the industrial classes were beginning to be sure of representation, and "something" must be done about the ballot. [*Greg, continues Martineau, is unreliable on the French (in "Difficulties of Republican France," 2: 22–62 [rpt. from* Edinburgh Review *92 (October 1850): 504–33]) because he has no faith in men "unless they be capitalists and gentlemen." Greg values Louis Napoleon for the order he has brought (in "France in January 1852," 2: 157–218 [rpt. from* North British Review *16 (February 1852): 559–600]) but, Martineau claims, Napoleon rules with "vulgar and barbaric despotism." On social issues Greg is, within limits, "a sound economist . . . and . . . a most conscientious, earnest, and humane man." His own and his family's record of the treatment of laborers is good, and Martineau praises Greg's treatment of mutual duties (in "The Relation between Employers and Employed," 2: 252—302 [rpt. from* Westminster Review *57 (January 1852): 61–95]).*]

The demand for the reprint of these essays proves that Mr. Greg is a writer of rising influence; for the dates of the articles are not old. Within his own circle of economical subjects, and within the class to which he belongs, he is eminent for clearness and good sense, and, as we have said, for earnestness and good feeling. If we wish for more expanded views, a more hearty general sympathy, and some substitution of candour for complacency, it is with genuine thankfulness for what we have got in a sincere and strenuous worker on some of the leading topics of the time.

Notes

    1. Macvey Napier became editor of the *Edinburgh Review* in 1829. Martineau echoes the *Westminster Review* (58 [July 1852]: 95–110), which noted the "entirely changed" (Whig) tone of the journal under Napier; see *Wellesley Index to Victorian Periodicals* 1: 420. For Martineau's view of Whiggism, "mere death in life," see also, *Autobiography* 1: 211–14. For the beginning of the *Edinburgh Review*, see "24 July 1854."

    2. Henry Brougham (1778–1868), Napier's most "difficult and demanding" contributor (*Wellesley Index* 1: 419); Thomas Spring-Rice (1790–1866), 1st Baron Monteagle; and Nassau William Senior (1790–1864).

    3. William Empson (1791–1852), Jeffrey's son-in-law, was editor from 1847 to 1852, followed by George Cornewall Lewis for two years and then by Henry Reeve (Martineau's cousin) from 1855 to 1895. Greg's first contribution was in January 1844; his second not until April 1849.

    4. The *Quarterly Review* was founded in 1809 by a conservative group that included Sir Walter Scott, the publisher John Murray, and George Canning, then foreign minister in the Tory cabinet—in reaction to the sometimes "Jacobinical" *Edinburgh Review*; see *Wellesley Index* 1: 696.

    5. "The Expected Reform Bill," 1: 422–517 (rpt. from *Edinburgh Review* 95 [January 1852]: 213–80).

    6. Martineau comments on Greg's ideas in a letter from "A Reformer," *Daily News*, 14 January 1854; and see "*Daily News*, 25 January 1859," note 4.

    7. Martineau next discusses Greg's "Representative Reform," 1: 518–94 (rpt. from *Edinburgh Review* 96 [October 1852]: 452–508).

8. Cholera at Newcastle

Introduction

The deadliest of the five cholera epidemics to strike Britain in the nineteenth century began at Newcastle-upon-Tyne in August-September 1853, alerting sanitary reformers headed by Edwin Chadwick at London. Newcastle was crucial because ships from northern Europe, where the cholera generally made its way overland from India, could bring cholera carriers to the port. The epidemic of 1847–1849 had started in nearby Sunderland.

The transmission of cholera bacteria (as is now known) by ingestion of fecal material from an infected person was suspected by a few men like Chadwick but flatly rejected by many doctors. Others referred to the cholera visitation of 1831–1832 as a punishment for sins like lewdness, drunkenness, and sabbath-breaking. Throughout his career, Chadwick aimed by means such as a clean water supply and the building of sewers to save ratepayers the relief money paid to widows and orphans of disease victims. Chadwick's innovations, however, caused friction with town and city officials, water company owners, and engineers. Newcastle, in fact, had voted not to participate in the Public Health Act of 1848 (largely brought about by Chadwick), that required local health boards to enforce preventive measures outlined by his central board.

Martineau had stayed in Newcastle as an invalid in 1839, when she interested herself in the city and in the public health work of her surgeon brother-in-law. She actively protested against the town's poor drainage system and smoky air. In Tynemouth, from 1840 to 1844, she watched the unsanitary habits of local people from her sickroom window, and organized the digging of a well and the building of a street drain. (For Martineau's Ambleside talks on sanitation and the formation, in defiance of local landowners, of a society to provide healthful cottages for working people, see "*Daily News*, 8 June 1852," above.)

* * * *

Daily News
24 September 1853

THERE has hardly been such an event at Newcastle since the civil wars as the turning out of the Sandgate people upon the Moor to live in tents. That old moor has been a tented field before now, in times when men were splitting into two parties to fight against each other. Now they are all uniting to fight against their common enemy—Death.[1] All the records of any such warfare promise victory to the tented party. Wherever the population of an ill-conditioned neighbourhood has been removed to a healthy site, this particular epidemic, and perhaps every other epidemic, has been at once reduced or extinguished.[2] As to the particular case of Newcastle—if the removal plan succeeds, there will probably have been a saving of life in the long run from the visitation of the cholera, terrible as the mortality has been at the outset; for the ordinary condition of Sandgate is dreadful. The respectable inhabitants of the town would rather go round than pass through Sandgate—the dirt of the street and houses, and the language and manners of the people are so offensive. Sandgate is the dreary spot in the rounds of a medical man. If he is called up to a case of midnight manslaughter—a man or woman thrown out of a window, or the like—he asks if it is in Sandgate. If a faint, sickening smell is wafted into the houses of certain streets and terraces, the inmates know that the wind comes from the Sandgate way. The place is now to be emptied, or half emptied; and the people are to taste pure air, scented perhaps with heather fragrance and the breath of cows, instead of the domestic reek to which they have probably become insensible through habit. It is to be hoped that the same plan will be pursued in many other places;—not only in crowded inland towns, but in fishing villages along the coast. There are no worse places than some of those villages,—huddled under cliffs, or thrust into clefts of the rock,—slippery with fish-scales, foul with offal, and with the drainage from the cottages dribbling away, and poisoning the sand. There is a plague of flies there, and a habit of ill-health among the people, as any one can tell who has lived much on various parts of the coast. We hear most of the large towns and their areas of danger; but the smaller places are in fact more difficult to manage, in regard to sanitary matters, from the greater slowness, prejudice, and egotism of the popular mind in secluded places, or small populations, where everybody knows everybody else, and nobody likes to be managed. True as it is that in towns like Newcastle there has been culpable neglect of sanitary conditions during the intervals between the visitations of the cholera, there are many humbler places where improvements have been made, and purification insisted on for a long time past. None but those who have witnessed the process can have any idea of its difficulty. In a large borough, when the magistrate discovers (as all magistrates will discover some day) that piggeries are the most poisonous of all ordinary nuisances, he issues his orders, and the pigs and their dwelling are swept away as by a decree of fate.[3] But when the same fiat goes forth in a little country town, the proprietor rushes into the market-place, proclaiming to all his acquaintance his civic injuries and the innocence of his own swine; and the clamour is great. Every man stands up for his domestic dunghill. When the doctor cannot cure any fever patients in a row of houses whose foundations are wet with an abominable ooze from the adjoining churchyard, he must expect the vengeance of the owners if he tells the reason why. Such are the places—those and the villages—where the paucity of cottages is the screw in the hand of the capitalist—where the artisan and labourer are kept subservient by their absolute dependence on the great men of the place for an abode; and such are the places, therefore, where overcrowding takes place—scarcely less fatally than in London rookeries—and where fever is always lurking, though the gushing of pure water in the brook and the sough of the wind in the trees are perpetually heard.[4] In such places especially may individual effort do great good, while nowhere, perhaps, is so much courage required to make the effort. In the larger towns, the authorities have the direct support of the public press, and of public opinion in every form; and there is an alliance of authorities—magistrates, boards of guardians, local health officers and others, which may easily carry all before it. We hear, accordingly, of the general willingness of the population to aid, as well as merely submit. The Shields people are lending a hand, with all heartiness, to pump up the salt water to wash their quays and mix the whitewash for their dwellings.[5] But the difficulty of getting any general observance agreed to in a village is incredible to those who have not tried. The more stringent, then, and the more honourable the duty of every enlightened inhabitant to watch over the health of his humble neighbours. There seems to be no doubt that the house-to-house visitation, for the purpose of detecting and checking the premonitory ailment, is the most effectual single measure that can be adopted.[6] If it can be done in such a place as Newcastle, it can be done very completely—only at a cost of more resolution and patience—where the habitations are fewer. It must be sedulously and frequently done, however; for the ignorance of a country population on such matters is indescribable. They will be off in the dusk to the gipsies in the green lane to learn their own fate and that of their neighbours; they will swallow anything that any tramping quack asks them to buy; they will take a world of pains about charms and mummeries;[7] but they will not be reasonable—they will not be temperate—above all, they will not be clean, unless watched over and stimulated with incessant care. Is it even so? some will ask; in our proud and prosperous England, can it be even so? Yes, it is so. We have not educated these people to fitness for self-guardianship, and their wiser neighbours are bound, at a time like this, to take that care of them that are unable to take of themselves.

It appears to those who give a moment's thought to an analysis of the population that if every industrial and official head looked after his subordinates during the present visitation, the disease might presently be checked. Some of the largest employers of labour in the kingdom have done this by engaging medical practitioners for the daily visitation of all their men and their families. If humbler employers would institute some such investigation, by themselves or deputy, a wide security would be ensured at once. Officers, and all others who have men under them; masters of merchantmen; village squires—all who can authoritatively ask questions and afford guidance, may now (it is not too much to say) save the lives of many about them. If they can stop any intemperance, even for a time, and teach the danger of long fasting, of imprudent eating, of dirt and bad air, they may be doing a good which will long outlast any visitation of the cholera, besides defying it successfully at the moment of its passage. Possibly they may themselves derive a good lesson or two—the shipmasters about accommodation for their crews—manufacturers about long hours of labour—and country squires about a paucity of cottages, compelling overcrowding, in the midst of nature's commons and broad meadows. The encampment plan, of itself, is full of suggestion. One way or another, everybody may easily learn something from the exigency of the time; and the visitation will not, we may hope, leave us unchastened and unenlightened by an opportunity which should yield us much wisdom.

Notes

1. In the English Civil War, Newcastle-upon-Tyne was loyal to the crown and in 1644 fell to the Scots (Charles I was brought to Newcastle when he yielded to the Scots in 1646). For an earlier cholera epidemic and the Sandgate area near the Tyne, "the perfect filthy ill-drained target for cholera," see R. J. Morris, *Cholera 1832. The Social Response to an Epidemic* (London: Croom Helm, 1976). By the Public Health Act of 1848, towns with a death rate of twenty-three per thousand or above had to set up local boards of health which would provide "houses of refuge" (and see note 2). On 21 and 22 September 1853, the *Daily News* reported the despatch of tents, granted by Ordnance; on 26 September 1853, a correspondent (taking his cue from Martineau) recommends the use of tents for a yearly cleaning of the slums (3, col. 2).

2. In Cornwall in 1849, six hundred people who were removed to tents escaped the cholera rampant in their town (see *Lancet*, 24 September 1853: 305–6). Sandgate had lodging houses where as many as

twenty-five people lived and slept in a room without access to a private privy. After inspection of the rooms in Sandgate, the Newcastle town council voted £500 to carry out the provisions of the Common Lodging Houses Act of 1851—meant to protect the health of "poorer" subjects (*Daily News*, 16 September 1853: 5, cols. 2–3). A week later, two churchyards and two lodging houses were closed and the people taken to a house of refuge (*Daily News*, 21 September 1853: p. 4, col. 6–p. 5, cols. 1–2). For Newcastle's earlier recalcitrance on public health, see S. E. Finer, *The Life and Times of Edwin Chadwick* (London: Methuen, 1980), 460; for public anger at the obstructionism of the town council, see R. A. Lewis, *Edwin Chadwick and the Public Health Movement, 1832–1854* (London: Longmans, Green, 1952), 355–56. See also Anthony Brundage, *England's "Prussian Minister": Edwin Chadwick and the Politics of Government Growth, 1832–1854* (University Park: Pennsylvania State U P, 1988).

3. Victorian sanitary reformers, noting the close relationship of human waste with disease, theorized that pestilence bred in mud; see, for example, Christopher Hamlin, "Providence and Putrefaction: Victorian Sanitarians and the Natural Theology of Health and Disease," *Victorian Studies* 28 (1985): 381–411.

4. For Martineau's practical efforts to improve working-class housing, see introduction. She addresses the problem of decent houses for agricultural laborers in a number of leaders; see, for example, *Daily News*, 6 October 1858, 26 December 1860, 30 December 1863 and—on a Society for the Improvement of the Dwellings of the Labouring Classes—5 October 1864.

5. The *Daily News* reported that after one death in North Shields, a river engine was pouring thousands of tons of salt water into the back lanes and that a hundred men were engaged in "sweetening" the town (22 September 1853: 6, col. 1).

6. House-to-house visitation, now started at Newcastle (*Daily News*, 22 September 1853: 5, col. 3), was meant to discover victims of cholera at the first, diarrhoeal stage. Sanitary reformers noticed that visitations markedly reduced the death rate—and gave them needed statistical evidence. See *Report of the General Board of Health of the Administration of the Public Health Act and the Nuisances Removal and Disease Prevention Acts, from 1848 to 1854* (P. P. 1854 XXXV).

7. Martineau makes the superstitious villagers try these folk remedies in her novel *Deerbrook* (London: Moxon, 1839).

9. Sydney Smith: Essays

Introduction

Sydney Smith's 102 articles, sermons, letters, and other pieces in this collection range widely. He attacks fuzzy-thinking individuals, public institutions like schools, and the repudiation of state bonds in America. Smith claims in his preface that he, Francis Jeffrey, John Archibald Murray, and Henry Brougham founded the *Edinburgh Review* to protest abuses prevalent in 1802.

To Martineau, Sydney Smith represented the idealistic Whig coterie she had admired as a young woman. In the 1830s when she was a literary "lion" in London, Smith often came to call on her. Later, he wrote to her while she was an invalid at Tynemouth. In her *Autobiography*, written a year after this review, Martineau draws her final, slightly disapproving portrait of Smith. It was not his pungent wit but his irreverence that troubled her. In fact, Smith's geniality fooled Martineau. She recalls his "vast envelopment of voice" and "his boast that I did not want my trumpet" when he came to call. Smith, on his part, remembered their conversations differently. When a friend asked Smith, during his last illness, how he had spent the night, Smith answered: "Oh, horrid, horrid, my dear fellow! . . . I dreamt I was chained to a rock and being talked to death by Harriet Martineau and Macaulay."[1]

Notes

1. Quoted by Hesketh Pearson, *The Smith of Smiths* (London: Hogarth, 1984), 323.

* * * *

Daily News
24 July 1854

LITERATURE.
THE NEW EDITION OF SYDNEY SMITH.
The Works of the Rev. Sydney Smith.
3 vols. Longmans.

It is with hearty satisfaction that we see the editions of Sydney Smith's works succeeding one another with a rapidity which seems to increase with time.[1] If he himself thought, or if any one else imagined—as was certainly the case formerly—that he was only an ephemeral writer, holding up the abuses of the hour to ridicule—the mistake is now manifest. Many of his topics were of permanent importance; and many of the abuses he ridiculed exist still, and are likely to render a repetition of his strictures a matter of social duty for a long time to come. But his merits are, for the most part, independent of his topics. No matter what the form of his utterance is, whether review, speech, or sermon; no matter what differences of opinion may exist about his topic; the fine sense, just and kindly feeling, and singular wit, which poured out from him whenever he spoke at all, are qualities which do not belong to date or subject, and which do secure to any man who is graced by them a permanent popularity, quite irrespective of the incidents which set him talking or writing. It is certain that persons of all ages, from those who read SYDNEY SMITH'S reviews when he himself was young, to the third generation which is now growing up to read them, there is a constant emotion of surprised gratification at the glorious sense, which even above other qualities, marks all his writings (with the exception of a few instances of prejudice, like that against the penny post). Now that people are beginning generally to agree, as wise men have ever agreed, that genius is sense in its highest form, and not anything incompatible with it, it is less a wonder than it once would have been that writings like those before us should be still living and spreading, while a mass of fine, laboured productions has sunk out of sight and memory. It would have been a prodigious surprise to a prodigious number of people, half a century ago, to have been told that the review articles which now appear to us so rich in matter, so true in spirit, and so beautiful in form, would be rising and spreading in reputation when the grand Johnsonian moralising, and the flimsy Rosa-Matilda sensibility which appeared to them so grand and lovely should have completely gone by. Sydney Smith began to write when it was still the fashion to say (in print, though not in conversation) everything that had to be said, or that could be said, in the most pretentious and roundabout manner. Sydney Smith certainly cultivated plainness—that is, clearness—of style, as carefully as other writers cultivated a resonant obscurity. As speech is the atmosphere, without which thought could not breathe and live, the wisest men have always seen that the best thing for thought is to render its atmosphere of style as clear as possible, even to the vanishing degree. That style is best which is not perceived to be a style at all—which is so direct and clear as to be unnoticeable. Thus is was with Goëthe, more and more till he attained the perfection of simplicity; and thus it was with Sydney Smith from the beginning, from those early days when fine people could see nothing in his writing because they were such as everybody could read.

It is not in the artistic view alone that this excellence of sense and of its expression is important to an estimate of Sydney Smith. It is of far more consequence that it arose from, and then subserved, the integrity of his mind in times and amidst circumstances which made the integrity of such a man a social blessing of high value.[2] In evil days, he called things by their true names, showed the real tendencies of the influences of the day—denounced wrong without passion, and presented the right with moderation, so as to make men, not so much his admirers at the moment, but, in a quiet way, so much the wiser for his wisdom.

This was a great thing to do, if it had died with the doing—if only the first set of readers had been influenced by him. It was a noble service to render at a time when, as he so strongly shows in the original preface to his works, "it was an awful period for those who had the misfortune to entertain liberal opinions, and who were too honest to sell them for the ermine of the judge or the lawn of the prelate." He braved at once the imputations of being a dangerous member of society and a common-place writer; and in so doing—in being at once a heroic citizen, and, if the world so chose, a martyr in literature, there is no doubt that the external uprightness of his style and method sustained the internal uprightness of his mind, from which it arose. When to these considerations we add the latest in the case,—that Sydney Smith's works are in increasing request at the end of more than half a century from the institution of the *Edinburgh Review*, it appears as if the honest and plain-spoken young clergyman of the beginning of the century would come out at the end of it one of its eminent blessings and graces. [*Martineau lauds Smith's stand in "Public Schools of England" (Edinburgh Review 16: 326–34; rpt. 1: 395–406) against the tyranny suffered by younger boys that, he says, has no value except to teach "hatred, suspicion, cunning, and a variety of odious passions" and approves his ideal of small, fairly supervised schools.*[3]]

In the same year, Sydney Smith gave forth his views on female education; and we believe his argument to have been about the first, and beyond all comparison the wisest plea on behalf of a full, fair, and free development of faculty wherever found.[4] After that came the long series of efforts in the service of the right, on behalf of freedom, personal and political, of simplicity and sincerity, in opposition to sentimentality and cant, which will bring new honour on his name in proportion as the right becomes dear to men. He was the friend of the negro, of the peasant, of the heathen, of the heretic, of the poor clergy, against the slaveowner, the squire, the vulgar order of missionaries, the sectarian inquisitor, and the ecclesiastical bully and self-seeker. He denounced the powerful, who might have made him a great men, "strutting in lawn," and pleaded the cause of the humble who could do nothing but bless him. And all this with infinite quietness, moderation, and good humour. So far was he from the fanaticism which has marked much of the moral effort of our century, that his enemies have tried to regard and represent him as a mere joker, a diner-out, a sayer of smart things which had no earnestness under them. They might have known, if they did not, what he was as a parish priest—attending his poor neighbours for rheumatism, he used to say, without trying to mend their case by doseing them with the Thirty-nine Articles. They little knew how grave, and even sad, were his quiet hours of work and thought, when the social evils which he did so much to amend bore heavily on his feelings and his faith.[5] None but an earnest man could have reached so many hearts; and, transcendant as was his wit, it will more and more give place, in men's impressions of him, to his benevolence, his sense, the depth of his convictions, and the earnestness of an utterance proceeding from so unfailing a sagacity. As not only an honour to him but a credit to society, we rejoice, and shall always rejoice, to welcome a fresh issue of the works of Sydney Smith.

Notes

1. At least six editions of the collected works of Sydney Smith appeared in Britain and America between 1839 and *The Works of the Rev. Sydney Smith. New Edition.* 3 vols. (London: Longmans, 1854), here reviewed by Martineau.

2. When the *Edinburgh Review* started, Smith notes, "The Catholics were not emancipated—the Corporation and Test Acts were unrepealed—the Game Laws were horribly oppressive—Steel Traps and Spring Guns were set all over the country—Prisoners tried for their Lives could have no Counsel—Lord Eldon and the Court of Chancery pressed heavily upon mankind—Libel was punished by the most cruel and vindictive imprisonments—the principles of Political Economy were little understood—the Law of Debt and of Conspiracy were upon the worst possible footing—the enormous wickedness of the Slave Trade was tolerated . . ." (Preface, vi–vii).

3. Smith's attack on the public school system attracted support that by the 1830s formed the basis of a movement for reform: see Alan Bell, *Sydney Smith* (Oxford: Clarendon, 1986). Cf. "*Daily News*, 30 March 1865," above.

4. In "Female Education" (*Edinburgh Review* 15: 299–315, rpt. 1: 372–94), Smith claims that seeming differences of understanding

between the sexes are entirely owing to the "circumstances" of their education. Women, who are kept doing trivial work like mending, need occupation for their minds. Education will not hurt them but make them happier mothers and adult individuals. Smith cites "Mrs. Marcet, Mrs. Somerville, and Miss Martineau" as honorably known *writers* as well as *readers* of books.

5. In her *Autobiography*, Martineau speaks of Smith's "failing spirits" before his death in 1845; she may have seen his daughter's account of how Smith, in his last illness, recalled his own words: "There are [some who] walk . . . against driving misery, and through stormy sorrows, over sharp afflictions . . . with bare feet, and naked breast, jaded, mangled, and chilled" (*A Memoir of the Reverend Sydney Smith* [privately printed at London: John Edward Taylor, 1854], 277). Smith had attended medical lectures at Edinburgh and later set up a dispensary for the poor of his Yorkshire parish.

10. Temperance

Introduction

Legislation to control the sale of liquor began in England in the middle of the sixteenth century as a means to curb unruly patrons of "common ale-houses and other... tippling houses." In the late seventeenth century, distilled spirits—brandy, gin, and whiskey (originally from France, the Netherlands, and Ireland)—began to be made cheaply in England. Public drunkenness, mostly from gin, reached such proportions that Middlesex magistrates petitioned Parliament for stronger restrictions on the retailing of distilled spirits. The resulting Gin Act of 1736 imposed high excise duties but greatly increased illicit consumption. More moderate acts followed. In the early years of the nineteenth century, "temperance" was the solution urged by Evangelicals and other groups such as Quakers. From 1828, hours of opening for public houses, hitherto closed only during Sunday Church services, were repeatedly restricted. To encourage the drinking of beer rather than spirits, in 1830 Parliament passed an act exempting the selling of beer from the requirement of a justice's license. Liquor laws for Ireland and Scotland were also passed over the years.

In summer 1855, a bill to extend the hours of Sunday opening for public houses, last set by a Beer Act of 1854, aroused lively public interest. One source of evidence for both advocates and opponents of the new bill (the latter including many temperance people) were the current prohibitory liquor laws in some of the United States. These laws were the direct outcome of an organized national temperance movement.

In the United Kingdom, a working-class temperance movement had begun at Belfast and Glasgow in 1829 and at Bradford in 1830. By 1846, the movement had gained enough strength to hold a World's Temperance Convention in London. The United Kingdom Alliance, formed in 1853, aimed at statutory prohibition—with local option as a first objective.[1]

Reminiscent of seventeenth-century English burgers' response to the effects of cheap gin, American temperance societies were formed early in the nineteenth century to combat the effects of the cheap rum (from West Indies molasses) and whiskey then flooding the country. New York passed a law prohibiting the public sale of liquor that lasted from 1845 to 1847. Under pressure from the formidable Maine Temperance Union, Maine passed a prohibition law in 1845. That law proving unenforceable, it was succeeded by the model Maine Law of 1851 (see note 7). But riots in the city of Portland, in June 1855, forced repeal of the Maine Law, not to be reenacted until 1858.

Martineau often wrestles with the question of the legislation of morals. As a scientific reformer, she opposed the idea of temperance movements that played on the emotions of the public but failed to treat the supposed social causes of habitual drunkenness (a view supported by contemporary leaders in *The Times*). In spite of her hardheadedness, in "Sarah Pellat, Florence Nightingale and Temperance" (*Daily News*, 22 November 1855),[2] she gives a romantic account of a female temperance crusader in the California gold camps. Her eloquence at the temptation to drink in the American wilderness as well as her vague and far-off solutions to intemperance in the working class seem equally uncharacteristic.[3]

Notes

1. See Brian Harrison, *Drink and the Victorians. The Temperance Question in England 1815–1872* (London: Faber and Faber, 1971).
2. Partly rpt. *Harriet Martineau on Women*, ed. Gayle Graham Yates (New Brunswick, New Jersey: Rutgers U P, 1985).
3. In private, Martineau expressed revulsion at the drunkenness she saw or knew about close to her home: see *Harriet Martineau's Letters to Fanny Wedgwood*, 102, 114–15.

* * * *

Daily News
7 August 1855

WE are past the middle of the nineteenth century of Christianity; and we, who believe our country to be the foremost of all the world, find the great problem of our social state to be, the treatment of drunkenness. The most complacent nation of all,—the people who most constantly call the world to witness their protestant and moral ascendancy over all the rest of mankind—the Americans,—are as perplexed as ourselves what to do with the drunkenness within their borders; and with yet more flagrant reason. Twenty years ago the divines and moralists of American society declared themselves so aghast at the sweeping devastation caused by intemperance, that, while fully aware of the false principle of tee-total association, they yet rushed into it, as the only immediate check to the ravage before their eyes.[1] No man was more thoroughly aware of the futility of expecting moral regeneration from mechanical association than Dr. CHANNING. He wrote upon it, he preached upon it, and he commanded the assent of many who yet formed or joined Temperance Societies, allowing their terror to overpower their clear convictions of the uselessness, and therefore ultimate mischievousness, of the means to which they resorted.[2] The same thing happened in Ireland during the active career of Father MATHEW,[3] and the same thing happens now, every day, in many a district of England and Scotland. The consequences are showing themselves very instructively on both sides the Atlantic; and all who are perplexed by the great moral problem of the time are thankful for instruction from any quarter.[4]

The United States labour under certain disadvantages which fix attention first on that country from the magnitude of the rate at which the vice augments there. The temptation and the supply are both enormous in the wild regions where new settlers suffer under bad conditions of health, and all manner of social privation; and the semi-barbaric state of the frontiers, and of the outcasts (chiefly from Europe) who infest the great rivers, is but too favourable to spirit-drinking as well as gambling. The same thing takes place in our newest Australian colonies, and, indeed, wherever the process of pioneering into wild places is going on. At the other extreme of the scale, in places and times, like Ireland before and during the famine, when men have no prospect and live from hand to mouth, intemperance flourishes. It prospers by the first social hope, and by the last social despair; when virgin regions are opening to the enterprise of man, and when exhausted territory presents to him nothing but a blank. In both cases, good men struggle against the spread of the vice; and something may be learned by the contemplation of their efforts.

In Ireland, Father MATHEW'S enterprise is but too well typified by the state of his Temperance Chapel at Cork, where the beautiful edifice is left, a wonderful abortion, to provoke the questions of strangers.[5] It stands unfinished and useless, an expensive disappointment, vexing the hearts of many who never doubted its success. In like manner, the Irish temperance, which created so much delight and hope, was first found to be a political affair, and then to be sustained only by the poverty of the people. When prosperity began to return, the vice encroached again; and it now appears that the only check which is effective in the slightest degree is the interest of some great purpose in life, which excludes the need and love of drink. The emigrants and the friends of emigrants can lay by their earnings and keep sober; and so can an increasing number of the tenants of Scotch, and English, and well qualified Irish farmers who have altered the face of the country very largely, since the break-up of the Wilderness of Encumbered Estates.[6] In the United States, the opposite method has been resorted to,—the attempt to exclude drunkenness by legislative precautions. When the Maine Liquor Law was first proposed, what we British had to say about it was that in a democratic republic, the people, being their own legislators and rulers, had a perfect right to impose what restraints on themselves they pleased; but that such legislation would not do anywhere else. Absolute rulers could not enforce such prohibitions as that law imposes; and in a constitutional country they could scarcely be proposed, still less enacted, and least of all enforced. It is true there are some few advocates of a similar law for England; but, shallow as must be the thought and

Temperance

knowledge of such men as to the function of law and the foundations of morality, they can hardly fail to learn something from the present state of the great controversy in America. In several states the law is wholly inoperative.[7] People drink, and buy and sell, spirits with as much impunity as if the law had never been passed; while they have become confirmed in that light view of the law which is the most deadly blight upon the citizen character. We regard with less pain the open and riotous rejoicing in other states at the throwing out of the law. It is bad enough, such a celebration; but it is better than the whited sepulchre of the law, which covers all manner of uncleanness.

Now, if our superficial moralists, who will not read the Gospel and the works of the wisest men, to learn how to exclude sin and treat sinners, but who prefer going to work like the old Pharisees,[8] cannot take a hint from the present course of the Maine Liquor Law in America, and from recent manifestations at home against promoting religion and morality by Act of Parliament,[9] they are bound at least to attend to other means of discountenancing the vice of drunkenness; and above all, to see what can be done by bringing existing laws to bear impartially upon the results of intemperance wherever they violate the law. This is usually done very fairly by the vigilant sense of justice of the people, and that vigilance must be carefully fostered. About fifteen years since a police magistrate in London was properly gibbeted in the newspapers till all England knew the story, for having sentenced some soldiers to an absurdly light punishment for an atrocious assault on a woman, on the ground that her door (which they broke open) was made of thin planks, and yet more, that the soldiers were drunk. So much was heard on that occasion of the judicial morality of excusing criminals because they were drunk, that few or no cases have occurred since where the culprits were of the rank of those who usually appear before London police magistrates. Wife-beaters get their six months with hard labour, however drunk they may have been when they knocked their wives to pieces; and no one but the culprits themselves, or their trembling victims, thinks of urging the lesser sin as an excuse for the greater. The point to be watched is that other judges than police magistrates are kept up to their duty in the same class of cases. [*Three recent cases of officers in the Crimea,* cashiered for drunkenness, have caused a sensation among the troops. Such examples keep others sober, Martineau feels. On the other hand, the case of a drunken ship's captain who endangered hundreds of passengers proves that prohibitory law on the use of liquor should be enacted in the "highly exceptional instance of ships on long voyages."] Whether that is done or not, the friends of temperance may employ themselves usefully in watching over the administration of law and the expression of sentiment when intemperance is found in a form in which it may be dealt with by law. That public opinion may restrain drunkenness is shown by the fact of the comparative infrequency of the vice among women, except in an order too low for shame.[10] Let public opinion sustain (as it will) the retribution on army and maritime officers, and the multitude will feel the check and be sober for a better reason than that they cannot get drunk.

Notes

1. Temperance as an organized movement in America began in Boston in 1826, but Martineau must refer to the national convention at Saratoga in 1836, when delegates adopted the principle of total abstinence.

2. Dr. William Ellery Channing, the charismatic religious leader whom Martineau met on her American tour, delivered an *Address on Temperance* in Boston in 1837 [Boston: Weeks, Jordan; 1837; rpt. London: John Green, 1837] that set a pattern for Martineau's pragmatic approach to the problem of alcohol abuse among the poor and laboring classes. Channing advocated better education, recreation, and mental and physical health practices for the poor. He urged the rich to set an example of moderation and to restrain the sale of alcohol to the poor. See Jack Mendelsohn, *Channing. The Reluctant Radical* (Boston: Little, Brown, 1971).

3. Martineau traces the career of Theobald Mathew (1790–1856) in *History of the Peace* 2: 294–97. He began to preach total abstinence among the Cork poor in 1838, convincing thousands throughout Ireland to take the pledge and travelling to England and America. He was said to have greatly reduced drunkenness and crime in Ireland.

4. In *Daily News*, 6 October 1856, Martineau cites the failure of legal acts to stop intemperance in states such as Maine. Drunkenness is not a problem in European towns or in Louisiana (where claret is

Temperance   81

cheap), she claims, and she recommends the sale of light beer and wines.

5. Martineau records her impression of Father Mathew's uncompleted chapel—a monument begun in "superstition and political enthusiasm"—in *Letters from Ireland* (London: John Chapman, 1852), 210–11.

6. In *History of the Peace*, Martineau points to the "unsoundness of the principle of societies for individual moral restraint" (2: 294). The Irish radical leader Daniel O'Connell perverted Father Mathew's followers, she claims, by encouraging them to believe in the cause of repeal of the union with England. In 1849, Parliament passed an act facilitating the sale of encumbered properties to encourage the improvement of agricultural lands.

7. The Maine Liquor Law of 1851, the model of similar legislation elsewhere, prohibited all sale of intoxicating liquor except for medicinal purposes. Offenders were fined and, on a third offense, jailed. Other states also stiffened earlier liquor laws, and by 1856 thirteen Northern states were restricting its sale. Martineau must have seen the arguments over the legality and enforcement of new liquor laws that appeared in New York newspapers from spring to summer 1855.

8. Martineau seems to use "Pharisees" in the sense of sticklers for the law but no doubt has Evangelicals and Quakers in mind.

9. Martineau refers to the bill in Parliament to extend Sunday opening hours for public houses in England. Her scepticism echoes that of *The Times*, which called temperance workers "Quixotic" and defended the right of most working men to innocent recreation in public houses. The remedy for intemperance, according to *The Times*, would be the spread of religion and education and increasing civilization. See, for example, 1 June 1855 (6, cols. 5–6), 30 July 1855 (9, col. 5) and 7 August 1855 (9, cols. 1–2). For a comprehensive discussion of English drinking habits and laws to restrict the sale of alcohol, see F. M. L. Thompson, *The Rise of Respectable Society* (Cambridge, MA: Harvard U P, 1988), 307–31.

10. One shocking aspect of the seventeenth-century "spirit-bars" were the female drunks seen on the streets.

11. Railroads: The United States, England, and Russia

Introduction

In October 1825, Britain's first daily passenger and freight train began service between Stockton and Darlington. Four years later, Robert Stephenson's steam locomotive, "Rocket," attained speeds up to 29 miles per hour (average, 14 miles per hour) on the Liverpool and Manchester line. In 1846, "railway fever" caused Parliament to pass 270 railway acts for the construction of 4,538 miles of lines. (In 1855, by contrast, 73 acts were passed for the construction of 363 miles of lines in England, Wales, Scotland, and Ireland.) G. E. Porter in *The Progress of the Nation* (1836–1838) notes the unique contribution of railways to English prosperity.[1]

In the United States, one of the earliest railroads (built 1826–1827) used horsepower to carry granite from quarries near Quincy, Massachusetts. By summer 1829, the Delaware and Hudson (canal) company was using a steam locomotive brought from England. Shortly after, the Baltimore and Ohio railroad— the first long line in America through mountainous country— began to use steam as well as horse-drawn carriages and carried 82,000 passengers in the first eight months of 1831. As rail transport caught on, local interest groups often built short (sometimes duplicate) lines that were connected by longer systems. Such longer lines also linked western states to the eastern cities. In 1850, the Illinois Central railroad was the first to receive a federal grant (pushed through Congress by the special pleading of Stephen A. Douglas and others) for a long connecting line. By 1851–1852, both houses of Congress had begun to consider bills for the building of a transcontinental railroad. Of five possible routes surveyed, Secretary of War Jefferson Davis in 1855 recommended a southern route. But growing alarm over the spread of slavery caused northern Congressmen to reject his choice.

Martineau romances the notion of an American transcontinental railroad in *Daily News*, 27 July 1853. Here she also focuses on technological progress as opportunity for middle-class investors. Her stance as expert on European and North American politics also requires that she watch for pitfalls for the uninformed.

Note

1. A later edition of the book claims that £700 million were invested in British railways in 1845 (followed by a severe crisis in 1847): ed. F. W. Hirst (London: Methuen, 1912), 546 and 551.

* * * *

Daily News
10 February 1857

OUR Special Correspondent at New York has presented us with some striking and portentous facts in regard to American railways, and we are glad of his promise to send more.[1] We may leave it to him to describe the expansion of intercourse taking place through the growth of the miraculous rail, and to suggest the political and social consequences of the laying open of the diverse regions of the great continent; but he has already said enough to suggest to us Europeans a new aspect of railways, which certainly was never dreamed of when they were projected, and which does not seem to be duly considered even now. It would be useful to us to consider railways, both philosophically and economically, as exponents of the social systems under which they arise, and are intended to work. If we

Railroads: The United States, England, and Russia

would but study the republican railway, in its contrasts with that of an autocratically or constitutionally governed country, we might not only save a great deal of money, but learn some things which may possibly be of greater ultimate importance than a safe investment of capital.

Our correspondent tells us that the small railways running, on the whole, north and south, or nearly at right angles with the great east and west line, are like ribs got ready first, and then formed into a system by running in the stout back-bone between them. It is just so wherever railways arise in the United States. And why so? Because they grow out of a republican condition of society. The process is this. Settlers sit down on the rich meadows of Ohio, or the broad table-land of Western Virginia, or the Illinois prairie, or the long-winding valleys of Western Pennsylvania and New York; and, according to circumstances, reclaim lands, or set up manufactures, or open mines, forming towns, or scattering along the river-side. The time comes when they want a market for their produce. Formerly they organised a road traffic, or detained the Irish as they came along to dig a canal, for which they might or might not obtain aid from the State legislature.[2] At present they resolve on a railroad. There need be no delay or difficulty about it, for the dwellers by the roadside are the majority of the proprietors. The road is chiefly made by them, and for their own purposes. Every man of them knows the cost of the wood and the iron and the labour, and the erection of the stations; and every yard of the line is made under the eyes of some proprietor or another who is on the watch to see that there is no waste or faulty work. The directors are the agents, in fact, of a vigilance-committee; and every bargain for land is made under a common desire to render the road as cheap as possible. Instead of a desire to obtain large dividends in return for a simple investment of capital, the main object with the proprietors is the development of the district and the expansion of commerce.[3] They care little about how much their rail pays in the way of dividend, in comparison with the value it adds to their estates and their produce. For every dollar they could possibly gain by the success of their line in the share market they may gain a hundred by the goodness of its working quality. Thus, the management is less ministerial and more personal than in any other country; the earners of the money which makes the road are the spenders on the road; and the enterprise may be a very profitable one to the local proprietors, even though it pays no dividend. Iron is dear there, and labour is dear; and foreigners shake their heads over the non-paying condition of American railways; while the country is fructifying under their influence; and thousands of citizens who have never pocketed a hundred dollars of dividend may yet say that their grandest stroke of prosperity was laying out their branch railway. This is so well understood in the Republic that the great Pacific Railway is to maintain itself, and to stretch out on its own resources, if it is ever to be accomplished at all. A strip of land on each side—now perfectly wild—is all that the projectors ask for:[4] and no one seems to dispute the soundness of their anticipation that the development of the more fertile portions will pay for running the road through the barren parts; and that the proprietary which will spring up beside the rivers will carry the scheme well over the desert portions. However this may be, there are before us the great facts that in the Republican case the branch roads come into existence first, creating their own proprietary and management; and that the main lines, with their old-world attributes of a proprietary which looks for gain from dividends, and a large body who expect profit from the process of construction, are losing concerns, almost in precise proportion to their departure from the Republican ground of creation and management. European capitalists, who put their money into American railways, have themselves to blame if they expect a handsome return for their investment without examining the fundamental conditions of railways in the United States.[5]

The proposed Russian railways are of the directly opposite sort. The bidding of the Autocrat brings them into existence; they will be constructed by bodies of men who have no other interest in them than making money by the process of construction, which will inevitably be as expensive as it can be made; and the capital will be supplied by parties whose claims will be an irremovable incubus on the enterprise.[6] The roads will stretch through vast wastes where no materials for traffic exist; and when they cross fertile regions where villages are least scarce, they will not be supported and animated by commercial competition and the energy of an organised society. Where there are none but nobles and serfs, no liberties, none of the productiveness and expansion which arise under the great natural laws of society, there can be no genuine success for enterprises which owe their origin to opposite conditions. The CZAR may make railways to subserve his military purposes, and he may find capitalists who will supply the capital under sufficient inducements; but the conditions of the scheme indicate as plainly as possible that the construction will be bad, the expense to the last degree exaggerated, and the natural profits *nil*. The prospect of any creation of wealth is most uncertain and remote, while there will be a crowd of claimants to divide—nothing. Whatever returns the Russian railways may profess to yield must be arbitrary and factitious: for it is an absolute condition of natural profits that the structure of society should first be wholly changed—that, in fact, the railways should cease to be an exponent of an autocratic system of society.

Between these two extremes lies the English system. If we had nothing better to show for our constitutional method of national existence than our railway management, we could not hold our heads very high.[7] As to our ostensible scheme of railway property, it is democratic enough; but it works rather autocratically in detail. We have not a despot commanding a road to stretch itself out for a thousand miles; but we have plenty of little despots who abolish in their own sphere the democratic constitution of proprietorship in railways. We admit Parliament into an affair with which, the Americans say, Parliament cannot have any natural concern—viz., giving leave for an industrial enterprise. We may, in return, point to the American abuse of competing lines, which cause much waste and ruin: but the truth remains, that we delude ourselves with the notion that parliamentary permission is itself a property. Here is one unproductive property, held by a great body of claimants. Another expects to make money by the process of construction, which is essentially unproductive. A yet larger body looks for dividends in return for investments; and great must be the productiveness to raise that sort of profit above the ordinary interest of capital. And finally, there is a highly expensive body of persons who hope to grow rich by the unproductive process of mere management. While so many claims are to be met, there is no specific party whose interest it is to watch over the details of construction and management like the body of local stockholders in America. The shareholders do not speak or act for themselves, and are anything but represented by the directors. Altogether, the whole affair is very like the old-fashioned "West India property," which was never a very good thing, and has long been a very bad one; where an estate is expected to maintain, first, the labour upon it; next, the overseer's establishment, with its house, its garden, its servants, its horses, &c.; next, the attorney of the estate, with his needs and accommodations; and finally, the proprietor in England, with his family, his mansion, his servants, his carriages, his foreign travel, and so on; while it is nobody's particular interest to cherish the productiveness of the estate.[8] There are fine features about our railway system; the durability and splendour of our engineering works,[9] and the facilities for forming at length an effective organisation; but the political aspect of that social department requires amendment most pressingly. While there are between 70 and 90 railways directors in Parliament, whence permission for railway construction must proceed; while various unproductive bodies of claimants press upon the yield of our railways; while the actual owners have no power over the management, or none that they can use with effect, or none that is in fact effectively used, we cannot regard with much complacency the comparison of our system with those of other countries. If we complain that our American investments yield precarious returns or none at all, the Americans point with amazement to our sheer losses, which amount to two-thirds of the entire expenditure on American railways thus far. Till the Americans can establish such concert as will obviate the formation of needless lines, they have something to be ashamed of. Till we can afford to our shareholders a real representation, or an effective control, we have little to boast of. As to the Russian scheme, its character is simply that of a costly imperial convenience, with which neither subjects nor aliens have any temptation to meddle. But in truth all the three nations may well desire to have their social structure judged by some more favourable exponent than their railway system.

Notes

1. The "Special Correspondent" was probably Edwin Lawrence Godkin (see William M. Armstrong, *E. L. Godkin. A Biography* [Albany: State U of New York P, 1978]). "New Aspects of American Railways" (*Daily News*, 5 February 1857: 5, cols. 2–3) warns British investors to pay closer attention to "continental" railroads in the United States than to local, zig-zag lines that can fail. The New York-Cincinnati route, for example, is to be part of a "great artery" of a "mammoth animal" and will eventually put St. Louis within 40 hours of New York. Shorter "ribs" will cross the major track.

   Martineau may also have seen "A New Pacific Railroad Bill" (*New York Times*, 13 December 1856: 1, cols. 1–2) and the series of articles and letters in the *New York Daily Tribune* that argue for and against the wisdom of building and/or of ceding public lands for a railroad to the Pacific (11 December 1856: 4, cols. 2–3; 12 December 1856: 5, col. 4; 16 December 1856: 5, col. 3; 29 December 1856: 4, cols. 3–4; 5 January 1857: 5, col. 2; 13 January 1857: 4, cols. 2–4 and 5, cols. 3–4; and 4 February 1857: 4, cols. 2–3 and 4–5, and 5, col. 2). The *Tribune* claims that American railroads pay a poor return on their stocks, partly owing (in New England) to the "petty local interests which they have been constructed to subserve" (4 February 1857: 4, cols. 4–5).

   For British investment in western American railroads, especially through the financial house of Baring Brothers, see Thomas C. Cochran, *Railroad Leaders, 1845–1890. The Business Mind in America* (Cambridge, MA: Harvard U P, 1953). Martineau obviously does not anticipate the panic later in 1857—see remarks that follow.

2. The idea of state aid for canal building and river improvement began in Virginia and Maryland under Washington; in Britain, railroads and most canals were built by unaided private enterprise. For local, state, and federal government help for railroads, see Carter Goodrich, *Government Promotion of American Canals and Railroads, 1800–1890* (New York: Columbia U P, 1960).

3. Cf. Martineau's report on British "railway mania" of 1845 in *History of the Peace* (2: 628–33) and as caricatured by Dickens in *Dombey and Son*.

4. Before 1850, private projectors of a Pacific railway asked for as much as a thirty mile-wide strip on each side of the road. A bill reported to the Senate of 1855–1856 asked for alternate sections of twelve miles on each side. In February 1857, the *New York Daily Tribune* recommended a continuous two mile-wide strip plus $50,000,000 in cash (4 February: 4, cols. 4–5). The act of 1862 for a Pacific railway granted ten sections per mile, later doubled to twenty sections on each

side of the road, plus other government support. See Lewis Henry Haney, *A Congressional History of Railways in the United States, 1850–1887. Bulletin of the University of Wisconsin*, no. 342 (January 1910).

5. Martineau probably wrote the *Daily News* leader of 18 January 1859 that urges British investors to devote their energies to improving administration of the safer British "Government, Railway, and other Home Securities" rather than seeking foreign projects for surplus capital.

6. Russia's first longer railroad, from St. Petersburg to Moscow, opened in 1851. It was built by the state and later sold to a private company. After the Crimean War, the government surveyed railroad lines that were constructed and managed by private companies, with help from the government. *The Times* had recently warned readers against investing in a French company contracting to build a railroad in Russia; see 30 October 1856: 6, cols. 2–3; 12 November 1856: 6, cols. 4–6; 25 November 1856: 8, cols. 3–4; and 19 December 1856: 6, cols. 4–5.

7. In 1867, Martineau was to berate the inept and unethical managers of the London, Brighton and Southcoast line, in which she had her money: see *Harriet Martineau's Letters to Fanny Wedgwood*.

8. Martineau uses this utilitarian argument against slavery elsewhere, as in *Daily News*, 25 October 1859 (on West Indian labor).

9. English locomotives had a reputation for strength and durability, and English rails were generally made of better-worked iron than American ones.

12. The National Association for the Promotion of Social Science

Introduction

The second meeting of the National Association for the Promotion of Social Science, an analogue to the British Association for the Advancement of Science, took place at Liverpool, 11–15 October 1858. Founded on the idea that "the science of promoting the prosperity, happiness, and welfare of the human race" was no less unified than the various branches of physical science treated by the British Association, the NAPSS met annually in different cities. (Unlike the British Association, it also welcomed women members and speakers.[1]) Ruskin, Charles Kingsley, and Florence Nightingale were among those who sent papers in 1858. From the five "departments" of the NAPSS: jurisprudence and amendment of the law, education, punishment and reformation, public health, and social economy, issues of special concern in 1858 were reform of the bankruptcy and insolvency law, open competitions for civil service, and the controversial movement for central authority in sanitary reform (cf. "*Daily News*, 24 September 1853," above).

The Times, sarcastic in the past about the British Association, devoted three leaders and ten articles to the meeting, announcing it as a "flood of light" upon the science "popularly termed 'social.'" Speeches by Lord John Russell, Lord Shaftesbury, Lord Brougham, and others were quoted in full, like parliamentary or constituency speeches.

In 1838, Martineau had attended a meeting of the British Association at Newcastle. That meeting she describes as spoiled by "coxcombs ... third-rate men ... and humbugs" (*Autobiography* 2: 137). In the case of the NAPSS, Martineau mistrusted the Whig politicians who ran it and usually disagreed on principle with *The Times*, which praised it.[2]

Martineau's report of opening day of the meeting (*Daily News*, 11 October 1858) sounds a political note: she deplores the national state of "helplessness" [under Palmerston] and calls for guidance in social reform. A study of recent history, she says, can help the middle class to see how reform was accomplished in the past, "to prepare and bring forward the hour and the man." (By the following year, Martineau had changed her verdict on the NAPSS: Lord Shaftesbury's message seemed cheerful and the state of social progress encouraging, in spite of the diversity and magnitude of remaining problems: *Daily News*, 11, 15, 18 October 1859). Even here, after censuring the NAPSS, she cannot resist spinning a parable to excuse its seeming failings.

On the day this leader appeared, Martineau wrote to a friend that she had "doubted its reception,—from its abstract character," but the editor had assured her it was "precisely what he had been wishing for."[3]

Notes

1. See Kathleen E. McCrone, "The National Association for the Promotion of Social Science and the Advancement of Victorian Women," *Atlantis* 8 (1982): 44–66.
2. For a claim in favor of Martineau as a social scientist in her own right, see Susan Hoecker-Drysdale, *Harriet Martineau. First Woman Sociologist* (Oxford: Berg, 1992).
3. *Harriet Martineau's Letters to Fanny Wedgwood*, 169–70.

* * * *

Daily News
25 October 1858

IT ought not to be a matter of surprise to any of us, that we are hearing on every side expressions of perplexity and vague uneasiness about the desultory and indefinite character of the results of the Social Science Meetings of last year and the present.[1] The impression ought not, we say, to surprise us; and the open manifestation of it in many directions ought to be hailed by us as a great good in itself, and as a promise of future benefits. There is a natural reluctance to find any fault, to express anything like discontent, when so much good has been intended and actually done; and when we agree all round that the scheme is a noble one, that the meeting of this year was a great improvement on the last, that much wisdom was uttered and substantial knowledge conveyed, and, above all, that the whole spirit of the assemblage and its proceedings was elevated and genial, it really goes hard with us to acknowledge any deficiency or disappointment. Yet is everybody wondering at the same phenomenon—"the floundering of the wisest people there" on some of the most prominent questions, and not the least on those which are regarded as their specialities. In the midst of more than one discussion it became suddenly understood that the question grew out of another below it which nobody was prepared to enter upon; or if the discovery was not made the case was the worse, because the study was then necessarily quitted in an unsatisfactory manner, and found unsusceptible of settlement—nobody knowing exactly why. In short, the whole scheme and all its component parts were fragmentary. Not only was there, as in the sessions of the British Association, a long list of separate topics (which is all very right), but, unlike those Physical Science meetings, there was no scheme of general facts—in other words, of laws—to which to refer the special facts.[2]

From the outset of this great and beneficent scheme of association there has been an omission which was certain to occasion such disappointment as is now expressed, and to cause, meantime, some loss of time and waste of words. In promulgating the description of the Association, as aiming at "the promotion of Social Science," its authors should have expressed their conception of the term "Science," that the public might know what to look for, and the members might come to some sort of agreement what to attempt. This omission (or rather the state of mind which occasioned the omission) we take to be the cause of the confused and fragmentary character of the achievements at both meetings. The general consciousness of the fact is much stronger after the Liverpool than it was after the Birmingham meeting; and another year or two will probably open the eyes of all the most intelligent members and observers to the real position of the Society and its task.

It should be remembered that there are practically, though not philosophically, two meanings to the word SCIENCE. The loose, popular, and deceptive meaning of the word is Knowledge. In this sense not only is the term used every day by people who prefer a fine word to a plain one, but by many who should be more accurate, but who like to regard as science any knowledge which relates to genuine scientific topics. Thus we used to hear Geology called a science a quarter of a century ago, when we were in possession only of a mass of facts, and of hypotheses which had not had time to show whether they were to drop off the stem of truth or to fructify into theory and law. In like manner Political Economy was called a science before men had agreed on any general facts whatever within its range, or any one principle was indisputably established.[3] In like manner the Association to which we are now paying deserved honour proposed, as the aim and reason of its existence, the "promotion" of something which actually remains to be created. Social Science does not yet exist, while knowledge on social subjects abounds more than it ever did before in any age, among the most advanced people in the world. In its true philosophical sense, science means a recognition of the bases of knowledge, of the laws of facts. If our Association really proposes to promote *this*, we have only to ask when it means to begin its task; for no approach towards such an attempt has yet been visible. It would be an affectation to put the inquiry in form; for it is obvious that this greatest work which remains for human reason to do is not one which can be ever undertaken by any desultory association of persons, philosophers, philanthropists or other. The due preparation is not made; the time has not arrived; and, if it had, the means are inappropriate. The true science of society is the establishment of the laws under which mankind live in society; and those laws must be derived from the nature of Man. This nature is not yet ascertained: that derivation has not yet been traced; and nothing can be further from the intention of the Society under notice than to undertake the study of either the one or the other.[4]

Neither is it their object, as far as they have yet shown, to collect and supply the means and materials of such science. This is the great point of difference between them and the members of the other great Association. However desultory were the proceedings and the achievements of the British Association for the Advancement of Science in its early days, every act of its existence did really tend towards the discovery or establishment of general facts—in other words, of laws—of Nature.[5] [*Martineau continues to praise the British Association for "progress . . . towards the evolution of the great laws of the Universe."*] The general facts which underlie physical researches are awful in their way, impressive, if not overwhelming to the human imagination; but there is, as far as our ignorance yet allows us to see, something infinitely more solemn and overpowering in the general facts which will constitute the social science of a future generation. It was the general instinct of this which caused so many shortcomings, so much abrupt recoil from ends to which all seemed tending. In fact, the heights of the science can be attained only by ways as yet unexplored, except, perhaps, by individuals who do not want to be telling travellers' tales, and whom the world does not solicit to do so. A large party have agreed to begin to scale the heights, and off they set, in fine spirits and good humour, hoping to do great things. At present they have got no further than a broad glacier. People on the watch at a distance wonder why they do not march straight on and up, instead of going zigzag, stopping very often and turning back always. People at a distance do not perceive the crevasses which open in all directions, and can have no conception what it is to look down into those dim abysses, nor how unsatisfactory it is to find them bridged in a way which will not bear any but the lightest tread. A guide here and there may show how to head them round; but in most cases there is nothing for it but to turn back, and try some other way, or to make the best bridge for the nonce. If their day is over before they have accomplished this, why blame them? Who is there that could have done any better? Let them try again and again, and, if they do not reach the summit—even any true peak of the whole range—they are exploring the way, and perhaps making something like a road. In plain language, the best hope seems to be that the members will work on at practical objects, improving in scope, in order, and in enlightened zeal as they are now doing from year to year. They will be brought, some day, into a position which will compel them to determine whether to go on into science, properly so called, or to break off. It will be given them in that hour what to speak, and resolve, and do. Till that hour arrives, we have only to desiderate what is practicable, and not to be dissatisfied with what is achieved, merely because it has been mistakenly ticketed with the description of a higher class than that to which it belongs.

Notes

1. The NAPSS, launched by Lord Brougham at Birmingham in 1857, aimed to encourage social reformers "to collect facts, to diffuse knowledge, to stimulate inquiry . . . and [to make] suggestions in aid of social improvement" (*Transactions of the National Association for the Promotion of Social Science. 1857*, xxviii); cf. McCrone. Martineau may overstate negative reaction to the meetings—see introduction.

2. For its "departments" and the special subjects the NAPSS addressed in 1858, see introduction. Its stated goals declare that "as much reliance was placed on the actual experience of social reformers as on that *à priori* reasoning which would strike any thinker on the subject" (*Transactions . . . 1857*, xxi). For Martineau's censure of the early British Association, see *Autobiography* 2: 134–38.

3. In spite of her early popularization of "Political Economy," Martineau makes the same accusation in her *Autobiography* (2: 244–45).

4. In her preface to *The Positive Philosophy of Auguste Comte. Freely Translated and Condensed by Harriet Martineau* (London: John Chapman, 1853), Martineau praises Comte for leading readers up to the highest [social] science, which he has "discriminated, arranged, and consolidated, so as to be ready to fulfil the conditions of true science" (ix). The NAPSS hoped to establish the interrelationship of the various branches of social science but was to find "the phenomena . . . so numerous and complex . . . that it [was] not possible by observation or induction to distinguish their exact relations" (*Transactions . . . 1884*, 1).

5. The British Association, established in 1831, aimed to encourage and direct scientific inquiry, to provide a forum for British

and foreign scientists, and to draw public attention to the objects of science. Papers on geology, astronomy, and the physical sciences predominated. The tenor of some early meetings may be judged from Dickens' "Full Report of the First Meeting of the Mudfog Association for the Advancement of Everything" (*Bentley's Miscellany* 2: 397–413). See O. J. R. Howarth, *The British Association for the Advancement of Science: A Retrospect, 1831–1921* (London: The Association, 1922).

13. Cotton Supply: India, U.S.A./Slavery

Introduction

Flemish refugees may have begun the spinning and weaving of cotton cloth in Lancashire in the second half of the sixteenth century. In 1727 Daniel Defoe could claim of Manchester—a market town where freedom from guild restrictions had earlier encouraged linen and woolen making: "the grand manufacture which has so much raised this town is... *cotton* in all its varieties."[1]

Most raw cotton, by the end of the eighteenth century, came from the British West Indies; from Spanish, French, Portuguese and Dutch settlements; and from Turkey. Innovative machinery for spinning (along with that for weaving, bleaching, and printing the cloth) soon allowed the popular short-stapled American cotton to be imported in quantities that swamped other suppliers. Within another thirty years, far-seeing men from Manchester and Liverpool began to warn against overdependence on American cotton. In 1848 John Bright, then MP for Manchester, headed a select committee that reported on Indian cotton. In 1857, the Manchester Chamber of Commerce spawned an offshoot Cotton Supply Association to act as a pressure group on the government and to encourage the growing of cotton wherever possible, especially in India.

Meanwhile from 1850 to 1873—a "golden age" of British trade and manufacturing achievement, the cotton textile industry reached its "highest peak of importance and prestige" as Britain's premier industry.[2] By 1850, three-fourths of the raw cotton came from the United States. Yet by the mid-1850s, cotton cloth consumption was increasing at a rate almost double the imports of American raw cotton, "cutting dangerously into the reserve stocks held in Liverpool" (Silver, 62, 77).

Cotton Supply Association spokesmen, among other critics of the (British) government of India, focused on the former East India Company's tepid interest in promoting railroads and canals.

In *Society in America*, Martineau records that she visited cotton plantations worked by slaves and heard of worn-out soil in southern states (cf. "*Daily News*, 25 November 1856," note 10). She also saw thrifty farms and settlements of non-slave-owning Germans there. Throughout her fifty or more leaders on cotton, Martineau decries the reliance on American slave-grown cotton and touts India as the best alternative source. She accepts the notion held by a vocal minority of the Manchester Chamber of Commerce and the Cotton Supply Association that, contrary to the workings of the law of supply and demand, practical steps must be taken to stimulate the growing of cotton in India (see, for example, *Daily News*, 24, 26 February; 30 June 1857; 29 January, 27 April, 29 October 1861; and 27 June 1862). American slavery, Martineau claims, changed economic laws (*Daily News*, 8, 14 July 1862), and British manufacturers had an obligation to keep their operatives employed (*Daily News*, 21 July, 9 August 1862).

Notes

1. Quoted by Edward Baines, *History of the Cotton Manufacture in Great Britain* (London: H. Fisher, R. Fisher, and P. Jackson, 1835), 107. See also, W. O. Henderson, *The Lancashire Cotton Famine, 1861–1865* (Manchester: Manchester U P, 1934).

2. Arthur W. Silver, *Manchester Men and Indian Cotton, 1847–1872* (Manchester: Manchester U P, 1966), 1.

****

Daily News
18 February 1859

IT is a matter of satisfaction that Lord STANLEY recognises the importance of Indian cotton to English prosperity. Now that we are about to hear what he has to say and propose, it is of the utmost consequence that the essential elements of the case should be understood and estimated at their true value.[1] If, for instance, we misapprehend the conditions in regard to American cotton, and entertain groundless expectations of a permanent supply from other countries than India, we shall make mistakes in regard to the Indian case. The *Times*, while explaining the importance of opening new sources of supply, has presented a picture of American cotton-growing so thoroughly erroneous that it must be corrected before we can be in a position to estimate our need of an Indian supply.[2]

The *Times* explains well the essential importance of our having plenty of cotton at command and in store; the subsistence of millions of our countrymen depending on it no less than on a sufficiency of corn. But, in proceeding to show why the cotton of the United States is, and always will be, our main reliance, the writer seems to be actually unaware of any change of circumstances in the cotton-producing States which can affect their production and commerce. The picture would not have been a true one ten or twenty years ago. Now it is perfectly untrue—at the very moment when mistake is practically dangerous in a high degree.

The *Times* says that the American planters have a great advantage over other cotton-producers in the excellence of their handling of the cotton. This is true. It is their one distinctive advantage. Long experience, constant practice, and the best gins in existence give them the preference in the market; and it requires a long course of folly on their part to annul such a privilege. Beyond this, the account of their qualifications in the *Times* is illusory. The boundless extent of fertile soil, the abundant capital, the agricultural improvements, the perpetual supply of trained labour do not exist, or are on the decline. The crumbling plantation-houses and degenerating lands show the deficiency of capital. The reports of the *Southern Conventions* of any year will show how this deficiency is felt.[3] Northern capital sustains such public enterprises as exist; and the acutest jealousy has not enabled the planter-class to run a single steamboat to Europe, as was proposed in indignation at the "encroachments" of New York.[4] The amount raised was enough to pay for coal for steaming an hour and a half—or a mile and a half, we forget which, without reckoning the vessel and her outfit. As to private business, it is mainly Northern capital which sustains it too, for the Southern estates are mortgaged, like those in the West Indies before the days of emancipation; and the mortgagees see their security crumbling away, under the pressure of debt, and the bad economy which attends slave-labour. While whole states are sinking into something like the barrenness of Virginia and North Carolina, there is no opening for new planting elsewhere, as we are apt to suppose. It was so once; but it is not so now. When Texas was annexed, we supposed there was no further limit to the spread of Southern production; whereas Texas has proved to be itself the barrier. Beyond it extends a barren territory, a dry desert, where even a railway is impracticable from the total deficiency of water for several days' journey. Nothing grows there, of course, and nobody lives there but a few wandering Mexicans and half-castes, who offer a safe refuge to escaping slaves. But the way in which Texas is itself a bar is that free white labour is gaining ground upon slavery there so as materially to affect the question of cotton supply. It is a pure good to us and the world that the German settlers find it easy, wholesome, and profitable to grow cotton with their own hands; and that they are living on an area level for the most part or slightly sloping to the sea, so as to afford every facility for sending us their produce by rail and steamer.[5] But it must be remembered that this supersession of slave labour by immigrant industry must break up so much of the routine of the other cotton-producing States as to occasion great disturbance in the supply. One indication of what must ensue is afforded by the present commotion on the subject of reviving the African slave trade.[6]

It is worth while to give a moment's attention to the latest account of the population of the leading cotton State, in order to see what we have to expect in a few years' time. While the fertile lands of Texas are more and more taken up and tilled by white immigrants, whose young children do more good work than the costliest slaves, the condition of South Carolina is this—according to the Report for 1857 just made to the Legislature. The white population of the State has not increased for thirty years; and the births among the blacks are three to one of the whites. It is well understood that the new generation are in large proportion Mulatto, as every Slave State is more or less a slave-breeding one: and the killing-off, or "using-up" of slaves in the rice swamps of South Carolina causes a higher mortality than usual among blacks, though not equal to that of Louisiana, where the sugar crop is yet more destructive of human life. On the one hand, then, the slaves die off fast in South Carolina; and on the other, they increase rapidly, through an extensive concubinage. The result is one with which we have a practical concern. The total population of the State is 668,507; and the majority of the slave population over the free is already 101,461, or nearly a sixth; while the births in that class are 3 to 1 of the free inhabitants. The excess of deaths among the slaves is 5,858; while the excess of births is 9,564. The anxious question is now asked, what will be the condition of the State after another thirty years? Here is no increase of white population in the last thirty—the deaths nearly equalling the births, the small surplus always wandering away from its unprosperous birthplace; and meanwhile the black element—which is the slave element, for there are no free blacks—steadily and rapidly encroaching upon the free. Now we see why there is such fierce opposition of opinion on the spot about the re-opening of the African Slave-trade [sic]. A country-bred, narrow, selfish proprietor, who knows only that the slaves in the market are far too dear for a man with a declining estate and insufficient capital, seizes upon the idea of importing savages cheap; and he bestirs himself to get the thing talked up at Charleston, and even at Washington. Wiser men, more conversant with affairs, and more awake to the perils of the State, see that it will be more than they and their sons can do to go on as they are, and to extricate themselves safely from their perils; and that it would be immediate destruction to introduce native Africans among a slave population already nearly one-third more numerous than the free race. The recent discussion in the Legislature is distinguished by an earnestness and solemnity which indicate the gravity of the case.[7]

When we remember that the same contrast between the prospects of free and slave labour is becoming conspicuous through the whole range of States, we shall admit that it would be rash in the extreme to depend for our cotton supply on a country already so disturbed in its industrial area, and so certainly destined to go through a most trying revolution in the conditions of labour. Meantime, the exhortations offered to South Carolina by sister States are strong and clear—to encourage the white element and repress the black—to invite free immigrants and get rid of slaves with all convenient speed. We know that this cannot be done. We know that free and slave labour cannot exist face to face. It is not our province to foretel what part the South Carolina planters will take. We have only to observe at present that their position and circumstances are something very unlike what the *Times* sets forth, and to take early care to secure a supply of cotton for our own needs, which shall prevent our being too much affected by any convulsions which may occur in the industrial system of the Southern States of America.

Notes

1. Edward Henry Stanley (1826–1893), later 15th Earl of Derby; currently Secretary of State for India (taken over by the Crown in 1858) in his father's second cabinet. Stanley told Parliament he intended to proceed with railroad and irrigation projects in India to be financed by private capital (*The Times*, 5 February 1859: 7, cols. 2–3, and 15 February 1859: 7, cols. 1–6—8, col. 1). Stanley's family had Lancashire cotton interests, and he had visited India in 1852.

2. On 7 February 1859, *The Times* noted that the law of supply and demand for cotton was not working: a sufficient store of cotton, now scant, could not be maintained by a limited supply of slave labor, in spite of the millions of yet uncultivated acres in the United States. Further, *The Times* said, the East India Company and a "close"

Cotton Supply: India, U.S.A./Slavery 105

government in India had not supported irrigation works, railroads, and other projects to insure a cotton supply (6, col. 6—7, col. 1).

3. The New York *Times* called the latest Southern Commercial Convention (held at Montgomery, Alabama) a farce. Among the proposals were retaliatory measures against Northern products and resumption of the slave trade. The first was illegal, said the *Times*, and would leave the South without products they couldn't produce. Most states' representatives opposed revival of the slave trade: some had left early in disgust. A trans-Atlantic steamship project was also reported on (14 May 1858: 4, cols. 3–4; 15 May 1858: 1, cols. 2–3 and 2, cols. 3–5). Articles on the convention also appeared in the New York *Tribune*, 20, 21, 22 and 29 May 1858.

4. Cf. the New York *Tribune*, 29 May 1858: 5, cols. 1–2.

5. For Texas and the account of German settlers there, Martineau may rely partly on Frederick Law Olmsted, *A Journey Through Texas* (London: Sampson Low, 1857). In earlier leaders she notes as sources of information on the South: Olmsted's *A Journey in the Seaboard Slave States* (1856), James Stirling's *Letters from the Slave States* (London: J. W. Parker, 1857) and Hinton Rowan Helper's *The Impending Crisis of the South* (New York: Burdick, 1857): *Daily News*, 19 and 20 July 1856 [review of Olmsted's *Slave States*], 13 August 1856 and 4 August 1857. While she stayed in New Orleans in 1835, Martineau was invited to settle in Texas to help write a constitution for the republic (*Autobiography* 2: 20, 51–54).

6. See above, note 3. For Martineau's attack on a French-inspired revival of the slave trade, see "25 November 1856," below.

7. On 3 December 1858, the New York *Times* rebuked the South Carolina legislature for discussing the slave trade (4, cols. 3–4); on 27 December 1858, the New York *Tribune* reported the introduction of bills in the same legislature to prevent slaves from doing mechanical labor or entering into contracts, posing a dilemma for South Carolina slave owners (4, col. 4).

14. Sheffield Outrages

Introduction

The "Sheffield outrages"—trade-union-inspired acts of violence against workmen and employers of the town's light metal-working industries—in 1867 led to a Royal Commission on Trades Unions. Through subcommissions on trade outrages, members of the middle classes hoped permanently to discredit trade unions. Although Sheffield hand-craftsmen such as knife-, file-, fender-, and saw-makers earned high wages, their special skills were threatened by the use of machines (readily employed in the new American industries). In fact, Sheffield's small workshops, employing men mostly known to one another, were a carry-over from past centuries that could not survive indefinitely.

In the mid-1860s, trade unions were in the public eye because "for the first time, large national amalgamated societies had arisen which were solid enough to survive trade depressions, or defeat in disputes."[1] Even in 1859, the carpenters' and joiners' unions had successfully defied a lockout by the London master-builders.

Sheffield craftsmen were unusually self-confident, owing to the high quality of their wares, and were defiantly loyal to union leaders who used harassment. Reports of two Sheffield outrages reached London newspapers in November and December 1861. In the "Acorn-street outrage," a tin box of gunpowder thrown through a house window at night (intended to intimidate a fender-grinder) injured two women, one fatally. The other incident, in nearby Thorpe Hesley, was the blowing up of a shop belonging to a strike-breaking nail-maker.

Martineau declares herself against trade unions in early tales like *The Rioters* and *The Turn-Out; or, Patience the Best Policy* (London: Houlston, 1827 and 1829); "A Manchester Strike" and "The Moral of Many Fables" in *Illustrations of Political Economy* (London: Charles Fox, 1832); and *The Tendency of Strikes and Sticks to Produce Low Wages, and of Union Between Masters and Men to Ensure Good Wages* (Durham: J. H. Veitch, 1834). She consistently opposes the right of workers to combine in restraint of trade and preaches "identity of interest" between masters and men.[2] Laborers, she urges, should save money and bring up their children to a variety of trades to be ready for trade depressions.

Martineau's latest sustained attack on unions had come in seventeen *Daily News* leaders, August to November 1859, over the London builders' strike. There she chides union leaders for inconsistent statements about the aims of the strike and for ignorance of political economy. The nine-hour working day, she asserts, is an impossibility. In "Secret Organisation of Trades" (*Edinburgh Review* 110 [October 1859]: 525–63), she explores new gains by the unions, condemning their "tyranny" and "audacious trickery" against true British liberties.

Although this short leader may have been edited, Martineau seems to have written it as a follow-up to her anonymous article, "The Last Sheffield Outrages" (*Once a Week*, 14 December 1861: 679–83). The narrator of that article, speaking to presumably naive readers, expresses surprise at the violence in a once-peaceful old town. He deplores the reversion to savagery by workmen in the midst of social advancement and the threat of "socialistic authority" on the part of unions.

By contrast, the *Daily News* leader abandons a pastoral tone and deploys favorite devices like alliteration, opposing details, and balanced phrasing.

Notes

    1. Sidney Pollard, ed., *The Sheffield Outrages. Report Presented to the Trades Union Commissioners in 1867* (Bath: Adams and Dart, 1971), vi.
    2. As Valerie Sanders has pointed out, Martineau's fictional characters fail, however, to demonstrate the latter principle: see *Reason*

over Passion: Harriet Martineau and the Victorian Novel (New York: St. Martin's Press, 1986).

* * * *

Daily News
26 March 1862

THE peculiar reproach of Sheffield has passed from being a matter of loose and vague censure, of dispute, and of display of various tempers, to some practical shape. The late trials at York have put an end to all uncertainty, real or pretended, as to why Sheffield outrages were perpetrated, and what sort of people perpetuated them.[1] It is well known that the prosperity of the town has been incalculably and irreparably injured by the protectionist policy and spirit which have been rampant in the self-styled representatives of the working men; and when the trade was mainly gone to America, and the capitalists retired in discouragement, or become virtually slaves to the working men, there was plenty of occasion for discontent all round. For a quarter of a century there have been serious objections to living in Sheffield for any man who valued his liberty of action, thought, and speech; for there was one set of subjects on which a man could not speak as he thought, tell what he knew, and act as he pleased, without danger to property, limb, or life. This could not, in a free country, go on for ever. It was always probable that some season of distress, or some new aspect of the local manufacture, would occasion a rate of outrage above the average, and bring on a thorough search, and an effective retribution. It was only a question of time; and it is not surprising that no one was found to precipitate the explosion when it was nearly certain that a private and particular explosion in his own house or shop would be the recompense of his public service.[2] Everybody must be glad that the exposure has come, allowing action against the evil, and putting an end to the silence of terror in which men sat waiting for new murders. As the mischief ceased in Glasgow and Dublin after a full disclosure of the facts, so it will cease in Sheffield, if all good citizens do their duty.³

The hideous revelations at York have let all the world know—what Sheffield was aware of throughout—that there has been a system of dictation and tyranny, enforced by assassination, weighing all this while upon the working class, and on the employers of the town and neighbourhood. At last, however, the men of Sheffield have taken heart, and are stirring to vindicate their freedom and their good name. Last Wednesday the operatives of the town met in large numbers, "to discuss the question of trades' unions."⁴ The subject was a large one, and, thus announced, looks vague; but a distinct and circumscribed character was given to it by the adoption of a resolution to form a committee for the purpose of routing out the offense and punishing the offenders, and for taking all requisite steps for the complete suppression of that crime which is the opprobrium of Sheffield. If those working men are wise, they will give no confidence to anyone who attempts to palliate the crime, or to discourage them in their efforts. If they are wise, they will work on, under the sanction of public opinion, till they have traced the mischief to its root. When they have done that, they will be ready to assert that liberty which now most needs assertion—the liberty of the working man to sell his labour to whom he pleases, and on the terms which suit him. When the Sheffield workman obtains this liberty, he will feel what it is to live in a free country. Meantime, he might as well live under the BOURBONS or BONAPARTES as under the dictator of his trade district, whoever that may be.

Notes

1. At the York assizes on 19 March 1862, three nail-makers were found guilty of letting the can of gunpowder down the shop chimney at Thorpe Hesley and were sentenced to fifteen years' penal servitude each. (Seventeen witnesses, including three policemen, swore the men were elsewhere on the night of the outrage and, on appeal, the three nail-makers were set free.) At the same sessions, on 20 March 1862, a workman from the fender-grinders union was acquitted of the murder

Sheffield Outrages 111

of the woman lodger in the Acorn-street outrage. See *Daily News*, 21 March 1862: 6, col. 5; and 20 March 1862: 6, col. 2.

2. For the long history in Sheffield of intimidation through violence, claimed as a right by union spokesmen, see Sidney Pollard, *A History of Labour in Sheffield* (Liverpool: Liverpool U P, 1959).

3. Martineau refers to the 1838 trial of five Glasgow cotton spinners sentenced to seven years' transportation for conspiracy, illegal combination, and writing threatening letters (a charge of murder was "unproven"); she also seems to refer to the denunciation of Dublin trade officials by Daniel O'Connell in 1838; see also, "The Last Sheffield Outrages," 681.

4. At a meeting of the Sheffield operatives on Wednesday night, 19 March 1862, leaders asserted the duty of trade unionists to protect their good name by organizing an inquiry into the recent outrages: *Daily News*, 22 March 1862: 3, col. 3.

15. Drainage

Introduction

Flooding in the fenland area between Lincolnshire and Norfolk caught national attention in May 1862, when spring tides helped to undermine embankments (some possibly of Roman origin) and poured into agricultural lands.[1] After the Romans, religious groups and kings took the lead in draining and embanking the fens. Floods and neglect that followed dissolution of the monasteries by Henry VIII then caused the area to revert to watery expanses and bogs dotted with islands. Although seventeenth-century attempts to drain the fenlands succeeded, they were opposed by native fenmen (at first supported by Cromwell), and the region was fully drained only in the later eighteenth and early nineteenth centuries.

Early in May 1862, a sluice in the embankment of the River Ouse near King's Lynn, Norfolk, burst and allowed mixed sea and river water to spread over 6,000 acres of rich fields.[2] Superintendents were later charged with having known for four years about leaks in the embankment. Pressure had gradually built up on the sluice and when it fell, tidal and river waters ran wild.

Growing up in Norwich, Martineau must have heard the colorful history of the fens, where French Huguenots like her own family settled in the sixteenth century. In 1845, Martineau bought land at Ambleside to build herself a house. On the small farm she added in 1848, she put into practice her belief in the scientific control of nature by careful planning, including draining.[3] From the late 1840s, she regularly read the Royal Agricultural Society journal[4] (see *Daily News*, 28 May and 11 June

1853) and works such as Thomas Gisbourne's *Essays on Agriculture* (London: John Murray, 1854).[5]

From the beginning of her association with the *Daily News*, Martineau took farming and rural labor as two of her special topics. She urges, for example, the importance of arterial drainage—the implied subject here—to be carried out by a (utilitarian) central authority. She argues the need for agricultural statistics (opposed by farmers), adequate dwellings for laborers, steam-powered farm machines, and the re-cycling of wastes for fertilizer. She reports on weather, harvests, food supply, and on Irish, French, and Italian agricultural progress. She recommends consumption of American corn (maize) and salted beef. She analyzes the onset of cattle murrain in Britain and warns against water mills.

Here Martineau also indulges her historical imagination. As in her "historiettes" for *Once a Week*, she shows universal events as they affect ordinary people. The teeming life in the fens with its past disastrous floodings takes on a modern aspect. Unlike George Eliot, who conveys human frailty at catastrophic flooding in *Mill on the Floss* (1860) [based on the Trent in Lincolnshire], Martineau looks for a practical explanation of events. In *History of the Peace*, she notes the need for an understanding of "the huge revolutions of nature" to gain "some determining power over the human lot" (2: 709). In this leader, she hints at the similarity of sinister forces from the past, like the figures hiding in neglected thickets, and the modern authorities who failed to prevent the disaster.

Notes

1. See *The Times*, 16, 21, 23, 26 and 27 May 1862.
2. The sluice gates kept seawater from fields that at high tide were below sea level. Cf. H.C. Darby, *The Changing Fenland* (London: Cambridge U P, 1983), 158.
3. "Our Farm of Two Acres" (*Once a Week*, 9, 16 and 30 July 1859) describes the experiment.
4. Martineau may take information for this leader from John Algernon Clarke, "On the Great Level of the Fens, including the Fens of South Lincolnshire," *Journal of the Royal Agricultural Society* 8 (1847): 80–133.

5. This included "Agricultural Drainage" from the *Quarterly Review* 86 (December 1846): 76–126 (see *Daily News*, 16 December 1853).

* * * *

Daily News
27 May 1862

TIME was when the sea and the land struggled for mastery over a wide area of the eastern part of our island, where the Wash cuts deep into the coast between Lincolnshire and Norfolk.[1] At low tides there was an expanse of many miles in circumference, extending to Peterborough, Ely, and even Cambridge, where there were tracks of stone or wood, just passable from one mud bank to another, affording access to dry elevations, so that country carts could pass, or packhorses, with the help of ferry boats where the hundreds of streams were too steep for fording. At high tides the whole expanse was one swashing sea, sprinkled with islands, on which arose, from belts and clumps of alders, churches with crocketted spires, and monasteries, surrounded by their well-drained and paved gardens, green with vegetable crops, and in spring flowery with blossoming orchards. Those were the days when companies of pilgrims arrived in processions of boats to pay homage at the saints' shrines, or obtain the benefit of religious offices from the monks. Those were the days when the monks were kept busy in attending the sick beds of sufferers by ague and fever, and in burying, in graves in which the water stood almost up to the surface, hundreds of children, and of men and women cut off in their prime by the diseases of the region. Those were the days when thieves hid themselves among the alder thickets and tall reeds of uninhabited islands; and when pirates ran in from pursuit at sea, and dodged their pursuers in the multitudinous channels; and when rebels lay close in the watery wilderness till skiffs from foreign vessels ran in by night to carry them away with their heads on their shoulders. The monks, who had what learning there was at that day, lamented over the lapse into wilderness of a part of England measuring sixty miles one way by forty in another. They said that there had once been a forest there, in which not a few people, and a vast number of wild animals, lived and throve; but the trees grew old and fell, and at every fall a watery hole was left, so that the whole area in time became the swamp that the monks saw it a thousand years ago.²

As the years passed on, one great man after another imagined that he could make use of this one or that of the eight rivers which ran through the district to carry off the waters from his territory, so that he might have orchards and vineyards like those of the monks; and he employed his retainers to raise dykes and make drains till he provoked the jealously of neighbours, who alleged that he flooded their lands to dry his own.³ Then there were feuds and fights, and attempts to destroy the dykes, till some great winter storm rolled over the country and swamped the occasions of strife, reducing all parties to the same helplessness against the encroaching sea. Then the mariners and merchants of Lynn rejoiced, because their harbour was deep, and fresh traffic came to their port.

As the state of English society changed, and wealthy citizens began to see the bearings and benefits of public works, they asked why the sea should be allowed to play fast and loose with land which had once afforded game to the sportsman, and shelter and habitation to the Britons when the Romans were everywhere else. One scheme of embankment after another was approved by kings, and praised by nobles, and blessed by bishops, and exulted in by adventurous capitalists; but one day King HENRY VI. heard, amidst other misfortunes, that the sea had washed away all the works. King HENRY VII. heard the same bad news, and sorely the news must have vexed his rapacious soul. Queen ELIZABETH'S servants had to tell her that the Wash had made a clean sweep of a mass of wealth invested in the soil, or growing out of it; and JAMES I. received the same bad tidings.⁴ Then many citizens said that their fathers had been right when they shook their heads over new speculations. Time after time it had been said that the disaster could never happen again, so well planned were the drains and so firm the dykes; yet the disaster always had happened again, and it no doubt always would. When men tried to raise the fruits of the earth from the domain of the sea, they deserved to be

Drainage

disappointed. It was impious not to accept the rebuke. There are always men, however, who will be sure that disasters are rebukes before they will fold their hands and submit. Some such men thought the rebuke applied to making dykes of loose soil, and stopping or turning streams, instead of helping them to flow away; and in the reign of CHARLES I. there was an Earl of BEDFORD who was of this turn of mind; and he and some comrades began the great scheme of drainage, by which his name became connected with a vast district of reclaimed land.[5] There was loose earth in the embankments still; and there was, moreover, a screw loose in society at that time, by which ravage was let loose on the new territory. During the wars in which a certain Huntingdon brewer made himself famous, it was a device against the Royalists to cut the dykes, and spoil what the sea had left of the great Bedford property. But the son of the enterprising earl set to work again, fifteen years after his father's first attempt; and he persevered till a regular system of preservation was organized, and a corporation invested with the care of the whole project.[6] The different stages of improvement since CHARLES II.'s time have been marked by Acts of Parliament, by which one practicable navigation after another has been secured, and the wide waste has been made the seat of towns, villages, and homesteads, of production and traffic, of industry, wealth, and, for many years, of supposed security. The traditions of the Bedford Levels tell of the admiration excited by the first array of windmills, as the keepers of the peace between the sea and the land; and of the disgrace of the windmills when the steam engines were brought upon the scene; and of the neglect of steam engines when science taught the lands and channels to take care of themselves and each other. In course of years men began to see that there might be a separation between the ideas of drainage and navigation, and, as drainage was pursued for its own sake, it utilised more and more soil from which the salt waters were withdrawn, and rendered the modern marsh land even more famous for fertility than the great levels had ever been.[7] Up to this month of May the region was one which Englishmen might be proud of. Instead of a sprinkling of islands, one in ten of which might produce corn, and wine, and fruit, there were miles upon miles of fertile fields, bearing heavy crops of grain, and roots, and showing pasturage as green and rich as the sleekest fields in Holland. There were large farms, with their stackyards crowded with plenty. There were substantial roads, well walled canals, and bridges and sluices which might defy any dash of the surf, if the surf could come so far. There were laden boats on the canals, and herds of cattle in the meadows, and a stout population in the hamlets, not wholly exempt from the evils of fog and damp, but a wonderful contrast to the ague-striken cottagers of ancient times.

This year, the ploughing was done, the sowing of grain was done, the blade was green in the weeded fields, and the farmers and their wives in their Sunday walks reckoned up their probable crops, and settled what should be done next year. So affairs went on till the Sunday which will be memorable— Sunday, the 4th of May—when the news spread over the six counties which have an interest in the Fens[8] that the Middle Level Sluice had blown up. Instead of the rage of a fierce surf beating against stone walls and stout gates, there had been the spite of a stealthy foe—of a hidden force of waters which had undermined the stone walls, and taken the gates in the rear. From day to day the salt flood surmounted more barriers, burst more banks, overwhelmed more farms and villages, and scoured more and deeper holes in levels and canal channels. We heard of ten thousand acres being submerged, of fifteen thousand, of thirty thousand, of sixty thousand, and still there was no check to the ruin. There were hundreds of men, women, and boys, collected here and there, throwing sacks filled with earth into the holes and chasms, and trying to bind the banks with willow withes, and to line the great holes with basket work which might hold the stuffing of bags and stones: but each tide rose higher than the last, and swept out to sea whatever was laid down in the water or pinned into the land. The scene needs no description—the frenzied industry of the residents, the awe of the strangers who came to see, the grief of sympathisers, and the despair of the ruined. Future inquiry will show how much time was lost, and why.[9] Any day may show what science can do, and how quickly, to stop the mischief first, and then to remedy it. After a few days of lower tides, during which no effectual barrier was raised, the rise has begun again, and every variety of

Drainage

prophecy is heard on the ground as to the amount of ruin which will be wrought before the salt water is driven home. The certain points of the case are that a complete retrieval might be effected by the improved science and skill of our time, and that there is meantime a vast amount of ruin to be borne by somebody. England is not a country in which men allow themselves to be beaten by forces which their forefathers mastered, nor in which a deluge of rain is allowed to overwhelm innocent people, without a helping hand being extended to them. There is a double duty to be done—to save the land, and to save the people upon it. But divided interests are bringing perplexity and weakness. This is a mischief for which a remedy must be found, and that quickly.

Notes

1. The Wash is a shallow bay of the North Sea bordering the silted-up area of more than a half-million acres known as the fens; cf. Darby.

2. In another account of flooding, *Daily News*, 26 December 1857, Martineau notes this early history of the "Bedford Levels."

3. Martineau uses her Ambleside experience. In one case, a neighbor accused her of causing floods on his land, "by the construction of a causeway a long way off" (*Harriet Martineau's Letters to Fanny Wedgwood*, 291). And see her *Two Letters on Cow-Keeping* (London: Charles Gilpin, n. d.), 15.

4. For historic floodings in the fens, from sea and/or fresh water, cf. William Dugdale, *The History of Imbanking and Draining of divers Fens and Marshes, both in Foreign Parts and in this Kingdom, and of Improvements thereby* (2nd edition), ed. Charles Nalson Cole (London: Richard Geast, 1772).

5. Francis Russell, 4th Earl of Bedford (1593–1641), headed an association under an agreement with Charles I to drain the great level of the fens of the Nene and Ouse rivers; it became the Bedford level.

6. The "Huntingdon brewer" was Cromwell. William Russell, 5th Earl and 1st Duke of Bedford (1613–1700), and others convinced the Commonwealth Parliament to pass "the first specific act of Legislation for the general drainage of the Great Level" in 1649. After the Restoration, a new act of 1663 "established the corporation of the 'Bedford Level.'" (Samuel Wells, *The History of the Drainage of the Great Level of the Fens, called Bedford Level; with the Constitution and Law of the Bedford Level Corporation* [London: R. Pheney, 1830] 1: 155 and 388) The

Duke was advised by an engineer from Holland, who divided the area into the North, Middle, and South Levels.

7. In 1844 Parliament passed an act for "improving the Drainage and Navigation of the Middle Level of the Fens" (Clarke, 98). In *Daily News*, 7 January 1858, Martineau cites an 1848 act incorporating a land drainage company in the west of England and South Wales. On the need for government action on a national system of arterial drainage, see *Daily News*, 13 June 1862 and 24 August 1864.

8. The six counties were Norfolk, Suffolk, Cambridgeshire, Huntingdonshire, Northamptonshire, and Lincolnshire (Wells 1: 2–5).

9. *The Times* leader of 21 May 1862 (9, cols. 3–4) cites inadequate measures by the Middle Level Commissioners: "Engineers . . . running about from place to place, and hundreds of men . . . employed in filling bags with clay and twisting lengths of willows, all of which are swept away as quickly as they are thrown into the torrent"; and urges MPs to ask for an explanation in the Commons. "The Floods in the Fens" (*The Times*, 23 May 1862: 5, col. 3) further reports that after a failed attempt to stop the waters, nothing had been done for three days.

16. Factory Act

Introduction

Continental visitors to Regency Britain wrote in glowing terms of the industrial progress they saw: five- or six-story steam-heated factory buildings of steel beam and brick construction, with gas lights gleaming through plate glass windows and ingenious machines for producing metal, wood, glass, and leather objects and woolen, linen, silk, and cotton cloth. The visitors descended coal mines and observed ships and tramways and bridges. (Laborers were mentioned only rarely, as drunken, dirty and miserable.)[1]

Historians argue that while inventions like the flying shuttle and the spinning jenny allowed ambitious handworkers to become wealthy, the new employers had to force operatives ruthlessly to make the system work.[2] As an alternative, some early water-powered mills—necessarily located in rural areas—employed pauper boys from London. This led Parliament to enact the Health and Morals of Apprentices Act of 1802. The act contained features such as the regulation of working hours and the provision of education, inspection, and a method of publicizing its terms. Volunteer inspectors flagged, however, and the act was ignored. With the advent of steam engines, hugely expanded plants were set up in cities. There children became an integral part of, especially, the cloth-making processes.

Victorian acts regulating labor in factories and mines aimed, among other benefits, to limit hours of work for children, "young persons," and women and to provide a workable system of government inspection. Beginning with the acts of 1833 and

1844 for the textile industries, Parliament gradually passed laws that protected laborers from inhuman hours, dangerous machinery, and unsanitary working conditions. (The act of 1842 forbade the employment of women and children under ten in coal mines.) Time off for—and the provision of—education continued to be badly enforced.

In fact, Parliament's piecemeal approach left many industries employing children partly or wholly outside the law. In 1862, a new Royal commission headed by Hugh Seymour Tremenheere began to take evidence on the Staffordshire potteries, as well as on other industries, that led to the Factory Act of 1864—a watershed act that showed there was no real limit to future regulation of employers. Because the Factory Act of 1861 had failed to regulate hand finishing in lace and hosiery making, the commissioners also took evidence on those industries. *Children's Employment; Factories [Reports from Commissioners]* (P. P. 1863 XVIII), the results of two years' work, appeared after the parliamentary session ending in July 1863. The report recommended that conditions of existing factory law be extended to six more industries.

Martineau spent her formative years as the daughter of a manufacturer. Part of her radical creed was that market forces should determine conditions of work and that working people should be allowed to sell their labor without restrictions. In *The Factory Controversy* (Manchester: National Association of Factory Occupiers, 1855), she notoriously attacks Dickens for presuming to meddle in the question of the "fencing" of dangerous moving parts and of employer liability for factory accidents.[3] Her *Daily News* leaders on the question at times verge on hysteria, despite her claim to be the voice of reason (see 12 February; 4, 27 March; 7 and 15 April 1856). For Martineau's attacks on unions, see "*Daily News*, 26 March 1862," above.

The factory bill of 1863 called up an unexpected, positive response from Martineau (see also *Daily News*, 11 August 1863 and 29 April 1864) but one that is true to utilitarian theory that the labor of children is not free. Although Martineau here slights much horrifying evidence in the report, she underscores her long commitment to child welfare and, indirectly, to a national system of education.

Notes

1. See W. O. Henderson, *J. C. Fischer and His Diary of Industrial England, 1814–51* (London: Frank Cass, 1966) and *Industrial Britain under the Regency* (London: Frank Cass, 1968).
2. See Maurice Walton Thomas, *The Early Factory Legislation* (Leigh-on-Sea, Essex: Thames Bank, 1948).
3. For Martineau's personal reasons to quarrel with Dickens, see K. J. Fielding and Anne Smith, "*Hard Times* and the Factory Controversy, Dickens vs. Harriet Martineau," *Nineteenth-Century Fiction* 24: 404–27; Peter W. J. Bartrip, "Household Words and the Factory Accident Controversy," *Dickensian* 75: 17–29; and *Harriet Martineau's Letters to Fanny Wedgwood*.

* * * *

Daily News
4 August 1863

THE task of retrieving the condition of over-worked and ill-conditioned children in the various branches of our industry is immeasurably less difficult at present than it was formerly. Considering what the results of our Factory Acts have been, from the imperfect one of thirty years ago to the most recent and improved, the wonder is that thousands of children and young persons should still stand outside of the pale of legal protection in their daily work.[1] In manufacturing districts, where crooked backs, bent limbs, haggard faces, and fevered skins have become a rare sight, and where, in seeing the young people at work we need no longer tremble at the thought of what the next generation must be, we have an admonition to carry the same protection which has wrought the change into every manufacture in which departments of the work are done by persons too young to protect themselves.[2] All the objections which can be offered to such care of the helpless have been offered before; time and events have answered them, and they can never, therefore, be so difficult to deal with as they once were. A much larger number of employers than formerly is in favour of a legal provision which shall save them from many difficulties and responsibilities; and, on the other hand, many of the parents have heard of the improved condition of such populations of children as have come under the Factory Acts—of their better health, better education, and better wages; and such parents are on the side of protection instead of being ignorantly and violently opposed to it, as was commonly the case on former occasions.[3] There can be little doubt that the much smaller changes which remain to be made will be accomplished with little difficulty. Thirty years ago the whole question of the rights and wrongs of children and young persons in their industrial capacity was one of our most embarrassing social jungles, which it seemed scarcely possible either to penetrate or leave untouched. Now, the state of things, according to the Report of the Children's Employment Commissioners, is this.

There is a manufacture which employs a certain proportion of children and young lads and girls to the men who are considered able to take care of themselves. While nobody inquired how things were going on, serious evils were endured every day, which continued by force of custom—wasting the capital of the employer, and the time of the men, and the health of the children. As soon as an interest is felt outside, and a stir begins within, it is found that by applying modern knowledge and new inventions the masters may get larger profits, and the men more wages, while the health and lives of a multitude of children may be saved. This is remarkably the case in the particular instance of the drying stoves in the Potteries. Children have perished in great numbers from being sent incessantly backwards and forwards between these stove-rooms and cooler places, carrying in the ware, and bringing out the moulds. Liberal employers have reduced the visits to the stove (often red hot) by providing a large stock of moulds, while stingy or inconsiderate masters have got through with the smallest supply, at the expense of sending the children as often as possible into the heat. Under the stimulus of complaint and inquiry it is found that all purposes will be better answered by a new kind of stove, which spares the children from exposure to the heat, cooks the ware more evenly, and saves fuel at such a rate as soon to repay its own cost. There are in the Report indications of such a stir about various new stoves, the cost of a

Factory Act

due supply of moulds, &c., as promises well for the children, even before they can be brought under the guardianship of the law. The case is the same in regard to inconvenient and unhealthy buildings and arrangements, where the mere presence of inquiry introduces economy of time and toil, raises the roofs, opens the windows, and seems likely to call up new edifices provided with means of true economy, in the form of proper conditions of health and convenience.[4]

One of the first things disclosed by inquiries is that each party concerned needs some aid against another. The memorial of the great Pottery firms to the HOME SECRETARY, expressing a desire for an Act applicable to the children in their employment, speaks for one party; and complaints were made to the Commissioners by some employers that their men, whom they could not control without the aid of a law on the children's behalf, were apt to keep the boys under them idle one day, and work them on the next into or even through the night.[5] As for the men, the best will not let their children work at the risk of health and life, while the worst will get what they can from their children's toil and peril. As for the helpless children, it requires no explanation how they need help. Thus it is admitted to be for the benefit of all parties but bad employers and bad parents that the interests of the children should be secured in a way already proved to be safe and beneficial; and the only debate is about the method in each particular case.

Six branches of manufacture are included in the regular inquiry here reported, and the chimney-sweeps' case is somewhat irregularly but most advantageously considered also.[6] We shall hear more about other industries hereafter, and it is well that the Commissioners have not delayed their disclosures about the young potters, and match and percussion cap makers and finishers, and fustian cutters, till they could report of all the rest of the tribe of young workers. Of the 17,776 whose case they report, 11,000 are in the Potteries; and large as the number is, this is a very manageable case, because the number of employers is small, and the district of manufacture measures only eight miles in length by one to three in breadth. Within this narrow space the amount of paralysis, asthma, and consumption, of dwarfing and deformity, of irksome life and early death inflicted on 11,000 children and young persons, is most painful to read of, and yet it might be saved by improving the methods of about 100 pottery works. There are only 180 works in the Staffordshire district, and they lie so closely together that nowhere could supervision be more easy or more effectual. The Commissioners recommend, in a case at once urgent, peculiar, and easy in comparison with some others, a special procedure. On the testimony of the twenty-six eminent employers who memorialised the Government we may assume that there is every willingness to follow up by reform the inquiry they have asked for; but they are most impressed with the moral mischiefs of the case; whereas the Commissioners properly insist that an improved physical condition is an indispensable preliminary to other reforms.[7] This involves changes which the employers may object to. Special knowledge of the manufacture is thus requisite in the inspector, and the recommendation is that a qualified medical inspector shall be appointed by the SECRETARY OF STATE for a term (probably two years will suffice), whose business it will be to see that the works are well ventilated, and the evils of dust, heat, and especially overwork, are suppressed, and to enforce his authority by sanctions proposed in the Report, after which the children and young people of the Potteries may pass under the existing Factory Acts, only very slight modifications of which will be required.

This is the leading case of the Report—the young sweeps themselves being only 2,000, and the finishers and hookers only 2,300 to the 11,000 potters. The further we look into each case, however, the more important it is seen to be, in relation to the future interests of the country; and, when the ravage of factitious disease and death is stopped, there is something else of not less vital interest to be looked to. In what we have said of the doom of the young potters we have only opened up the first aspect of a very extensive disclosure.[8]

Notes

1. The factory act of 1833 reduced the working hours for children (but was not successful as an educational measure); the act of 1853 established the principle that it was "the right, and indeed the duty of

Factory Act

the State to intervene between employer and employed" (Thomas, 327). Yet besides the fact that some large and many small industries remained unregulated, health and safety provisions could be rudimentary and arrangements for education unsatisfactory. Martineau gives opinionated accounts of early Victorian factory acts in *History of the Peace* 2: 90–92, 408–9 and 551–60.

2. Evidence before the children's employment commission told of boys and girls subjected to intense heat (and/or sudden changes of temperature) and long hours in the potteries, of youths contracting "necrosis of the jaw" from phosphorous in lucifer match manufacture, of bodily distortion from fustian cutting, and of injury or death from explosions in percussion-cap making. In a few factories, virtual Dantesque conditions prevailed.

3. Proprietors usually agreed government regulation would be "good for the country" but had reservations on the grounds of staying competitive. In *History of the Peace*, Martineau attacks parents for "selling" their children to excessive labor before 1833. She cites "guilty neglect" by the Church in having failed to educate parents and by the state in regulating food (i. e., by Corn Laws, repealed in 1846), so parents had no choice but for their children to work (2: 90, 552). See also Martineau to Richard Monckton Milnes, 1843 [?] (MS Trinity Library Cambridge 16/56).

4. The report recommended the appointment of a medical inspector (see below) with the "power of entry (as under the Coal Mines Regulation Act)," who would serve notice of deficiencies and if necessary call up a committee of arbitration: specified improvements to be made within two years of the act.

5. The memorial from twenty-six pottery firms noted that children were taken from school before they were ten to work in the potteries and that this caused "moral and physical evils" such as illiteracy, stunted growth, consumption, distorted spine, and a high death rate. Because all manufacturers would not agree not to hire young children, the memorialists asked for an inquiry and a law to prevent early employment and to secure a minimum of education for the children.

6. In addition to pottery, lucifer match, percussion-cap manufacture and fustian cutting (see note 2), the report of the commissioners focused on "paper staining" [for wallpaper] and finishing and "hooking" [folding] of cloth. Besides chimney sweeps, Martineau excludes lace and hosiery making (see introduction), where evidence nevertheless revealed that children as young as two-and-a-half worked crammed together for long hours in dim light, often ill and suffering eyestrain.

7. The "moral mischief" was a "vast amount of ignorance [as shown by] that fact that out of 670 working children . . . 185 (or 27.6 per cent) professed themselves unable to read" (*Children's Employment; Factories*, 322).

8. Martineau surely means a (non-Church-dominated) system of national education. For her frustration at the Dissenters' opposition to Home Secretary Sir James Graham's factory bill of 1843 (providing for compulsory education for children in the manufacturing districts), see *History of the Peace* 2: 555–58.

17. Education: Rural Laborers

Introduction

Before the Education Act of 1870, children in Great Britain who were not privately taught went to elementary schools provided by the Church and other religious groups. Early attempts to help educate the burgeoning pauper and working-class population included Bell's and Lancaster's monitorial systems (starting 1797 and 1798) and Robert Owen's "institution for the formation of character" of 1816. When the liberal Whig leader Samuel Whitbread proposed in 1807 to use public money for a national system of education, he was treated as unrealistically "visionary" and his plans "sneered away."[1] Contemporary belief in the possibility of human enlightenment was supported by Utilitarians, who saw popular education "as the essential concomitant of the growth of factory production" (Simon, 138). Lord Brougham's reform-minded committee on the "Education of the Lower Orders in the Metropolis," also of 1816, exposed the misuse of endowment funds, mostly by the clergy, and the lack of schools for the poor. Yet his 1820 bill for universal compulsory education met opposition not only from the Church and the Dissenters, but from manufacturing interests dependent on child labor (152). In 1833, Parliament at last voted £20,000 to aid voluntary education societies to build school houses for the poor children of Great Britain.

A parliamentary committee reporting in 1838 still found education for the poor in England and Wales "lamentably deficient." Factory acts that specified the release of children to attend classes (see "*Daily News*, 4 August 1863," above) did not provide funds for schools. Sir James Graham's factory bill of

1843, which would have made education compulsory for factory children (with agricultural workers' children left for later), was defeated by Dissenters still objecting to control of schools by the Church.

In 1858, the Newcastle commission was formed "to inquire into the present State of Popular Education in England, and to consider and report what measures . . . are required for the Extension of sound and cheap elementary instruction to all classes of the People." From the commission's report came the Revised Code of 1862, largely drawn up by Robert Lowe, vice-president of the parliamentary Committee of Council on Education. Lowe aimed to reduce government spending on education and to make grants to individual schools dependent on how well pupils performed on examinations in reading, writing, and arithmetic (rather than on general reports by school inspectors). In spite of objections from men like Matthew Arnold (a school inspector), the new utilitarian "payment by results" prevailed.

As an early reader of the works of Priestley and Hartley, Martineau acquired a strong faith in the all-powerful influence of education. Virtually all she wrote aimed to "teach," including stories for children like *Traditions of Palestine* (London: Longman, 1830) and the *Playfellow* series. In *Household Education* (London: Moxon, 1849),[2] she explores the psychology of learning, beginning with physical care of the infant, the child's emotional development and its preparation for "intellectual training." With illustrations—partly from her own traumatic childhood, she traces the development of the "faculties," including "reasoning," and gives special attention to the education of girls. "Care of the habits" comes last.

In *History of the Peace*, Martineau usefully surveys government involvement in education over the past forty years. She pays tribute to Brougham for his "first comprehensive and definite proposal for the Education of the People of Great Britain" (1: 263–64) and praises the Church for giving up more than the Dissenters over the proposed factory bill of 1843 (2: 556–58).[3] Unstinting, she notes that the "sectarian spirit which is the curse of English society has thus far condemned the children of the nation to a defective education, or to total ignorance" (2: 712–

13). In *Endowed Schools of Ireland* (London: Smith, Elder; 1859),[4] she summarizes the report of a four-year study of endowments for middle-class education in Ireland, but also comments on the scheme of national (elementary) education in force there since 1832.

Martineau dedicates almost fifty *Daily News* leaders, 1853 to 1865, to the question of a national system of education, education in Ireland (5 July, 2 August 1853; 17 January 1858 and 29 January 1864), and the local system in Birmingham (5 January 1857). She recommends clear objectives about what children need to know (see 14 April 1857), the teaching of British law and history (see 5, 17 November 1855) and a range of domestic skills for girls (see 4 December 1856). The state, she claims, should act in the role of parent instead of policeman ("Transportation and Education," letter from "A Practical Reformer," 16 July 1853). Martineau's other writing on education for the *Daily News* concerns reform of the now rigidly stratified middle-class schools (see "*Daily News*, 30 March 1865," above). Her focus on schools for the children of agricultural workers in this leader backs her repeated claim that they are less well off than the children of factory workers.[5]

Notes

1. See Simon, *Studies in the History of Education 1780–1870*; and *History of the Peace* 1: 75–78.

2. Partly from the *People's Journal*; see Valerie Pichanick, *Harriet Martineau. The Woman and Her Work, 1802–76* (Ann Arbor: U of Michigan P, 1980).

3. For her letter attacking the Dissenters, written "for circulation or publication" but withheld by friends, see Martineau to Henry Crabb Robinson, 8 March 1844 (MS Dr. Williams's Library).

4. Reprinted from the *Daily News* of autumn 1858 and meant for MPs.

5. See Martineau to Richard Monckton Milnes [1843] (MS Trinity Library Cambridge 1656/6–7) and especially, Martineau to Henry Crabb Robinson, 11 May 1844 (MS Dr. Williams's Library), on Lord Shaftesbury's misdirected efforts for factory workers.

****

Daily News
11 November 1864

EVERY two or three years we witness a stir about the education of the rural labourers, and hear the most dismal reports and prophecies of the mischiefs of the hopeless ignorance of that class. Any incident of the time will serve for the introduction of the topic. At present there is the rick-burning in the Yorkshire Wolds.[1] Ten years ago there was the widespread protest against the spending the money of the taxpayers on capital schools, furnished and provided with all the requisites of a good education, but nearly or quite empty. There was no getting the parents to send their children, as long as they could make any sort of use of them at home, or obtain the smallest weekly sum from their earnings. The Inspectors' Reports of ten years ago are full of complaints of getting labourers' children to school at all, and of keeping there any above eleven or twelve years of age, or even younger children for more than a year or so at any one school.[2] Then, when the poverty of the clergy and the pay of curates is the topic of the day, we hear again of this dead weight of the rural schools, the chief expense of which is borne by the local clergyman, and the results of which are a poor consolation to him for the privations his own children may have to undergo under this heavy charge on his income.[3] A sort of panic seems to have seized on a part of society this autumn about another feature of the case. Not only will the rural children stay away from the schools; not only will those who go be in a hurry to get away again, but those who attend for seven or eight precious years of youth, and are considered by their teachers and by themselves to be well-educated, bring away little or nothing that will ever do them any good; little or nothing that they will not have utterly forgotten in two or three years. According to the croakers who have lately been making their plaint through various newspapers there is nothing but failure on every hand, wherever the enlightenment of the rural labouring class is concerned; and the fires in the farmsteads of the Wolds are

Education: Rural Laborers

interpreted to be a sort of burning in effigy of our ideal of a regenerated peasant class.[4] This seems to us so far from being a sound view of the case, that we really cannot countenance the despondency of those friends of the rural class who declare themselves disheartened.

The evils complained of have all been true in their turn; and many of them are in full operation now; but each has its cause; the causes are known; and this in an age of progress is nearly the same thing as saying that they are sure of being remedied. It is perfectly true that a hedger and ditcher who earns 9s. a week must set his boys to work in the field as soon as they can earn anything. It is perfectly true that parents so poor, if they yield, in some hopeful time, to the admonitions of the clergyman or the Squire's lady, to send their children to school, may too probably be obliged to take them away again before a year is out. The lowness of wages is the mischief here; and the natural remedy is to be looked for in those changes which are daily improving the quality and the wages of agricultural labourers, wherever the new influences extend.[5] If it is really true that there are many such schools as "S. G. O." describes, where the children have their memories crammed with useless facts—facts useless to them in their present and prospective state of mind—the remedy lies in the reform of the managers and teachers of those schools, who are not giving the education the parents have a right to expect, but something else, less valuable to them than what they would learn in the course of their field labour. Common sense and sympathy in the patrons and conductors of the schools are the requisite here. The same thing may be said about the failure of the evening schools, where they have failed. We hear a great deal about the night schools being a worn-out system—a plan which yields no result, a hopeless enterprise, and so forth—but, if the boys leave school at twelve, having made a beginning in reading, writing, and arithmetic, there is every natural reason why an evening school should be the very thing for them—the appropriate remedy for the curtailment of their day schooling. And such a blessing as this many a night school still is, where the right elements and necessary conditions are present, viz., a decent peasantry, sufficiently fed and clothed to be open to the inducements of knowledge; a modest and sensible scheme of study; and managers and teachers who have patience and perseverance enough to do justice for years together to such an enterprise.[6] When it is once seen how dozens or scores of young men and boys and girls make a certain amount of progress from year to year, and are succeeded by others till the influence tells on the intelligence, morals, and manners of the parish, there will be no lack of the benevolence and self-denial requisite for the full working of such an institution.

While the croakers are insisting on the desperate condition and prospect of the rural intellect and manners, they are apparently blind to everything on the brighter side. In the recent discussions of the deplorable case of the labourers' children, from infancy upwards, we have not met with one single reference to the greatest educational proposal for many a day—the Half-Time System.[7] Do not the croakers know that well-taught scholars learn as much of ordinary school learning in three hours of the day as in six? Do they not perceive that, good as this discovery is for everybody, it is a blessing above all to the poor labourer, who can thus let his boys earn and learn at the same time, with less fatigue and disadvantage than if they did either without the other? Are these croakers unaware that this plan of alternate school and field work has been tried, and is in practice now, with the best results?

Again—do not these despondent good people take the trouble to attend to the results of such experiments in school gardens as we and others have pointed out as succeeding admirably at Alnwick and Eyemouth, and some other places?[8] Have they not observed that where that plan has been tried, the boys stay at school two or three years longer than they do elsewhere? This is one application of the half-time system which may be very widely extended in connexion with rural schools.

In proportion as the earlier schooling becomes more genuine, rational, and appropriate to the class it comprehends, the night schools will show that they are very far from being "worn out;" that, in fact, they have never yet had a fair chance, except in particular cases, where success has been the natural consequence. The influence of the Revised Code may be expected to extend beyond the schools which it controls—restoring the old estimation of the three first, great studies.[9] This

Education: Rural Laborers

being assumed, or at least hoped, all else that is requisite for the education of the labouring class (whether in town or country) is in actual existence, and only needs extension in proportion to the demand. Children may obtain a good plain education, in conjunction with work, up to fourteen or sixteen. Then the night school may take them up, and carry them on to a point from whence they can manage for themselves.

Further, the improvement in the science and art of agricultural is from year to year elevating the mind, the character, the position, and the fortunes of the rural labourer. The very aspect of the class, as one encounters them at agricultural meetings, is already so changed that the ghosts of their grandfathers would not know them. The children of a class so rising will not long be left in ignorance, or permitted to learn things that are, to them, hollow and useless. At the close of the Rev. J. P. Norris's last year's Report, as School Inspector, there is a passage which should shame the croakers, by showing what the lot of the rural labourers' sons might be under the very disadvantages complained of. Our readers may remember that statement of the rise in life of many sons of the poorest order of cottagers—youths by the score, who have risen to good positions in shops and warehouses, in the army, on the railways and in engineering works, on farms, as bailiffs or tenants, in the public service, or on good salaries in private establishments; and some in business for themselves, and rising in the world. The particulars are so interesting that it would be a kindness to refer all croakers to that Report.[10] Even the most disheartened of them could not but see that if such a lot is even now within reach of so many of the class, there is nothing that may not be hoped for even our rural labourers, when the new agricultural improvements have spread over the whole country, raising wages everywhere to the present highest point, and when parents of that class shall see plainly, and use eagerly the means which exist for making their children wiser than themselves, and the equals of the children of any other class which lives by its industry.

Notes

1. In five or six items in October 1864, *The Times* reports incendiary fires which "have last year and this so devastated the [Yorkshire] Wolds" (rick burning occurred in other places, too). A leader and correspondents dwell on "education and strikes": see 24 October: 6, cols. 3–4 and [letter from S. G. O.] 7, cols. 4–5.

2. See P. P. 1854–55 XLII. One inspector noted that boys over 7 in country parishes worked three to five months of the year and at 10 or 11 were taken out of school, some farmers even forcing laborers to put their children to work (391–92).

3. *The Times* printed at least seven letters in August and September 1864 on the "low remuneration and despair of preferment" among curates.

4. See note 1; also in October, a *Times* leader and various correspondents comment on rural schools. In "The Education of the Labouring Classes" (10 October: 7, cols., 4–5), S. G. O. claims school managers aim too high, forcing dull brains to memorize facts they will never use; W. E. R. (13 October: 10, col. 5) agrees, as does the Rev. Henry White (12 October: 6, col. 6), but he urges the need for night schools where students do more than sleep. (A *Daily News* leader of 11 October ridicules S. G. O.'s idea of *over*-education and says all should help societies for self-education.)

5. In his letter of 10 October (see note 4), S. G. O. quotes the prospectus of a school for artisans, farmers, and the like that includes not only reading, writing, and arithmetic but grammar, composition, history, geography, bookkeeping, accounts, conduct, formation of character, political economy, physiology, sewing, and other subjects.

6. In "Night Schools" (*The Times*, 14 October 1864: 9, col. 2), correspondent Charles Whitbread claims six years' success teaching only basic subjects and sponsoring a club with prizes and free beer—for working men and boys.

7. Half-time schools for farm boys were reported in 1854 (P. P. 1854–55 XLII: 544), and an inspector in 1864 notes the "wise provisions" of half-time schools where the factory acts were in force (P. P. 1864 XLV: 113; see "*Daily News*, 4 August 1863," above). In fact, a paper was read at the September 1864 meeting of the NAPSS on further extension of the factory act "with special Reference to the Half-time System" and its beneficial effect on future workmen (*Transactions of the National Association for the Promotion of Social Science* [1865], 479–80).

8. Eyemouth, near Berwick, does not figure in 1864 school inspectors' reports; Alnwick, near Newcastle, only slightly (108).

Education: Rural Laborers 137

9. I. e., reading, writing, and arithmetic. The Code did not apply to private schools or those of too low a standard to qualify.

10. The Rev. J. P. Norris served as school inspector from 1849 to 1864; his reports probably inspired Robert Lowe to press for the Revised Code (see D. W. Sylvester, *Robert Lowe and Education* [London: Cambridge U P, 1974], 55–56). Norris lists occupations of upwardly mobile "sons of Labourers" from one of the "best parish schools in Shropshire"; his list of thirty girls shows most to be "in service." (P. P. 1864 XLV: 121–25).

III. The Crimean War

18. Czars

Introduction

A new crisis in the relations of some of the European states with the Ottoman Empire (the "Eastern Question") arose when Roman Catholic monks, backed by France, disputed access to the Palestine holy places with Orthodox monks backed by Russia. Czar Nicholas I (1796–1855) demanded of the Turkish Sultan the right to act as protector of Orthodox Christians in all the Ottoman dominions—a direct affront to the Sultan's sovereignty. An agreement on the holy places, worked out in April 1853 by France, England, and Russia, proved useless: Russia insisted on the protectorate and, a week after this leader, invaded the Danubian principalities, part of the Sultan's sovereign territory (see introduction, "*Daily News*, 26 December 1853").

Martineau sets out her view of Russian imperialism in *History of the Peace* and *Introduction to the History of the Peace, from 1800 to 1815* (London: Charles Knight, 1851): Russia was a barbaric, essentially Asiatic, state, not to be trusted by Western nations. In this leader, the first of the one hundred and eighty-odd Martineau wrote on the Crimean War, she launches her campaign to educate the British public with a brisk overview of Russo-Turkish history of the past two centuries. In spite of her claim to be objective, Martineau's hysteria at the Russian czar persists throughout the leaders on Russia. (See "*Daily News*, 25 August 1854," below, also on Russian history.)

****

Daily News
15 June 1853

AT a time like the present, when the scales are trembling to a decision between war or peace for Europe, the best possible way of forecasting the event is to place ourselves, free from passion or prejudice, at the point of view of the person or party with whom the decision rests. In the present case, the decision rests with NICHOLAS of Russia. Or, if there be truth in the rumor that he is in the hands of the old Russian party who let him mount the throne on sufferance, the case is, to us, practically the same.[1] Whether the EMPEROR stands solitary at his point of view, or is surrounded, as he was on ascending the throne, by a circle of bayonets, does not immediately matter to us. As long as he is there, we had better, for a moment, stand there with him, see with his eyes, remember with his memory, and thereby forecast his decisions. And in order to see with his eyes, we must bear in mind that Autocrats have a peculiar sense, or sentiment, or persuasion of a transmigration of souls, or a transmission of qualities, whereby all the ambitions and the aims, all the glories and the mortifications of their most eminent predecessors become their own, and accumulate till the brain of the man, or the patience of the world, sinks under the burden. This is the process by which, under the great natural laws that are their instruments, the gods craze those whom they are about to destroy. There is a proclamation extant, addressed by Russia to the Circassian Chiefs in 1837, which indicates that the process had then gone pretty far in the mind of the Autocrat. "Are you not aware," said that proclamation, "that if the heavens should fall, Russia could prop them with her bayonets? The English may be good mechanics and artisans, but power dwells only with Russia. No country ever waged successful war against her. Russia is the most powerful of all nations. If you desire peace, you must be convinced that there are but two powers in existence—GOD in heaven, and the EMPEROR upon earth."[2] The Circassians are not convinced of all this yet; but there is every reason why the EMPEROR should believe it even more now than he did sixteen years ago.

He feels and remembers, as if he had been there himself, no doubt, the first war with the Porte, in 1678, when Russia, having then no port in Europe but Archangel, made some exchanges with the Turks by which she was left in possession of the Ukraine.[3] He feels and remembers, as if he had himself been the negotiator, the acquisition of Azof, by which Russia first obtained a port on the Black Sea.[4] This was before the Czar PETER is known to have been struck by that idea which cannot but affect the destinies of the world for centuries to come—the idea that the nations of Western Europe were more advanced than his own, and that there was no reason why he should not bring up his own people to the level of European civilisation. All his successors have inherited his ambition, with modifications suited to their respective characters. One may have thought more of an ostentation of luxury, as CATHERINE did; and another might glory, as PAUL did, in being the head of the Northern Confederacy against us; and another, as ALEXANDER, in organising a Holy Alliance; and another, as NICHOLAS, in subordinating the Western to the Eastern principles of government; but all have sympathised in the Czar PETER'S first wistful gaze westward, as to a promised land.[5] They have all feasted their retrospective imaginations with the spectacle in the Finnish marshes, when the waving bulrush and flowering reed were mown to make way for the trim metropolitan gardens that PETER had planned, and when the stagnant lakes began to dimple and stir and drain off towards the Neva; and when the huts of the fowlers were pulled down to make way for the granite embankments on which a new European capital was to stand. And all these Sovereigns turn, as PETER turned, to the southern extremity of his empire, and see, as he saw, that his growth as an European Power, would be accelerated in a vast proportion by his owning the whole of the Eastern length of Europe, from sea to sea. He had Archangel and Azof, and he wanted only Constantinople to extend his empire from the Arctic Sea to the Mediterranean. By his will he enjoined his successors to obtain Turkey, and to foment such quarrels among the western nations as would give time and opportunity for Russian enterprises. This was the real beginning of the conflict, which has yet little more than begun, between the principles of Oriental Despotism and Representative Government in Europe; the conflict, which must come at one time or another, and on the issue of which the fate of Europe hangs.[6] [*Martineau summarizes the aggression against Turkey by Catherine and Alexander and related events up to 1829.*]

When, in 1829, the Russians swept the banks of the Danube, and poured down the southern slope of the Balkan, Turkey might seem more helpless than ever before: and the fall of Adrianople without a shot being fired in defence, and the yielding up of every post on the Black Sea, might well make the CZAR suppose that the prey was his at last. And he did obtain concessions and privileges which constitute the difficulty of the case at this hour.[7] But a change came over the spirit of the warfare, in consequence of the very weakness of Turkey, which may be the source of future strength. When nothing remained to be taken but Constantinople, and when the sacred flag failed to raise the faithful in sufficient numbers for defence, Turkey found she could accept Christian aid. Before, the war had been treated as a religious war. The introduction of political assistance altered at once the relations of Turkey to Russia. It has not only sustained Turkey to this hour; but, when the truth comes to be known, it may be seen to have improved the resources of the country, and stimulated the minds of the people, and made a war with Russia something very different from what the CZAR himself may anticipate if, in adopting the traditions of his race, he overlooks the new circumstances of the age. Placing ourselves at his point of view, we think it probable that he does overlook this, and a good deal more, which it is extremely important for him to remember.

The one great point which he appears to overlook, because PETER and CATHERINE overlooked it, is that Russia is separated from Western Europe—as a Russian nobleman was himself heard to say—by a thousand years of civilisation. It is little more than 400 years since Russia was invaded by barbarians; whereas it is 1,400 years since Western Europe underwent that infliction.[8] PETER and CATHERINE, not measuring the abyss thus existing, thought to bridge it over in a day. PETER imported *savans* and artisans; and CATHERINE had villages run up impromptu by the road-side; and they supposed this to be civilisation. Whatever may have been done since, the chasm has not been bridged over. Russia stands on the eastern side, rude, heterogeneous, ill-compacted, and only outwardly disciplined in her great strength; despotic, violent, on the side of physical rule; dead, or not yet alive, on the side of rational political government. Government is, with her, a religious institution, upheld by arms—the EMPEROR standing before the eyes of his people as their warrior priest, and in their catechism as a god.[9] In Western Europe, meanwhile, where government is a purely political institution, the popular mind has become, amidst many alternations, more and more infused into it. There can be no possible amalgamation between the two systems—no truce between the two principles, when once either has made aggression upon the other. If the EMPEROR, in pursuit of the antique purpose of annexing Turkey to his empire, raises a hand against the Christian allies of Turkey, he should be aware what he is doing—firing his cannon over an abyss of 1,000 years, and compelling Europe to wage the war to which there can be no truce. When the principles of freedom and the very sense of civilisation are put on their defence, we, who know their strength, can have no doubt of their victory. He does not know their value, nor that they have a traditionary history much more imposing than his own. We stand at his point of view; but ours is inaccessible to him. We can sympathise, in a manner, with his ambition and his hereditary delusions: and it is therefore in no mood of passion or prejudice that we declare our conviction that the prospects of Russia, never so brilliant as he supposed, are affected by lapse of time; and that, whatever may be the fluctuations of war about portions of territory, he can never succeed in intruding himself and his mediæval policy into the councils and the sufferance of the peoples of Europe.

Notes

1. In "The Czar's Birthday. A Royal 'Festival' in St. Petersburg" (*Daily News*, 10 July 1854; rpt. *Biographical Sketches*), Martineau reviews details of Nicholas's life: the probable murder of his father, Paul I; his

education during a time of conspiracy among the nobility; his inheritance of the throne over his second-eldest brother by the secret will of his eldest brother; and finally, Nicholas's severe punishment of the conspirators upon his succession. Cf. *Daily News,* 13 January 1854 (on the Czar and Napoleon) and "26 December 1853" to "19 November 1856" *passim.* For a sympathetic modern treatment, see W. Bruce Lincoln, *Nicholas I: Emperor and Autocrat of All the Russias* (Bloomington: Indiana U P, 1978).

    2. For the Circassians, see "*Daily News,* 18 January 1854," below. Martineau first quotes this speech of General Williamneff in *History of the Peace* (2: 369) and often alludes to it.

    3. Martineau chooses a puzzling date: during the reign of Czar Alexis (d. 1676), Russia acquired the northeast Ukraine from Poland; forty years later, after the unsuccessful insurrection of the Cossack leader Mazeppa against Peter the Great, all the Ukraine became part of Russia. Archangel (Russian Arkhangelsk), on the White Sea, was for long Russia's main seaport. For Martineau's history of the pro-English trading settlement, founded in the sixteenth century and taking its name from the nearby monastery of the Archangel Michael, see *Daily News,* 17 July 1854.

    4. Peter the Great (1672–1725) conquered Azof in his second attempt in 1696; see "*Daily News,* 25 August 1854," note 7.

    5. Catherine the Great (1729–1796), friend of French *philosophes,* tried to bring European culture and art to Russia; Paul I (1754–1801) was responsible in 1800 for the Northern Convention of Russia, Sweden, Denmark, and Prussia directed against British rules on neutral shipping; Alexander I (1777–1825?) entered into a Holy Alliance, after the fall of Napoleon in 1815, with the Emperor of Austria and the King of Prussia. Martineau uses Voltaire for her portrait of Peter the Great and for the building of St. Petersburg, following: see "25 August 1854," note 7.

    6. Martineau often refers to British statesman George Canning's feared "War of Opinion," for which she blames Russia in advance: see *Introduction to the History of the Peace,* iii; *Daily News,* 27 November, 13 December 1854; and "*Daily News,* 26 May 1859," below.

    7. By the Treaty of Adrianople of 1829, the Danubian principalities Walachia and Moldavia (modern Romania) were to pay tribute to Turkey but be under Russian protection. Among other concessions granted to Russia were exclusive rights over the Palestinian holy places and the protectorate of Christian subjects of the Sultan. For efforts in summer 1853 by Austria, France, Britain, and Prussia to reaffirm these concessions—part of the "Vienna Note"—see Lincoln, 338.

8. Martineau several times repeats this idea, probably first seen in Richard Monckton Milnes, "The Marquis de Custine's *Russia*" (*Edinburgh Review* 79 [April 1844]: 351–66). Cf. *History of the Peace* 2: 637, and "*Daily News*, 2 March 1854," below.

9. As part of his ruthless reform of Russia, Peter abolished the patriarchate and replaced it by a holy synod with himself as head. For Nicholas's religious fanaticism, see "*Daily News*, 16 May 1854," below.

19. Cromwell vs. Aberdeen

Introduction

In June 1853, Russian troops had taken possession of the Danubian principalities of Moldavia and Wallachia, formerly under the joint protectorate of Russian and Turkey (see "*Daily News*, 15 June 1853," above). European diplomatic protests brought no solution, and on 5 October 1853, Turkey declared war on Russia. Britain, France, Austria and Prussia—negotiating the dispute at Vienna—tried to delay Turkish hostilities. Then on 30 November 1853, Russia shocked Britain and France by sinking an entire Turkish fleet with loss of 4,000 men at Sinope on the Black Sea.

British Prime Minister George Hamilton Gordon (1784–1860), 4th Earl of Aberdeen, headed a coalition government of Peelites and Whigs. In a leader of the week before, Martineau upbraids Aberdeen for his failure to act against Czar Nicholas I. She calls Aberdeen "the wet blanket which is turning the national fire into smoke" (*Daily News*, 19 December 1853).

Martineau's leaders on Russia from June to December 1853 treat the nationalistic fanaticism of the Czar and Russia's two-hundred year history of aggression against Turkey. This "Letter to the Editor" employs a favorite Plutarchian biographical/historical contrast: cf., for example, the Czar and Napoleon (*Daily News*, 13 January 1854), Admiral Charles Napier and Admiral Nelson (*Daily News*, 22 June 1854), the Czar and Queen Victoria (*Daily News*, 11 August 1854), and Russia and England (*Daily News*, 1 December 1854); see also, "Turgenev vs. Everett, *Daily News*, 4 June 1858," below.

Martineau's rationale for choice of the "letter" form is not always clear. Here it allows her to roam freely through English history to support her case against the government. For her picture of Cromwell and Milton when they heard of the Waldenses, cf. Thomas Carlyle, *Oliver Cromwell's Letters and Speeches* (New York: Charles Scribner's Sons, 1903) 3: 204–6. Martineau was to revert to the Waldenses in *Daily News*, 12 January 1855.

* * * *

Daily News
26 December 1853

THE FOREIGN POLICY OF CROMWELL AND THAT OF LORD ABERDEEN

SIR,—The Waldenses have opened their new Church at Turin. The letter of your correspondent made the fact known in England some days ago.[1] Well; what of that? What is that to us? So the thoughtless might ask: but the informed and patriotic among us know, by a certain pain of heart that seizes on them at the news, that it is something to us. The very name of those people, distinguished by a faith which has come down pure from the highest Christian antiquity, raises in every true Englishman's mind the image of the time when his country stood first in authority and honour in the whole world. When the news arrived one day that the Waldenses were driven from their valleys and slain, the tidings wrung the earnest heart of CROMWELL, and that of the people he was worthy to rule over.[2] He shed bitter tears, and set to work to right the oppressed. The mere countenance and word of England were strong enough to do so then. CROMWELL gave 2,000£. out of his private purse towards the relief of the Waldenses: the nation subscribed in proportion. MILTON wrote letters to all the Protestant rulers in Europe; the Duke of SAVOY was compelled to draw back his cruel hand, and the persecuted were escorted back to their homes by the fidelity and courage of England. Such are our associations with the name of the Waldenses: and now that they are prosperous, it cannot but strike us how our name and authority have sunk in Europe since the time of that great transaction.

In the case of protection afforded by the strong to the weak, more than in any other case of aid, "he who gives quickly gives twice." When the news came CROMWELL went to his purse, sent his views to the press, and summoned MILTON to his desk. There was no hesitation or delay, causing needless deaths among the Alpine snows, or false encouragement to the tyrant. But now, how many months have our existing rulers been whispering with the oppressors of Europe, without our knowing what they have been saying, while thousands of the aggrieved Turks have been thrust under ground, and sent to the bottom of the sea?[3] Instead of a CROMWELL, who dashes away the few tears wrung from a manly heart, and cries, "to arms, for right," we have a Prime Minister of whom the enemy have (for reasons best known to themselves) no dread. Instead of a MILTON, rising up as a *Vates* to declare the gospel, and sing the great epic of liberty, sending abroad his summons to all our allies to come up to the battle with despotism,[4] we have leisurely old gentlemen, inditing now sentimental private letters, and now wordy and formal cabinet notes, while there is not a day to lose, when every hour of waiting upon the pleasure of the despots may cost a thousand lives, and every act of subserviency to Russia is a new blot on our dimmed fame, and a treacherous forfeiture of virtual promise to Turkey.[5] Instead of a Protector— which CROMWELL was in the widest sense of the word—must we say that we have a government of Betrayers? Instead of pressing forward on behalf of the right, are we holding back for the sake of dynastic interests? The fear of the hour is, not that the innocent should be trodden down, but that the thrones of Europe should be shaken. The determination is, not that the oppressed shall be avenged and sustained, but that the oppressor shall not be offended, nor our personal convenience encroached upon. CROMWELL would have shed bitterer tears than those if his *Vates* could have foreshown that, in the day when the Waldenses should open their temples in Turin and Genoa, and enter the Parliament of Sardinia, and contemplate the conversion of the

Princes of Italy, we, the people of England, should be writhing under the suspension of our national honour, and the consciousness that our action is that of a catspaw, our position that of the pillory, and our alliance another name for dupery in a double sense. Our present rulers seem to be able to bear this degradation. At the mere prophetic tidings, CROMWELL'S noble heart would have cracked. At the mere prospect, MILTON'S mental vision would have been blinded like his bodily eyes, and he would have prayed to see no more.

The day is passed for the national principle and spirit to settle on the religious ground. It was liberty in the form of Protestantism that inspired us then; and the inspiration prevailed over the length and breadth of the land. It is liberty in another form and sense that is the cause—to those worthy of living for a cause—at the present day. While the Waldenses are still adhering to their apostolic faith and forms (not being Protestant, because they were never Catholic), having neither images nor altars, but merely a noble edifice fit for the sublimest speaking and hearing of the gladdest tidings, we have our St. Barnabas, with its half-and-half Heathenisms, and a pretence of supporting a Christianity in the East, to which the Popery of CROMWELL'S time would have appeared to him pure and simple.[6] The feeble attempt to give a religious colour to our faithless conduct rests wholly on the pretense of supporting Christianity in the form of the Greek Church; whereas that Church is, in spirit, in form, and even in doctrine, further removed from the Christianity of the Bible than Mahometanism: and no one who knows what the two really are will for a moment question this.[7] Here is the Christianity actually prevalent in the battle-field, among the armies of Russia. When the Russians invaded Hungary, the talk of the Sclavonian soldiers round their bivouac fires showed how overmastering was the idea, held out by authority, of the Greek Church. "If we are wounded," they were heard to say, "somebody lays a handful of grass upon the place; and then we die, and we are shoved away a few inches into the ground, in a hurry. But when the CZAR'S own soldiers are wounded, the surgeons make haste to take care of them, and use silver instruments, and put linen to their wounds; and if they die, there is a POPE to bury them, and there are prayers for their souls. It is the CZAR who can do everything; and it is the greatest thing to serve the CZAR; for the CZAR is the son of GOD."[8] Those are the translated words spoken on the soil of the Hungary which we allowed to be subdued by this blasphemous aspirant to divine honours; and it is on behalf of such claims to divine honours that we are desired to leave Turkey to her fate. We [may] yet see a Greek Church built next, beside St. Barnabas; and few would be sorry if it should be the means of showing us who are the psuedo-Christians who want to make us traitors to the liberty with which Protestantism has made us free. If the name of Protestantism is now dropped out of the programme of our international action, the cause of Liberty remains not the less sacred. Whether Pope or Kaiser is the oppressor, we are pledged in conscience, in honour, in policy—by every consideration that can actuate sane men and a constituted nation, to stand by the liberties of Europe, attacked in any quarter, from the aggressions of a barbaric despotism. This is admitted by the presence of our ships in the eastern seas; and we do not choose that it should be made doubtful by the conduct of our rulers at home. We, the English people, are now suffering under the consequences of our permission of diplomatic secresy in regard to our international policy. We are chafing in shame and indignation at our helplessness under the mysterious management of our own public servants. We must put a stop to this, and take care that it never happens again. The first object, when Parliament meets, must be to learn, without permitting disguise or suppression, what has been done in our name during the last year; and we must then proceed to put an end to that practice of diplomatic concealment which is utterly unconstitutional in its spirit, and under which our common duty, safety, authority, and reputation are pawned or destroyed by our own servants. Meantime, we would put to them one question—are these the days when it is safe so to endear past times to the English heart as that a festival of the Waldenses in Sardinia shall fire that heart with the thought of the glory of our Commonwealth in the eyes of the world, and of a Protector as its champion?

Z.

Notes

1. In "Waldensian Church (Protestant) at Turin" (*Daily News*, 21 December 1853: 5, col. 5), "Subalpinus" reports on services at the "Lombardo-Gothic" church, in French and Italian, on 15 December, attended by Catholic refugees and a few Swiss, Germans, and English. Turin, capital of the kingdom of Sardinia (made up of Savoy, Piedmont, Nice, and Liguria—including Genoa), 1814–1865, was the center of the Italian national liberation movement (see note 3, below). Martineau's sympathy for the small, heretical sect, sometimes thought to be descended from the earliest Christians but named after the twelfth-century preacher Pierre Valdes, surely has roots in her early Unitarianism. For the Pope's opposition to the Waldenses, see *Daily News*, 12 January 1855.

2. In 1655 the Waldenses living in French and Italian alpine valleys were brutally attacked by forces under the Duke of Savoy and the incidents reported in English newsletters; see E. A. J. Honigmann, ed., *Milton's Sonnets* (London: Macmillan, 1966), 162–66.

3. For Martineau's attacks on secret diplomacy between Britain's aristocratic government and European despots, see *Daily News*, 11 July 1854 and 28 May 1855.

4. John Milton, Cromwell's Secretary for Foreign Tongues, wrote letters of protest to the Duke of Savoy and to other European rulers; he also wrote Sonnet XVIII, beginning, "Avenge O Lord thy slaughter'd Saints...."

5. In November 1853, Britain and France concluded an offensive and defensive alliance with Turkey against Russia.

6. St. Barnabas, Pimlico, was accused of "Popish practices": see letters in the *Daily News*, 8–21 December 1853. Martineau scoffs at both High Church leaning toward Roman Catholicism and then government permissiveness toward the Czar as head of the Orthodox Church.

7. Martineau read George Sale, *The Koran ... Translated into English ... with Explanatory Notes [and] a Preliminary Discourse* (1734, 1825) for one of the prize essays she wrote for the Central Unitarian Association in 1831 (*Autobiography* 1: 152).

8. In June 1849, Russian armies invaded Hungary at Austria's request (see "*Daily News*, 18 January 1854," note 8; and "*Daily News*, 2 March 1854," note 9); the country of the Sclavonians or Slavonians (Serbo-Croatians) had become part of Austria in 1848.

20. Circassians

Introduction

From 1829, when Turkey ceded to Russia her nominal sovereignty over the peoples living in the Caucasus mountains, Europeans closely followed the struggles of the Circassians. A tribe of distinct origin and language, they carried on a guerrilla campaign against the Russians, who built defensive forts along the eastern coast of the Black Sea. Although converted to Mohammedanism in the eighteenth century, the Circassians held to a mixture of chivalrous and savage customs that included selling their own and others' kidnapped children into slavery. From the beginning of the Crimean War, romantic histories of their leader Schamyl (1797–1871) appeared in Europe; see, for example, Thomas Henry Huxley, "Schamyl, the Prophet-Warrior of the Caucasus," *Westminster Review* 61 (April 1854): 480–519, a review of German and English books on Schamyl and the Circassians. For a post-war account of the Circassians, see *Daily News*, 13 May 1856.

After Russia's sinking of the Turkish fleet (see introduction, "*Daily News*, 26 December 1853"), on 3 January 1854, French and British squadrons entered the Black Sea. Martineau wrote two leaders in early January on the Crimean War: on the problem of providing British forces with up-to-date weapons and on the two "dreads" of the nineteenth century—the Czar and Napoleon. Czar Nicholas, the mere type of all past Russian leaders, seems to her less frightening than Napoleon because of the predictability of his behavior. She scoffs at his failure to subdue the Circassians.

In this leader, Martineau appeals to two Victorian penchants: love of a hero and sympathy for an underdog, such as a nation fighting for its liberty.

* * * *

Daily News
18 January 1854

ONE of the first consequences of the presence of the Combined Fleets in the Black Sea should be an ample supply (from *somebody*) of ammunition to the Circassians. After their long war with Russia—a war which will be ever memorable in the world's history—it would have been a sad and terrible result had the Circassians been forced to succumb at last through our remissness in not keeping the Black Sea open for the passage of auxiliary vessels. In the ordinary times of that war,—that is, for half a century or so,—they managed to get supplies of powder and ball, and whatever else was absolutely necessary. In fact, there have been Turkish merchant captains who have traded between Sinope or Samsûn[1] and the Circassian coasts for five-and-twenty years together, in spite of the Russian blockade; sometimes stealing through the blockading vessels; sometimes getting away astern in boats; but never giving up, even to this day. Of late SCHAMYL and his patriotic followers have been so badly off for ammunition that they have been driven to that mode of warfare which the Russians do not particularly relish, and which is likely to become common in proportion to the improvement taking place in firearms—that of picking off the officers, so that every shot may disconcert as many as possible of the enemy by the fall of one. But they have got a supply of ammunition now, and may fight as it best pleases them.

The more the interest of this Eastern question deepens the higher rises one's curiosity and admiration of this singular people—the Circassians. They are admirable for other reasons than their resistance to Russia. The best rulers and soldiers of the East come from Circassia, as the history of Egypt, Syria, and Turkey will show. But their conduct in the great struggle of the

Euxine affords, perhaps, the completest test of their quality. In 1793 Russia obtained the Crimea and the Cossack country, from the Sea of Azoff [sic] to the Caspian; but Circassia lay between the Kuban and the Black Sea, and spoiled much of the satisfaction of the acquisition.[2] The one Mahommedan country that lay between Russia and Turkey was gained; but this other held out. Russia crept round to the south-east, and in 1802 obtained Mingrelia.[3] She then transgressed the Persian boundary, annexing Georgia and other provinces, till her dominion comprehended the whole territory between the Caspian and the Euxine, below Circassia, as it had done before above it; but still Circassia was unsubdued. By the treaty of Adrianople the who,le of the coast of the Black Sea—"tout le littoral de la Mer Noire"—was ceded by Turkey to Russia: and Russia in consequence laid claim to the whole of Circassia.[4] But the inhabitants had something to say to that: and what they did say was that Russia might come and take them if she could. Their rulers and judges travelled through the country, and held councils in all the provinces, and administered everywhere the oath which has been so faithfully kept—never to come to terms with the enemy but by universal national consent. Twelve provinces joined in the league; and there they are, to this hour, maintaining the war successfully without a single ally.

Though they have no allies they have some curious reinforcements. The CZAR seems not to have known exactly what to do with the young Poles whom he dared not leave in their own homes after the revolution of 1831.[5] He sent Polish boys of ten or twelve years old by thousands into Georgia; and the Poles who have deserted from the Russians say that there are multitudes more now in Circassia. There are also large numbers of Russians, who have deserted. If many of the Russian soldiery prefer death to military life on the shores of the Black Sea, there is reason to hope that the Circassian forces will be strengthened by more such recruits. They say that they are treated at home worse than the dogs of other nations; and the Circassians believe it. When the CZAR was off one of their bays in 1837, and touched at one of his own forts, to survey the preparations made by his magniloquent General WILLIAMINEFF for the winter campaign, a fire broke out, and consumed everything in the way of provisions and stores—everybody being aware that it was a case of arson, adventured to prevent the CZAR seeing how horrible was the state of the bread, and how little there was of it.[6] That fire is vividly remembered as having saved the Circassians some warfare, and the usual proportion of Russian troops from death by dysentery. Many of them are living now, as Circassian soldiers. Anapa, which it cost the CZAR so much to reduce, was formed by the settlement of fugitives from the Crimea: and thus it is with every annexation he makes.[7] He grasps the thistle; but some winged seeds always fly off, and alight and germinate elsewhere; and he has to try again, and not always with success. He has not succeeded in his endeavours to obtain a *quid pro quo* for these immigrants. Again and again have the chiefs of the more exposed parts of the Circassian territory been invited over the frontier, to hold conferences and so forth; and when, not daring to refuse, some of the weaker-spirited have gone, they have been detained till, as they are told, they have sworn allegiance to the CZAR; that is, as hostages for the neighbouring population. But nothing has been gained by the procedure. Sometimes the hostages have been rescued, with damage or destruction to sundry Russian villages; or, if they have been already carried too far into the interior, they have brought nobody after them. Being regarded as lost, their place is supplied by new leaders, who are more on their guard against the trick.

How should a people be conquered who have a spirit as noble as the Hungarian, and mountains, instead of plains, for a battlefield and a refuge?[8] "If England and Turkey abandon us," exclaimed one of their chiefs (the one who originated the oath of the league), "we shall burn our houses and property, and retire to the high rocks, and there defend ourselves till the last man falls." And this was not the momentary enthusiasm of one man. In congress and councils it has been repeatedly declared that if the Russians succeeded in erecting forts in every bay of the coast, the inhabitants would never yield. "We have abundance of mountains," they have often said; "and to these we will retire and defend ourselves, if we are unable to retain the coast." They have, however, made stupendous efforts to retain the coast, and, on the whole, with success. Their rocks and trees are incessantly all alive with human eyes. If a friendly vessel arrives with salt (their great want) or other commodities, out rush a string of men into the sea to seize the rope; or boats full of armed men to row round the vessel and divert the Russian fire. If the Russians draw near to cut out a vessel or storm a fort, there is sure to be some breastwork, if only of hurdles filled with shingle, and concealing a trench; and from behind the aim taken is always deadly. Their songs are a curious contrast to the Russian hymns of the soldiery—a contrast which reminds the traveller of that which is on record in the case of the siege of Jerusalem, when the Roman trumpets in the camp sounded harsh and mechanical in comparison with the wild Hebrew music which swelled from the city walls.[9] The Russians chaunt the hymns prescribed and taught. The Circassians have their bards, who exhort and prophesy. "Young men, rush forth to the battle; for brave youths love war. If you fall, you are martyrs. If you live, you have half that glory." This is no mere romance. It is about the most solid and significant fact of the last half century, this successful defiance of Russia by Circassia alone, when all the rest of the world gave way. That little country has weathered the long, dreary storm; and now the worst is, we may hope, past. The Black Sea is opened, never more to be closed. All western Europe—the foremost peoples of all the earth—are to be the allies of Circassia. She asks only salt, ammunition, and a clear sea; and she must henceforth have them all. And how much more—how much of reinforcement and of commerce—how much of the gratitude of Turkey and the admiration of western Europe and America, a few years will show.

Notes

1. Sinope and Samsun are on the south coast of the Black Sea.
2. Circassia, in the northwestern part of the Caucasus, included the portion between the mountain range and the Kuban river on the north and the Euxine or Black Sea on the west.
3. A region in Western Georgia on the Black Sea. See also "*Daily News*, 25 August 1854," note 1.
4. For the Treaty of Adrianople in 1829, see introduction.
5. A revolt of Polish military cadets at Warsaw in November 1830 triggered a national rebellion against Russian rule. When it ended in autumn 1831, Czar Nicholas took fanatical measures against Poles of all

classes. Martineau summarizes these events of 1830–1831 in *History of the Peace* (2: 175–77, 368–69)—and refers to them in her leaders on eastern Europe. For a view of European revolutionary ideas in Poland, suffering under rule of the Czar's elder brother, see Lincoln, *Nicholas I: Emperor and Autocrat of All the Russias*, 135–43.

6. Czar Nicholas' insistence on total responsibility for the glory and welfare of his people is sympathetically portrayed by Lincoln (see last note). Martineau's sarcastic epithet for the Russian General Williamineff refers to his challenge to the Circassians (see, "*Daily News*, 15 June 1853," note 2).

7. The Crimea was annexed to Russia under the Czarina Catherine II in 1793 after struggles among the Tatars who inhabited the peninsula; Anapa is on the northeast coast of the Black Sea near the entrance to the Sea of Azof. Cf. "*Daily News*, 7 November 1854," note 12.

8. Martineau probably refers to the Hungarian followers of Kossuth, who in 1849 fought against Austria and the Croats for the rights of the Magyars.

9. Martineau also uses the idea of the Jews sustained by their music (when Vespasian besieged Jerusalem) in *Daily News*, 13 November 1854.

21. Allies

Introduction

After Czar Nicholas ignored the ultimatum from Britain and France to evacuate the Danubian principalities (see introduction, "*Daily News*, 26 December 1853"), both nations declared war on Russia at the end of March 1854.

From 20 January through 1 March 1854, in nine of her twelve leaders and "letters," Martineau keeps up a pro-war momentum, informing, cajoling, and reminding her readers how to interpret Russia's behavior in light of its past acts.

Here Martineau touches on another favored theme—friendship toward Britain on the part of the French people, kept in the dark and beguiled by their emperor, Napoleon III. Now Britain needed the French to help stop Russian barbarism and territorial ambitions.

Martineau's disgust with the current government (see "26 December 1853") may cause her sarcasm at Tory mismanagement in the last days of George III. In *Introduction to the History of the Peace*, written three years earlier, she gives a milder account of the same period.

Daily News
2 March 1854

ON the opening of a new chapter in our national history it is natural to compare our reputation as a people fifty years ago with what our character is now, as a nation engaged in war. We say fifty years ago, rather than forty, because it was PITT'S War Administration that decided our character in the eyes of foreigners; and WELLINGTON had not yet had opportunity to manifest the very qualities which we were ridiculed for being without.[1] Fifty years ago, then, JOHN BULL'S simplicity and gullibility were the amusement of one-half of the world, and the vexation of the other half. The old King always insisted on everything going on, throughout the universe, according to his direction, and he was excessively wroth when the universe went on some other way. He said a loud "amen" to his Chaplain's preachings about resignation, submission, etc., but was not the less constantly amazed at his intentions ever being frustrated. Mr. PITT was as sanguine as the King was self-willed. He had but one notion about making war. It always failed in practice; yet he was always perfectly certain that it would succeed next time. In private life, there is something attractive in that kind of temper; and when a merchant or shopkeeper is always positively certain of making his fortune by some favourite venture that never pays its expenses, we say that he is nobody's enemy but his own, and like him rather the better than the worse. But it is a very different matter for a statesman to have that sort of temper; for he is more the enemy of a nation, or of a world, than his own. PITT died heart-broken; but he did not exhaust the retribution of national credulity and conceit. We are suffering under it at this hour—certainly in the weight of the Debt, and, we are rather disposed to believe, in other ways too. Our reputation abroad, in regard to the statesmanship of the last year is not very high; and we rather imagine that we must show some signs of our wits being sharpened before we can get rid of the old impressions of JOHN BULL'S gullibility. We must remember that FOX was just

Allies

as sanguine as PITT; and his genial, unsuspicious, noble temper exposed him to hold out longer than an inferior man would in the hope of peace, when NAPOLEON kept him waiting and negotiating with TALLYRAND all the summer of 1806, while TALLYRAND'S master was negotiating and signing a treaty with Russia.[2] Our Coalition Ministry of that day were honourable men, strongly disposed for peace; but no match for the TALLYRANDS and the despots of the time. The Duke of PORTLAND and Mr. PERCEVAL did not much improve our reputation for sagacity and good sense; and the Tilsit treaty came next to make us blush—*we* said for our enemies, who could behave in such a manner—but *they* supposed, reasonably enough, for ourselves.[3] We were, to be sure, miserably outwitted, for a long course of years, by everybody who chose to be tricky, or lax about engagements. The commonplaces on such occasions are amiable and quite incontestable; that it is better to be the wronged than the wrongdoer; that our simplicity and hopefulness are morally graceful, and all that. But we see no occasion to be wronged, if we can help it, any more than to be the wrongdoer, and we should admire our simplicity more if it had some shrewdness with it, and our hopefulness if we had sound reason to give for it. We are now again engaged with parties as sly, as unscrupulous, as heartless, as any of the men of fifty years ago; and we have the advantages that might perhaps have made our fathers wiser and more competent. We have a reasonable Sovereign and a comparatively reformed Parliament, a people doubled in numbers, and with a much larger proportion of citizens who understand and have a voice in public affairs. Instead of a TALLYRAND there is a METTERNICH (not the less powerful for being behind a curtain); instead of a NAPOLEON, there is a NICHOLAS; and the Austrian Emperor of our day is under strong temptation to imitate the conduct of the ALEXANDER of 1806.[4] We must take care that we do not get tricked, insulted, betrayed, and ridiculed as our fathers were.

The English in Paris tell us that the good understanding which has long been growing up between the French nation and ourselves has now become so striking an amity as to be visible even in the streets. Our lively neighbours have indulged longer than we have in the amusement of quizzing their old foes. JOHN BULL has been their stage joke till now; now, when we have to go to work together about a very serious business, there is at once an almost entire cessation of stage caricatures of the English; and our officers are cheered in the streets. Our relations with France are sound and clear, and reliable, as far as human wit can see; and there is no ground whatever for distrust of the French people. Their object is the same as ours; their interest in the restraining of Russian aggression is the same; and we and they agree in our view of what should be done. We may fairly indulge our national temper of honourable trust in that direction; and, as far as we see, the only call to suspicious vigilance in our relations with the French is from the constant danger of an old enmity and prejudice breaking out to injure our harmony and co-operation. If the common foe can do anything to set us at variance, he will do it: and every statesman and citizen at home, and every officer, soldier, and sailor abroad, must remember that duty and patriotism require good temper, good manners, and a liberal kindliness towards every Frenchman he meets or has to deal with.

As for the common enemy, we have really treated him like a gentleman and a Christian too long, for the good of our reputation.[5] Let us have no more commonplaces about the satisfaction of having trusted the CZAR as long as possible—of having left no means untried, and so forth. He has had his own satisfactions in the last year of abortive negotiations. He has gained time, and afflicted his enemy, and organised his means, and inspired the lower orders of his people with fanaticism; and we, meantime, have given the Turks too much reason to fear, and Austria and Prussia to hope, that we should not really do anything effectual.[6] They have seen us tricked and insulted, as of old, and they find some of our public men can still go on talking of peace, when peace is out of the question, just as greater men did before them. Now, we must have no more of this. If our credulity and mismanagement cease from this hour, we will consent to treat our last year's weakness historically, as we treat that of fifty years ago, and let it drop as a matter of rebuke and complaint. But this is on condition that we have no more of it. It is the truth, and we must never lose sight of it, that our foe is half-savage; and there is nothing on earth like the half-savage for cunning.[7] If we really must go on priding ourselves on our innocence of guile, we must take care he does not yet cajole us. What we say is, that we must adapt our means to our ends, and, in national business, as well as private, use those faculties to which the occasion appeals. The CZAR has no business with our simplicity and magnanimity. His appeal is to our shrewdness, our wariness, our indignation, and our hearty contempt. In the strength of these faculties and feelings, let us deal with him as the enemy and disgrace to civilisation and morals that he really is.

As for Austria—knowing what we do of the opposition between her inclinations and her fortunes, we shall be weak indeed if we regard her as in any genuine sense a comrade in this business.[8] The French nation are our allies and comrades; but what and where is the Austrian nation? With whom are we to fraternise as we fraternise with the French? Is it with the Hungarians, or with the Italians? With all our hearts; but where will they be, and what will they be doing while we are fighting the Russians? Is FRANCIS JOSEPH going to put himself at the head of the refugees in Turkey, whom he quarrels with the Porte for sheltering?[9] Alas, no! The Austrian troops sent to this war will be those only who can be spared from keeping guard over the Italians and Hungarians; and our alliance is to be, not with them, the oppressed, but with their head gaoler.[10] "It will not, and it cannot, come to good." Nobody doubts, we believe, that the Austrian empire is destined to undergo great changes on the first opportunity. It requires no more shrewdness than even we English have credit for to see that. We must take care—in Parliament and out of it—that we English are not entrapped into any countenance of any oppression of the free nations which Austria is pleased to call hers. Most people think it odd enough that we did not countenance their efforts for independence. If we not only refuse to help, but do anything that may hinder them, the world must have liberty, not only to laugh at us for our simplicity, but to reprobate us for our treason to the principles of liberty.

Thus, we have an enemy to sharpen our national wits upon us in front; and an ally (as we suppose we must say) to keep our vigilance in exercise;—an ally, not on our left hand, as France is on our right—but standing, at once sly and irresolute, halfway between the barbaric and the civilised forces.[11] We must repose no trust in that direction; and in all directions, beware of an ambush. If JOHN BULL has shrewdness, let him rally it all, and vow never to be bamboozled again.

Notes

1. In *Introduction to the History of the Peace*, Martineau faults William Pitt the younger (1759–1806), prime minister in 1804, for his lack of judgment of men and for his policy, when threatened by Napoleon I, of seeking continental alliances and subsidizing smaller European states. She laments Pitt's early death, just after the return to England from India of Arthur Wellesley (1769–1852), later the Duke of Wellington. (lxxxix–xc, xcv–xcvii, and cxix–cxx)

2. Charles James Fox (1749–1806), foreign minister in Lord Grenville's coalition government in 1806: one of Martineau's Whig heroes, especially for his role in helping to abolish the slave trade. Charles Maurice de Talleyrand-Périgord (1754–1838) served as Napoleon's minister of foreign affairs until 1807. For Martineau's account of these events of summer 1806, see *Introduction to the History of the Peace*, cliv–clxvii. See also *Daily News*, 12 October 1854.

3. William Henry Cavendish Bentinck (1738–1809), 3rd Duke of Portland, leader of a Tory government, 1807–1809; Spencer Perceval (1762–1812), Chancellor of the Exchequer in the Duke of Portland's cabinet which, Martineau claims, allowed Napoleon I and Czar Alexander I to sign the Treaty of Tilsit in 1807, carving up Europe between them and declaring commercial war on England (see *Introduction to the History of the Peace*, clxxxviii–ccix).

4. Prince Klemens von Metternich (1773–1859) had retired as Austrian foreign minister in 1848. In "Metternich and Austria" (rpt. *Biographical Sketches*), Martineau attacks Metternich for duplicity and for supporting European despots. She must mean that Franz-Josef I (1830–1916), Emperor of Austria since 1848, would be tempted to sell out to Russia as Czar Alexander I did to Napoleon (see last note). For Martineau's use of balanced biographies, see introduction, "26 December 1853."

5. For Martineau's assertion of the Czar's "unchristian" treatment of minority groups and for "idol-worship" and the "heathenish"

Allies 167

practices of the Russian Orthodox Church, see *Daily News*, 3 February 1854.

6. Martineau must refer to the Vienna Note—drawn up by Britain, France, Austria, and Prussia in summer 1853—which attempted to settle the dispute between Russian and Turkey (see introduction) but which was rejected by Turkey and then Russia. In late September 1853, Britain convinced France not to accept a modification of the plan evidently agreeable to Russia and Turkey. (See Lincoln, *Nicholas I: Emperor and Autocrat of All the Russias*, 338–39) But for Martineau's scepticism of the peace strategies of the Aberdeen government, see also "26 December 1853."

7. Cf. "*Daily News*, 15 June 1853," note 8.

8. Martineau's often-cited roster of retrogressive European states included Austria, Prussia (probably), and, of course, Russia. For Austria's untrustworthiness as an ally and, from summer 1854, the mistake of letting Austria occupy the Danubian principalities, see *Daily News*, 8, 15, 22 April; 29 May; 4, 8, 11, 15 July; 3, 14, 29 August; 29 September; 14 November 1854; 6 August 1855; 21 April and 24 May 1856.

9. In autumn 1849, Hungarian refugees including Kossuth (see "*Daily News*, 18 January 1854," note 8) who fled the revolution across the border into Turkey became a point of issue between Russia (the real power to crush the revolutionaries) and Turkey. In 1850 Austrian and Russian demands for the return of the refugees were discussed briefly in Parliament.

10. A reference to Austria's threatened hold over Hungary as well as over the states of Italy, where freedom attempts were made in 1830 and 1849.

11. I. e., between Russia and France.

22. The Baltic Sea

Introduction

By early April 1854, Britain and France had landed forces at Gallipoli on the Dardanelles and thence at Constantinople and Scutari. On 20 April, allied forces bombarded Odessa, on the north coast of the Black Sea. Also in spring 1854, a British naval squadron under the command of Vice Admiral Sir Charles Napier (1786–1860) entered the Baltic, where part of the fleet captured Russian merchant vessels and destroyed supplies in the Gulf of Bosnia, the northern arm of the Baltic Sea.[1] By late June, Napier had blockaded a Russian fleet in the Gulf of Finland. Yet British expectations that Napier would soon take Cronstadt, the island fortress before St. Petersburg, were disappointed owing to lack of support for Napier by the Admiralty (97, 158–72). The allies' other important action in the Baltic in 1854 was the capture in August of the Russian fortress on the Aland Islands (see *Daily News*, 16, 23 and 26 August 1854).

Martineau wrote more than twenty leaders on the campaign in the Baltic, from 24 March 1854 through 20 August 1855; see also "*Daily News*, 19 November 1856," below. Thirteen years earlier, in *Feats on the Fiord* (London: Charles Knight, 1841; third of *The Playfellow* books for children), she vividly described Scandinavian scenery, taking her information from Henry David Inglis, *A Personal Narrative of a Journey through Norway, Part of Sweden, and the Islands and States of Denmark* (Edinburgh: Constable, 1829) and Samuel Laing, *Journal of a Residence in Norway* (London: Longman, 1836).

Among Martineau's topics of March through early May 1854, she analyzes problems of commerce and supply for both the Russians and the allies. Her leader of 17 May 1854, for example, contrasts to this imaginative one: she urges the allies to take Archangel (the Russian port on the White Sea) for the summer, so inhabitants can carry on their customary trading.

Here Martineau takes inspiration from letters and reports from the Baltic: see, for example, *Daily News*, 8 May 1854: 5, col. 5; 13 May 1854: 8, cols. 4–5.

Note

1. In *The Crimean War. British Grand Strategy against Russia, 1853–56* (Manchester: Manchester U P, 1990), Andrew Lambert argues that the war in the Baltic was of far greater significance than the war in the Black Sea.

* * * *

Daily News
16 May 1854

THE crisis of the Baltic enterprise seems near at hand. Under date of the 3rd of May we hear of bitter east winds and thick-falling snow; of the 4th, of Stockholm steamers running, with crowds of citizens, to see the fleet; on the 5th, of fog so thick, that the ships could not stir.[1] In Finland, meantime, the season is mild, and vegetation is rapidly advancing. The month of May is always the season of suspense at St. Petersburg—the time when it is said the restless CZAR, who sleeps only by snatches, looks out, or goes forth, almost before anybody else is stirring, to observe the aspect of his watery realm, and see which way the wind is. The suspense is about the wind; and even now, in this most solemn spring season of all the fifty-seven he has known, the movements of the wind are of more consequence to NICHOLAS than even those of the allies. A long continuance of strong east winds would do more for him than all the preparations he can make. A rush of west wind would ruin him more speedily and thoroughly than all his united enemies could,

The Baltic Sea

without its help. The suspense is about this. The fog is the token that the crisis is at hand. The fog precedes the breaking up of the ice in the Neva; and it will be succeeded by those singular twilight nights, of unequalled beauty, which are the only charm of the desolate region in which St. Petersburg stands.[2] While the fog lasts the sentinels on the watchtowers in the city look out in vain, some towards Lake Ladoga, some up the Neva, some towards the sea. They can hear something, but see nothing. So it is with the CZAR, listening in his balcony; and with the commandants at Sveaborg and at Cronstadt: and perhaps with our "CHARLEY" walking the deck, and talking to himself. What he is listening for is the arrival of the French squadron, which will enable him to proceed to his work when the fog-curtain rises.[3] What the Russians are listening for is, first, the wind. To some it comes sighing over the peaty plains which stretch to the margin of the gulf, whence they look like a mere drift upon the waters. Over that barren bleak expanse the wind comes sighing through the rushes, with an occasional bark of the wolf, or bursts of the din of the waterfowl in the pools which are already melted. To others the wind comes vibrating like mournful music through the pine forests, which, surrounding the capital with their black belt, nowhere further off than twenty miles, approach much nearer in some directions. There are sounds which come to the ear on May nights when the wind is from any point of the compass; for there are swamps and pine forests everywhere. It is the voice of the waters that the watchers listen for with hearts that stand still. As long as the hollow moaning goes on, the moaning of the imprisoned winds below the ice, the suspense is complete. Sooner or later comes the crack, which tells that the hour of crisis has come. The cracks of the ice are naturally most impressive and sound the loudest in the night. The CZAR and his sentries are already on the watch; but now the citizens rise, and look out in vain through the fog. Some dress and go to the wharves, though it is much too soon to conjecture how high the waters will rise. Next comes the crash of the ice, driven up in heaps in the river, or against the wharves; and then the more anxious sound—the swash of the driven waters. The thing most desired is a moderate east wind: and this is what usually happens. A violent east wind brings down the inland ice and flood too fast; and every inch that the waters rise above the iron rings in the granite embankment is so much danger. But the fearful thing is a strong west wind, turning back the flood on its way to the Gulf. Then it is less the swash of waters pouring down than the roar of the sea coming up; and when the tides meet, the consequence is what the world saw in 1824. The vessels that were not capsized by the meeting of the floods were carried over the wharves, and stranded on the sands which were arable fields the day before. The nine rivers and seven canals on which St. Petersburg is seated all overflowed at once; and the flood poured into the upper chambers of the best houses in the capital. At Cronstadt, a large vessel was drifted into the main street of the town, and left there. Every successive year adds to the peril of such a chance: for every year does St. Petersburg settle lower in the swamp. Amidst the stagnant silence maintained there about all disagreeable facts, this very disagreeable fact is well understood. The mallet is heard, driving new piles incessantly— that is a sound that cannot be muffled. The blocks of granite on the quays settle unequally: that is an irregularity which the martinet CZAR himself cannot prohibit or punish. The walls of palaces crack, and hovels sink down endways into the bog, and all the world may see them melt down or be shored up. The destruction will be horrible some day: and every inhabitant knows it, and only hopes that the place may last his time. But, if a west wind should carry up—not the sea only, but those who are now riding that sea—what then? This is what the CZAR is listening for; the one other sound—the boom of cannon—which might for once rival in terror the roar of the sea. From Cronstadt, 16 miles off, the spire of the Admiralty and the glittering cupolas of St. Petersburg may be seen on a clear day. Cronstadt is nearer to St. Petersburg than Gravesend is to London. From St. Petersburg the boom of such cannon as we have sent there may be heard from Cronstadt, if we have the west wind for our herald of approach. By that time the fog will be gone, and the transparent twilight of that latitude will have set in. The admirals will then have no more time for listening like the CZAR.[4] Such a chance as that wind would fill the channels for them, and obviate their chief difficulty. A very few hours of such a tide would suffice for their attempt upon Cronstadt. The gun-

The Baltic Sea

boats of the enemy, ambushed among the islands, and watching with intense curiosity and awe the great floating fortifications that we have sent against their stationary one, must not, in such a case, come out, unless they would be run down; and the sentries on the bastions at Cronstadt would see with dismay how rapidly the ordinary watermarks are disappearing. Such a wind would be the best of allies. But, without it, we are disposed to believe that Cronstadt is, as is now hinted from the scene of action, "not impregnable." We hear much of the shallows there: but it is certain that the largest Russian ships of war are built at St. Petersburg, as far as the hulls are concerned, and then brought into the Cronstadt harbours to be finished. They are brought by the old-fashioned machinery of "camels" down the river, and then, by means of the great ship canal at Cronstadt, into the heart of that place. That canal—the one running from the Middle Harbour—holds ten large ships of war at once. The shallows before Acre were thought to be an insurmountable difficulty before Sir C. Napier made a wreck of that marvellous fortification.[5] We shall soon see whether, with the added resources of 14 years of naval improvement, he cannot deal with the shallows of Cronstadt. The CZAR permits no sounding of the Neva. To sound the Neva is death to Russian subjects; but it is given out that the average depth is nine feet on the bar, and twelve within. We all know what Russian figures are worth, and we may be sure that the shallowest depth that can be believed will be the one reported. We know too that the range of difference between the highest and the lowest water is very great, and that the period of highest water is just at hand. "CHARLEY" knows all this, and very much more; and while he is walking the deck, and talking to himself, he has his own plans for making wind and tide serve him we may be sure. Everything is said to serve the NAPIERS (as it generally serves other people) when they are at their work.[6]

And the watcher at the other end of that Gulf, who knows all this, and very much more, how is it with him? Thus far in life, he has never heard the truth on ethical subjects—has never conceived that he could be in the wrong—has never doubted his being able, if he chose his time well, to do what he would, in and with the world. Is the transparent twilight of the spring night the time when the reality of his own mind and life is to dawn upon him? As the fog draws off, is it carrying away the mists of passion and delusion which have hitherto clouded his mind? In that dim light, do the ghosts of his evil deeds rise before him, and promise to sit heavy on his soul to-morrow? Do the hanged come down from their gallows, and the knouted up from their bloody bed; and the buried alive from the depths of the mine; and the exiled from the shores of the Polar Sea? Are the women of Warsaw there, demanding their children with heart-broken voices? Do the insane shake their chains at him? Can noble and serf for once speak their minds to him? Does the "sick man," not dead, come and show him his brawny arm?[7] Is this the vigil that the despot keeps while listening for the boom of our cannon? If so, he is calling on all his saints to help him. But to the hollow-hearted, saints and diviner beings than saints, are but ghosts also. To so great a sinner, in the hour when fear brings conviction, there is nothing present but his sins—the whole array of them—promising to "sit heavy[. . . ."][8]

Notes

1. Napier thought the fog the thickest he had ever encountered and feared for safety of the fleet: see *The History of the Baltic Campaign of 1854. From Documents and Other Materials Furnished by Vice-Admiral Sir C. Napier, K. C. B.*, ed. George Butler Earp (London: Richard Bentley, 1857), 133.

2. Martineau describes the building of St. Petersburg, on the islands and shores of the mouth of the Neva, in *Introduction to the History of the Peace*, iii. She repeatedly alludes to this project of Peter the Great: see, for example, "*Daily News*, 15 June 1853," above, and "*Daily News*, 25 August 1854," below. Lake Ladoga, mentioned below, lies on the border with Finland, northeast of the city. Sveaborg, the island fortress close to Helsinki on the Gulf of Finland, taken by the Russians in 1808, was shelled by an Anglo-French fleet only in 1855 (see *Daily News*, 20 August 1855).

3. Sir Charles Napier was spoken of as Black Charley from his dark complexion or Mad Charley because of his eccentricities. A French squadron had sailed for the Baltic in mid-April.

4. Besides Napier, the British Rear-Admirals Corry and Plumridge and the French Vice-Admiral Parseval-Deschêmes.

The Baltic Sea 175

5. In November 1840 Napier sailed with an allied fleet that fired on and took Acre (on the Syrian coast), in support of the Turkish Sultan against his rebellious Egyptian vassal, then occupying Syria. Napier disobeyed orders in positioning his ship, however, and was later accused of endangering the success of the action.

6. Martineau followed with keen interest the careers of the five Napier brothers who were cousins of Sir Charles: see "Lieutenant-General Sir William Napier, K. C. B.," *Daily News,* 15 February 1860 (rpt. *Biographical Sketches*).

7. The "watcher" is Czar Nicholas in St. Petersburg, at the end of the Gulf of Finland. The Marquis de Castelbajac, French Ambassador to Russia and a close observer of the Czar, reported: "In his painful indecision, his religious scruples on one hand, and his humanitarian scruples on the other; in his wounded pride, in the face of national feeling and the dangers which pursue his Empire; in the violent struggle with these various feelings, the Emperor Nicholas has aged ten years. He is truly sick, physically and morally." (General Castelbajac to M. Thouvenel, 11 February 1854; quoted in Lincoln, *Nicholas I. Emperor and Autocrat of All the Russias,* 341). For trees hung with corpses along the Circassian coast, see *Daily News,* 4 October 1854; for the flogging of Polish cadets at Warsaw in 1830, see *History of the Peace* 2: 175; for the Czar's taking away of Polish boys and his exile of Polish nobles to Siberia in 1831, see *History of the Peace* 2: 175–77; "*Daily News,* 18 January 1854," above; and *Daily News,* 10 April 1854. See also, *History of the Peace* 2: 368–70 and *Daily News,* 20 May and 5 July 1854. When Czar Nicholas came to England in 1844, he reportedly said to Lord Aberdeen, in confidence of their two nations' mutual interests in Europe, "Turkey is a dying man. We may endeavour to keep him alive, but we shall not succeed. He will, he must die. . . ." (Baron C. F. von Stockmar, *Memoirs of Baron Stockmar,* trans. G. A. M., ed. F. Max Müller (London, 1872), 107–8.

8. "on his tomb"?—text of the leader incomplete.

23. Russian History

Introduction

In May to June 1854, French and British troops landed at Varna (in modern Bulgaria) on the Black Sea, close to where the Turks were routing the Russians along the Danube. Enthusiasm for the war ran high in Britain and France: the Russian fleet and its base at Sebastopol were declared the next targets. Meanwhile, cholera spread through the camps in the summer, making the men apathetic and resentful. For a vivid account of the period, see Christopher Hibbert, *The Destruction of Lord Raglan: A Tragedy of the Crimean War, 1854–55* (London: Longmans, 1961).

Martineau conscientiously read history, both as a young woman and later. Like most Victorians, she idealized Greek and Roman writers. In her first published book, *Traditions of Palestine*, she used events of the New Testament as historical background for short tales. She also wrote an historical novel, *The Hour and the Man* (London: Moxon, 1841; on Toussaint L'Ouverture), "historiettes" for *Once A Week*, 1862 to 1865, and other tales about fictional commoners and historical aristocratic figures. Her view of the Crimean conflict as instructive, in this leader, is true to her utilitarian concept of history.

Daily News
25 August 1854

EVERY day now fixes attention more and more on the movements in the Black Sea, whence news of importance may be expected at any moment. There is nothing like travel, people say, for teaching geography; and it appears now that there is nothing like a war for substantiating historical knowledge, and deepening impressions derived from early study. How many of us have gone through half a life reading and talking about the trade the Greeks carried on to Colchis and the Chersonesus, without identifying the track, in the first case, with that which the CZAR had in view at the time of the siege of Herat and our wretched Affghan war; or, in the second case, with the provisions of the treaties by which he appropriated the navigation of the Black Sea.[1] Now that we are ourselves at war there, the old classical names slide into a curious identity with the uncouth words, which we have been wont to regard as part of the bore of the interminable Eastern question. The old Apollo sheds a fresh light upon those table lands of Georgia, gilding the fleeces of the common sheep in memory of old days. That headland of the Chersonese catches a gleam where IPHIGENIA served in the temple on the steep, and, at the command of the chaste goddess, sacrificed all the youthful adventurers who were cast on that inhospitable shore.[2] If there is an interest in such associations to us at home, much more stirring must they be to the officers of the fleets there—to those who have already run down the Circassian coast, and seen from the sea that Caucasian summit where PROMETHEUS is still, as people say, steeling his soul against his long agony; and to those again who have surveyed the noble precipitous coast of the Crimea—now finding it extremely like the glorious coast on either hand the Giant's Causeway, and now straining their eyes to catch the last gleam from the lighthouse, which through the gloom of night might easily pass for the temple where IPHIGENIA was tending the vestal fire.[3]

Then there are the religious associations. In the Asiatic direction of the war there is old Ararat; and without diverging so far as to the Seven Churches, there is Armenia, with its ecclesiastical history, and the Manichean controversies which have left behind them the great sect of devil worshippers:[4] while, in the European direction, there are the fastnesses of the Crimea, where the persecuted confessors of many faiths have taken refuge. If we so land our troops as to attack Sebastopol from behind and above, our officers may see—and when they have taken Sebastopol they may visit—the caves in the freestone rocks where the Arians retreated, to worship in their own way, without hourly danger of martyrdom.[5] The mountains of the Crimea, split into precipitous ranges by deep valleys between, have been found in all ages as proper for the abode of anchorites and fugitives as those of the Arabian desert: and the peninsula of Sinai scarcely contains a greater number of caves, or a greater variety of hermits and monks, from the Sabaites to the Greek churchmen, than does the Crimea.[6]

And yet there is room there for a very different set of associations. Here—in this wild place—while the high civilisation of the Western world was enjoying itself at Paris, Vienna, and London, little thinking what was doing down there among the Crim Tartars—here, in the Cimmerian darkness of these remote shores, was the yoke flung, with a vigorous hand, which so coupled Europeans with Asiatic destinies as to give us at this hour the task of throwing it off with accumulated pain and trouble. While the wild fowl were plashing in the pools, and the bittern was booming among the reeds where St. Petersburg now stands, PETER himself came down hither, and picked up the notion of making Russia a maritime power. The Genoese and the Venetians were busy about Greece and the Bosphorus, and had brought some of their light boats up as high as the Sea of Azof, as they well suited its shallow waters. The Crim Tartars were occupied in threatening the Polish frontier, and receiving checks from that then powerful nation. The Czar PETER came down as a volunteer with his own army to free the Tanais from the lodgments of the Turks which had taken place there.[7] PETER then, as NICHOLAS now, could trust only foreigners in command; and one of his foreign officers, exasperated by

Russian discipline (by having been knouted) went over to the Turks (as some of his successors may now do any day), and defended Azof, for that time with success. This disappointment induced PETER to take some Calmucs into his pay, to act as his light horse; and it was they who led on his desires to the acquisition of the Crimea. His second attempt against Azof succeeded; and as he stood on the shore of the muddy sea, and saw how well the light caiques that had fallen into his power navigated those shallow waters, he made up his mind that Russia should be a maritime power. Our Baltic admirals are now pitted against the main naval force of Russia; but it is DUNDAS and HAMELIN who have to destroy the Muscovite maritime force in or near its birthplace.[8] Before PETER began his travels—before the first drain disturbed the fish and fowl in the meres which were filled from Lake Ladoga—PETER made a harbour at Azof, to hold vessels large enough to win for him the Cimmerian Bosphorus, or Straits of Caffa, through which, again, he might possess himself of the Black Sea—through which, again, he might extend his empire to the Mediterranean. His scholars told him that MITHRIDATES once kept up great naval armaments there, and he therefore tried what he could do.[9] He left thirty-two armed boats before Azof—the originals of the famous gunboats which have since done such good service to Russia in her locked seas. There were fifty larger vessels presently ready for service: but it was these armed boats which coasted and watched the shores of the Crimea, in preparation for driving away the Turks and subduing the Tartars, and giving Russia the command of the Mediterranean trade by the sea channel on the one hand, and that of Persia and India, by the table lands of Georgia, on the other. His scholars told him that this was the trade which the Greeks carried on to Tauris and Colchis, and again he thought he would try what he could do. Our correspondents in the Black Sea tell us now of Russian ladies and their children basking on the shore of the Crimea, apparently fearless of our fleet, while Sebastopol is safe.[10] They have come down from the interior for their summer bathing. Their blossomy gardens and fruitful orchards, and vineyards that grow all the grapes under the sun, slope down from the precipitous mountains to the blue sea: the ladies sit reading on the shore—the children pick up shells—under the care perhaps of an English or French governess, here and there, who looks out wistfully at that fleet, with her countrymen clustering on the decks, and wonders who will be masters of this splendid peninsula next summer.

This is the point which the present autumn ought to decide. When PETER returned from his conquest of the higher Bosphorus he had the first Russian medal struck, and distributed as he entered Moscow under triumphal arches. That medal exhibited Azof, with a legend which told that PETER OF MUSCOVY was "Victorious by Fire and Water." As he marched, he glanced northward to the Baltic, and resolved to have a harbour and a fleet there also. He sent sixty young men into Italy, and forty into Holland, to learn how to make those useful boats which he had left behind, and the large ships with which maritime nations sweep the broader seas. Growing impatient, he soon went forth himself for some years of travel, and took up the mallet with his own hand in the shipyard at Saardam.

He made the mistake which enables us now to undo his work—a work too perilous to the peace of nations to be allowed to indulge itself unchecked. He was more ambitious of extension abroad than of elevation at home. Hence the hollowness which has spread through the whole overgrown carcase of his empire. It is well known to have extended to his beloved shipping. What would he have thought if he could have foreseen that his successor NICHOLAS would lock up his two navies within booms, and sentinel them with forts and guardships—afraid to trust them out of harbour because the worm is in the wood, and the rot in the rigging, and probable bad faith in the foreign commanders, and craven fear in the native serf seamen?[11] What could he have said but that such would be the hour for the overthrow of that maritime ambition which is a blessing if grounded on considerations of domestic welfare, but a curse if it ministers to aggression abroad? That maritime ambition it is the business of our Black Sea Admirals to strangle in the cradle of its birth.

Notes

1. Colchis, the mythical home of Medea and goal of the Argonauts, sometimes identified with Mingrelia (cf. "*Daily News*, 18 January 1854," note 3); for the Chersonesus, see next note. Herat, in Afghanistan, was besieged in 1837–1838 by Persia backed by Russia (see *Daily News*, 16 January and 7 March 1856); Britain was drawn in because of the threat to her Indian territories. In *History of the Peace*, Martineau accuses the Czar of sending out secret tentacles into all parts of the world: she recounts the events of 1837–1838 in 2: 368–70 and 496–516. In *Daily News*, 13 January 1854 she notes the Czar's building of a highway through Asia Minor, nominally for pilgrims to Jerusalem but really, she claims, for his soldiers. In 1833, after Russia helped Turkey put down her Egyptian vassal (see "*Daily News*, 16 May 1854," note 5), she forced Turkey to agree that no armed vessel could pass from the Mediterranean to the Black Sea without Russian permission.

2. Martineau follows Euripides (*Iphigenia Among the Taurians*) and other ancient writers who say that Iphigenia was rescued from sacrifice at Aulis and wafted in a cloud to the Tauric Chersonese, to become chief priestess in the temple to Artemis on the southwestern tip of the Crimea. Sailors cast on shore were said to be sacrificed to the goddess.

3. The Giant's Causeway, a spectacular basaltic-column formation on the north coast of Ireland, noted in *Letters from Ireland* (London: John Chapman, 1852). In *Daily News*, 14 October 1854, Martineau tells that the allies have relighted a lighthouse at Chersonese.

4. Martineau casts a wide net in her biblical associations: Mount Ararat, in Turkey; the Seven Churches in cities of Roman Asia mentioned in Revelation; the independent Armenian Church, with a history of differences with the Orthodox and Roman Churches (Martineau notes the Armenian convent at Jerusalem in *Eastern Life, Present and Past* 3: 126 and 128); "devil worshippers"—followers of Mani, third century prophet of dualism?

5. A reference to the Arian Visigoths? See *Daily News*, 2 October 1854.

6. Probably followers of the fourth-century monk Santa Saba, whose convent near the Dead Sea Martineau visited in 1847, noting "the innumerable holes in the rocks" where from 10,000 to 14,000 of the anchorites were said to have lived (*Eastern Life* 3: 158–59).

7. Martineau's account in this and the following paragraph follows Voltaire's *The Life of Peter the Great, Emperor of Russia* [trans.] (Frederick-Town: John P. Thomson, 1813) in the old forms of names, the selection of details, and even in verbal echoes of the English translation. She refers first to the seventeenth-century capitals of Louis XIV, the

Holy Roman Emperor Leopold I, and William and Mary. The Tartars established an independent khanate in the Crimea in the fifteenth century (Crim Tartars) but were soon conquered by the Turks and finally lost their kingdom to Russia in 1783. The Cimmerians were ancient inhabitants of the Crimea, but Martineau may mean simply "mysterious" shores. Voltaire records that Peter marched, as a volunteer with his armies, down the Tanais, or Don, in 1695 and attacked two Turkish forts en route to Azof at the mouth of the river. Voltaire also notes Genoese and Venetian traders in the Black Sea area. Poland—after her golden age in the sixteenth century—fought wars with Sweden and Russia. Martineau outlines the Czar's ambitions in Turkey in "*Daily News*, 15 June 1853," above.

8. Voltaire tells of the desertion of Peter's artillery officer Jacob, a Dane, and his defense of Azof; of his hiring of Calmucs (modern Kalmyks, mongols who migrated from Chinese Turkestan in the seventeenth century); and of the taking of Azof in 1696. Vice Admiral Sir James Dundas (1785–1862) and Vice Admiral Ferdinand-Alphonse Hamelin (b. 1796), commanders of British and French naval forces in the Mediterranean.

9. For Lake Ladoga, near St. Petersburg: see "16 May 1854," note 2; the Straits of Caffa, or Cimmerian Bosphorus (modern Kerch Strait), leads from the Sea of Azof to the Black Sea. Mithridates VI, first to second-century B.C. King of Pontus who fought the Romans and retreated to the Crimea. According to Voltaire, "The Czar's scheme was to drive the Turks and the Tartars forever out of the Taurica Chersonesus, and afterwards to establish a free and easy commerce with Persia, through Georgia" (95).

10. Martineau uses the vignette of Russian ladies basking in the Mediterranean sun again in *Daily News*, 25 September 1854.

11. Reportedly to serve as a battery, Russian ships had been anchored off St. Petersburg (*Daily News*, 8 May 1854: 5, col. 5). Blockships were later sunk across the entrance to the roadstead at Sebastopol. Martineau may partly base the idea of a poor Russian navy with many foreign commanders on Henry Reeve, "The Russian Empire," *Quarterly Review* 94 (March 1854): 423–60.

24. Sebastopol

Introduction

At first expecting to take Sebastopol easily, French and British troops landed on the Crimean peninsula in September 1854. Three battles—at the Alma in September, Balaclava (where the "charge of the light brigade" took place) in October, and Inkerman on 5 November—seemed to prove the tenacity of the Russian forces, now pouring into Sebastopol in preparation for a siege. In a bombardment of Sebastopol by British, French, and Turkish ships on 17 October, every ship in the British fleet was damaged. Allied commanders were accused of mismanagement of the war; thousands of men were disabled or died of illness and wounds.

Martineau's leaders do not usually respond to the latest bulletins from the front. She gives political, historical, and sociological background for the war and draws inferences for future European reform. Throughout her career Martineau also wrote on sanitation and water supply: see, for example, *Daily News*, 26 September 1853, on the use of peat charcoal to filter sewage water.

In *Daily News*, 28 August 1854, Martineau comments on the precarious water supply at Sebastopol, likely to be cut off by the allies. Although her analysis of sanitary conditions and military problems here would seem to heighten rather than relieve public anxiety over the coming siege, the notion of apocalyptic, even physically disgusting, punishment for the Czar takes precedence. Her romantic view of the rest of the Crimea, though wildly inaccurate, follows that of *The Times*. She partially qualifies that view in *Daily News*, 29 November 1854.

* * * *

Daily News
7 November 1854

NOWHERE has more extreme precaution against plague been exercised than at Sebastopol. The CZAR has lavished there all ingenuity and all money that could preserve the city of his pride from the ravage of imported pestilence. The water which comes down through the Inkermann tunnel he has had filtered for the use of the sailors and inhabitants, by being passed through a mass of sand and charcoal. Under the care of the UPTONS—his English engineers there[1]—he has had as much done as can be done in Russia towards clearing away accumulations of mud in the hot season, and getting rid of the refuse which is apt to poison a large town in a deep valley, inhabited by a filthy people. And now, it is this very CZAR who has caused this city of his pride to stink with a more horrible refuse than ever infected it before. The stench from dead bodies began early to be mentioned in the accounts of the siege. The deserters and prisoners tell of it, and there is no reason to doubt the statement. The great filter lies dry; for no water now comes down from the tunnel. It is cut off by the besiegers; and the townspeople would be without water but for the compassion of the Allies, who permit the women and children to steal out to the wells, beyond the walls, every morning. The heat is still great down in the valley—enough to breed a pestilence from the mud and refuse which no one can now carry away, and for which there is now no proper receptacle.[2] The cutting off the stream by the Allies, and the blocking up the harbour by the Russians[3], leave the town to be a great plague and fever hole; and there is no doubt that Sebastopol will follow the usual course of misfortune in war, and be laid to waste by pestilence when fire and slaughter have done their work.

This is an anxious consideration for us, who have been contemplating the occupation of Sebastopol by our troops for the winter. They have suffered enough by cholera this year, and must not run into any fever trap that can be escaped. Whoever next occupies Sebastopol will have a dreadful task to do in making a clearance of the dead, who must probably be carried out far to sea, in boatloads, and sunk weighted, because so many cannot be safely buried on land. They would pollute the shore if put under the sand, and anywhere else near the city the earth is too shallow above the stone to admit of interment on so large a scale.

Considering the danger on this ground of structure, and the circumstances of the Crimean climate, we cannot but hope that the allied forces will be quartered all along the "south coast," as the region below the rocks is technically called, and perhaps at Simpheropol,[4] and as few as can be permitted at Sebastopol. It is not premature to be speaking of this now. Everybody believes and declares that Sebastopol will be taken, and there have been conflicting accounts as to where the allied armies are to winter when the place is theirs. It seems to be a prior question where the Russians now in the Crimea are to winter. They will have to be encountered in battle, it is agreed, when the siege is over, and driven somewhere. Now, though the weather remains fine, and the climate mild, on the south coast, under the precipices, it must already be becoming wintry everywhere else. The steppe is considered impassable for bodies of men—for all but the Imperial couriers and such favoured personages—after the third week in October. If more Russians cannot come by that way, neither can those now in the Crimea escape by it, except into the very jaws of destruction. The blasts and snow-drifts and suffocating tempests of the steppe can be sustained by no body of men in the winter months. The disposal of the enemy we must leave to the best wisdom of the allied commanders.[5] The disposal of our own defenders for the winter is a subject of too deep and close an interest not to be discussed at almost every fireside in England.

Supposing that the contents of Sebastopol harbour are so treated as to make all safe there, we should hope that a considerable part of our navy would winter in the harbour of Theodosia, which never freezes, and is in all respects admirable. Special engineers are gone out to the East with their apparatus for blowing up the sunken ships at the mouth of the harbour of Sebastopol, to make room for some of ours.[6] Others may be well sheltered at Balaclava;[7] but Theodosia has the best climate and other qualities of the three. As for the land of the Crimea it consists of three kinds of scenery—Russian plains, Tartar defiles, and the south coast for whoever can get and hold it. The Russians cannot hold their plains in winter; and those plains, it must be remembered, stretch from far in the interior to Simpheropol. The Tartars who live in the defiles, building their villages on the shelves of the rocks, like wild bees setting up their honeycombs in a hollow tree, hate the Russians with the deepest hatred, and certainly will not make them welcome to their perilous strongholds. There was a day when every reigning Prince of the various Russian states had to go to the Golden Horde for investiture, and to do homage for his dominions to the Tartar Khan.[8] In those days, when the Tartar Khan sent his tribute gatherer to those Princes, each one had to lead the collector's horse by the bridle and feed it with oats out of his cap of state. The Tartars know, to a man, that there was such a day, and they regard the Russians accordingly. They have shown their willingness to help our armies to food and horses from the time we landed; and so conspicuously that the Russians are hanging every Tartar who can be detected in, or suspected of, supplying provisions to anybody but themselves. These Tartars know, and will readily tell, what food there is stored up in their valleys. The other cultivators are Germans, with a good many Bulgarians, who, if once tempted so far by the prospect of gain, prove themselves a wonderfully gainful people. Their neighbours say of them that they work like horses, scrape together like magpies, and live like hogs; in other words, they have stores of produce ready for our market. Along the coast there are fishermen, who catch mackerel enough in their autumn plumpness to send into the very centre of Russia, to the point of encounter with the fish of the Baltic. Many of these fishermen are wrecked mariners of all nations, who will be well pleased to deal with our soldiers while the Russian roads are stopped.[9]

There is an immense quantity of game in the forests of the valleys, and on the slopes under the precipices. These grey precipices are capped with snow, at a height of 4,000 feet above the sea, when below the pastures are green, and the vines and pomegranates need fear no injurious frost. The daws, owls, eagles, and smaller cliff birds come out and sun themselves at the mouths of their holes, when the Scythian north wind[10] is blowing out to sea over their heads; and the small game and sheep, goats, and cattle below, know nothing of winter. Now, it is under these precipices that, in spots properly chosen, handy and prudent men may winter perfectly well. The beech woods and other forest trees abound sufficiently to afford shelter and fuel for as many soldiers as will want to be there. The weather is fine enough there, up to Christmas or later, to allow of the building of huts to any extent required. If care be taken to choose the dry sunny slopes, instead of swampy valleys, the men will have a better chance of health than they ever had since they left home. Good winter clothing is on its way to both armies; and there seems to be no reasonable doubt that stores of food could be laid up, or obtained when wanted.[11] There are granaries in various ports of the Sea of Azoff [sic], always full when exportation is checked, because the roads become impassable too early to allow of the corn being sent back into the interior. These ports surround a sea which is usually as calm as a lake—its depth being nowhere more than 42 feet. With half a dozen granaries set round a little sea like that, Anapa forsaken,[12] the Black Sea our own, and craft of all sorts at our command, it is inconceivable that resources enough, in addition to those of a singularly fruitful country, should not easily suffice for the support of as many men as are wanted to hold the Crimea through the short and mild winter which makes the south coast so curious a contrast with the steppe which lies behind it.

Notes

1. Martineau refers to the nine-hundred-foot tunnel which formed part of an aqueduct also used to supply the system of locks and dry docks originally devised by Colonel Upton. William Upton supervised the building of a dam to supply the aqueduct.
2. For the Victorians' connection of pestilence with mud, see "*Daily News*, 24 September 1853," note 3.
3. See "*Daily News*, 25 August 1854," note 11.
4. By "south coast" Martineau must mean the coast east of Balaclava; Simpheropol (or Simferopol) is 37 miles northeast of Sebastopol on the Crimean peninsula.

5. For Martineau's concern over the welfare of the Russian soldiers, including a suggestion to send them to colonize elsewhere, see also *Daily News*, 8 September; 14, 18 October; and 29 November 1854.

6. Theodosia (modern Feodoysiya), a Black Sea port in the eastern Crimea. Cf. "25 August 1854," note 11.

7. Martineau's assertion contrasts with Hibbert's picture (among many others) of congestion and military chaos already at Balaclava: *The Destruction of Lord Raglan* (Penguin, 1985), 113.

8. In the thirteenth to fourteenth-century Mongol Empire of the Golden Horde (named for their gleaming tents pitched along the Volga), covering most of Russia and ruled by a descendant of Genghis Khan, Russian principalities paid tribute to the khan. Martineau seems to use "Tartar" to refer both to the Turkish-speaking people originally from northeast Mongolia and to all subjects of the khan.

9. For more comment on the variety of races in the Crimea, past and present, see *Daily News*, 25 September and 2 October 1854.

10. The area of the ancient Scythians (barbarians to the Greeks) extended from the Danube to the borders of China.

11. A week later, on 14 November 1854, a hurricane destroyed ships and supplies at Balaclava, including boots for most of the army and 40,000 greatcoats.

12. See "*Daily News*, 18 January 1854," note 7; the fortress at Anapa was blown up by its Russian defenders in early June 1855.

25. Raglan's Successor

Introduction

From mid-November 1854 the condition of British and French troops in the Crimea worsened: freezing rains alternated with snow; men fell sick and died for want of food, clothing, or shelter; no military gains against Sebastopol were made. Reports by war correspondents like William Howard Russell of *The Times* angered the commanders by their descriptions of suffering and the breakdown of military supply. Soon the tide of public support for commander-in-chief of the British forces, Lord Fitzroy Somerset (1788–1855), 1st Baron Raglan, and his staff turned to accusations of negligence and incapacity. A motion in Parliament at the end of January to inquire into the condition of the army before Sebastopol led to the fall of Lord Aberdeen's government. Lord Raglan, however, refused to fire two of his generals as the new war minister urged. With the coming of spring, shipments of clothing and food bolstered army morale. Then an attempt to take Sebastopol on 17–18 June failed with terrible loss of life. Lord Raglan seemed broken by the disappointment after enduring months of hostile criticism, and died probably of cholera on 28 June. His chief of staff, General James Simpson, took temporary command, and the struggle for Sebastopol ended without distinction for the British, in September 1855.

Martineau wrote a short biography of Lord Raglan, at the time of his appointment as field marshal in 1854 (rpt. *Biographical Sketches*), in which she praises the "man of rank," who for years "worked like a clerk" for the nation's defense under the Duke of Wellington and was the obvious choice for imparting "the old spirit into the new war." But here her muster of past military heroes who faced crises in their careers suggests that, unlike them, Raglan failed to recoup his losses. For her attraction to comparative biography, see "*Daily News*, 26 December 1853," above.

* * * *

Daily News
3 July 1855

THE successor to Lord RAGLAN'S office has that destiny open before him which all great warriors, in all times, might well have coveted. At the close of the career of all great captains, their success, and the labours which won it, seem easy to account for; and we care more to study their characters than to marvel at their achievements. This is because the most essential quality of a great captain is to turn obstacles into advantages, so that Fortune appears, by the results, to have favoured him: whereas, if we could study his career from its starting point instead of its goal, we might regard the hero as the step-son of a cross-grained Fortune, which had complicated his difficulties to the utmost. The reader of the history of every great warfare ought, in order to estimate its hero properly, to have that sympathy of imagination which would enable him to forget the known catastrophe, and proceed *pari passu* with the soldiery, to be perplexed by their difficulties, cast down by their reverses, and exhilarated, like them, by hopes which are never to be fulfilled. We talk glibly of GONSALVO DE CORDOVA, of TURENNE,[1] of CORTES, of WASHINGTON, of WELLINGTON, when we think of them as conquerors, resting under their laurels; but the true way of appreciating them and their career is to pass on with them from the outset of the struggle, and plunge with them into their abysses of difficulty. We should lose our breath in the struggle of the Spaniards on the Mexican causeway, on the "mournful night" of their expulsion, and see CORTES blinded with dust, blood, and the slime of the canals, before we can judge of the true character of his re-entry and rebuilding of the city. We should see TURENNE stemming the flight of his troops at Mariendahl before we can judge how Fortune favoured him at Turkheim, or in his sweep of the Palatinate. We should read WASHINGTON'S quiet but heart-touching letters about the shoeless and hatless state of his troops, and their perpetual return to their homes when he had most need of them, to understand the marvel of the fact that there was any American war at all. In like manner, we cannot compare any opening career with that of WELLINGTON, if we look at him riding through the southern provinces of France as the allies were converging from all other quarters upon Paris; or as directing operations at Waterloo, with the absolutism which he had won by seven years of patience as remarkable as his action.[2] We must look at him now superseded in his command, now disappointed of his supplies; now speculated on by incapables in the House of Lords, and compelled to march for food when he wanted to halt, and now compelled to halt when he wanted to be marching, through the withholding of everything necessary to his advance. All the great captains won their honours and changed the aspect of the world by pressing on through fog and darkness, among snares and pitfalls; and the probability seems to be that no man can rise to fellowship with them by other means.

Yet does the death of Lord RAGLAN seem to offer the dignity of his high post on conditions morally easier. There will never be any lack of difficulty in such a position, of course; but the worst evils, those which impose helplessness, are not present in the camp before Sebastopol, and are not likely to arise. The woes and failures consequent on long inexperience of war are over; and the new Commander sees his troops comparatively well fed, clothed and provided with arms and ammunition; and likely to continue so, from the rousing of the national will in a way that WELLINGTON never had the benefit of. Our French Allies in the Crimea are worth our Spanish Allies in Spain ten times over; and the Turks are now at least as good as the Portuguese were in 1809—excellent auxiliaries as they afterwards became.[3] In these essential preliminaries of success the new Commander is more fortunate than perhaps any great captain that could be pointed out. His difficulties will be just those which must be dealt with by the genius of the man. His enterprise is provided to his hand, while it rests with him to achieve it in his own way. He has brave and competent allies, and a ready and eager soldiery of proved courage and constancy. It is for him now to show what professional ability he can bring to bear amidst circumstances so favourable. A *médiocre* general may take Sebastopol, with the aid of his allies and other appliances. A great captain will do it soon and thoroughly, and make the achievement a stepping-stone to others and get other victories, till the war is closed—so far as Russia is concerned. By clearness of aim, by concert and promptitude, it must be possible to bring to satisfactory terms an enemy now so punished as Russia, with a soldiery so renovated as our own. And a great captain will look beyond the strict limits of this task. He must know well, at this moment (if there be a great captain now in the British nation), that the taking of Sebastopol in the autumn— when, as we now find, it might have been ours—would have determined the policy of several of the governments of Europe, so as to save the dire conflicts which are now almost certain to arise.[4] He will feel that by the careful promptitude of genius, other evils may now be obviated which a dilatory warfare will bring to birth. He will see that, in the present condition of Europe, his word of command in the field will decide matters in the Cabinet no less; and that every moment lost by him in hesitation is an advantage given to the despotisms kindred with Russia, to join their forces, and build up their barriers of political obstruction. A Captain of the highest order might now show the world the noblest specimen of the military hero ever seen. In proportion as ours is an age of peace, and the military phases of social progress are known to be left behind, may the glory of a great captain of the 19th be greater than that of any former century. The present conflict is not one of an interminable series of wars, all like one another to the end of time.[5] Ours is, as the wisest men tell us, a final struggle of united physical and moral force to put down in Europe the brute force which has still to fulfill its term in Asia. The greatest captain will see how to do this best, by the largest admixture of the highest intellectual and moral qualities of the hero and statesman with such a quality of physical force as the nation has now put into his hand. The old method, enfeebled by the encrusting influences of a long peace, is gone, we may hope, with the veterans who have shown abundance of fine soldierly qualities in an unavailing sort of way. A man worthy of the occasion may now drive back the Russian power within the limits at which the Czar PETER found it—at least in the south.[6] He will get the Principalities emptied of Austrians, while politicians at home are thinking what they shall say at Vienna about it. He will overawe Germany, not by apprehension of force, but by the majesty of right; and at the same moment, the POPE and King BOMBA will slink into themselves, while constitutional Sardinia will send abroad the reviving influence of her spirit of freedom.[7] Under a General of the highest order, the way may be opened at once to the majestic establishment of the right, and tyranny and faction may be shamed and discouraged everywhere, as they were by WELLINGTON, when he was the greatest statesman as well as warrior in Spain.

The way stands open. Lord RAGLAN is dead. Everybody agrees as to what is wanted in his place. Whether the man is to be had is the anxious question. If the man exists, and can be installed, it is certain that never before had a true commander so prodigious an opportunity.

Notes

1. Gonzalo Fernández de Córdoba (1453–1515), Spanish general, "the Great Captain," fought in the civil wars at the time of Isabella I, in the conquest of Granada, etc., and improved the Spanish infantry. Henri de la Tour d'Auvergne (1611–1675), Vicomte de Turenne, skilled French general, fought in the Thirty Years' War; and see note 2.

2. Hernán Cortés (1485–1547) was driven from Mexico city on the *noche triste*, 30 June 1520, after the death of Montezuma; he recaptured the city in 1521. Turenne fought model campaigns in Germany. After a defeat at Marienthal in 1645, he reorganized his troops and conquered the foe; fighting for Louis XIV, he devastated the Palatinate (Germany) in 1674 and defeated an army at Turckheim (eastern France) in 1675. Washington was forced to make use of the militia, whom he could not control; his worst ordeal was the winter at Valley Forge, 1777–78. Wellington defeated Napoleon's army in Spain in autumn 1813. When Napoleon abdicated in April 1814, Wellington was summoned to Paris to confer with the allied sovereigns about Spain. The battle of Waterloo,

1815, came seven years after he was prevented from following up a victory over the French in Portugal in 1808. See also *Daily News,* 20 January 1854 and 4 January 1855.

3. Martineau steadily defends the Turkish leaders, especially their commander Omar Pacha (see *Daily News,* 23 May, 1 September, 3 October 1854; 20 January, 25 May and 13 November 1855) and Turkish soldiers (*Daily News,* 3 August 1854, 20 January and 6 December 1855) even though they fled at the battle of Balaclava. English and French troops generally disparaged the underfed and undisciplined Turks.

4. A reference to the unwillingness of Austria (see "*Daily News,* 2 March 1854," note 8; and below), Prussia, and the Scandinavian countries to side firmly with the allies against Russia. Martineau wrote approximately thirty leaders, from April 1854 to May 1856, on Austria and Prussia and the Czar's manipulation of their "sympathetic despots." In about twenty leaders on Denmark, Sweden, and Norway during the same period, she emphasizes the distinction between their freedom-loving people and their rulers. Her mention of the cabinet, below in this paragraph, points to her disgust at "aristocratic dilatoriness": see "26 December 1853," note 3, and *Daily News,* 28 May 1855.

5. The notion of historical phases was widespread in the nineteenth century; Martineau then refers to the British statesman George Canning's "war of opinion . . . by which Oriental Despotism is finally to measure its force against the Western principle of Self-government by Representation" (*Introduction to the History of the Peace,* iii), for which she blames Russia in advance. See "*Daily News,* 15 June 1853," note 6; *Daily News,* 27 November and 13 December 1854; and "*Daily News,* 26 May 1859," below.

6. Martineau repeatedly uses Peter the Great's ambition to own "the whole of the Eastern length of Europe . . . from the Arctic Sea to the Mediterranean" (see "15 June 1853" and "*Daily News,* 25 August 1854," above) as a basis for her attacks on Czar Nicholas. But she overstates her case: when Peter the Great came to power in 1689, the southern boundary of Russia was roughly a hundred miles north of the Caucasus Mountains in the east and even farther north of the Black Sea. Russia had no outlet at the mouth of the Don in the Sea of Azof (cf. "25 August 1854," note 7) or on the Black Sea.

7. Austria had been occupying the Danubian principalities since summer 1854 (see "2 March 1854," note 8). Representatives from Britain, France, Austria, and Russia met in the winter and spring of 1855 at Vienna but failed to reach an agreement to end the war. Pope Pius IX (1782–1878), elected 1846, at first supported political reforms but became reactionary and anti-liberal after the revolutions of 1848; King

Bomba—Ferdinand II (1810–1859), despotic ruler of the Two Sicilies, was so nicknamed from his bombardment of Sicilian cities in 1849. (For Martineau's review of English actions towards Sicily in the nineteenth century, see *Daily News*, 2 October 1855.) Sardinia (see "26 December 1853," note 1), under King Victor Emmanuel II entered the Crimean War on the side of the allies in summer 1855.

26. The Czar and Scandinavia

Introduction

The Crimean War ended officially in March 1856 with the signing of the Treaty of Paris. At the evacuation of the allies from the Crimea in July 1856, Russia regained the peninsula. Czar Alexander II, eldest son and successor of Czar Nicholas (who died in March 1855), helped to negotiate the treaty.

Martineau wrote several leaders in 1856 on the peace terms and on the economic future of Russia, but other topics such as the war with Persia and the battle over the settlement of Kansas (see introduction, "*Daily News*, 24 September 1856") now absorbed most of her interest.

During the Crimean War, Martineau repeatedly refers to the friendliness of the liberty-loving Scandinavian people and the Czar's long-standing designs on their territories—signaled by Russia's takeover of Finland in 1809—and of an "aristocratic coterie" in Sweden who sympathize with the Czar. (See also "*Daily News*, 16 May 1854," above.)

Here Martineau draws on lively details in a recent book on Scandinavia to remind readers that Russia still posed a threat to European freedoms.

Daily News
19 November 1856

IT is interesting, and somewhat rare, to be present as it were at the creation of a tradition—to be the first hearers of an apologue which will be related from generation to generation for centuries. Here is one—dating from 1853. Let the date be observed, lest the story should be supposed a prophecy made after the event. In 1853, an English clergyman (the "Oxonian in Norway") was at Wadsöe, when a mannikin of the Fins there told the following story.[1]

He said the CZAR had sent to the King of SWEDEN to give notice that he meant to annex Sweden and Norway to Russia, and that there was no use in making any opposition to his scheme. King OSCAR,[2] in a great fright applied to Queen VICTORIA, and she sent to warn the CZAR against attempting anything of the sort. The CZAR wanted to fight the British immediately; but Queen VICTORIA said it would suit her better the next year. NICHOLAS, in a rage, sent her a sack of barley, saying that there were more grains than she could count, but not more than he would send soldiers against her; and if they were not enough, he had ready as many more. Queen VICTORIA sent NICHOLAS a peppercorn, and bade him put it in his mouth; and this was her message with it: "My army is small, and so is this peppercorn; but this corn bites sharp, so my army will be sharp—much sharper than you will like." So the CZAR put off fighting for another year.

Such was the story which was going the round of the Lap tents in that summer when they were in such tribulation about their reindeer pastures. It will be remembered that in the preceding year (1852), the CZAR had suddenly abrogated the treaty of a century old, which professed (in 1751) to be "for all time to come," and which declared that the Norwegian and Finnish Laps should have a common right of passing the frontiers to graze their reindeer. The pretence was that the Finnish Laps belonged to Sweden when the treaty was made;

The Czar and Scandinavia

and that Swedish engagements were not binding on Russia. One wonder was that this had not been found out before; and another, what could be the object of the abrogation of the treaty now.

The state of affairs on that frontier at the time throws light on the latter question; and as the aspiration of every good citizen on the frontier is "I wish these things could be told in the London newspapers,"[3] it may be well to show how the land lies. It is true the decisive act of guaranteeing the Swedish and Norwegian territory from foreign encroachment has been accomplished by the Western Powers since 1853, and Russia has for the present been baffled in her prowling about the Finmark frontier;[4] but till Russia earns a reputation for good faith, it is as well that the English public should understand the precise facts of each case of collision, in order to support and stimulate their Government, to the satisfaction of Turks, Roumanians, Swedes, Laps, or whosoever may be threatened next.

The Russians have a peculiar sort of geographical perception. Like persons with colour blindness or colour squint, who despise the rest of the world for saying that the British clothing is not drab, and that the grass is not the same colour as the sky, they assume that all maps but their own are bad, and think it enough, when making treaties, to lay open Russian gazetteers and books of travel. A recent Russian traveller describes Vardohus as commanding the entrance of the Varanger fiord, the Varanger fiord being the harbour coveted by Russia, and Vardohus the last Norwegian fort in that direction.[5] Vardohus is nine Norwegian miles from the entrance of the fiord, but of the readers of Russian books of travel not one in a thousand has the means of checking their statements. Norway is so far from commanding Varanger Bay by that fort, that she must do it by other means, and cannot do it too carefully. But if Russia has peculiar geographical conceptions, she has yet (or had when Finland became Russian) an insufficient knowledge of some facts relating to climate. She had not studied the effects of the Gulf Stream enough for her political purposes. The promontories next the Russian frontier were barricaded with the ice of centuries; and, ignorant that a better coast lay beyond, the Czar NICHOLAS, on his accession, made haste to settle his frontier—before left indeterminate—and drew his line just to the east of Varanger fiord, which, from its relation to the Gulf Stream, never freezes. In 1840, that northern region became wonderfully attractive to Russian officials, who could not see too much of midsummer night sunshine, or row and sail enough about the rivers and harbours, or satisfy their curiosity and memory by too much sounding of the waters and sketching of the shores. The fashion was something like the flight into Egypt of our tourist countrymen of late years; or the resort of our sportsmen to the Norwegian rapids and forests. Some careless official, however, put a wrong direction on a Government circular, by which it reached the hands of a Norwegian magistrate. It disclosed the significant fact that these pleasure-seeking tourists were emissaries of the CZAR, sent by him to explore the coasts, and report on the fitness of certain harbours for the reception of a fleet, the convenience of the rivers for navigation, and the proper track of military roads throughout the region. This was all clear enough; but the late CZAR went further still, in his reliance on the timidity and Russian leanings of the King of SWEDEN. He offered to Norway a considerable tract of territory elsewhere in exchange for the small north-east corner which contains Varanger Bay. The pretext was of course the interest of the fishermen, and some merely nautical objects; but the disclosure about military roads stultified all such pretences. The negotiation was never completed; and, in 1852, the poor Laps were prohibited, as has been said, from carrying their reindeer over the frontier into a district which had always been considered neutral ground. The calculation evidently was that the Laps, who care more for their deer than for kings and nationalities, would be quite willing to become his subjects, rather than see their herds hungry. The notice, bearing date June 22, 1852, declared the intention of the CZAR to punish all crossing of the frontier by the deer, whether their keepers were with them or not, by a seizure of a tenth part of the deer for a fine, and as many more as might be assessed for damages to the pastures. If the herd were not gone back by the day fixed, the forfeiture was to be repeated. If a river or other natural boundary marked the frontier, the deer might be seized immediately on crossing; and if an arbitrary line marked the frontier, the point of trespass would be half a mile within the line. The Laps threatened by this arrangement owned about 80,000 reindeer, for whose maintenance the pastures of the neutral territory were absolutely necessary. They must reduce their herds, or see them pine with hunger, or become Russian subjects; and it is not surprising that the CZAR reckoned on their choice of the last alternative.[6] But he was not aware of the hatred excited against him and his rule by his insolent subjects on the frontier—his drunken soldiers and tyrannical placemen; nor did he reckon on the immediate effect of his insult to Norwegian pride. Up to that time the poor people near the frontier had been neglected by their Government, and regarded rather as colonists than as an integral part of the nation. They were left dependent on Russia for grain, meal, cordage, and other necessaries, and Russian officials had the whole business of the region under their hands.[7] The Norwegian residents had no power of resistance, and no hope of redress under the daily wrongs and insults they were subjected to by tipsy Russian crews, and trespassers who fished in their waters. At first there was some fear that even this last encroachment would not suffice to rouse the Government. There was some talk of an appeal to the Western Powers; but King OSCAR desired to keep the matter quiet. Then the CZAR went, as in other cases, one step too far. He threatened to blockade the Norwegian frontier if his demands were not granted. There was an end of secrecy, and consequently of the reserve of Sweden. While the White Sea was shut up, the Government sent up supplies of grain to the inhabitants who had been left to depend upon Archangel:[8] inquiry was made into a certain claim of the CZAR'S on a bit of Norwegian land as one of the "Holy Places," and the alarm was fairly taken by the Western Powers. The "Oxonian in Norway" was shown how the Russians had effected a lodgment on the Norwegian side of Jacob's river, by first sending some Russian Laps to live on a portion of land there—then building a Greek chapel for them—and then claiming the little territory as a "Holy Place," belonging to "Holy Mother Russia," on that account.[9] All this was preparatory to obtaining a splendid naval station within easy distance, by a new route, of the British Islands and the Norwegian coasts. It was too much for the apathy or timidity of King OSCAR; and now the frontier residents have something better to do under Russian tyranny than getting tipsy in drinking ill luck to the Heir of Norway, and cursing the CZAR's officials under their breath, while publicly bowing and scraping to them as formerly. They may now appeal to a Government ready to listen, and to Allies willing to fulfil their engagements. As for the rest, we may learn from this story what to expect and what to do when any Czar takes liberties, either in an Isle of Serpents, or before a Bolgrad, or with his eye on Skagerö;[10] and Queen VICTORIA knows that whenever another sack of barley is sent to her, she must have her peppercorn ready.

Notes

1. The Reverend Frederick Metcalfe, *The Oxonian in Norway* (London: Hurst & Blackett, 1856), a genial account of travel and hunting experiences (see 2: 187–89). Vadsoe is on the north shore of the Varanger Fjord [Warranger Fiord], an inlet of the Barents Sea, northeast Norway (cf. Metcalfe 2: 175).

2. Oscar I (1799–1859), King of Norway and Sweden from 1844, began a mild reform program unpopular with the upper classes; Martineau notes his problematic neutrality in the Crimean War (*Daily News*, 27 April, 8 May, 7 June, 29 September, 6 December 1854; 21 May, 20 August and 20 November 1855.

3. Reported in Metcalfe 2: 184.

4. In 1853, King Oscar declared he would not form a coalition with Russia; in 1855, in return for a promise of help in case of a Russian attack, he concluded a treaty with Britain and France pledging not to cede territory to Russia.

5. Vardohus fortress, on the island of Vardo, just off the coast in the Barents Sea.

6. On the Czar's edict, see Metcalfe 2: 189–91. In *Daily News*, 29 September 1854 (first leader), Martineau comments on the Czar's turning back of the Laps' and Finns' reindeer herds.

7. Metcalfe 2: 186–87.

8. Archangel (Russian Arkhangelsk), on the White Sea, for long Russia's main seaport, only open from May to October. For Martineau's history of the pro-English trading settlement, founded in the sixteenth century and taking its name from the nearby monastery of the Archangel Michael, see *Daily News*, 17 May 1854; see also introduction, "16 May 1854."

9. Metcalfe 2: 207–8.

10. Russian claims, after the Treaty of Paris, included Serpents Island at the mouth of the Danube, claimed by both Turkey and Russia; Bolgrad, a town on the new frontier of Russia with Moldavia (part of Romania); and Skagerö (a small Scandinavian island), not otherwise identified.

27. Sidney Herbert

Introduction

After the failures of the British army administration during the Crimean War, Sidney Herbert—abetted by Florence Nightingale—led a crusade to reform the army medical department. As Secretary at War, in charge of army finances and accounting in Aberdeen's cabinet, Herbert had resigned as a result of the debacle at Sebastopol in the winter of 1854–55. In 1859, he became Secretary of State for War, responsible for the whole War Office. Though Herbert achieved reforms in army training, equipment, and barrack amenities as well as of the militia during his career, Nightingale and others blamed him for not trying harder to reform the privilege and abuse-ridden war ministry.

Martineau had used the "Reports" on army sanitary reform sent her by Nightingale (see introduction, "*Daily News*, 23 February 1865," above) for *Daily News* leaders on 14, 18, 26 January; 1, 11, 16 February and 5 March 1859; and for *England and Her Soldiers*. She then supported Herbert's efforts to reform Indian army service (see *Daily News*, 27 June, 15 July and 26 August 1859).

In January 1861, when Herbert retired from the House of Commons to become Lord Herbert of Lea, a letter from Nightingale (Britiish Library Add MS 45788: f 103–10) evidently spurred Martineau to urge that Herbert be allowed to carry out reform of the War Office (see *Daily News*, 9 January 1861). Later, Martineau was to return to the question of Indian army health and welfare (*Daily News*, 16, 22, 27 July 1863; 3, 17 June, 18 October and 2 December 1864). After a celebration honoring

Herbert in September 1865, Martineau was to report continuing abuses in army service in spite of sanitary and other reforms Herbert achieved (*Daily News*, 27 September 1865).

In her obituary of Herbert (*Daily News*, 6 August 1861, rpt. *Biographical Sketches*), Martineau romanticizes Herbert's Russian family connections[1] and praises his private philanthropy. She summarizes his political career, including his request to Nightingale to take nurses to the Crimea and his reform efforts at the War Office.

Unfavorable estimates of Herbert also appeared. The office of the commander-in-chief and the military authorities, "the Horse Guards," had balked at any infringement of their privileges. Others, like the permanent under-secretary of the war office, helped to baffle Herbert's reforms.

On 4 October 1861, Martineau wrote indignantly to Nightingale:

> No harm can come of an attempt to shame the Horse Guards. I have consulted my editor, and if I can obtain a sufficiency of clear facts, I will gladly harass the Commander-in-Chief as he was never harassed before— that is, I will write a leader against him every Saturday for as many weeks as there are heads of accusation against him and his Department. We don't want to mince matters.[2]

Nightingale claimed not to know where the Horse Guards were thwarting Herbert's plans but sent Martineau her sketch of Herbert's achievements (also sent to Gladstone).[3]

In November 1861, a grand meeting to decide how to honor Herbert gave Martineau her cue to write a second, more specific account of Herbert modelled on Nightingale's memoir of him (see below, note 7).

In spite of Nightingale's unwillingness to send information on the Horse Guards, Martineau here points to them as villains of Herbert's heroic failure. Nightingale was to write to Benjamin Jowett the following summer:

> in one short year Sir G. Lewis has dragged down the War Office to the position of contempt, out of wh. S. H. was 5 long years in dragging it up ... the War Office has never

been at so low an ebb of intelligence, the Horse Guards at so high a flow of folly and insolence as now.... [4]

Notes

1. Cf. *Daily News*, 24 November 1854 on his grandfather Prince Woronzoff.
2. Quoted by Sir Edward Cook, *The Life of Florence Nightingale* (London: Macmillan, 1913) 2: 6.
3. Florence Nightingale to Harriet Martineau, 24 October 1861 (MS National Library of Scotland 1890: f 16).
4. British Library Add MS 45788: f 3–12, TS copy of original now perished. Quoted in *Dear Miss Nightingale: A Selection of Benjamin Jowett's Letters to Florence Nightingale, 1860–1893*, ed. Vincent Quinn and John Prest (Oxford: Clarendon, 1987), 17.

* * * *

Daily News
2 December 1861

IT would seem impossible that any description of a man's character could be fuller, or any appreciation of his gifts and virtues more thorough than that which we read in the speeches in honour of Lord HERBERT at the meeting at Willis's Rooms last Thursday. Yet we miss in those collective addresses any accurate estimate of the precise service to which he proposed to devote his life. All that was said of his character and manners is true, and was grateful to the feelings of those who knew him; but the public, who regarded him in connexion with public affairs, have not found in the words of his eulogists any clear representation of Lord HERBERT'S aims and proposed services as a minister and citizen.[1]

With him began Military Administration in England. We need not go back beyond the Crimean war to show that there was then nothing worthy the name of administration at the War-office. We used to hear of the great services of the Duke of York in the military department:[2] but there never was a time, nor an occasion, when the British army was not at the mercy of accidents in some direction or other; when its forces were not wasted by mismanagement; when its precious lives were not extinguished by thousands by disease and misadventure in barrack, camp, and field; when its affairs were not conducted in a desultory way, or left to chance; when, in short, military administration in England was not a chapter of accidents, and found to be so on occasion of any unforeseen trial.

The last time this was discovered by the people of England was when they had to call a coroner's inquest on their first Crimean army.[3] Lord PANMURE tided over the crisis by the most lavish use of the most lavish means ever afforded to a broken-down department.[4] He brought our second army through; but the military department remained what it had been. It must be recreated. It was SIDNEY HERBERT who saw most clearly what had to be done; and to him we owe, in the first place, whatever has been done towards instituting a real Military Administration.

It is but little that has been done towards that particular object; but whose fault is that? Much has been done towards saving the life and health of our soldiery, elevating their character, and ameliorating their lives; but in other directions, much has been proposed that has never been accomplished—much promised that has been withdrawn; and the main object—the reorganization of the War-office—seems to be no nearer than when SIDNEY HERBERT first meditated the method of it. Perhaps some of those who on Thursday spoke his praises may be unaware of what he desired and strove to accomplish, but there were others who must have known how and why he was baffled, and even dishonoured in the eyes of Parliament and the country, by having engaged for more than he was permitted to effect. There must have been some present who were, or ought to have been, conscious that the labours so lauded had been held vexatious, troublesome, inconvenient to the department; that the devotedness so extolled over his grave had been rebuked or mortified when he was in life; that the zeal for which the people were called on to praise him had survived so many attempts to quench it as to prove itself unquenchable but by death,—the death which follows upon overwork when the work is mixed up with anxieties and failures. There must be some who at this hour know how it is that SIDNEY HERBERT'S intentions and promises about the purchase system remain unfulfilled;[5] and by what gallantry of spirit it was that he took on himself the blame of failures which disappointed him more than any of us.

Looking in somewhat of an orderly way at what he achieved, we are better able to understand what he failed to effect, and why; and, as it is of importance to the country that the case should be understood, in order to its being effectually dealt with, we may just glance at the list of SIDNEY HERBERT'S effective services in the military department.

Lord PANMURE'S sanitary commission, on the return of the army from the Crimea, was conducted by SIDNEY HERBERT.[6] His Report was the beginning of the internal reform of the army. Out of it arose, at his suggestion, four commissions, which occasioned reforms in as many departments of the military service. One undertook the subject of barrack and hospital reform; one the reorganization of the medical department; one the reform of the medical statistics of the army; and the other the organization of a School of Army Hygiene at Chatham. SIDNEY HERBERT conducted all these commissions while waiting for his proper office as War Minister. These four commissions were worth more than might be supposed by persons who regard them as working merely towards the health of the army. They have reduced the mortality of our soldiery one-half; but that is only a part of their value. They established the essential principles of administrative reform, and thus half achieved other reforms which appear to have no connexion with the life and health of our army.

The new Warrant for the Army Medical Service, which gave new virtue, capacity, and dignity to our army physicians and surgeons in a body, was the work of SIDNEY HERBERT. He proposed it, and drew it up, and got it issued by General PEEL.[7] Who it was that afterwards tampered with it, and succeeded for a time in undoing a work of singular importance and benefit, will be known some day, perhaps soon. Meantime, the medical statistics of the army have become the best in Europe, and will save hosts of lives, and advance medical science for all time to come. The regulations by which the medical and sanitary reorganization was made effective in our whole military department were issued by him two years since, in a model code, of which foreign governments are eager to obtain possession.[8] The school at Chatham was opened by him in October, 1860. Last January he completed the new arrangement of the Purveyor's Department, by which the sick and wounded are made secure of all needful provision in all situations. Later still he completed his reforms of the hospital service, so that the scandals of Scutari can never recur. The General Hospital at Woolwich will properly bear his name, in memory of this signal service. It is his doing that there are already two hundred camp cooks trained at Aldershott, and that there will be wholesome and economical cookery in the army henceforth. Whatever exists, and will exist, in the form of soldiers' institutes, soldiers' homes, day rooms, reading rooms, is his work; and whatever sobriety, cultivation of intellect, and improvement in manners which may result from such institutions must be attributed to him. The unheard-of lowness of the mortality and sickness of our army in China, and the reforms in the health, temper, and spirits of our troops in India, were his work. Instead of sixty dying in the hundred, as in the Crimea in 1854, only three per cent. died in China;[9] and if we can keep up an army of requisite strength in India, it will be by his having shown us how to deal with the causes of mortality there.

What he did in reorganizing our national defences—the Militia, the Volunteers, and the Indian Army—the people of England are more aware of than of his services in the War-office. What they have chiefly to attend to, in justice to his memory, is that every step he took in his office was in the direction of reform, in a department in which it is singularly difficult to achieve reforms.

What he did *not* do was to reorganize the War-office. Hence his failures, hence his mortifications—hence such censures as he incurred, hence the anxieties which are worse to bear than any amount of labour. Why he did not achieve this central work, why he had to account for promises unfulfilled, why he was baffled and humbled, and beset by difficulties, will have to be explained. His nature was modest; his spirit was generous; his temper was above the reach of irritation; and he

Sidney Herbert

was therefore a safe subject for thwarting. He was one who might be trusted to uphold dignities, and take censures upon himself. But the people of England must now look to these things for themselves; and they will choose to know the precise operation of the Horse Guards upon the War-office; and why engagements of vital importance to the character of our military service remain unfulfilled; and how much the breath of praise over the dead is worth when it comes from those who contravened the efforts, and played fast and loose with the honour, of the statesman who rests from his labours. When the true history of SIDNEY HERBERT'S life becomes known it will disclose some passages of some other men's lives which it concerns Englishmen to be acquainted with. Meantime the more he has done for us the more resolute we must be to obtain what he desired, but failed to achieve. His best monument will be the carrying out of his work in a thoroughly honest, just, and able administration of military affairs.

Notes

1. The meeting in Willis's rooms, conducted by the Duke of Cambridge, commander-in-chief of the Army, resolved to raise a subscription for a statue of Lord Herbert and to endow exhibitions in his honor at the new army medical school at Chatham. Speakers included Palmerston, Gladstone (Chancellor of the Exchequer), General Peel (see note 7, below), the Bishop of Oxford and the Duke of Newcastle. *The Times*, 29 November 1861: 7, cols. 1–4.

2. Frederick Augustus, Duke of York and Albany (1763–1827), became commander-in-chief of the Army in 1795. Though not successful in the field, he rid the Army of certain abuses in discipline and administration and enhanced Army spirit. The headquarters of the commander-in-chief at the Horse Guards building, Whitehall, also dated from 1795.

3. In January 1855, a motion to investigate the condition of the Army in the Crimea, including the hospitals, caused the fall of the Aberdeen government. Herbert resigned as Secretary at War. See "*Daily News*, 26 December 1853" and "*Daily News*, 3 July 1855," above.

4. Fox Maule, Baron Panmure (later Earl of Dalhousie; 1801–1874), became Secretary for War under Palmerston. Panmure sent three sanitary commissioners to the Crimea to carry out reforms in the

hospitals. However, he was blamed for mistakes and misfortunes to the Army preceding the fall of Sebastopol. Herbert continued his reform efforts, receiving reports from Florence Nightingale at Scutari.

5. In March 1860, Parliament voted against changes in the systems of promotion and purchase of commissions in the Army.

6. Watched over by Nightingale working behind the scenes, a Royal commission began work after six months' delay in May 1857. Herbert's *Report of the Commissioners appointed to inquire into the Regulations affecting the Sanitary Condition of the Army, The Organization of Military Hospitals, and the Treatment of the Sick and Wounded, with Evidence and Appendix* (P. P. 1857–58 XVIII) revealed the shocking rate of mortality in the Army from preventable "sanitary" causes.

7. At the advice of the royal commission, Herbert framed an army medical officers warrant to insure military doctors suitable rank and pay for their services: see Florence Nightingale, *Army Sanitary Administration and Its Reform under the Late Lord Herbert* [read at the London meeting of the Congrès de Bienfaisance, June 1862] (London: McCorquodale, n. d.), 7 (under pressure from the Horse Guards, the warrant was withdrawn in 1864). General Jonathan Peel (1799–1879), Secretary for War under Palmerston in 1858.

8. The new code of regulations for sanitary service of the Army, issued by Herbert in 1859, focused on caring for the soldier's health rather than sickness. It defined the duties and responsibilities of the commanding and medical officers and set out regulations for general and regimental hospitals. For Martineau's collaboration with Nightingale in sending the regulations to the American Secretary of War, cf. *Harriet Martineau's Letters to Fanny Wedgwood*.

9. Partly at Nightingale's instigation, reforms based on experience in the Crimea in army diet, accommodation and medical equipment were carried out with the British expeditionary force sent to China in spring 1857 (Nightingale, 8). For reforms of the whole structure of army administration following the Crimean War, see John Sweetman, *War and Administration The Significance of the Crimean War for the British Army* (Edinburgh: Scottish Academic, 1984), 128.

IV. Politics and Foreign Affairs

28. Gervinus

Introduction

Martineau wrote two early leaders on the German martyr to academic freedom Georg Gottfried Gervinus (1805–1871), a literary and political historian from the University of Heidelberg whose *Introduction to the History of the Nineteenth Century*[1] traced progressive stages of political freedom in the Western world according to a scheme taken from Aristotle. In his short book, Gervinus expressed admiration for English constitutional monarchy and for American democracy. Gervinus's book drew the wrath of the Grand Duke Frederick of Baden, whose (once-liberal) father had been forced into exile by Radical uprisings in 1849.

From spring 1851 to autumn 1853, Martineau worked at *The Positive Philosophy of Auguste Comte. Freely Translated and Condensed* (London: John Chapman, 1853). Although Martineau was to object to Comte's later elaboration of Positivism, she admired his systematic treatment of knowledge—which she saw as crucial to "the intellectual and social needs of the time" (*Autobiography* 2: 371). Comte distinguishes three stages of intellectual development in man: a theological stage where man attributes cause to supernatural forces, a metaphysical stage where man sees metaphysical abstractions as causes, and a positive stage where man views phenomena scientifically. Comte's plea for the reform of society based on the facts of man's behavior in the past, i. e., scientific history, supplies Martineau's defense of Gervinus.

On 14 February 1853, also, the *Daily News* printed Gervinus's defense to a charge of high treason, that his work was a *scientific* study (5, col. 4).

Note

1. From the German. With a brief notice of the author, by the translator (London: H. G. Bohn, 1853).

* * * *

Daily News
14 February 1853

GERVINUS has made his preliminary reply to the charges against him—as will be seen by the news in another column. The little German potentate, and his little court who are prosecuting him, can hardly be aware of what they are undertaking. It may be said that potentates who attack liberty of speech and the press never are aware of what they are undertaking—it being proved that men will speak, and that the world chooses to hear them. This is true: but there is a more special sense in which it is to be said that these Baden prosecutors do not see what they are about. They might, with comparative safety, put down utterance about MAZZINI and the Austrians in Lombardy, and about the French at Rome,[1] and discontent and conspiracy everywhere—they might even interdict with more safety the good old democratic classics, and their favourite horror, PLATO'S Republic; but when they meddle with scientific history, they show, by their rashness, their own ignorance of that very interesting modern study. It is a study of such recent invention that it has still all the charm of novelty; it is so picturesque that it is welcomed as an inexhaustible poem; it is so true that the Grand Duke of BADEN might as well attempt to hush up the Newtonian philosophy; and it so nearly concerns all thinking men that, if driven to make the choice, they will be found ready in many cases rather to give up their Princes than this grand new power of interpreting the past, discerning the present, and foreseeing the future of human history.

It is one of the multitude of facts confirmatory of scientific history that the genuine and the spurious scientific historians are meeting with a widely different fate at this hour. It is only within the present century that history has assumed a scientific form— that it has really passed from the character of chronicle to that of philosophy. Considering the critical character of our age, intervening between the old Order and the new Progress, it is not surprising that the first attempts at philosophical history should be highly metaphysical and very slightly scientific, and it was quite inevitable that the metaphysical would be followed by the scientific. This is what is happening now, and no fact of the case is more suggestive, more pregnant with meaning to students of history and politics, than that which is before our eyes of the different treatment met with by the metaphysical and the scientific historians. One of the former, who has spun a prodigious bundle of historical politics out of his own brain in his own closet, giving a halfpenny worth of fact to a monstrous quantity of doctrine, and who once avowed that he constructed his system out of a choice fact, as CUVIER would delineate a skeleton from the measurement of a tooth, is living very comfortably in the light or shadow (there is no saying which) of a despotic throne, while a fellow-citizen of his, who has established the true value of hypotheses, and has a hundred historical facts to show for every principle asserted, is now hunted from office and in want of bread.[2] And there is GUIZOT again, with his half merits and his spoiled promise,—his account of civilisation in Europe, true where his imagination and knowledge enable him to group facts in an illustrative way, and false when he sets to system-building, and has to look for final causes,—he is safe and easy, after all that has come and gone,[3] while GERVINUS, a humble disciple of fact, of unquestioned political integrity, and a character lofty in every view, is under prosecution for—not doctrine spun out of his own brain but inferences—large general truths arising as inevitably from the unobscured surface of human history as light radiates abundantly from the surface of many waters. The Sovereigns of Europe are shrewd enough in thinking that the metaphysical historians and politicians will do no harm to anybody—will do nothing but retard for a space the progress of the science of history. The Sovereigns of Europe are right, also, in seeing that the promulgation of scientific history is hostile to their hopes and efforts to continue a retrograde policy. Their mistake—that which makes us suppose that they do not know what they are doing—is in not seeing that their safest course is to let the matter alone. If the Grand Duke of BADEN does not perceive the foolhardiness of opposing his notions or his will to the testimony of long-drawn ages—to the dying warnings of feudalism, and the posthumous instructions of a whole worldful of despotisms,—there is nothing to be said but that he does not understand his own case, and had better enter himself as a student under Professor GERVINUS as soon as possible.

If the GRAND DUKE did so, one of the first things he would learn from his teacher would be that the metaphysical condition of politics and history is the most revolutionary, and the scientific the most permanent and the only invincible one. The facts of the life of GERVINUS bear testimony to the sincerity of thus much of his doctrine. Among the wild spirits of Germany, in this most critical period, he has always been remarkable—and universally allowed to be so—for his calm and good sense, his sobriety of views, and moderation of temper; and the rampant ideologists that the French EMPEROR so abhors never had a more declared and effective opponent than GERVINUS. He is a sober citizen, of sufficient fortune and established position. His moral quality is found to wear well; for every year of his virtuous life has raised him higher in the respect and love, first of his university and city, then of his duchy, and for a long time past of all Germany. He was one of the three Göttingen professors who were banished by the King of HANOVER when he annulled the constitution, and the university refused to elect a representative till the constitution was restored. The exiled professors were accompanied to the frontier by their students; and, as fast as professors were deposed, more came forward as candidates for deposition.[4] It is curious that, on that occasion, nearly sixteen years ago, Baden was the first state in Germany which remonstrated against King ERNEST'S proceedings; and that Bavaria and Saxony were the next that followed. It is curious, because it was at Munich that the booksellers were, last month, subject to domiciliary visiting, for copies of GERVINUS'S book; and the news now arrives that it is searched for and suppressed at Leipsic. When Baden was the first to protest against the invasion of Hanoverian liberties, Heidelberg University offered a welcome to the exiled Professor; and there, it seems, he has been almost ever since, devoted to his proper business. It was on behalf of a constitution that he had subjected himself to exile; and his teachings for all these years have tended to make the students sober and rational constitutionalists. After 1848, he was a member of the Frankfort Diet, till it became certain that the union of Germany under constitutional rule was out of the question; and then he returned to his chair at Heidelberg. His historical studies have been resumed, not now undertaken for the first time, as the authorities seem to choose to think. It is very probable—indeed, it is inevitable, that the reactionary proceedings of the last five years have quickened his perceptions of some of the facts of history: but the clearer his perceptions, the calmer is his language and the more serene his temper. He takes his stand upon his book, as his book takes its stand upon the studies of his life.

And what is this terrible book—so tremendous that booksellers must give up the names of all purchasers of it, or have their ledgers seized till the names are found? The book is an Introduction to the History of the Nineteenth Century.[5] It is so scientific in its form and method that none but thinkers are likely to read it; so that unless the GRAND DUKE has for subjects a population worthy to associate with that pensive parrot which was so lost in reverie as to have nothing to say but "I think the more!" he had better have left the book wrapped up in the shadow of professorial lore, than have advertised it as he has done in all the newspapers in Europe and America. It tells a good many things that the Mannheim officials will find it a rather ridiculous business to contradict.[6] GERVINUS sees that great natural laws are for ever at work in politics as everywhere else. Will the Mannheim jurists deny this? He thinks that the sufferings of men under the aristocratic prerogatives of the middle ages made absolute sovereignty a refuge, necessary and welcome in its day, but no more made for permanency than aristocratic government, or any other of those modes that have passed away. He sees that the British have emerged into a system which suits them well; but he thinks their position singular, and no rule for Continental nations, in which, we should think, the GRAND DUKE will be quite ready to agree. The Professor goes on to think that there is a character of generality and simplicity in the principles of American republicanism which marks it for extension, with local modifications, over any part of the civilised world which desires to naturalise it. Here, we suppose, is the High Treason with which the Professor stands charged. Or is it in another idea of his which it seems to us we have heard before, and pretty long ago—that retrogression is a preparation for advance; and that after every attempt to repress liberty in a nation once in the way of progress, there ensues a reconquest of lost ground, and an acquisition of something more? We doubt whether this be altogether new. Is there not an illustration of it somewhere used—something about the tide on the shore?[7] Had not we English once a King CHARLES and a King JAMES, who taught us some thing of this sort? And have not some of us,—though we may not pretend to know so much as GERVINUS,—said something of the kind, about the reactionary governments of Europe, and what will become of them if there be really any science of history at all?

Whatever the Mannheim jurists agree in or differ from, we cannot see what business they have with the Professor's historical conclusions, put forth as science, and not as preaching. Whether they have any business with them is the point which GERVINUS has now submitted to the law-faculty of his old University, Göttingen. We shall soon see whether they will give an opinion, and, if they do, what it is. The accused has returned to his home to meet his fate, whatever it may be. We must remember that the charge is the inciting to High Treason.[8] Nobody thinks of pitying such a man in such a position, in such times, when every act of endurance on his part may be for the healing of the nations. We must keep our pity for the GRAND DUKE, for if his prosecution fails he will hear all the world laughing at him; and if he succeeds he will hear something

Gervinus

worse—we need not tell him what. His choice is only between the scorn and the reprobation of all who can be called men.

Notes

1. Martineau refers to recent events in the movement for Italian liberation: Giuseppe Mazzini (1805–1872) returned to Italy from exile in London to organize an (unsuccessful) insurrection against the Austrians in Mantua and—on 6 February 1853—in Milan, Lombardy. In 1849, French troops had defeated the newly proclaimed Roman Republic and restored the government of Pope Pius IX.

2. By metaphysical historian, Martineau may mean Louis Adolphe Thiers (1797–1877), (inaccurate) historian of the French Revolution, eulogist of Napoleon and the bourgeoisie, and recent returnee from exile to France under Louis Napoleon. Martineau includes Comte's discussion of George Cuvier (1769–1832) on the permanence of species in *Positive Philosophy* 1: 413ff. By fellow-citizen, Martineau must mean August Comte (1798–1857), who in 1842 lost his job as examiner of applicants to the Polytechnique at Paris and now lived mostly on support from his friends.

3. François Guizot (1787–1874), brilliant young historian and political theorist, later conservative statesman (arch-rival of Thiers). Among his many works was one Martineau may just have re-read: *History of the Origin of Representative Government in Europe*. Trans. Andrew R. Scoble (London: Henry G. Bohn, 1852), originally published in 1821–1822.

4. Gervinus was a professor of history and literature at the University of Göttingen in the duchy of Hanover when Ernest Augustus (1771–1851), Duke of Cumberland (fifth son of George III and a reactionary Tory), became King of Hanover in 1837. Ernest Augustus canceled the liberal constitution of the duchy and demanded an oath of allegiance to his absolute sovereignty. Seven professors including Gervinus and the two Grimm brothers protested.

5. *Einleitung in die Geschichte des neunzehnten Jahrhunderts* (Leipzig: W. Engelmann, 1853).

6. Gervinus was tried on 24 February 1853 before the Mannheim Court Tribunal in the duchy of Baden.

7. Gervinus noted, in one of his writings, that the French Revolution signified "the reaction of nature against oppression . . . the bound from extreme to extreme" (see Emil Lehmann, *Georg Gottfried Gervinus*. Trans. Edith Dixon [London: Chapman and Hall, 1872], 29). Martineau must then refer to Shakespeare's "tide in the affairs of

men,/Which taken at the flood leads on to fortune" (*Julius Caesar* IV: iii) and finally to the intransigence of Charles I and James II.

8. In her *Daily News* leader of 14 March 1853, Martineau compares Gervinus's trial to that of Galileo at Pisa. Though the law faculty at the University of Göttingen thought the attempt "too ridiculous to be proceeded with," the Grand Duke had Gervinus tried in a court "crowded with professors and scholars from Heidelberg, and jurists who forced their way through snow-drifts . . . to witness a trial so little like anything . . . in the nineteenth century." The verdict was "seditious libel" rather than "high treason" with a sentence of four months' imprisonment.

29. Robert Burns

Introduction

The centenary of the birth of Robert Burns was celebrated by festivals, dinners, suppers, balls, and tea meetings in Scotland, England, Ireland, the colonies, the United States, and Europe. Speakers quoted from Burns and offered poems and commentaries of their own. At the Music Hall in Edinburgh, for example, where a banquet for "seven hundred persons" (with five hundred ladies in the galleries and orchestra) took place, readings included a letter from Lord Brougham pointing to Burns as a product of the superior education from a Scottish parish school of his day. In London, thousands of admirers crowded into the Crystal Palace at Sydenham, pressing around glass cases of Burns' relics while bands played and singers performed. An original ode by a (surprise) winner of a prize of fifty guineas was also read. In New York, famed clergyman Henry Ward Beecher spoke to an audience of three thousand at the Cooper Institute (about Burns' temptations and melancholy), and William Cullen Bryant presided over a dinner of the Burns Club at the Astor House.

Martineau takes the occasion of Burns' centenary to urge the cause of Parliamentary reform—first proposed in 1852 but not to be carried out until the Second Reform Act of 1867. She focuses on the least happy period of Burns' life, as an exciseman in 1792, when his sympathies for American patriots and French republicans gave his enemies an opening to cause him trouble.

Martineau's spirited defense of Burns demonstrates her ability for trenchant and memorable biography. She also shows her skill at writing interestingly on a set subject. This leader is one of about a dozen she produced for special days, including Christmas and Valentine's Day.

* * * *

Daily News
25 January 1859

AMONG the many and sore troubles which embittered BURNS' decline, the sorest (by his own account) was the dread of an unfavourable posthumous reputation. He apprehended that his faults would be the most conspicuous features of his character, as they were to himself at the moment; and that the world could not fully sympathise in his lofty democratic view of Man in Society. Never was a last estimate of self and one's kind more mistaken! The veriest pedant and puppy, who dies pitying the world for the struggle it will have to get on without him, is not more deluded in one direction than BURNS was in the opposite. He was not irrational in his view, however, though wholly mistaken. Those who surrounded him were much engrossed with his faults towards the close of his life; and his views and opinions were treated by his employers, as well as others, with not only displeasure but contempt. It was intimated to him that "his business was to act, not to think."[1] And this was said, not as a check upon political agitation, or any extreme demonstration of any kind, but in reply to a statement of his views which had been drawn from him by accusation. He did not desire a republic in Great Britain, he said, because Britons have all the means of rational liberty and social welfare. He wished for no change in our form of government, but for a reform of the "system of corruption between the executive power and the representative part of the legislature, which boded no good to our glorious constitution, and which every patriotic Briton must wish to see amended." After this, his "superiors" could not denounce him as a republican, so they informed him that his business was to act, and not to think; and he, valuing his thought, feared that there would be no sympathy with it or him after he was gone, and that he would be known by his infirmities, if at all. On this day, the centenary of his birth, the whole world that speaks or reads our language is rejoicing because he lived and thought, and told what he thought. The homage of united kingdoms, of clusters of colonies, and of several foreign nations is paid to his memory to-day. So much for his posthumous reputation! As to his being remembered by his faults, the most touching and glorious tribute of all is, perhaps, the teetotal celebration of the day. If he could but have foreknown it in his hour of deepest remorse, what a solace would this have been!—what a pregnant reply to his worst misgivings! There is to be a "tea banquet" in the Edinburgh Corn Exchange today, "under the auspices of the Total Abstinence Society."[2] We hear it with gratitude and glee. So much for his being remembered only by his faults!

There could not have been a better conjunction between the date and public affairs than that which we witness. It could not have happened better as an express reply to BURNS' yearning after sympathy in his aspirations for society. The festival would, no doubt, have been held under any condition of public affairs. The man binds us to him by so many ties that we should have been ready with our homage in the midst of a war, or under a PITT and ELDON Government,[3] or under a return of the STUARTS, or under a Republic—whether amidst the deepest adversity, or in a condition without a care. The response of men's passions, sympathies, sentiments, to his song would have been loud and clear amidst any turmoil of conflict, or merrymaking in peace and prosperity. But there is a peculiar aptitude in the spirit of the hour for honouring BURNS. His irrepressible thought about the mutual relations of men in society, and his clear view of the necessity of making their representation in Parliament an honest one, are the very thought and the very view which our minds are now occupied with, and on which we are at present daily called upon to speak.[4] So much for the sympathy which he dared not anticipate!

Far be it from us to dwell exclusively on the Poet's darkest hours, or on the controversiest which embittered them. When men talk of BURNS they do not (except, very naturally, in the United States) consider whether he was a Republican, or a Whig, or a Tory. They think of the *Cotter's Saturday Night*, or of

Highland Mary, or of *Tam o'Shanter*. They think of the dirge, the reaping-song, the war hymn, the prayer, and personal penitence. They think of the plea for the weak, and the rebuke of the haughty. They regard him as the poet, the lover, the mourner, the wit, the comrade, the sinner, the sufferer, rather than as the politician. Yet, the chief bond between him and other men—the grand security for his possession of the sympathies of all generations, is his estimate of Man as Man, under all conditions.

Some may praise his "Republican boldness" of speech, and others may exalt his generosity towards the lowest and most helpless: his employers might call him dangerous, and his fine acquaintance might caution him against noticing the vulgar: they have all agreed from the beginning, and all men will agree to the end, in feeling to their hearts' core his estimate of what is due to Man as Man. One morning he shook hands with a peasant on the Leith road, and talked with him some time, in the presence of a fop, who afterwards rebuked him for showing his friendship for a man dressed in homespun. "Why, you fantastic gomeral," cried BURNS, "it was not the grey coat, or the scone-bonnet, or the boot hose, that I spoke to, but the man that was in them:" and he proceeded to develop his view of the comparative quality of the three men who composed the group. His song, "Is there for honest poverty," is the expression of his daily habit of mind throughout his life.

> The rank is but the gu-nea stamp:
> The man's the gowd for a'that,

is the doctrine and the sentiment by which he lived, and which made him the immortal poet he is. That song is certainly the most widely known of his pieces at present. Familiar as we all are with half-as-hundred of his strains which range from lofty devoutness, through the whole series of affections and passions, to the most homely fun, we all feel that that song is the truest exponent of the man to the greatest number of his kind. Under the virtual censorship of his day, it was not permitted to be sung in the streets of our northern towns—a strange fact to us now! But it was sung in the reaping-field and in the cottage; and now it is known by heart wherever our language is spoken and Lowland Scotch is read. He made no secret of his having achieved a personal discovery on the subject of that song. He said, "I remember in my ploughboy days, I could not conceive it possible that a noble lord could be a fool, or that a godly man could be a knave. How ignorant ploughboys are!" In the same way, the high-born and the pious (self-called) could not, in those days, conceive of a peasant as being wise, or a poor man dignified. This song is an admonition as valuable for the one mistaken class as for the other; and who can say how much it may have done towards bringing them into the happier understanding of our day?

One of BURNS' long-standing regrets was that he could not enter Parliament. He had much to tell there, and much to ask; and it might have been of advantage to us in several ways if he could have had the opportunity. That wish of his, and the reasons for it, are natural recollections for us to-day, when we are in the midst of an enterprise to obtain a voice and a hearing in the House of Commons for men of BURNS' class. He had perceived that, in our country, while there is no obstacle to the entrance of the low-born rich into society, and into Parliament, there is great jealousy of the low-born who rise, or are qualified to rise, by other powers than that of wealth. The owners of boroughs in those days were great men, whether they were born in the mansion or the cottage; but the poet, the scholar, the politician, was repressed by an insolent or a timid aristocracy. BURNS had keen reason to know this, and his craving for an opportunity of utterance in Parliament was a natural consequence. We live in an improved age, when there is a fairer field for desert, without any fatal inquisition into origin. We live, accordingly, under a growing necessity of admitting to the representation men whom BURNS would have called his equals before the law and the throne; and whatever BURNS said about the claims of such men is valuable to us, not only on this day, but on every other.

We have no right to appropriate it, however, without being clear as to what he meant by peasant life, when he asserted its claims. Its poverty was obvious enough. On this day hundred years, he was born in a ricketty clay hovel, which was blown down a few days afterwards, when he and his mother were carried out into the storm from among the ruins. But it did not follow that this peasant family would, like some of our country neighbours at this day, ask whose son the Prince of WALES is, or demand wages which will rise with the price of bread, or insist that the QUEEN should "do something" for everybody who is badly off.[5] BURNS had a father who read with him, and a mother who sang to him—sang songs which brought out the poet and patriot elements in him. The Scotch peasantry then were at least as intelligent as our shop-keeping or best artisan class now. When we see that our rural neighbours are as intelligent, we shall delight in expressing their aspirations in BURNS' words.[6] Meantime, the way is more open now than it was then, while we have not a peasantry capable of his ambition. When he died it was asked, in all simplicity, by those about his door, "And who will be our poet now?" This need never be asked by the peasantry of a later century. As sure as they rise into a capacity for seeing that

> The pith of sense and pride of worth
> Are higher ranks than a'that.

and show their claim to equality before the law and the government—the answer will be, "BURNS shall be your poet now."

Notes

1. The members of the Board of Excise at Edinburgh sent this message through the official who came to investigate Burns when he was accused of being "disaffected to the Government" (see introduction).

2. At least 1,500 people drank tea at the "grand citizen banquet" in the Corn Exchange, where the chairman expressed regret at the high price of tickets to the Music Hall to honor a "man of the people." A total of four large meetings, in a descending scale of grandeur, and twelve smaller ones took place in Edinburgh. For full reports on many of the 872 recorded meetings worldwide, see James Ballantine, *Chronicle of the Hundredth Birthday of Robert Burns* (Edinburgh: A. Fullarton, 1859).

3. Martineau means under conditions during the repressive laws of 1793–1798, drawn up by the prime minister William Pitt (cf. "*Daily News*, 2 March 1854," note 1) guided by the reactionary Tory and (then)

attorney general, John Scott (1751–1838), later 1st Earl of Eldon, Lord Chancellor (cf. "*Daily News*, 24 July 1854," note 2).

    4. Here and at the start of the paragraph, Martineau refers to the reform of Parliament promised by Lord Derby's government for the coming session (to be opened by the Queen on 3 February 1859) and much discussed by the press and at public meetings sponsored by advanced liberals like John Bright. For a review of the political background of Britain's crucial adjustment of its institutions to meet the emergence of a powerful working class, see Francis Barrymore Smith, *The Making of the Second Reform Bill* (London: Cambridge U P, 1966). Martineau argues, in her leaders on Reform, 1859 to 1860, that artisans, tradesmen, and other responsible members of the newly-educated working class *valued* English institutions and property and deserved political rights: cf. "*Daily News*, 27 January 1853," above.

    5. Examples of incredible ignorance of fact and economic "law."

    6. Martineau often expresses disgust at sottishness and ignorance among the rural poor (see *Harriet Martineau's Letters to Fanny Wedgwood*, 114–15), in contrast to the industrious working people of towns. The artisan, shopkeeping class interested her most of all.

30. War of Opinion: Italy

Introduction

At the defeat of Napoleon in 1815, continental monarchs resumed their prerogatives and determined to keep a European balance of power. The English Tory government, faced with economic depression and social unrest, continued to be repressive and reactionary in domestic policy but aimed at a careful neutrality and the preservation of peace abroad. Later revolutions in Spain, Portugal, and Italy posed a dilemma: how could Great Britain, which took pride in its republican institutions, fail to support liberal constitutionalists in revolt against despots?

The brilliant Tory statesman George Canning then stepped onto the stage of this international drama. While serving as foreign secretary, 1822 to 1827, Canning eloquently defended a decision to send a British squadron to support the Portuguese Infanta Isabella, under threat by absolutists who were backed by Spain. Although Britain had gone to the aid of an old ally, Canning recognized the danger of involvement in any war greater than a territorial dispute. Spain was now waging a "war of opinion" against Portugal, he claimed: "this new power in any future war which excites my most anxious apprehension."

Martineau makes Canning a hero of her *History of the Peace*. More significantly, her foreboding of a coming struggle between reactionary upholders of privilege and the defenders of freedom and progress forms a contrapuntal theme to the celebration of peace. By 1855, Martineau could refer to the impending American Civil War as part of the "war of Opinion which Canning foresaw ... a war between Asia and Europe,—between despotism and self-government" (*Autobiography* 2: 450–51). At the time of the threat to the Portuguese Infanta, in 1826, Canning had stressed that Britain must not lightly show her "giant's strength" but could best act as "umpire" between "violent and exaggerated doctrines on both sides."

Throughout her writing on European affairs, Martineau harks back to Canning's feared "war of opinion." Here she applies the concept at the beginning of a final stage in the war for the unification of Italy, a cause that captured the imagination and sympathy of mid-century Victorians—but not their willingness to be officially involved.

* * * *

Daily News
26 May 1859

IN many quarters men are anxiously asking whether the conflict which is now beginning is *the War of Opinion in Europe* which has been the impending fate, the recognized doom of the European nations for nearly forty years.[1] When it was found that the arrangements of 1815 were working differently from what had been intended and expected, it became clear to reflecting men that the real crisis was only deferred—that the final settlement of the Governments of Europe remained to be made.[2] There has been a remarkable absence of dispute about this. Liberals have agreed in anticipating an ulterior crisis; and the retrograde party has not denied that it must come, but rather, by its fear of all expression of Liberalism, has disclosed its reluctant faith in the prophecy. It is true the Liberals are taunted with having cried "Wolf!" pretty often: and a succession of efforts and alarms has passed over without effecting any permanent settlement: so that the Emperor of the FRENCH may be excused for having fancied, up to a very recent date, that the impending war would be a short and circumscribed one, bearing no relation to the great one which must come sooner or later. Ten years since, people who read of what was passing in Berlin, Vienna, Milan, Florence, or anywhere in Hungary or Sicily, or along the

Elbe and the Rhine, believed the war of opinion had broken out, and found it a false start; but all the world knew it was only adjourned.³ This may be the true wrestle between the powers of progression and resistance; and if so, there will be no truce now—no further adjournment of the conflict—no pause, even till the one or the other is laid low. The occasion is too solemn for any amusive speculation—for any vanity of prophecy. All Liberals, and we among them, have a steady faith that truth and justice, and therefore liberty, will finally prevail; but we decline to promise or specify anything more definite. It is one thing, however, to foretel events in the shrouded future, and another to exhibit the relations of the elements visibly at work in the present, and to interpret their lessons of duty, and the hopes and menaces they hold out. We offer no suggestions as to who will win battles, and how much the losers will lose. We will not undertake to say how far the results of the war will correspond with its beginning, its theory and intent: but we would exhort all rational and conscientious men to contemplate the parties involved in the struggle, and decide for themselves what all have to aim at, to expect, and to do; both the combatants and the bystanders.

The Governments of Europe are of three classes. Some are behind the nations they rule in political principle and spirit; some are in advance of their people; and one or two are a fair expression of the national mind. The results of the impending struggle must be widely different to the members of these three groups; their duty at the moment is different; and it is highly necessary that all should recognise their own proper part in such a crisis. The Governments which, like those of Sweden and of Portugal, are, on the whole, in advance of their people, have no concern whatever with this new war. If the bigoted acts of the Swedish Government are still too liberal for Swedish Protestants, and if the King of PORTUGAL cannot induce his people to profit by the advance of knowledge and the development of the arts of life, those kindly rulers have their proper duty at home in educating their subjects, and preparing them for a genuine political existence.⁴

As for the large group of States in which the people are in advance of their rulers, they are the natural and appointed combatants in this great opening war. However distinctly the proclamation may be framed, and the challenge delivered, as of a strife between one Sovereign or Cabinet and another, it is universally understood that the real fight is between oppressive rulers and oppressed peoples. It begins with an antagonism between oppressed Italians and Kaiser, Pope, King, Grand Duke, or whoever may have oppressed any Italians; and the serious part of the affair to Austria is that there is a Hungarian nation, and many restless tribes behind who may rush into the fray.[5] Nobody doubts that they will do so, and when once the strife has assumed its true aspect, of a struggle between peoples and tyrants, between resolute freedom and obstinate despotism, all the despots will be on one side at last, though they might have begun as opponents, and either the free nations on the one hand, or the despotic rulers on the other, will stand or fall together. It matters little to thoughtful men that there is an absolute ruler on each side at the outset.[6] Before long the question must be, whether the people of the various Italian States (and probably other peoples, over a wide area of Central Europe) shall live under modes of constitutional government of their own choice, or whether they shall be over-ruled by the will of despotic Sovereigns; and it will be a matter of inferior importance whether the despotism comes from Vienna, or any other centre of absolutism. How ever little they may intend it now, all the despots will be in the same boat before the hurricane is over; and if one goes down, so will the rest. That group of States, then, has to perceive clearly what the true ground of conflict is, and to consider the tremendous issue involved—whether every nation that is qualified for freedom, from the Baltic and the Channel to the Mediterranean, shall finally cast off the yoke of despotic rulers, or be finally enslaved. If this is really the "War of Opinion in Europe," it cannot end in a success divided between despots and free peoples. If any tyrant remains victor, liberty is beaten. If free Italians have achieved their aims, all will be over with all the despots.

    How is it with the remaining class—with those States in which constitutional government is a fair expression of the mind and will of the nation? England is, of course, the chief figure of that group. Prussia is some way behind, but will by-and-by be by her side. Norway is equally free, but out of the field of observation.[7] Sardinia is free, but with no option, as she is the party attacked. What is the duty of the Constitutional States not involved in the war? No duty ever was clearer. It is a case in which example and testimony may afford more aid to the right than "blood and treasure." It is the duty of England to maintain a stern testimony against the tyranny of despotic Governments wherever their victims complain, and emphatically against Austria, and the Princes of Italy who have opposed themselves to Piedmont. Without reserve or qualification England must pronounce against Austria in this quarrel, and give her warmest sympathy and heartiest testimony in favour of Piedmont. But she could not march to the field side by side with a French absolute ruler. The British mind on the subject of the controversy is known wherever the name of England is known. England stands as a kind of arbiter when all others are going to fight. She stands ready to be appealed to—to be relied on—to represent the political condition aimed at by the Liberal party in this strife; and in proportion to her isolation from the strife will be her eventual authority, and power to strengthen and sustain.

Notes

1. In January 1859, King Victor Emmanuel II of Piedmont, supported by Napoleon III of France, initiated a new effort to drive the Austrians out of Italy and, eventually, to unify the country. In April and May, Austria invaded Piedmont, France declared war and on 20 May defeated Austrian troops at Montebello. For a summary of French machinations over the Italian struggle, see James F. McMillan, *Napoleon III* (London: Longman, 1991).

2. Italy had been repartitioned by the Congress of Vienna in 1815: Victor Emmanuel of Piedmont became King of Sardinia (cf. "*Daily News,* 26 December 1853," note 1); Ferdinand I of Naples became King of the Two Sicilies, including Naples; the Pope regained control of his former central Italian states; and Austria incorporated Lombardy and Venetia and either controlled or hoped to control the rest.

3. Martineau refers to revolutionary false starts such as those in Italy in the early 1820s and 1830s, and to the revolutions of 1848 in the capitals of Prussia, Austria, Lombardy, Tuscany, and elsewhere in Europe.

4. King Oscar I of Sweden, who succeeded in 1851, inspired reform of antiquated marriage and inheritance laws. Under King Pedro V of Portugal, who succeeded in 1853, the country acquired new railroads, a reformed educational system, and other improvements.

5. See note 2, above. After the revolution of 1848, Austria renewed the attempt to Germanize her other ethnic groups and became more repressive and isolated among European powers.

6. I. e., Franz Josef, Austro-Hungarian emperor, and Napoleon III, French emperor.

7. Prussia, currently under a regency owing to the madness of King Frederick IV, in 1851 adopted a constitution that divided parliamentary electors into classes, by property qualification and/or position. Norway in 1815 became a "free and independent" kingdom under the Swedish king, with its own national assembly.

31. Syria

Introduction

The nineteenth-century revival of interest in Jerusalem and the Holy Lands, among Western Europeans, had furnished a *causus belli* for Napoleon III that led to British involvement in the Crimean War, 1853–1855. In the years following, while Western visitors and investors moved freely through Turkish dominions including Syria and the Holy Lands, Britain failed to urge Turkey to carry out promised government reforms. Then, in spring 1860, fighting broke out in Syria between the Moslem Druses and their Christian Maronite enemies. Turkish soldiers of the Pacha were accused of complicity in a series of atrocities that culminated in the massacre of, reportedly, several thousand Christians and Jews in Damascus in early July 1860. Throughout the summer, reports and letters about the slaughter of Christians in Syria appeared in British newspapers.

Martineau travelled through the Holy Lands in early 1847; she gives an account of the places she saw in *Eastern Life, Present and Past* (cf. "*Daily News*, 25 August 1854," above). In various *Daily News* leaders from July to October 1860 and in *Daily News*, 21 August 1861, she reports on violence among the religious sects in Syria. (She also notes the benefits and dangers for British investors in mulberry or cotton plantations and other enterprises.)

Martineau's opening allusion to Thomas Paine, a favorite kind of rhetorical device, and her seemingly coherent account of confusing events support the case for a stronger British presence to balance that of the French under Napoleon III.

Daily News
25 September 1860

TIMES, such as the last few weeks in Syria and Palestine, try men's souls, and enable those who stand outside of the immediate trial to do justice to the merits of the wise and faithful. British residents in the Levant, and especially British consuls, hold in their hands a vast power over the progress of civilisation, and over the immediate peace of the world; and we cannot too well understand the position and conduct of our officials, in the midst of the late reign of terror, nor too highly value the merits of those who have worthily upheld the reputation and influence of our country.[1]

Jerusalem, being out of the track of bloodshed, has been longer in becoming a subject of study to us than the Syrian settlements which contain even a smaller number of European residents. Yet the everlasting interest which hangs around Jerusalem must render it an all-important element in seasons of strife between Christians and anti-Christians. And now that the intelligence is beginning to arrive in full detail it is as profitable for guidance—and possibly for reproof—as could have been imagined.

It is quite understood among British travellers, and all who have attended to Eastern affairs, that the genuine English in Jerusalem have a good deal to bear with, in the best times, from the prevalent persuasion and assumption that England does not hold the place in Europe that she once did, and that it will be the duty and pleasure of Russia, Germany, and France, some day soon, to compel her to fight for the Christian faith. However foolish this provincial sort of error and vanity may be, it does constitute something of a trial to British residents in Jerusalem; and it becomes of grave importance in such critical seasons as that which has just passed. The Mission and its Bishop, we need not say, have much to do with the growth and prevalence of this persuasion, and it is needlessly strengthened by the ill-judged parsimony with which our affairs at Jerusalem are conducted.[2]

Syria

Consulships are not all alike in importance, or in extent of business, and that of Jerusalem is of eminent importance in the present state of the East; yet our Consulate can afford only one dragoman, when the French has seven, and every other four or five; and our Consul has not even a secretary or assistant. Amidst all criticism, in Parliament and out of it, of Civil Service expenditure, there is no wish among those who provide the revenue that such a Consulate as that of Jerusalem should be beggarly in its circumstances, to the deep injury of the Consul's powers, and of the influence of the country he represents. From all causes combined, the expectation has grown up in Jerusalem that England will not long maintain her footing of peace and friendliness, but will be compelled to oppose or desert the Moslems, who in Palestine generally are as devotedly attached to England as the Syrian population for the most part are to France. The traveller who ventures across the Hauran, or pitches his tent among the ruins of Tadmor, can tell how England is worshipped by the desert tribes; while in the Lebanon France is the centre of all expectation.[3] In Palestine, the love for England is shared by the Jews, and especially in the district which surrounds Jerusalem. Under the agitation of the late news from Syria, it may be imagined what the excitement was when one set of people gave out that the hour was come for England to be coerced, and the rest felt that with the free policy of England would vanish their safety and all their hopes. During the early part of July it was told in the streets of Jerusalem that in a little while there would be an end of everything English there. Life, property, influence, would all be destroyed, and Palestine must get on as she might without the English. The one banker at Jerusalem did not mend matters. Money affairs were already in a bad state, from the Pacha—a sensible man where political economy is not concerned—having depreciated the currency in spite of all remonstrance; and when panic seized upon the banker, who pressed for his money from his debtors, and prepared to fly, with his family, a mischievous alarm spread among the Europeans in the city. The Consul, well acquainted with the Pacha, and with the effective control he had over his soldiers, as well as with the good will of Moslems and Jews towards the English, felt no alarm, and did his best to keep down the panic. On Monday, the 16th of July, the news of the Damascus massacre arrived, and upset the small fortitude of the alarmists. Some shut themselves within their houses; and many ran all day about the streets, and from house to house, spreading the most absurd rumours, and kindling a frantic terror. Some who should have set an example of calmness, courage, and reasonableness, received with greedy ears the wildest tales, and with busy tongues sent them abroad; and when obliged to retract them, they could not undo the mischief wrought by their folly. One of these stories was, that the Pacha in disguise had, the evening before, found the guard at the Zion Gate giving up the keys to the Siloam peasants. The Consul at once traced this story to its chief propagator, who confessed it to be a false rumour. The Moslems were quiet enough; but it was reasonable to apprehend that the conspicuous panic of the Christians might put mischievous notions into the heads of the evil disposed of any faith. Therefore it was that, when the evil threatened to become uncontrollable, the Consul issued the proclamation which we print in another column.[4] One of the Mission schoolmasters fled with his family; and four other households were known to be ready to start. Housekeepers of twenty years' standing were hastily packing up their effects and casting bullets. The Superintendent of the House of Industry was off to Alexandria, with wife and children; and the inmates were found, in trembling terror, sharpening axes, and repairing any implements that would do the execution.[5] All this alarm was without any justification whatever from facts. The Consul, and some temporary residents who kept their senses about them, were naturally on the look out for the threatening appearances; and as long as they could perceive no symptom of disturbance, and knew the Pacha to be both willing and able to keep order, they felt it a duty to discountenance the alarmists to the utmost. At the moment when the slightest accident in street or house might have brought about a collision, the Christians refused to open their shops on the Friday, having been informed that a general massacre of their body was to begin on the return of the Moslems from the mosque. No efforts were spared to show them the folly of thus inviting attack; but they did not open their shops, nevertheless. The Consul, dreading an artificial commotion, induced by the dread of one, had written to Beyrout, to request that a man-of-war might be sent down to Jaffa, simply to restore confidence. To avoid bad effects from disappointment, he said nothing of the step he had taken; and on the Friday, the 20th, the news of the arrival of the Mohawk, Captain HOWARD, off Jaffa, gladdened everybody, from the trembling domestic in a German household up through the Jewish merchants to the Moslem Pacha, who at once countermanded all the special arrangements he had made to meet the unnecessary perils of the day.

The facts of those few days speak more strongly than any narrative. None of the terrible stories could be found to have any solid foundation. While some Christians were preparing for flight, or siege, or massacre, others were going about as usual on their private affairs, one lady riding in from the country, seven miles, and back again on her ass, with only her donkey boy, and meeting with no token of Moslem displeasure.[6] We are safe enough at Jerusalem; we have a great duty to do there, not only to immigrants and Jews, but also to Moslems. There is no real obstacle to our living in friendship with them. They look up to us with respect and reliance; and to keep up a good understanding with Moslems in any centre of influence is to support the Turkish empire in the best way, and to strengthen the chances of peace in Europe; but, to do our duty fully, we must support our representative somewhat more liberally. Our Consul should not be restricted as to assistants and servants in the presence of the representatives of other powers. We are so fortunate in Mr. FINN, whose energy, frankness, and manly liberality towards all sects and all men have long commanded the confidence of native residents of every creed, that nothing should be spared to strengthen his hands and render the honour and influence of England entirely safe under his administration.

Notes

1. Martineau took particular interest in the British consul at Jerusalem, James Finn, who served from 1846 to 1863 and whom she met in 1847. See note 2 and *Daily News*, 11 April 1858.

2. For the Protestant bishopric established jointly by Britain and Prussia in Jerusalem in 1841, see Owen Chadwick, *The Victorian Church* (London: Adam and Charles Black, 1970, 1972) 1: 189–93. The Reverend Samuel Gobat (?1795–1879) currently served as head of a small congregation of Protestants, including a few converted Jews, and of the schools and House of Industry supported by the mission. For news of the panic among foreign residents of Jerusalem after the Damascus massacre, Martineau was indebted to a letter from her friend Emily Anne Beaufort, later Viscountess Strangford, who also told Martineau about Finn's embarrassment over the cost of entertaining Prince Alfred when he came to Jerusalem in 1859. For Martineau's appeal to the Queen through Lord Russell (Foreign Secretary) on behalf of a grant for Finn, see *Harriet Martineau's Letters to Fanny Wedgwood*, 197–200. Martineau labels the Protestant mission a "mistake" in *Daily News*, 10 April 1858.

3. Martineau assumes readers' familiarity with biblical associations: the Hauran, in southwest Syria, was conquered by the Israelites; Tadmor (Palmyra) mistakenly said to be founded by Solomon, attracted European tourists by its impressive ruins, including a vast Temple of the Sun. France acted as informal protector of (Christian) Maronites in the Lebanon. Under corrupt and inefficient Turkish rule in Syria, British and Prussian representatives vied with Roman Catholic and Orthodox representatives, and Britain took on the special protection of the Jews. For attacks on Orthodox and Catholic missions, see *Daily News*, 4 July (5, cols. 5–6), 11 July (5, col. 4) and 12 July 1860 (5, col. 4).

4. See "Jerusalem" (5, col. 3): Finn calls upon British citizens not to spread rumors but to "uphold our national character"; he threatens British subjects and other protected persons who abet the panic with imprisonment. The article claims there was no panic among British citizens, although others around them were terrified.

5. The House of Industry taught poor boys and Jewish converts trades such as carpentry and shoemaking; see note 2.

6. European residents of the Levant often stayed in the hills to avoid the summer heat of the cities. Martineau's friend Emily Beaufort and her sister, for example, took a house in a small village outside Beyrout in summer 1859: see Emily A. Beaufort, *Egyptian Sepulchres and Syrian Shrines; including Some Stay in the Lebanon, at Palmyra, and in Western Turkey* (London; Longman, 1861).

V. The United States: Antislavery

32. *The Times*: Kansas and *Dred*

Introduction

With its appeal to middle- and upper-class opinion, conservative in politics and religion, *The Times* during the 1850s reached the peak of its influence within British society.[1] Crawford also notes that "opinions which *The Times* sought to represent were ultimately responsible for shaping the political and economic decisions upon which Anglo-American progress depended" (19). Yet *The Times'* ignorance of American institutions and geography meant that it often failed to report accurately on American affairs and was not prepared for the secession crisis in 1860–1861. Though in favor of progress and of the elimination of slavery in America, *The Times* opposed abolition because of the jolt to society and the economy it would cause. The fighting in Kansas that broke out after the opening of the territory to settlement in 1854 (see "*Daily News*, 15 November 1856," below) confused and provoked *The Times*. By 1862, according to Crawford, *The Times* simply lost control of any grasp of developing events in the United States (132–33).[2]

In spring 1856, three events shocked the American nation. On 21 May, a proslavery mob sacked and burned Lawrence, Kansas; on 22 May in the Senate chamber, Representative Preston Brooks of South Carolina severely beat Senator Charles Sumner of Massachusetts; and on 24 May, John Brown and his men slaughtered five proslavery settlers at Pottawatomie Creek, Kansas. Earlier fear that Kansas would be overrun by proslavery settlers from Missouri had inspired men like Eli Thayer and Amos A. Lawrence of Massachusetts to recruit groups of antislavery settlers for Kansas, providing them with information, reduced transport rates and help in setting up mills, hotels, schools, and other facilities. Similar groups were organized in other states.[3] Meant to be both philanthropic and profit-making, the Emigrant Aid Company was accused of flooding Kansas with free-state settlers in time for the March 1855 election of a territorial delegate to Congress. In retaliation, armed Missourians swarmed across the border to vote, and proslavery forces carried all but one district. Thus began the saga of "bleeding Kansas."

Martineau habitually points to *The Times'* superficiality and failure to possess all the facts. In *Daily News*, 23 January 1856, she accuses *The Times* of "convenient blindness" on American affairs. *The Times*, she says, seems to think the President's discussion of Constitutional provisions for slavery mere irrelevancies, when the most significant crisis of the union has arrived. In *Daily News*, 18 September 1856, she scoffs at *The Times'* stupidity over American Senate and House functions in relation to Kansas. Here she continues the thrust of those attacks with a glance at the timely publication of Harriet Beecher Stowe's new antislavery novel.

Notes

1. See Martin Crawford, *The Anglo-American Crisis of the Mid-Nineteenth Century. The Times and America, 1850–1862* (Athens: U of Georgia P, 1987).

2. See also, Leslie Stephen, "The 'Times' on the American War: A Historical Study" [London: William Ridgway, 1865] rpt. in *The Magazine of History with Notes and Queries* 37 (Tarrytown: William Abbatt, 1915).

3. See Samuel A. Johnson, *The Battle Cry of Freedom. The New England Emigrant Aid Company in the Kansas Crusade* (Lawrence: U of Kansas P, 1954).

* * * *

Daily News
24 September 1856

THE more serious the news from America becomes, the more necessary it is that English opinion should not be misled or perplexed by the misrepresentations or mere ignorance of journalists, who ought to have more honesty or more knowledge than they have yet shown in their treatment of the existing American crisis. We had occasion last week to point out some absurdities put forth by the *Times*. There have since been more and worse—in the review of "Dred," and in the leading article of last Saturday.[1] It seems to be the aim of the *Times* to make its readers believe that there has been a pitched battle on the political ground of Congress; and another, of the physical force kind, on the soil of Kansas.[2] This leading assumption is entirely untrue. The aggressive party has made its onslaught, after half a century of express preparation; and the other party receives the attack as a summons to collect and organize its forces, and gird itself up for the conflict, which is now to begin in earnest.

First, as to the political struggle. The Southern elections have for many years been conducted with the sole view of sustaining slavery, and overpowering the numbers and the energies of the North; whereas, the Northern elections have had every conceivable aim rather than that of attacking slavery and humbling the South. With the exception of a very few constituencies, the North has carefully chosen men who would not trouble the South and imperil the Union; so that Congress has in fact represented the pro-slavery element of Northern society almost exclusively. The most thorough abolitionists, indeed, abstain from voting;[3] and thus, not only is Congress the representative of a state of opinion of some years standing, but it is the exponent of only a special element of public opinion on this particular subject. By one of those apparent accidents which open the sluices unexpectedly of all revolutions, it was discovered last winter that there was anti-slavery force enough in one House of Congress to resist the insults and aggressions of the South, and the immediate consequence was, the election of Mr. BANKS to the Speaker's Chair.[4] A very fair resistance has been made for several months, considering the inferiority in numbers of the Republican members; and that the PRESIDENT has met with any check at all from the federal legislature is quite as surprising as that free trade measures should make progress in an European Parliament returned under a Protectionist Ministry for Protectionist purposes.[5] No doubt it is abundantly disgraceful to the Northern constituencies, that they should not have made this great question the first instead of the last in their political programme; but, as a matter of fact, it has hitherto been so, and it can never be so again. The struggle is now forced upon them; they cannot evade it; they no longer think of evading it; and the world will be shown, through the whole series of the coming elections, what their strength really is. Meantime, they have not been beaten; for they have not yet gone out to the political war. A few members of Congress made a stand in a tentative spirit, and on a special occasion. These scouts have given the alarm; but the battle is not yet begun. The marshalling of the forces looks well thus far. Maine is the first New England State which can announce the results of its elections, and the other New England States usually follow its lead. The tidings from Maine are unexpectedly good. None hoped for more than a bare success for the Republican candidate for the office of Governor, and few expected that much; but Mr. HAMLIN, the Republican candidate, has been elected by a majority of 11,000.[6] As Maine leads New England, and the New England States lead the whole North, it is reasonable to anticipate the irresistible preponderance of the Republican party, and an anti-slavery strength in Congress proportioned to the numbers, the education, and the wealth of the North, and the importance of the vindication of its free labour.

As for the military conflict, in which the *Times* assumes the North to have been vanquished by the South, there has been no such measuring of strength. It is not true that the "vehement spirits" of the pro-slavery and anti-slavery parties went to Kansas to fight out the quarrel. The pro-slavery force there in part consists of bands of so-called immigrants, who have gone with—not ploughs, teams, seed, and cattle—but rifles, revolvers, and bowie knives. They are, truly enough, the vehement spirits of one party; but they are far outnumbered by the ruffians of the Missourian population, who, living at hand, have crossed the frontier for marauding purposes.[7] To these two elements of the pro-slavery population in Kansas must be added the federal soldiery, sent by the PRESIDENT to take the side of the slave-power, for his own personal objects. To meet this composite force, what troops has the anti-slavery power sent to Kansas? None whatever. The free-settlers of Kansas have been *bona fide* immigrants, carrying with them wives and children, farming stock and utensils, or tradesmen's wares. Those who did not go on their own resources, were despatched by the Emigrant Aid Society;—a speculative association, organised for purposes of gain. When the immigrants were found to be exposed to injury from Southern marauders and border ruffians, certain citizens, individually or in companies, sent them arms, ammunition, and other resources, and organized more bands to follow them. These were intercepted: the arms and supplies given to the marauders; the men and women turned back after being stripped; and the ferries stopped and rivers guarded to prevent all access to the territory. A new route has recently been organised, out of reach of the Missourians; but it was not available prior to the late conflicts.[8]

Thus, instead of "vehement spirits," leaders of anti-slavery enterprise, the free-soil party in Kansas consisted of disarmed and plundered immigrants, cut off from aid and reinforcement by the interposition of Missouri between them and the free States. To speak of this as a first victory in the sectional warfare now beginning is as absurd as it would be to say that Greece is conquering Turkey because a party of brigands has routed a company of merchants or drovers. Nobody doubts what the result would have been if any kind or amount of pro-slavery force had invaded any one of the free States, from Illinois to Maine. But the free settlers in Kansas did not go there as soldiers but as industrial adventurers. They risked much, not for any political object, but for making their fortunes; and, losing their game, the speculators have been shot as abolitionists. None knew better than they that abolitionism had nothing to do with their enterprise, and that it never received any aid or furtherance from the abolitionists. The North has yet to show what it can do, in the military as in the political field. When it is remembered that of the twenty-six millions of the United States' population less than a half a million are slaveholders, and that those slaveholders will scarcely suffice to restrain their own slaves, in case of commotion, there can be no serious doubt in any man's mind as to who will conquer when it once comes to fair fighting.

The inequality is so prodigious that it can hardly be seriously supposed that the South will encounter the enemy it has roused. The most conservative, ease-loving, apathetic, and timid of Northern citizens are fairly stirred at last. The coming elections will be the first evidence of their awakened vigour, and the next necessity will be, apparently, for the South to choose between the only two courses open to her—secession from the Union, or submission to the primitive conditions of Union, developed to meet modern requirements. The first can scarcely be practicable, for two reasons among others: that the North can interdict and prevent the secession, if it so pleases; and that (as the South well knows) it is only her connexion with the anti-slavery North which preserves her from a servile war. If she cuts the cable, the next hour the crew will rise, throw their tyrants overboard, and sail to rejoin the fleet. No Southern newspaper says this, nor probably any Northern one: but every man—north, south, east, and west—knows it.

The reviewer of "Dred" in the *Times* exhibits an ignorance, geographical and historical, which is perfectly astonishing when he pleads, on behalf of the South, the concentration of the negroes there. He says the Northern States poured their negroes into the Middle States; and that these last are emptying themselves into the Southern. So far from this being the case, the North has sent no negroes southwards. The tendency is all the other way. The coloured population of the North is abundant and prosperous beyond what European travellers have any means of witnessing. The census informs us that their numbers do not diminish, even now under the atrocious legislation of recent years,[9] and notwithstanding the large emigration to Canada and foreign shores. [*Travellers to the North see only a few blacks in servile occupations (not members of the "merchant and shopkeeping class"), Martineau claims, and blacks sent South from the* "impoverished" Middle Atlantic states are "bred for the purposes of sale."] Thus it is with Virginia and the rest of that group of States. The South has to deal only with the slaves she chooses to purchase and rear. Having chosen an unprofitable mode of living, through which she finds herself falling behind the world from year to year, her last desperate chance is to stop the competition of free labour with slave labour by engrossing the area of production, and hedging in the numbers and enterprise of the North. Her programme to this effect is before us, and we may perhaps present it to our readers some day soon.[10] We need not show why the project is as hopeless as it is desperate. Our present purpose is simply to warn all who take an interest in American affairs against supposing that any "victory" in "fair fight" has been obtained by the slave power. The North is stirring, but it has not yet taken up a position in either field—of politics or civil war.

Notes

1. Martineau refers first to *Daily News*, 18 September 1856, where she reacts to *The Times'* review (13 September 1856: 6, cols. 3–4) of Josiah Quincy, *Address [on] the Nature and Power of the Slave States, and the Duties of the Free States* (Boston: Ticknor and Fields, 1856). She defends Quincy as an "eminent citizen" standing forth in the crisis of events but not trying to tell slaveholders "how to deal with slavery." *The Times'* review (18 September 1856: 10, cols. 2–6) of Harriet Beecher Stowe, *Dred, A Tale of the Dismal Swamp* (London: S. Low, 1856), comments at length on the slavery dilemma. *The Times'* leader of 20 September 1856 (6, col. 2–3) declares that the proslavery party is succeeding in the "great battlefield" of Kansas. In almost all of her leaders on the United States in 1856, Martineau touches on the bloody struggle in Kansas between free-state settlers, partially sponsored by the Emigrant Aid Company of New England, and proslavery settlers, who were abetted by "border ruffians" from Missouri. Her long *Daily News* article of 23 June 1856, re-issued in pamphlet form as *A History of the American Compromises. Reprinted, with Additions, from the* Daily News (London: J. Chapman, 1856), gives an account of political moves by the slavery party that led to the crisis in Kansas. See note 7, below.

2. Cf. *The Times*, 20 September 1856. On 23 September (not yet seen by Martineau), *The Times* denigrates the struggle in Kansas and on

24 September, says the North must fight or dissolve the Union. See note 7.

3. A reference to the Garrisonian abolitionists of Boston: cf. *Daily News*, 4 January and 16 September 1856; "15 November 1856," note 6; and "*Daily News*, 9 January 1866," below. The arguments just above form the basis of the Quincy pamphlet.

4. Nathaniel Prentiss Banks (1816–1894), elected 2 February 1856 by a plurality vote, later seen as the first national victory of the Republican party.

5. Democratic President Franklin Pierce (1804–1869) had tried unsuccessfully to please all factions of his party and was not now supported by Congress. For Martineau's sympathy with the new Republican party, cf. introduction, "*Daily News*, 25 November 1856."

6. Former Democratic senator Hannibal Hamlin (1809–1891) served as governor only a few weeks before he rejoined the Senate. He later served as Lincoln's first vice-president.

7. Over the past months, Martineau had repeatedly explained the struggle for Kansas, including the shocking Sumner-Brooks episode. On 26 September, she elaborates on the "border ruffians" from Missouri; on 27 September, she notes the President's proslavery words and actions on Kansas; on 30 September, she identifies three divisions in the North—abolitionists, free-soilers, and the non-committed and cites trade sanctions muted by the South; on 10 October, she explains Northern resistance to the Kansas-Nebraska Act; and from 27 October to 13 November 1856 (six leaders), she summarizes the Report of the Congressional Commission on Kansas.

8. In *Daily News*, 7 August 1856, Martineau reports that a road is being built for free immigrants, the waterways being held by "ruffians." For the sending of arms to antislavery settlers, cf. "*Daily News*, 11 November 1862," note 3.

9. A reference to the Fugitive Slave Law of 1850: see "15 November 1856," note 5.

10. Martineau must mean the re-opening of the slave-trade: see "25 November 1856."

33. Presidential Election

Introduction

The American presidential election of 1856 marked a final stage in the growing incompatibility of North and South over slavery. The events of spring 1856 (see "*Daily News*, 24 September 1856," above) affected the political parties in different ways. Meeting in early June, the Democrats nominated James Buchanan of Pennsylvania, a safe candidate who could carry the South. In February, the American—Know-Nothing—Party had nominated the colorless Millard Fillmore, who was also endorsed by the Whigs. Both these candidates accepted the Kansas-Nebraska Act of 1854, designed to allow for popular sovereignty on slavery as new states were admitted to the union. The new Republican Party, formed in opposition to the Kansas-Nebraska Act and the extension of slavery in the territories, attracted many members of the elite, eastern establishment who had not before participated in politics. Meeting in mid-June, the Republicans nominated Colonel John Charles Frémont. Frémont was known for his life as an explorer and surveyor of the west and for his controversial court-martial over American military actions in California.

For Martineau's leaders on the United States over the past year, cf. 24 September 1856, notes 1 and 7. In this leader, Martineau repeats past warnings that add to the sense of impending crisis. Her final thrust at the proslavery party foreshadows protests against the Confederacy by major contemporaries like John Stuart Mill.

Daily News
15 November 1856

OUR suspense about the issue of the Presidential election is drawing to a close. [*Martineau warns of probable disputes over election results like those of the October elections in Indiana and Pennsylvania (both won by Buchanan Democrats), yet Buchanan will likely become President.*] While there was universal talk of ferment and excitement, there was in fact so profound a calm—or, to speak more accurately, so tremendous a tension—that it had the practical effect of a lethargy. There was nothing more to be done, except by individual efforts. To pass the time, there were torchlight processions and a great deal of talk; but men knew that this was but pastime, inadequate to beguile the heavy care that was weighing down hearts within. The pro slavery party, and their antagonists, who have not yet acquired courage to accept the name of anti-slavery, were straining their force against each other, in intense dread of the moment which must decide the victory. If the Czar PAUL'S proposal to decide the affairs of Europe in 1801 by single combat had been accepted,[1] and the eyes of a quarter of the globe had been fixed on the issue of the closing effort, the suspense could hardly have been more terrible than that which weighed upon the spirits of the American people but ten days ago. Through all disguises of passion and of levity, of dispassionateness and indifference, this was understood by those who know the Americans best, and the best Americans acknowledge the fact the most freely.

It should be remembered, however, that the most decisive events in human history are those which are unexpected. It should be remembered that what we take for issues are often not so, and that we are always overrating the importance of what we bring before our own eyes, and of the work which we do by our own hands. It is well that we do so, for otherwise our work would never get done, and our powers would never be roused to the extent of their capacity; but the tendency should be remembered and guarded against in crises like that on which our attention is now fixed. Careless men are saying as seriously as the most earnest, that the American conflict is beyond all comparison the most important phenomenon of the time. Aristocratic Europeans, who never before sympathised with anything republican, and who have been long weary of the low and trite subject of anti-slavery, now volunteer the observation that not even the present complications of events in the Old World can compare with the interest of the struggle in the New. If this is felt on our side of the Atlantic, what must be the tension on the other? Yet it is not the less true that the crisis has yet to deepen, and that the Presidential election can (however it may have ended) go but a little way towards deciding the future of that great country. The controversy is too deep, too broad, too vital to be settled by the ascendancy of one party, or the powers and virtues of one man. If any one of the three candidates carried every State, or if a heaven-born President condescended to the chair at this moment, the issue must still lie some way forward into the future: for the one party is pledged to the principles of the degradation of industry, the necessity of an aristocracy, and consequently of a resumption of the African slave trade,[2] and government by a self-appointing oligarchy; while the other is pledged by the very existence of the republic to the principles of the dignity and value of industry and of equality before the law, and consequently to repudiate slavery, to uphold the Bill of Rights of the free States, and perpetuate a republican form of society. An antagonism like this cannot be reconciled, nor placed in abeyance, by any electoral victory; and if it is ever possible to interpret events in the midst of their course, it may be safely said now that the revolution just entered upon cannot be less important to the world than that which transformed "the provincials" of a century ago into citizens of the first Republic in the world. Such a disruption can no more be settled by an electoral victory than our affairs could be settled in 1640 by a royal proclamation on the one hand, or a parliamentarian decree on the other.[3]

If BUCHANAN is to be President he can be nothing more than the tool of the democratic leaders. He is already nicknamed "Platform," and he can neither speak nor do anything beyond nor within the Cincinnati "platform" which he began the election by accepting.⁴ He must oppress Kansas, connive at the resumption of the African slave trade by South Carolina, insult the principles of republican government, and degrade his country to the level of a buccaneering State, or else do nothing, and sit still while his party are redeeming his pledges. In no case can he govern the free States. They have too loudly complained of the loss of their rights, and the infamy and disgrace of the Southern policy, ever again to countenance such a policy abroad, or bow their necks to such a yoke at home. They will accept Mr. BUCHANAN as President if the majority (with the assistance of the slave element—the three-fifths suffrage) elect him; but they will never allow his policy to be realised. In this case, the struggle is not even modified by the election of BUCHANAN. It will be renewed by every act of his; and if his Southern masters put arms into his hands wherewith to enforce the obedience of the North, the North will abide the onslaught with arms in their hands. Nobody expects this; for the bluster about a military procedure has never yet produced a cannon shot. The alternative is—a dead lock, and a renewal of the crisis.

If FILLMORE becomes President, his course will simply be an exaggeration of his former one, or something worse. He is a known man— avowedly "a Northern man with Southern principles"—secure of a place in history as the PRESIDENT who passed the Fugitive Slave law. No one dreams of his approximating to Northern principles, and he himself makes no profession of doing so. His hope appears to be to evade the great conflict by drawing attention to minor matters, persecuting catholics, making immigrants uncomfortable, and so forth.⁵ Of course the South will not allow this, nor will the North consent to a further term of degradation under disabling laws and a vitiated constitution. A temporising President must displease both parties in such a juncture.

It is natural and inevitable that Englishmen should desire the election of FREMONT, because he represents the party which is most nearly republican, most nearly anti-slavery, most nearly honest and respectable. But it would be highly dangerous to suppose that all would go well if FREMONT were President; and those patriots may be the wisest who are beforehand reconciled to the prospect of his defeat, while yet endeavouring to obtain

Presidential Election 259

his return. The man himself can (as far as can be foreseen) do little or nothing. A mighty genius lodged in him may show this supposition to be a mistake: but it is difficult to see what any mortal man can do, by the act of ruling for four years, to solve the controversy. He may abstain from foreign aggression, and give fair play to parties at home; but, beyond this, it appears that he must be either a tool or a dictator, or a revolutionary leader. The Presidential office has become but too like a treadwheel whereon a man must step, and can only step in one way. If so, he must wholly disappoint his party, unless indeed his party, as a whole, should in that case decline to his quality. It must be distinctly remembered that the most genuine republicans in the country are of no party at all—some standing aloof, the reserve awaiting the real crisis, and others aiding the FREMONT party without sharing in its pledges.[6] These are of opinion that the cause would on the whole gain by the defeat of FREMONT, because should he be elected his party (surrounded by temptations) would be timid, conservative, and unprincipled, whereas defeat would rouse them to courage and animate their political virtue.

While we are thus contemplating the various phases of the case, the decision (temporary or permanent) is made, and the tidings are on the way. In a few hours, many eyes will be straining to see, through the November fogs, the signal that the news-bearing ship is approaching its port.[7] In a few days we shall know whose election is accepted as valid by the country at large. In a few months some old man, of no superhuman endowments, will be charged with a superhuman weight of duty, compared with which that of WASHINGTON himself was light. In a few years, citizens, too grey-haired for their time of life, will be telling their children how their boasted republic was no real republic while all men's liberties were affected by the claim of some men to hold other men as property, and describing the fearful shocks and bitter griefs which attended the regeneration of the corrupt into the pure republic. Or, if the other issue be decreed, in a few generations the sons of the sainted PILGRIMS, the revered FOREFATHERS, will be roving land and sea, in pursuit of rapine and the wild license of barbarism—the Ishmaelites of civilization, keeping alive singular traditions of a

WASHINGTON and a FRANKLIN, who did something great for them which they can no longer understand or remember. In a few centuries history will tell of a noble opportunity for wise and good government once missed through inexperience and heedlessness, a vitiating element being implicated in the settlement, and of another such opportunity occurring before it was too late, and seized or repudiated—on the one hand justifying the confidence of all friends of human progression; or, on the other, plunging the most promising of nations into a retrograde course, and giving a new lease of life to the powers of evil.[8]

What shall be told in those remote traditions? What shall be written on that future page?

Notes

1. Czar Paul I, despotic and unbalanced father of Czar Nicholas I, whom Martineau attacks for causing the Crimean War (cf. *Daily News*, 13 January 1854, and almost all leaders on the Crimean War, above).

2. Cf. "*Daily News*, 25 November 1856," below.

3. Martineau refers first to the members of the thirteen British colonies in America that became the United States, then probably to King Charles I's dissolution of the Short Parliament in spring 1640 and the citation of the King's misdeeds—the Grand Remonstrance—by the Long Parliament, November 1641, which failed to prevent the English Civil War. Cf. Macaulay on Charles I and James II in his famous *Edinburgh Review* essay of 1825.

4. The Democratic Convention, meeting in Cincinnati on 2 June 1856, declared against "renewing . . . agitation of the slavery question" and in favor of the Kansas-Nebraska Act. James Buchanan (1791–1868) received the nomination after Stephen A. Douglas, the most outspoken Democratic leader, withdrew his name.

5. Millard Fillmore (1800–1874), elected Vice President on the Whig ticket of 1848, became President at the death of Zachary Taylor in 1850. He helped push through the series of acts referred to as the Compromise of 1850, which included heavy penalties for aiding or interfering with the recovery of escaped slaves: the Fugitive Slave Law. Martineau also refers to Fillmore's nomination by the Know-Nothings, originally a secret society aimed at restricting immigrants and the influence of Roman Catholics in public life (see, for example, *Daily News*, 4 July and 12 December 1855).

6. Martineau refers first to the followers of William Lloyd Garrison of Boston, who refused allegiance to a "corrupt" Constitution that allowed for slavery, and then to the many clergymen, intellectuals and literary figures—including Emerson, Longfellow, and Bryant—who publicly supported the Republican declaration against the spread of slavery: cf. *Daily News*, 4 January 1856, "25 November 1856" and elsewhere.

7. A transatlantic telegraph cable laid in 1858 was to last only a month; a successful one was laid in 1866.

8. For a similar outburst at Southern secession, cf. *Daily News*, 24 January 1861.

34. Slave Trade/U.S. Newspapers

Introduction

Results of the American elections of 1856 gave Frémont, first presidential candidate of the Republican Party, 33 percent of the popular vote (the Republicans carried all but four of New England's 67 counties), while Buchanan, the Democratic winner, gained fewer popular votes than the combined total of the Republicans and the Know-Nothings or American Party. Among the new Republicans were former antislavery Whigs as well as a number of other groups including former antislavery Democrats.

From 1835, Martineau identified herself with the radical American abolitionists of Boston led by William Lloyd Garrison. As American specialist for the *Daily News*, she used the letters she received from Americans like Garrison's follower Maria Weston Chapman, plus newspapers and other American publications, to form her opinions on American events.

In *Society in America* (London: Saunders & Otley, 1837), Martineau clearly sets out her view of the inadmissibility of slavery in a nation dedicated to free labor. The Republican Party readily gained her sympathy, moreover, not only because it opposed slavery but because it supported liberal capitalism.

One of Martineau's chief targets in her antislavery writing before the Civil War was the continuing traffic in African slaves to destinations such as Cuba and the French Caribbean islands. In 1858, for example, she was to write nearly twenty leaders for the *Daily News* and an article, "The Slave Trade in 1858" (*Edinburgh Review* 108: 541–86), on the *Regina Coeli* incident. This incident involved French slave traders in collusion with the

President of Liberia (founded by the American Colonization Society to offer a home in Africa to former American slaves).

Martineau probably added the first paragraph, on the presidential election, after the rest was written.

* * * *

Daily News
25 November 1856

THE latest news from the United States presents all that could be desired as to the political spirit and temper of the Free States. The remarkable diminution of the Democratic majority manifested by the recent election is, as it ought to be, enough to sustain the confidence and invigorate the nerve of the Republican party,—inexperienced as a great proportion of that party is in political action. Clergymen, Quakers, literary men, men engrossed in trade, men who have never before taken part in an election, have swelled the Republican vote to proportions so large as to make the Democratic victory a hard one to win, with the aid of the Irish element, and of every advantage of organisation and prestige. Instantly on the decision becoming known the Republicans began their preparations for bringing in a free-soil President in 1860. What we have to direct the attention of our readers to at this moment is the fact that the South is no less on the alert, and that European observers ought to watch the action of the South with no less earnestness than that of the North.

The newspapers of the leading Southern States have come out, seemingly with one accord, in favour of a *revival of the African Slave Trade*. This indication should not be passed over as an electioneering outburst—a flash of Southern fire and fury. The incident should be studied with its antecedents, and not lost sight of, like an occasional notice of the reappearance of the sea serpent.[1] From 1806 (when the African Slave Trade ceased in the United States) till now, there has been an occasional threat from some bully, or clique of bullies, that the Southern planters would get what they want direct from Africa, if any difficulty was made about their inter-State traffic in slaves. But, since the passage of the Fugitive Slave Law, and the consequent proof that property in man had become insecure in the Union, the proposal to restore the African trade has become more frequent, and more definite.[2] Now, instantly on the announcement of the smallness of the Democratic majority, the Southern newspapers openly adduce the policy of slave trade revival as the true ground of separation from the North. The readers of OLMSTED'S recent work on the Seaboard States will remember that before its publication two grand juries of South Carolina had "solemnly recommended a renewed importation of slaves from Africa," and that "a Committee of the Legislature, to whom the subject was referred, had given its approval to the measure, on theological, moral, and economical grounds," while doubtful whether the time for such action had arrived.[3] These facts ought to have excited more attention on both sides of the Atlantic than they appear to have done. The recent decree of WALKER, as President of Nicaragua, ordaining the introduction of slaves into his territories from any quarter where they can be had, does strike even careless people as something portentous; and so does the reviling by Americans of all Mexicans and native Texans who may be found within their newly annexed dominions.[4] Mexico had abolished slavery before the southern annexations began; and the inhabitants of all the Mexican provinces see with grief the institution reintroduced wherever the Americans have encroached. The American proposals to "root out" all Mexicans as abolitionists harmonise remarkably with WALKER'S late decree; and it would be a serious mistake to slight such indications on the ground that WALKER is an adventurer whose fortunes are precarious in the extreme. Matters stood thus a week or two ago. Now we have more warnings what to expect and prepare for.

The *Carolina Times*[5] remarks on WALKER'S proclamation:

> For our own part, we are highly pleased with the decree, for we are decidedly in favour of reopening the slave trade in order that the price of negroes may be reduced to such figures that every industrious man may purchase, and become a slaveholder. We regard the course pursued by General Walker as not only correct, but challenging the approval of the entire mass of people inhabiting the

southern States; and we believe that they will sustain him in the position he has assumed. Hoping and believing that the confederacy now known as the United States of North America will soon be dissolved, we look upon this movement of General Walker as that of a statesman; and we hope the day is not far distant when Central America, embracing the Island of Cuba, will form part of the Southern confederacy.

The *New Orleans Daily Delta*[6] gives a similar approval, adding:

> There is another step further along, however, more difficult, it may be, but scarcely less important, as a prime auxiliary in making the first effective—that is, opening Nicaragua to the African slave trade. We have not time here to elaborate, but a glance at the statistics of slavery will show the great importance of the measure. Labour is in too great demand in our Southern States to allow many to be withdrawn for Nicaragua; the Cooly trade, devised by British policy and carried on by Boston philanthropists,[7] is too hypocritical, too treacherous and inhuman for the civilisers of Central America to think of for a moment; and therefore the African slave trade and African slavery, conducted on humane principles and regulated by law, must have the preference over every other form of compulsory labour.

The *Charleston Standard*[8] opens a new campaign thus:

> Near three years ago we avowed ourselves in favour of the slave trade, and as this had at least the merit of being a new proposition, it may be interesting and instructive, perhaps, to look upon the changes, if any, in Southern opinion that have since occurred. It is not too much to say that the position was an extreme one. Men were generally disinclined to make a standard of slavery. We had slaves, and as against all others, we had a right to hold them; but there was the feeling that, in some sense, they were plunder, which it was enough to get out of the way with. And, solicitous to sustain ourselves within the existing social sentiment of the world, we were unwilling to revolt against it, and we were rather inclined to brave the world in the practice of an acknowledged wrong than promulge the social principle upon which our acts were to be

rendered right. This we thought unwise. We believed it not only possible, but necessary, to erect a standard of our own. Though slavery was possessed of every element necessary to a living social system, we felt it never could be defended upon pre-existing principles of opinion; but that, to its vindication and establishment, there was the necessity of distinct organisation and intelligence; that, instead of a flank, we must present a front—instead of fear, we must have hope—instead of endurance, action—and, to the end of changing our attitude in the contest, and of planting our standard right in the very faces of our adversaries, we propose, as a leading principle of Southern policy, to re-open and legitimate the slave trade.

The journal from which we have just quoted admits that the South could not compete with the North in the settlement of Kansas, because it had not free men enough to spare, and also because such whites as might go there would probably become converts to free-labour principles.[9] To meet this and other difficulties, the following scheme is proposed by the *New Orleans Delta*:

One other measure we are in favour of, though we fear its announcement may throw some of the "ancient fogie men" into almost epileptic consternation. Nevertheless, we shall announce it, and here declare that we not only desire to make territories free, slave territories, and to acquire new territory into which to extend slavery—such as Cuba, North-Eastern Mexico, &c.—but we would re-open the African slave trade, that every white man might have a chance to make himself owner of one or more negroes, and go with them and his household gods where-ever opportunity beckoned to enterprise. But the North would never consent to this; they would dissolve the Union rather than grant it, say the croaking impracticables. Gentlemen, you do not know the North, oracular as you look when dubiously shaking your heads. It would not oppose any more bitterly a large demand like this, boldly made, than the smallest one faintly and politely urged. Try it. There is nothing to lose by the experiment. At all events, if the attempt to re-open this trade should fail, it would give one more proof of how injurious our connection with the North has become to us, and would indicate one more signal advantage which a Southern confederacy would have over the present heterogeneous association called the Union.

We could fill many columns with repetitions of the same proposal in various forms. The question is—what will follow from the demonstration? That is what we would commend to the attention of society on both sides of the Atlantic.

It is true that the Southern States have been ruined by slavery; that everybody knows this; that all recent evidence shows those States to be in the most hopeless condition which have been most dependent on slave labour; and that the richest and freshest soils have not averted ruin where slavery has been most thoroughly worked.[10] It is true that all of the world knows that it is not labour which is the deficient element in the South, but that capital has always failed of due reproduction there, owing to the wasteful quality of the labour. All this is true and thoroughly known; but it does not necessarily follow that the Southern States will not actually attempt a revival of the Slave Trade. Something must be done. They are sinking in fortunes, and threatened with political reverses. The idea of surrendering their peculiarities is intolerable; and to form a small Union among themselves without some distinctive new policy, they know to be hopeless. They have but too much reason, as recent incidents have shown, to rely on the services of slave traders in New York, Baltimore, and Philadelphia.[11] For these and other reasons it seems too probable that some attempt may be made to evade or defy the Federal interdict of the African slave trade; and if so, it would be no comfort to the rest of the world to know beforehand that at this time of day, and in the vicinity of the most prosperous free labour in the world, the experiment must turn out ruinous. We have done and suffered much to extinguish the African Slave Trade, and it is our duty to let no movement towards its revival pass unheeded.[12] The old excuse—that the Americans inherited negro slavery from us—was annihilated when the Missouri compromise was repealed.[13] A new and deliberate choice of slave institutions was then made; and the present movement is a spontaneous confirmation and repetition of that choice.

If the scheme becomes more or less practical, the North will be on the side of justice and humanity. The unworthy among its traders will betake themselves to Southern ports, as the wisest and best of the Southern population will migrate to the North. The Southern Union, if it should take place, will be the lowest in the rank of so-called civilised communities. Nevertheless, if all this be ever so true, it would be no compensation for the re-opening of the African Slave Trade. Let the movement, therefore, be watched closely and betimes.

Notes

1. For sightings of sea serpents that sometimes proved to be giant pieces of seaweed, see for example *Annual Register*, 1840 (75) and *The Times*, 26 September 1856 (5, col. 6).
2. The Fugitive Slave Act of 1850 not only set heavy penalties for helping escaped slaves but was meant to settle the question of slavery in United States territories: see "*Daily News*, 15 November 1856," note 5.
3. Frederick Law Olmsted, *A Journey in the Seaboard Slave States in the Years, 1853–1854* (New York: Dix & Edwards, 1856) [an antislavery account], 521.
4. "General" William Walker (1824–1860), American filibuster [freebooter] who invaded Nicaragua in 1855 and declared himself president in July 1856. As part of his scheme to develop a military empire in Central America, in September 1856 Walker repealed a former act that abolished slavery. Texas became a state in 1845 and was now dominated by planter-settlers, dependent on slavery.
5. The *Daily Carolina Times*, Charlotte, North Carolina, 1854–1870.
6. The *Daily Delta*, New Orleans, 1845–1863.
7. Coolies (unskilled Asian contract laborers) began to be brought from India to British Caribbean sugar colonies after the abolition of slavery in 1834, and from China about 1845. Because of abuses, the bringing of laborers from China was made illegal on British ships after 1855. The reference to Boston philanthropists must be a gibe at the radical abolitionists, some from wealthy Boston merchant families.
8. Charleston, South Carolina, 1851–1858.
9. Cf. *Daily News*, 3 November 1856. Kansas had become a territory by the Kansas-Nebraska Act: cf. "15 November 1856."
10. Olmsted notes the deterioration of Southern land. Martineau first mentions it in *Society in America* (2: 107) and often cites it as a utilitarian argument against slavery.

11. Articles about the arrest and sentencing of slave traders in Baltimore and New York appeared in the *New York Times*: 16 July (1, col. 6) and 19 August 1856 (3, col. 6), and there were many others.

12. Martineau refers to the successful campaign in Parliament against the slave trade in the late eighteenth and early nineteenth centuries. Slave trading was also prohibited by the United States and eventually by most European nations. Britain paid Spain £400,000 and Portugal £300,000 to stop their trade. By the Ashburton Treaty of 1842, Britain and the United States agreed to the joint maintenance of squadrons to stop slavers off the west coast of Africa.

13. The Missouri Compromise of 1821, which confined slavery to below 36° 30', was repealed by the Kansas-Nebraska Act.

35. Turgenev vs. Everett

Introduction

On issues that concerned both the United States and Europe, Martineau often took cues from American newspapers. Edward Everett (1795–1865), the illustrious former congressman, governor, ambassador, secretary of state and president of Harvard was currently under attack in the North for touring Southern cities with his patriotic orations on the life of Washington and other talks. By his tour, Everett hoped to raise money to preserve Mt. Vernon and to salve growing Southern anger—against the North—in defense of slavery.[1] Four years earlier, Everett had resigned from the Senate after failing in a late night session to vote against the Nebraska Bill, the new compromise on slavery.

Martineau must have met Everett socially at Washington, in winter 1835, and apparently stayed with him in Boston in August of that year.[2] By the following autumn, she had met the Garrisonian abolitionists of Boston and endorsed their anti-Whig stand on Everett. In letters to her friends and elsewhere, Martineau berates Everett for his failure to help stop slavery.[3] In her *Autobiography*, she accuses him of "burning incense to the south" for his own "political aspiration" (2: 63–64).

Martineau had studied Russian history to write *History of the Peace*. In her leaders on the Crimean War, she focuses on Czar Nicholas as villain and instigator of the conflict (see "*Daily News*, 15 June 1853," above).

The *National Anti-Slavery Standard* reprinted this example of balanced biography—a good versus a failed hero—on 26 June 1858 (2, cols. 1–2).

Notes

1. For example, see "Mr Edward Everett in the South," *National Anti-Slavery Standard*, 1 May 1858: 1, col. 1, and 8 May 1858: 1, col. 3.
2. See William R. Seat, Jr., "Harriet Martineau in America," *Notes and Queries* 204: 207–8. In *Retrospect of Western Travel* (London: Saunders & Otley, 1838), Martineau tells only that the party she stayed with in Washington included a Representative from Massachusetts (1: 236) and later that she called on Everett at Cambridge, Massachusetts (3: 53).
3. See Martineau to Richard Monckton Milnes, 10 July 1843 (MS Trinity Library Cambridge 16: 33); *Daily News*, 12 September 1854 and 26 February 1856; and *A History of the American Compromises*.

* * * *

Daily News
4 June 1858

A CONTRAST: RUSSIAN SERF-EMANCIPATION, AND AMERICAN SLAVE-POLICY: TOURGUENEFF AND EVERETT

WE had occasion to mention recently the position of the Russian Legation at Washington, where the CZAR'S Ambassador, lately so popular, could not put his head out of doors without risk of insult.[1] We need not explain that the reason of the change is the Russian policy of serf-emancipation. Long before the last war exhibited the fact to all the world, it was no secret to well-informed persons that the Russian alliance was the favourite one in the United States.[2] That it should be so was the most natural thing in the world. There is practically more resemblance between life in Russia and life in the United States, than between that of either of them and of any other country. Under their respective despotisms their inhabitants bear much the same relation to public affairs, and occupy their days with much the same interests and amusements. The two countries agree singularly in their foreign territorial policy; and their intimate alliance has always been renewed and re-invigorated at all occasions of meeting in the heart of continents and in far corners of the sea. The Czars have been affable patrons of American citizens, wherever such were encountered; and all the physicians, artists, diplomatists, and other travelled Americans who have visited St. Petersburg have been eloquent, on their return home, on the graces of Russian hospitality, the virtues of the Imperial family, and the confidential admiration of the Czar of the day of American institutions.[3] We need not add that the Serfage and Slavery of the two countries formed a peculiar bond between them. Their tacit compact to sustain one another against the disapprobation of the world was as special a ground of mutual attachment as "the secret known to all" of their policy in the North Pacific.[4] It is true, that European observers have always seen that Russian serfage and American slavery were essentially different institutions; have always doubted whether the Americans would be ultimately satisfied with the respective shares of the game to be played from the opposite coasts in the North Pacific; and have long seen that each Czar made a convenience of his far-western ally by creating a commotion (always on the subject of pro-slavery policy) in the United States whenever he was about to make an attack on his neighbours' liberties in Europe. But, if some Americans perceived this, they were not statesmen who could bring it into practical notice. The displeasure or suspicion which should long ago have been excited by the flatteries and selfish cajoleries of former Czars is roused at last by the virtuous intentions of the new EMPEROR,[5] who may fairly tell his American allies that, according to their own political theory and professions, they, above all men, should rejoice in what he is trying to do. Instead of applause, however, he meets only rage, disappointment, and insolence—not from the nation at large, let us hope; but from those who represent the nation to him and to his embassy—the Congressional public at Washington.

Under these circumstances, there is something extremely interesting to observers, and as instructive as interesting, in comparing the career of a Russian and of an American statesman, both whose names are just now conspicuous in Transatlantic journals. The most cursory glance at the lives of these two men, scholars and gentlemen both, each a Minister of State for a part of his career, and each brought into prominence by the events of the moment which embitter the alliance of their respective countries, will show wherein the instruction and interest consist.

M. N. TOURGUENEFF was born into the class of serf-owners, and saw what serf life was during a childhood spent on the family estates. He studied at Göttingen, travelled in Germany, France, Italy, and England; and returned to Russia with his countrymen after the peace of Paris, carrying with him, as hundreds of others did, those aspirations after liberty which became the great difficulty of ALEXANDER[6] for the rest of his days, and NICHOLAS for the whole of his reign. TOURGUENEFF was charged by ALEXANDER with the business of providing for serf-emancipation; but he was his advisor in other matters also—a Councillor of State, Finance Minister, and the author of various books and state papers on economical and administrative subjects.[7] When his health gave way, and he was ordered to the German baths, the CZAR told his other Ministers that he would sacrifice everything to retain TOURGUENEFF beside him; that he knew enough of his opinions as a Liberal to destroy him, if he trusted his judgment to others; but that it was enough for him that TOURGUENEFF was an honest man. The Russian Minister STEIN, whose amenities were scarce, declared that TOURGUENEFF'S name was the synonym of integrity and fidelity. When he was departing, in search of health, his Imperial friend warned him against the infection of revolutionary ideas, so prevalent in foreign countries; while both were fully aware that the patriot's ideas could hardly be more liberal than they had always been known to be. During his absence, ALEXANDER died, and NICHOLAS succeeded to the throne amidst a tempest of—not revolution, but demands of more liberties; and, among the rest, the emancipation of the serfs. TOURGUENEFF was at Edinburgh when he heard, by a sort of accident, that he was included among the conspirators summoned to trial. The Russian sub-consul at Leith was invited to play the spy upon him, and indignantly refused. Mr. CANNING received proposals to deliver him up, and returned no answer to that paragraph of the despatch. TOURGUENEFF obtained a promise from the CZAR, through his friends at St. Petersburg, of personal safety if he appeared for trial, and he was starting for home when he was stopped by the CZAR'S withdrawal of the promise. Every movement of the patriot's life was known to ALEXANDER; his love of freedom was the utmost that ALEXANDER, with all of his desire to free his serfs, could endure; and it was too much for NICHOLAS. From that time forward TOURGUENEFF was in exile. He has lived at Paris, giving his assistance to every effort for freeing slaves in any country where there were any, and rendering effectual service by his life-long knowledge of the institution, and his statesmanlike experience in dealing with it. At present the American newspapers exhibit a letter from him, full of instruction and of cheerful anticipation about the fulfilment of the great object of his life. His day of triumph has come, and his name will be immortally connected with the emancipation of the serfs of Russia, whether it takes place now or hereafter.

While TOURGUENEFF was sinking into proscription and exile, the American, EDWARD EVERETT, was coming forward, after a collegiate course in Germany in the career of political ambition.[8] So ripe a scholar, and a man of such winning manners, and so eloquent a gift of lecturing, seemed formed and trained for University life; and probably no one now so mourns as EVERETT himself that he did not rest in peace in the Greek professorship at Harvard, and become the chief of University Presidents in New England, and therefore in the whole country. But a lower ambition took possession of him; and he sacrificed much more than his university interests to go to Washington. With all his ability, he did not discern the true issues of the politics of his day; and with all his tendencies to irresolution, he did not shrink from a conflict to which he should have felt himself unequal. The slavery question has wrecked him, as so many others; and the more painfully, because he had not the ignorance and audacity to propose a course on behalf of slavery. At the outset of his Congressional career, he said (being pressed, as a New England man), that in no cause would he more willingly buckle on his knapsack and shoulder his musket than in preserving their slaves to the Southern masters. When Governor of Massachusetts, he admonished the citizens to keep silence on the subject of Slavery, "leaving it to an allwise

Providence" to abolish it without human aid.[9] When Ambassador in England, he spoke of Slavery as Englishmen do; and when Secretary of State, on his return, he wrote that extraordinary letter on the annexation-policy of his own country, which elicited the well-remembered epistle of rebuke from Lord JOHN RUSSELL, (February 16, 1853).[10] After rising thus far in office, if not in honour, EVERETT missed the great object of his life, and, instead of becoming President, began to sink; and now he has sunk so low that the barest mention of the facts is all-sufficient to indicate the case. He had not courage to take his part with either section of the commonwealth; and he mixed himself with both. He advocated the great Southern sham—the Colonisation Society—in a public address in which he wooed the North by descriptions of the developed abilities of the negroes, which alarmed and exasperated the slaveholders, who do not consider the negro human.[11] He propriated the South, in 1854, by virtually upholding the Nebraska Bill on the ground that the climate would exclude slavery, though the latitude is the same as that of Virginia and Missouri; and he evaded voting, on the plea of weakness from a spinal complaint inducing him to retire early.[12] The subject of "backbone" has never been dropped; and the indignation of his constituents was so strong that he resigned his seat in the Senate. On occasion of the assault on Mr. SUMNER—his fellow-citizen and friend, and the occupant of his seat in the Senate—he seemed to be strengthened to feel as a citizen of Massachusetts should; and he signed an address of sympathy, together with most or all other men of mark in the State. Presently after he began his series of deliveries of an oration on WASHINGTON, designed to raise funds for the purchase of Mount Vernon, the WASHINGTON estate. His oratory, not strong and clear enough for Congress, is a popular exhibition in the great country of lecturers; and EVERETT has been in the habit of courting the multitude, and gratifying his own thirst for plaudits, by delivering his studied orations in an itinerant fashion which makes his old college comrades blush. On the recent occasion he ventured South on the strength of the virtual support he had rendered to the slaveholders in Congress; and they greeted him at first as the CICERO of America—Patriot, Sage, Priest of the Union, Laudator of WASHINGTON, and so forth. But the signature in the SUMNER case! Something must be done when that question was asked, or all would be over, and the Orator in peril; so his "most intimate friend" publishes Mr. EVERETT'S own explanation—that he signed that document when he was "under the confusing influence of an anodyne."[13] Mr. EVERETT adds, that when he discovered the strength of the language of reprobation of the act of PRESTON BROOKS, he wrote to friends in the Southern States to explain away his signature. Enough! The same newspapers which give us TOURGUENEFF'S letter of exhilaration about freedom in Russia present us with EVERETT'S dismal excuses for appearing to countenance the same cause in America. Verily, each has his reward!

Notes

1. Édouard de Stoeckl became Russian minister at Washington in 1857; he had married an American wife and moved freely in Washington society.

2. Martineau echoes an article in the New York *Evening Post*, "The End of Russian Influence at Washington" (24 February 1858: 2, cols. 1–2) [rpt. *National Anti-Slavery Standard*, 27 February 1858: 2, col. 3, and *Liberator*, 30 April 1858: 1, col. 5]. The article calls Russia "quite a pet of the Southern oligarchy" and Russian influence hitherto "a sort of fourth estate in our Federal Government." As evidence, it cites the American invoking of neutrality laws during the Crimean War. It also quotes speeches from a banquet at Moscow in January 1858 in honor of the czar's request to his nobles to plan for emancipation of their serfs.

3. Martineau directs her sarcasm at defenders and apologists for slavery. Recently, a letter from the president of the American Colonization Society, dated St. Petersburg, December 1857, had appeared in a Washington newspaper (*National Intelligencer*, 20 February 1858: 1, col. 2).

4. In *History of the Peace*, Martineau notes the Russian presence in the American northwest before final settlement of the Columbia River boundary by the British-American treaty of 1846 (Boston: Walker, Fuller, 1866) 2: 354–56 and 4: 115, 487–89).

5. Alexander II (1818–1881) succeeded his father, Nicholas, in 1855 (cf. introduction, "*Daily News*, 19 November 1856").

6. Alexander I (1777–1825); the peace of Paris, November 1815, followed the final defeat of Napoleon.

7. Nikolai Ivanovitch Turgenev ([Tourgueneff] 1789–1871) held various government posts and served in the Ministry of Finance from 1819. His three-volume economic and social analysis, *La Russie et les Russes* (Bruxelles: Meline, Cans, 1847), addressed the problem of the emancipation of the serfs, as did his *Un dernie mot sur l'emancipation des serfs en Russie* (Paris: A. Franck, 1860) and other pamphlets.

8. Turgenev and Everett both studied at the University of Göttingen, Turgenev from 1808 to 1811 and Everett from 1815 to 1817—to earn the first Göttingen Ph. D. awarded to an American. At nineteen, Everett had become minister of the (Congregational) Brattle Street Church in Boston. Two years later, he was appointed Professor of Greek Literature at Harvard and allowed two years' study in Europe. He served as president of Harvard from 1846 to 1849. See Paul Revere Frothingham, *Edward Everett: Orator and Statesman* (New York: Houghton Mifflin, 1925).

9. In his first prepared speech to the House, in March 1826, Everett gratuitously pledged to defend Southern slaveholders against a "servile insurrection"; in his inaugural address as governor, in January 1838, he urged toleration of slavery for the sake of the Union.

10. During his four months as Secretary of State under President Fillmore, in 1852 to 1853, Everett wrote the reply to a British-French proposal of a tripartite guaranty of Cuba. He cited (as reasons for rejecting the treaty) "the law of American growth and progress" and a possible future wish to buy Cuba from Spain. Lord John Russell, British foreign minister, objected to Everett's long-winded explanation and defended British and French concern for Cuban safety from attacks by American marauders. See *Correspondence on the Proposed Tripartite Convention relative to Cuba* (Boston: Little, Brown, 1853).

11. On 18 January 1853, Everett told the American Colonization Society (see introduction, "*Daily News*, 9 January 1866") at Washington he did not believe the retarded progress in Africa showed any natural inferiority of the people but that leadership from the outside seemed needed. Accounts of heroic slaves, he said, proved the capacity of the colored race to civilize Africa.

12. For Everett's failure to vote on the Nebraska Bill, see introduction.

13. For Sumner, cf. introduction, "*Daily News*, 24 September 1856." Martineau reflects taunts in American newspapers, such as "Everett's Defence. His Compliment to Mr. Sumner Explained—Yeardon's Researches in Boston" [Richard Yeardon of the Charleston *Courier*] and "Vindication of Edward Everett," New York *Evening Post*, 4 May 1858: 1, col. 1, and 5 May 1858: 2, cols. 1–2.

36. The Isthmus of Panama

Introduction

First suggested by a Portuguese navigator in 1550, the idea of a canal to connect the Atlantic with the Pacific Ocean received sporadic support until the nineteenth century. After the British-American War of 1812 and the Napoleonic wars—and the Central American republics gained their independence from Spain—interest in a canal intensified. Americans and Europeans both proposed schemes including the use of natural waterways and overland passages. The discovery of gold in California in 1848, in Australia in 1851, and in New Caledonia (British Columbia) in 1858 confirmed the commercial value of a transit between the oceans. The Panama Railroad, for example, earned more than two million dollars for its American owners from just 1852 until it opened fully in 1855.

British interest in Central America dated from the buccaneers who preyed on Spanish ships carrying gold and later precious wood. British trading settlements grew up in Belize and along the Mosquito Coast. American and British conflicts of interest in the region were temporarily solved by the Clayton-Bulwer Treaty of 1850, by which any canal built by either country would be under the joint patronage of both. In 1858, further negotiations by the United States and Britain with Nicaragua for a right-of-way across the isthmus met opposition from the French agent M. Belly. Belly convinced the leaders of Nicaragua and Costa Rica to give his company the commission for a canal to improve a waterway in fact being used by a New York company started by Cornelius Vanderbilt.

Martineau combines several pertinent topics in this leader. She responds to a popular bill on British Columbia going through Parliament, she continues her attacks on American slavery (her writings on Central America form a part of that campaign), and she reminds British investors that she is alert to their interests. For the details of Americans jostling for power in Central America, Martineau probably draws on articles like those appearing over the previous months in the New York *Daily Tribune*.

* * * *

Daily News
27 July 1858

WE may be excused for our uncertainty as to what is to be done about an effective transit route in Central America, while it is clear that nobody in the United States can answer for any plan being fixed, and no two authorities in Central America tell the same story.[1] The facts must be got at by some means or other, for the time has arrived for union on one point—for agreement in discontent that a proper mode of crossing the Isthmus has not been provided before this time. The interest is quickened by our Colonial Secretary's scheme for the settlement of New Caledonia.[2] However eagerly we may forward our emigrating countrymen by the great lakes, and by the rivers and passes of the existing Hudson's Bay Company, and however the energetic people of the United States may push their waggon trains through the Nebraska territory towards the Columbia, both parties will be well aware, like all the rest of the world, that round by the Isthmus is the nearest way home to our colony after all. Those who go to seek the gold have every reason to desire a passage by sea, however long, in preference to plunging through the wilds, with all their liabilities of hunger and thirst, hostile Indians, and an untried climate. No man of any nation is safe where Americans of the United States and the Indians of any tribe are within hail and scent of each other—their natural antipathy imperils all other men.[3] While this lasts, while there are Indians in the wilderness and companies of American citizens crossing them, no other men, of any country or complexion, can reckon on a safe journey from either Lake Superior or the Missouri to Oregon. For many years to come, till there are Pacific railways across the continent, the Isthmus must be the popular route to the shores of the North Pacific. Much more will it be preferred for bringing the gold or other products home, either to the United States or to Europe. There could be no doubt about this if the Indians had not learned the value of gold. Now that they are grubbing in the river bottoms, and setting scouts and pickets to keep off intruders, and burying their gold dust till they can find a qualified purchaser, it must be hazardous in the extreme to depend on any land route for returning eastwards, either with the actual gold or with the reputation for carrying it. With these new interests rising up, and at the very time when the European and American allies are busy on the further shore of the Pacific, throwing open China to the trade of the world,[4] no one country, and no Government of any country, can tell what is the real prospect about crossing the Isthmus.

We have shown before that there are four parts in which the crossing is believed to be practicable on a large scale, by railway or canal; and that the Panama railway, and the Nicaragua route, by river and lake, are the two in use—both being inadequate, from the want of good harbours in the one case, and the scanty means and difficult water route in the other. There is a perfect hubbub of schemes, amidst the new pressing need of a good one. Mr. SQUIER'S Honduras Railway is exalted by one party, and M. BELLY'S Nicaraguan ship canal by another; while the old dog-in-the-manger Company—who have held the route without fulfilling the conditions by which they obtained it—are protesting, in a variety of newspapers in many countries, that they have got a further term of possession, and will yet show what they can do.[5] American speculators declare that they will keep the ground and the work in American hands, whereas it appears that there are American capitalists concerned in all the schemes afloat. Mr. SQUIER'S organs say the interests of the Honduras Railway are divided between English and American capitalists, though the material and labour for the road are to be furnished exclusively from the United States: to which other informants add the particular that the labourers, to the number of 6,000, are to be armed. M. BELLY declares that he has succeeded in forming an American connexion in support of the great ship canal, which is, according to the recent convention, to be protected in its neutrality by England, France, and Sardinia.[6] Mr. VANDERBILT, again, claims to have been beforehand with M. BELLY, and to have obtained from the Nicaraguan Government the entire control of the route, and the possession of the property of the former companies, in consideration of certain loans to the State of Nicaragua. Once more, the Transit Company protests that Mr. VANDERBILT has no more business there than M. BELLY; that the route is theirs, and they mean to keep it, being actually promised by that same Nicaraguan Government that nobody shall interfere with them till the beginning of 1859. Where are we to turn for information amidst all these boasts and contradictions? Are we to believe WALKER, who pretends that he shall step down into Nicaragua and take the matter into his own hands?[7] Are we to believe the text of the Convention by which the route and its neighbourhood are put under the protection of three European nations, against WALKER and American filibusters in general? Are we to believe that M. BELLY is or is not acting under the authority of the French Government? He is now said to deny that he ever had any such authority. If so, what connexion has he with the new Convention, and how is it that two French vessels of war will remain on the spot during the formation of the route?[8] Can the American PRESIDENT give us the information we want? He says the route shall positively be opened, and he will support whatever party shall prove its valid right—thus intimating that he cannot or will not say to whom the right belongs.[9] Can the Nicaraguan PRESIDENT tell us what to believe?[10] One would think he could, if any one. We find him (by the reports of the respective parties) first renewing the term of the company in possession; then making over the scheme to another set of speculators, in return for pecuniary assistance; then showing favour to M. BELLY, and appealing to the European Powers in his dread of American aggression; then receiving telegraphic menaces from Washington on behalf of the first Company, and finding himself charged with being bribed by France through M. BELLY; and then seeing M. BELLY start for New York and Washington, to form an American connexion, and delight Mr. BUCHANAN with enthusiastic accounts of the brilliancy of the enterprise which American capital and energy are to complete, for the boundless advantage of American interests.[11] Are Costa Rica and Nicaragua reconciled and allied for mutual defence against northern aggression, or is that report a fable?[12] Are France, England, and Sardinia to keep the transit open impartially to all the world? or is that a fable, and "the text of the convention" a forgery? There is one person who can tell us what to believe; and that is Lord MALMESBURY.[13] He must be questioned; for really it is more than time that we knew what is going to be done. If any scheme is settled, there can be no objection to letting the world know it. If no scheme is settled, it is, if possible, more important that we should know it, that we may rate at their true value the boasts of speculators, each one of whom declares his supporters to be masters of the situation. Armed vessels are at each extremity of the route, we are told. Of what nations are these, and how many are there of them? Why are they there, and how long will they stay? Above all, is there certainly to be a great ship canal? and when will it be ready for use, and under what conditions? Mr. BUCHANAN is determined that there shall be one, we are told. Are other potentates equally determined to the same effect? And are they all acting together to make a common highway for the world? or are they instituting a mutual check and control, for political purposes apart from considerations of the transit? These are things which it is indispensable that we should know; and members of both Houses should charge themselves with the inquiry while they are yet face-to-face with Ministers.[14]

Lord MALMESBURY can hardly need to be reminded of the debts long owing to British bond-holders from that region. The creditors have waited in silence, or with only occasional complaints, while Nicaragua was in the depths of every kind of adversity.[15] A firm establishment and wide opening of this route must enrich the territory through which it passes; and Nicaragua may, with common prudence, become one of the most flourishing countries in the world. In prospect of this, stipulations ought to be made for the liquidation of all British claims, in proportion as the means arise, under British countenance and protection. The bond-holders should go to the Minister, to ask their own questions; but inquiry should also be made in Parliament, to satisfy a more general curiosity and interest.

Notes

1. Martineau describes four possible routes across the isthmus in "*Daily News*, 6 July 1858;" see also "*Daily News*, 15 October 1858," below, and note 5.
2. On 8 July 1858, Colonial Secretary Sir Edward Bulwer Lytton proposed a bill to establish a government under a governor and council of the territories controlled by the Hudson's Bay Company north of the American border between the Rocky Mountains and the Pacific. Accounts of rich gold finds in spring 1858 had created a rush to the area by American, British, and native Indian prospectors. The bill passed the Commons on 24 July and the Lords on 29 July; the name of the colony was changed to British Columbia on 27 July 1858.
3. In spring 1858, stories of Indian hostilities on the Snake River and elsewhere in the Northwest appeared in American newspapers beside stories of gold finds: see, for example, the New York *Daily Tribune* for July 1858. Until then in British Columbia, the Hudson Bay Company had maintained good relations with the Indians, from whom it bought furs.
4. The Earl of Elgin, British Plenipotentiary, concluded a trading treaty with the Emperor of China in spring 1858.
5. The northernmost of the four routes, surveyed for a canal and with "the beginning of a railway, of American workmanship," ran from the Gulf of Campeche on the east coast to the Gulf of Tehuantepec on the west coast of Mexico. Next on the north, Ephraim George Squier, former American chargé d'affaires in Guatemala, proposed a railroad to run from "Puerta Caballos, in the Bay of Honduras, to the ... harbour of Fonseca." The "Nicaragua route" ran by ship from Greytown (San Juan del Norte) on the east coast along the San Juan River to Lake Nicaragua and then overland to the west coast. (See *Daily News*, 6 July 1858.) For the southernmost route, the railroad across the isthmus of Panama, see F. N. Otis, *History of the Panama Railroad: and of the Pacific Mail Steamship Company* (New York: Harper, 1867); cf. introduction. For Félix Belly, agent of a French company, see next note. For the "dog-in-the-manger"

company, owned by former associates of Cornelius Vanderbilt, see William Oscar Scroggs, *Filibusters and Financiers. The Story of William Walker and His Associates* (New York: Macmillan, 1916) and Albert Z. Carr, *The World of William Walker* (New York: Harper & Row, 1963). Vanderbilt's original Atlantic and Pacific Ship Canal Company had contracted to complete a canal along the route now given to Belly's company; a San Francisco-based faction of his (subsequently formed) Accessory Transit Company then tried to wrest control from the New York group, which also broke into factions, cutting out Vanderbilt. For the relevance of the transit schemes to Britain's Central American claims, see Mary Wilhelmine Williams, *Anglo-American Diplomacy, 1815–1915* (Washington: American Historical Association, 1916).

6. Belly convinced Nicaragua and Costa Rica to accept the guaranty of "the three powers which had guaranteed the Ottoman Empire" (see note 8). For Sardinia as an ally of Britain and France in the Crimean War, see "*Daily News*, 3 July 1855," note 7.

7. For William Walker (cf. "*Daily News*, 25 November 1856," note 4), an ally of the San Francisco-based faction, see William Oscar Scroggs, "William Walker and the Steamship Corporation in Nicaragua," *American Historical Review* 10 (1904–05): 792–811, and next note. For Martineau's latest attacks on Walker—whose actions revealed the strength of the proslavery party at Washington, see *Daily News*, 21 January, 1 March, 2 April, 12 May and 26 August 1858; and cf. "15 October 1858," below.

8. Dreading Walker's return, even after he was twice arrested and sent back to the United States, the presidents of Nicaragua and Costa Rica on 1 May 1858 jointly announced the concession of the canal and transit route to Belly. In a separate document they empowered him to arrange for "European vessels of war" to be stationed off the coasts of Central America. See Scroggs, *Filibusters and Financiers*, 258–63 and Carr, 245–46.

9. For Martineau's scepticism of President Buchanan's intentions, see "*Daily News*, 15 November 1856," above. The Nicaragua route was closed in 1857 after Vanderbilt's men, in collaboration with the president of Costa Rica, seized the river steamers to keep a boatload of Walker's volunteers from reaching him from the east.

10. President Tomás Martínez of Nicaragua favored Belly's scheme, but the route was to remain closed with isthmian travel diverted to the Panama Railroad.

11. For further maneuverings of Vanderbilt's former associates over the ship canal route and Belly's unsuccessful search for American backers, cf. "15 October 1858."

12. See note 8.

13. James Howard Harris, 3rd Earl of Malmesbury, Foreign Secretary.

14. For Martineau's exasperation over the unaccountability of ministers between parliamentary sessions, cf. "*Daily News*, 26 December 1853," note 3, and "15 October 1858."

15. Cf. *Daily News*, 6 August 1858 (where Martineau cautions "Central American Bondholders" and "Nicaraguan Bondholders"); "15 October 1858;" and *The Times*, 11 August 1858: 5, col. 2, on Venezuelan bonds.

37. The Isthmus of Panama

Introduction

Although only a few stories on Central America, the transit schemes, or American filibusters appeared in British newspapers from August to October 1858, the machinations of various groups to gain control of the Nicaragua route continued.

In *Daily News*, 6 and 26 August 1858, Martineau reviews details of the four existent or proposed transit routes across the isthmus and warns Britain not to let American cupidity or vainglory take away the right of other nations to passage through the isthmus. Here she offers a clear rationale for her return to the isthmus question and the improbable developments there.

* * * *

Daily News
15 October 1858

WE make no apology for recurring to the topic of Central American politics, as affecting the transit route, because there really is no other way, under our system of secret diplomacy, of securing the interests of our foreign bondholders, and the honour and advantage of England abroad, than that of extending the protection of the Fourth Estate to such interests. In the recess, especially, our foreign affairs are altogether in the hands of Ministers; and before they have to render an account, the time for a wise and popular policy may be past, and the mischief of any shortcoming may be irretrievable.¹ For many months past so little has been publicly said on the subject of the Nicaraguan transit route that there was no certainty that the affair would be duly watched by the public, and cared for by Ministers, unless the newspapers chronicled every change at Washington and New York, and every movement on the Isthmus. For several months we have shown what was going on, as far as it could be ascertained, and now, at length, we have reached a point, both of time and policy, which indicates that a critical settlement of this great highway of the world cannot be far off.

The Americans have never ceased their agitation of the question of the proprietorship of the route. In order to draw the whole world into their interest, they have projected four routes, each of which had special recommendations for one class or more of capitalists. One would lead nearest to Mexico, and would serve New Orleans and the southern seaboard; another would better suit the northern shippers and those of Europe, while it would keep the command of Honduras for the Americans; a third was incomparable as a waterway; and the fourth for its shortness and speed.² Through all phases of the scheme the intention of the United States to appropriate the command of the Isthmus, or the Isthmus itself, was firmly held, and occasionally disclosed, in the form of a reference to "the MONROE doctrine" (a doctrine which would astonish MONROE himself more than it need alarm Europe). Without going over again the projects and the manifestations which have been offered on the other side of the Atlantic since the opening of the year, we may just remind our readers that the real perplexity—the mystery which most concerned us—has been as to what really took place in May and June last about opening a ship canal, and securing the use of it to the world.

What was the authority of M. BELLY? What was true about the Convention between certain European Powers and Nicaragua and the United States, protecting the formation of the canal, and guaranteeing its neutrality? And what were we to think of the engagement, on the part of England, France, and Sardinia, to protect Nicaragua and Costa Rica against aggression from the United States?³

The Isthmus of Panama

Whatever were the conjectures formed in Europe and America, it is now clear that the decisive moment is at hand in which the assumptions ascribed to the Washington Cabinet must be clearly ascertained, and finally reconciled with the interests of other nations, and especially with the rights of the inhabitants of the Isthmus.[4] The American newspapers have published past transactions, present agitations, and assumptions for the future. The case is before us; and we must give it the attention its importance demands.

The Nicaraguan government holds itself free to accept a new Transit scheme, the old American contractors having forfeited their possession of the existing water-way by the non-observance of the main conditions of their bargain.[5] These parties refuse to retire, claim to retain their position till 1859, and propose to institute their promised works before that date, though warned that the term of permission expired long ago. This Company, like other American parties in the case, attempts to throw discredit on M. BELLY, as an unauthorised adventurer. Thus far, all is as it has been for many months past. Next, the VANDERBILT scheme seems to be at an end altogether. It was too precipitately concluded that the President of NICARAGUA could not refuse a *douceur* of 100,000 dollars; but the dollars and their donor have been returned to New York—and this disposes of another project.[6] Next, it is announced from New York that the grand scheme which was said to have attracted so much English capital, and which was characterised by the remarkable stipulation that 6,000 armed American labourers were to be employed on the line—the great Honduras Railway—is considered to be abandoned.[7] Money is asked for to provide, instead, a modest cartroad. This closes another branch of the question.

Then there is WALKER and his filibuster force—what are we to think of his prospects? There has been no saying lately whether he was here or there, up or down, the soul of the enterprise, or cast out of the game. After his recent disclosures of his employment by the Government against Mexico, in aid of designs upon Cuba, it seems impossible that he can ever recover the countenance of Government; and it is to be expected that the Washington Cabinet will answer his allegations, and take care that he does not imperil the honour of the Republic by his aggressions in the Isthmus: yet it is certain that the inhabitants are in desperate fear of invasion by a force under WALKER, sustained by his Government.[8] After everybody believed that WALKER was gone to the Isthmus last month with men, arms, and ammunition, it was discovered that he was still in the Northern States, and certainly within reach of a prohibition from head-quarters. The next inquiry is why we do not hear of such a prohibition? What we do hear—not once or twice, but from month to month, and almost from week to week—is that the PRESIDENT only waits to be convinced which of the American claimants can establish the best title to the Transit route, existing or prospective, in order to support with the whole power of the United States, the best claim; being resolved, however, that the claim he will support shall be an American one, as he will take care that the United States shall hold the command of the Isthmus. The last item of news under this head is, that the PRESIDENT may be expected to offer himself for re-election next year, partly because his "policy" has not been so easy of achievement as he anticipated, and will require a longer time; and partly because his candidateship may ward off the extreme peril to the Union of the critical antagonism of the North and South in the next election.[9] If this news is true, it is considered equivalent to an engagement to obtain Cuba, and get the command of the Isthmus. If the announcement should turn out false, it will appear that the wish has been father to the thought.

All this time there has been much blind speculation at Washington as to the function and real objects of Sir WILLIAM GORE OUSELEY.[10] Some of the best informed persons in the political world believed that he was placed at Washington to keep within bounds, or to overrule, the sympathy of Lord NAPIER with the PRESIDENT in his Kansas policy,[11] if not even in matters of international debate. Whatever Lord NAPIER'S sympathies may be, on points of American policy, this was not like our English ways of proceeding; and it now appears that Sir W. GORE OUSELEY has been keeping watch over the interests of the Isthmus, and that the European Governments—or one of them at least—may have really been duly vigilant during this critical year, which has rendered the free passage between the oceans more important to the world in general, and ourselves in particular, than it has ever been considered before, though the forecast of centuries has been directed towards it. The reply of Lord MALMESBURY (June 11) to M. BELLY, declaring that, in his opinion, the treaty for the Ship-canal (dated May 1) is in accordance with the CLAYTON-BULWER treaty of 1850, has come out;[12] and the remarks of the French journals indicate that the EMPEROR'S Government is in agreement with ours,—is pledged, in short, to sustain the independence of the Central American States, and to protect the free and neutral character of the transit route, as a highway for the whole world. We shall take an early opportunity of commenting on the treaty between this country and Nicaragua, which is understood to be the model on which treaties with the neighbouring States will be framed.[13] It will now be seen whether the Government of the United States will be satisfied to share with other Powers the advantages of the Central American route, or whether it will make any special demands. It seems to have experienced, as yet, none of the "calm" anticipated by Mr. BUCHANAN as the characteristic of his rule. In the north and west, at sea and on land, troubles have sprung up, and clouds have gathered thick.[14] It seems scarcely credible that new turmoils should be instituted to the south of the Gulf for purposes of ambition which have no warrant in reason, policy, or international law. A short time must now show what attitude will be assumed by the PRESIDENT: and his allies have only to consider how the rights of the Central American States can be most thoroughly established, with or without the aid of the United States. *With* their aid, let us hope, for the honour of nations and the welfare of the world.

Notes

   1. For British investors in Central American bonds and the non-accountability of ministers, cf. "*Daily News,* 27 July 1858," notes 14 and 15.
   2. For the four routes, north to south, cf. "27 July 1858."
   3. For Belly's unproved claim to represent Emperor Napoleon III of France, see Scroggs, *Filibusters and Financiers;* for his return to

Nicaragua in February 1859, see *Daily News*, 19 April 1859; for the other points, cf. "27 July 1858" and *Daily News*, 6 and 26 August 1858.

4. Cf. "27 July 1858;" Martineau must now refer to Secretary of State Lewis Cass's negotiation of the Cass-Irisarri Treaty to reopen the Nicaragua route under American protection, and to Secretary of War John B. Floyd's reported encouragement of Walker to help precipitate a war between Mexico and Spain to prepare for American annexation of Cuba.

5. Vanderbilt's company, now under control of his former eastern associates, made no attempt to improve the route, as originally agreed: see "27 July 1858," notes 5 and 9.

6. Vanderbilt reportedly made the offer to get back the contract for the route now held by his former associates.

7. Squier's Honduran railway scheme failed because President Martínez refused to sign the Cass-Irisarri Treaty; see "27 July 1858" and note 4, above.

8. Walker published his claim to covert support from Secretary of War Floyd in the *Mobile Register*, 19 July 1858: see note 4. For Walker's attempts to return to Nicaragua with new "colonists," see Scroggs, *Filibusters and Financiers*, and Carr, *The World of William Walker*. After he was acquitted for violation of the neutrality law, Walker went on a lecture tour and began to gather new volunteers. A circular published in Mobile in early October 1858 announced that his Southern Emigration Society would sail in November. On 30 October 1858, President Buchanan issued orders to stop such illegal enterprises. (Yet in spring 1860 Walker evaded authorities and sailed to Honduras, where he was executed after intervention by the British.)

9. For Martineau's opinion of Buchanan at the time of his election, see "*Daily News*, 15 November 1856," above. Buchanan said in his inaugural address that he would not become a candidate for re-election but would serve his country to be gratefully remembered. Martineau refers to the next presidential election, in 1860, repeatedly after this, often in support of the new Republican Party.

10. Sir William Gore Ouseley (1797–1866), British diplomat sent to negotiate a treaty of commerce and navigation with Nicaragua and to settle claims on the Mosquito Coast but delayed for months at Washington, D. C. His failure to obtain the treaty was partly owing to the arrival of Belly: see Williams, *Anglo-American Isthmian Diplomacy*.

11. Lord Francis Napier (1819–1898), British Minister to the United States, sympathetic to Buchanan's strict Constitutionalism over the slavery issue in Kansas. See "15 November 1856."

12. For Belly's proposals, see "27 July 1858," notes 6 and 8.

13. Martineau gives the terms of the treaty with Nicaragua, learned from a New York newspaper, in *Daily News*, 22 October 1858: Britain was to have free use of the route and would help to protect it.

14. Martineau refers to troubles with the Indians in the Northwest, with the Mormons in Utah, and between free and pro-slavery settlers in Kansas: see *Daily News*, 31 December 1858.

38. Sale of Pierce Butler's Slaves

Introduction

On 9 March 1859, the New York *Daily Tribune* published a full-page account of the sale in Savannah, Georgia, of slaves belonging to Pierce M. Butler, divorced husband of the English actress Fanny Kemble.[1] Written by the popular sketch-writer Mortimer Neal Thomson, the article's heavy-handed sarcasm and cynicism about the feelings of Southern whites echo the antislavery stand of the *Tribune's* editor and publisher, Horace Greeley.

Though Martineau closely followed reports of the growing disgust at slavery in the North, she had a special reason for interest in the fate of Butler's estate. In autumn 1834, she met Fanny (Kemble) Butler in Philadelphia and commented so disapprovingly on portions of Fanny's yet unpublished journal (on her American theatrical tour with her father) that Fanny withdrew them.[2]

Pierce M. Butler had courted Fanny Kemble for the two years of her tour. They married in June 1834, without Fanny's being aware her husband was a slave owner. After a painful court battle, they were divorced in 1847. Fanny's divorce further prodded Martineau (in her *Autobiography* and elsewhere) to censure the volatile and talented young actress. A succinct account of Fanny Kemble's marriage and of the Butler ownership of the Georgia plantation and its slaves appears in John A. Scott's introduction to *Journal of a Residence on a Georgia Plantation in 1838–39 by Frances Anne Kemble*.[3]

Martineau here reduces the six-column *Tribune* special on the slave sale to less than one and one-half columns. She picks illustrations from Thomson's rambling anecdotes on slave buyers, spectators, hangers-on and individual slaves to suit the shift from his ironic, slangy style to her thoughtful scene-painting—enhanced by pathos and a sense of grim honesty.

A week later, on 12 April 1859, *The Times* printed a condensation of the factual material (omitting comments), taken directly from the New York *Tribune*.

Notes

    1. Reprinted as a pamphlet by the American Antislavery Society, entitled *Great Auction Sale of Slaves at Savannah, Georgia, March 2 and 3, 1859* [n.d.].
    2. *Journal. By Frances Anne Butler* (Philadelphia: Carey, Lea & Blanchard, 1835).
    3. (New York: Knopf, 1961).

* * * *

Daily News
4 April 1859

    Deep and gradual social changes throw up from time to time picturesque incidents which fix the attention of the light and careless, and strongly attract the thoughtful who understand their significance. In every great political and social revolution—the slowest as well as the most rapid—dates stand out to catch the eye or help the memory, marked by illustrative scenes and adventures; and not less now, in our days of paper and print, than when traditions passed down from generation to generation. There must be something remarkable about a slave auction, to which the leading New York newspaper sent down a special reporter almost to the shores of the Gulf. There are slave auctions every day, somewhere in the country; and they were till lately seen at Washington, by multitudes of Northern citizens.[1] What could there be in such an auction down at Savannah, to take people a thousand miles without any intention of making purchases, or expectation of seeing anything sold but the black

Sale of Pierce Butler's Slaves

men, women, and children who may be seen under the hammer anywhere south of the Ohio? It was because this particular sale marks the dying out of an old time and the coming in of a new; the estates which answer to the antique and picturesque idea of "the patriarchal institution" in America are becoming fewer and fewer; and the breaking up of every such camp in the wilderness, and the dispersion of the tribe, has a combined romantic and political interest which may well carry observers a long way to be present at the catastrophe. When Mr. PIERCE M. BUTLER[2] was familiar in English society, well known as the husband of an accomplished Englishwoman, and observed with curiosity as a representative of one of the most ancient and wealthy families in the Southern States, it had not entered anybody's head that he would call together his neighbours, and all who had long purses, to draught off his clan, and destroy one of the few remaining centres of what the residents call "chivalrous civilisation." The thing has happened, however; Mr. PIERCE M. BUTLER'S great sale of negroes has taken place. Nothing like it has been known for many years as to mere extent of sale: but this is not the most marked circumstance belonging to it.

Old Major BUTLER was known by name all over the Union as a wealthy planter, and a man of great consequence in Georgia. He left estates valued at more than a million dollars, which were divided between two nephews, of whom Mr. PIERCE M. BUTLER was one.[3] Cotton and rice were the products; and the Negroes sold the other day amounted to 436, a prodigious number to be sold otherwise than by transfer with the land. While the old estate remained under the old family, while the slaves lived on the same ground where their fathers were born, and their children would live after them, there was some exterior appearance of truth in the romance with which strangers were entertained about patriarchal modes of living. Any one who has ever read the American Sketchbook called "Swallow Barn," by Mr. KENNEDY, has obtained the best and most favourable view of life on a Southern plantation, during its bright and fortunate days.[4] This Savannah sale shows the upshot of it. It must occur to every one that the ancient "patriarchal" mode of life would never have been possible for many years together on a prescribed landed estate; and the illustration is seen in slave-holding countries, where the land wears out, and the owner moves westwards with his tribe of dependents. Now and then, but rarely, the whole tribe is dispersed by partition and sale; but such a dispersion as this from the auction block is very rare. Mr. BUTLER lived in public during the week; he was seen here, there, and everywhere; and it could not but be a subject of speculation among his acquaintances whether he was fully sensible of the significance of what was going on. He made no secret of his case. He did not live on his estate, but at Philadelphia; he had speculated and lost; he delivered over his plantations to General CADWALLADER[5] and other claimants, brought his negroes to the Savannah raceground to be sold, and looked after his own interests himself. There was the usual comedy of auction meetings, and the unparalleled tragedy of slave auctions, though the theory was that families were sold together. The young lover, all smiles and confidence, overflowed with gratitude to his new master for being willing to buy his sweetheart, and to everybody who had put in a word on his behalf: but the sweetheart was put up as one of a lot; and the new master could not buy them all: so JEFFREY is gone to the Great Swamp rice-fields, and DORCAS to hoe cotton in South Carolina. This is one specimen; there are others of the partings of the old and young, comrades and relatives; but we will quote no more. One bit of conversation, however, should be cited, because there are still many readers who do not believe in the truthfulness of Mrs. STOWE'S expositions, even when supported by the documentary proofs contained in the KEY which she published for the purpose.[6] The New York reporter supplies the precise words which he overheard uttered by a party of men on the ground, on the appropriate subject of "managing niggers." Each told his own method, when finally a listener who had only put in an occasional nod, gave his view, as one who had had experience, and ought to know. "You can manage ordinary niggers by licken' 'em, and givin' 'em a taste of the hot iron once in a while, when they're extra ugly; but if a nigger really sets himself up against me, I can't never have any patience with him. I just get my pistol, and shoot him right down; and that's the best way." Assenting nods followed from many of the by-standers.

Sale of Pierce Butler's Slaves

Now, these are illustrative incidents which show the character of the time. In the comparatively genuine patriarchal days when the soil was fertile, and work was easy, and debt did not press on the estate, and politics went easily, in the State and at the centre, no man talked in this way, nor would have been tolerated if he had done so in his cups. The land is changed, the negroes are changed, the owner, the laws, the politics and the temper of the State, are all changed. The aristocratic seat in the province has become a scene of sordid slave-driving; and the encroachment, and yet more the dread, of free labour, destroys the ease and composure assumed by old-fashioned planters to reign throughout their domain. It is too late now to preserve the institution, except as a transient resource to keep up the value of negroes. Whatever there once was of human in the negro in his owner's eyes and heart disappears with every breaking up of these old estates; and the dispersed labourers sink lower in the cattle-pens with their transfer to each new driver. When the last hereditary plantation is deserted a distinct period will have passed away, for the old relation is not one which can be formed afresh, or through the agency of the auctioneer. For economical reasons it is impossible. For social reasons it is becoming more clearly impossible from year to year. For political reasons, the small faction of the slaveholders is clutching desperately at the sundering fragments of their power, fortune, and *prestige*; but the hopelessness of the struggle is becoming more evident from day to day.

The BUTLER negroes had never been sold before. They were remarkably black. Both these circumstances added to their value. They had never been taught to look sharp, knew nothing of the world beyond their native plantation, and had no intermixture of a higher quality brain. When the dismal four days' rain ceased, and the evening sunshine cast the shadows of the race-stand on the course, the negroes crowded round Mr. BUTLER, who gave them a dollar apiece in saying farewell. Then came the partings. Then steamers and trains started off, each with some parcel of the chattels which had been bought by the passengers. Those passengers were negro-traders from all the points of the compass, young planters (the old would naturally stay at home), and such strangers as desired to see one of the characteristic sights of the country. The old house and fields will probably sink into ruin, as the custom is in such cases. One after another, the few remaining seats of the old aristocracy must go; and the only alternative will be their lapsing to wilderness, or blooming and blossoming again under the operation of free and willing labour. As negro-plantations, there is nothing before them but the destiny of "Old Major BUTLER'S great property." And when that doom is reached, what next at Washington!

Notes

1. Thomson (see introduction) had joined the *Tribune* staff in 1855; his humorous "letters" and sketches were highly prized. Slave auctions stopped at Washington, D.C., with passage of the Fugitive Slave Law (cf. *Daily News,* 7 May 1862).
2. Pierce Mease Butler (1810–67)—originally Butler Mease; he took the name as a condition for inheriting his share of his maternal grandfather's property (see next note).
3. Major Pierce Butler (1744–1822) came to America in 1766 as a member of the British army, married a South Carolina heiress, and twice served as United States Senator from South Carolina. He later moved to Georgia, taking most of his slaves with him. His Georgia property came to Pierce M. Butler and his (deceased) brother at the death of a maternal aunt (see John A. Scott, xxii–xxiii).
4. John Pendleton Kennedy, *Swallow Barn, or, A Sojourn in the Old Dominion* (New York: Putnam, 1851).
5. General George Cadwallader, described as the representative of the creditors.
6. Harriet Beecher Stowe, *Uncle Tom's Cabin* and *The Key to Uncle Tom's Cabin; presenting the original facts and documents upon which the story is founded, together with corroborative statements verifying the truth of the work* (Boston: 1853). Cf. "*Daily News,* 22 April 1853," note 2.

39. Emerson: The *Atlantic Monthly*

Introduction

Though aloof from politics in his early years, Ralph Waldo Emerson had responded sympathetically to the abolitionists. By the time of the Fugitive Slave Law of 1850, he shared the revulsion sweeping New England at slavery and its Southern defenders. Emerson "pleaded the cause of peace" and "believed that war might be finally abolished once the individual citizen acquired the proper degree of mental and spiritual culture." Yet at Boston in January 1861, he tried unsuccessfully to speak before a near-riotous meeting of the Massachusetts Anti-Slavery Society, and when hostilities broke out he set out to "help win the war."[1]

Lincoln's preliminary announcement of the emancipation of slaves in conquered territories (to be effective on 1 January 1863) did not fully satisfy Emerson. In spite of his celebratory essay, "The President's Proclamation," on 8 December 1862 he cried out to Carlyle

> our President Lincoln will not even emancipate slaves, until on the heels of a victory, or the semblance of such. . . . Here we read no books. The war is our sole & doleful instructor.[2]

Nevertheless, "Emerson's manifesto in the new 'Atlantic Monthly'" was immediately hailed by Martineau and others.[3] Emerson and other high-minded writers had helped launch the magazine five years earlier.[4] The November 1862 issue, besides Emerson's anonymous tribute to Lincoln, includes a mixture of fiction, poetry, and articles on the North's problematic success in the war, the emancipation of serfs in Russia, and Carlyle's *Frederick the Great*, Vol. III. (Julia Ward Howe's "Battle Hymn of the Republic" appeared on the first page of the February 1862 issue.)

Martineau stayed with the Emersons in Boston in October 1835, and Emerson stayed with her at The Knoll in 1848. He refers to her as a "sweet-tempered sensible lady"—though later as a "masculine woman." In his journals, he praises her religious speculation (in *Eastern Life, Present and Past*) but not her "paid" political economy writings. Martineau calls Emerson"noble & serene, & humane to uttermost degree."[5] In *Retrospect of Western Travel*, she describes him as an essential American to know and quotes at length from his 1837 Phi Beta Kappa oration, "The American Scholar" (3: 228–40).

Martineau's admiration for Emerson outlasted her close ties to the Carlyles. Her admiration for President Lincoln kept pace with the view of other Garrisonians. For the nineteenth-century habit of extensive quotation in reviews, cf. "*Daily News*, 27 January 1853" and "*Daily News*, 24 July 1854," above.

Notes

1. Ralph L. Rusk, *The Life of Ralph Waldo Emerson* (New York: Scribner's, 1949), 410–11.

2. *The Correspondence of Emerson and Carlyle*, ed. Joseph Slater (New York: Columbia U P, 1964), 535–36.

3. See *Daily News*, 3, 10, 15, 21, 23 and 29 October 1862; and *Harriet Martineau's Letters to Fanny Wedgwood* [2 November 1862], 233.

4. See Mark A. deWolfe Howe, *The Atlantic Monthly and Its Makers* (Boston: Atlantic Monthly, 1919).

5. Martineau to Henry Crabb Robinson, 8 June 1844 (MS Dr. Williams's Library).

* * * *

Daily News
11 November 1862

[*Martineau opens with a salvo at "perverse" English supporters of "a slaveholding society in America," who were sure to protest "whenever the North should fairly disentangle itself from its trammels" to emancipate the slaves. Though "tens of thousands" have died, at least the war has now been "placed on its right ground."*] It is mournful that a republican nation should have been so entangled by its own former faults as to have infinite tribulation to go through before it could address itself to its true work, and combine its forces of mind and heart for the effort which was needed. But when these sins and shortcomings and griefs are left behind it is no time to begin lamenting them. It is rather the time to leave off lamenting them, and to rejoice in the good time that has come. Such must be the feeling of all who read with an open mind and a genial heart the contrasting utterances of such a man as EMERSON on the one hand, and of the spokesmen of despotic government on the other, in the early days of November 1862.[1] While the Free States were more or less in slavery to the South there was little for the large-minded men of the Republic, who lived retired from political strife, to say or do in public. They felt that the false game must be played out, and the clamour of false patriots be exhausted before they could speak to any purpose, except on special occasions; while they steadfastly trusted that the time would come when the true issues would be apparent to all, and when all good citizens might rejoice together. That time has arrived; and EMERSON hails it in a tone so lofty, and with a joy so cordial and so calm, that no minds and hearts that have not lost their simplicity and integrity can fail to be animated and cheered as they have not been for many a day. At the same moment that this worthy citizen of the Republic is so speaking, some of his own pro-slavery neighbours, disconcerted and alarmed, and some British journalists, rashly committed to the pro-slavery cause, are raising a lament over the greatness of past misfortunes, exaggerating them to the utmost, in the hope of making their readers suppose them irreparable. There could hardly be a finer political and moral lesson than reading Mr. EMERSON'S celebration of the Emancipation measure in the "Atlantic Monthly" for this month, and, in contrast with it, the TIMES leader of Saturday.[2] Which state of mind any man would rather be in, which point of view a philosophical statesman would rather hold, there is no need to conjecture. On the one side is the hope which grows out of righteousness; on the other is the despondency, under the mask of compassion, which follows upon the baffling of intrigues, and shrinks from the retribution which awaits a long successful tyranny.

"What is EMERSON doing?" is the question which has been often heard within the last two years. Everybody who knew him or his writings might know pretty well what he was about. When the actual conflict took its rise, thirty years ago, with the first co-operation of the Abolitionists, the question was asked, "What is EMERSON doing?" He was not joining in the organization, because he never joins any organization. He was doing more outside it than he could have done within it. Wherever he happened to be—in a lecture room, on board a steamer, travelling, or tea-drinking, he said what he thought, and especially he vindicated the liberty of speech of all who had anything to say. He denounced the tar-kettle and the burning of lecture-halls, and was the champion of every hunted Abolitionist, and the seconder of every citizen who moved that men's souls were their own. When Mr. SUMNER was struck down in the Senate, EMERSON stood forward in public meeting, and said the one true thing which was in fact a statement of the whole question. He said it remained to be shown how a barbaric and a civilized state of society could exist in union. When the Territories were to be saved by the free settlement of Kansas, he was the friend of the free settlers, in word and deed.[3] During the long melancholy struggle of Northern society to halt between two opinions he has never been heard of in that society; he was not of it; and he knew that it must learn for itself that the struggle was in vain. He waited, as wise men do wait—not in utter silence, but in patience—till the moment came for speech to be of use; and now that the right path, so long indicated, is taken, he hastens to clear away impediments which distress some weaker minded men. The difference between the large-minded and the narrow-minded man appears in the magnanimity and generous sympathy with which he treats of the delays and imperfections of President LINCOLN'S measure, while his rejoicing in the main scope of the Proclamation cannot be exceeded by that of the most "fanatical Abolitionist." He pays no heed to the clamour of parties over the details, and the collateral issues. He looks over the heads of the wranglers of the hour, being aware, as he says, that "at such times" (the times of great and high-principled political acts) "it appears as if a new public were created to greet the new event;" and we learn "that mankind are greater and better than we know." "Life in America had lost much of its attraction in the later years," he says. "The ill use of power makes life mean and the sunshine dark." But now "a day which most of us dared not hope to see, an event worth the dreadful war, worth its costs and uncertainties, seems now to be close before us. October, November, December will have passed over beating hearts and plotting brains; then the hour will strike, and all men of African descent who have faculty enough to make their way to our lines are assured of the protection of the American law."

The pith of the matter is, in his view, its being simply a righteous deed. "The force of the act is that it commits the country to this justice. This act makes that the lives of our heroes have not been sacrificed in vain. It makes a victory of our defeats. Our hurts are healed; the health of the nation is repaired. With a victory like this we can stand many disasters ... It relieves our race once for all of its crime and false position. The first condition of success is secured in putting ourselves right. The Government has assured itself of the best constituency in the world. Every spark of intellect, every virtuous feeling, every religious heart, every man of honour, every poet, every philosopher, the generosity of the cities, the health of the country, the strong arms of the mechanics, the endurance of farmers, the passionate conscience of women, the sympathy of distant nations—all rally to its support." Surely this is an odd time and occasion to choose for bewailing the woes and destiny of the people of the North, as our Secessionist journals are doing.[4]

A few words of EMERSON'S (and no man knows the negroes better) show that there is a good deal of mistake here about the Yankee feeling towards the nigger. "Meantime that ill-fated, much injured race which the Proclamation respects, will lose somewhat of the dejection sculptured for ages in their bronzed countenance, uttered in the wailing of their plaintive music—a race naturally benevolent, joyous, docile, industrious, and whose very miseries sprang from their great talent for usefulness, which, in a more moral age, will not only defend their independence, but will give them a rank among nations."

How infinitely mean do the flatterers of a slaveholding aristocracy appear in the presence of a contemplative philosopher whose contemplation and philosophy make him a patriot!

Notes

1. By "spokesmen of despotic government," Martineau could mean simply correspondents and leader writers in *The Times*, 2–8 November 1862, who describe misery and brutality in the "barbaric" North (whose cause is said to be hopeless) as opposed to a joyful, sure-to-be-successful spirit in the South. For Martineau's next sentence, cf. "*Daily News*, 24 September 1856," above.

2. In "The President's Proclamation" (10: 638–42), Emerson lauds Lincoln's "poetic" act as one of the "moments of expansion" in modern history. The unexpected proclamation, he asserts, shows the political sagacity of a hitherto under-appreciated Lincoln. *The Times*' leader of 8 November 1862 (8, cols. 5–6) accuses Lincoln and his party of assuming despotic powers in issuing a proclamation "which is to excite, if possible, an ignorant race to deeds of murder, lust, and rapine."

3. See "24 September 1856" and "*Daily News*, 15 November 1856," note 6. A free Kansas figured as part of the Republican platform of 1860; Kansas became a state in 1861. In 1856 Emerson had subscribed to the Concord relief fund for fighters in Kansas, and in 1859 he eulogized John Brown: (executed 2 December 1859 for his raid on Harpers Ferry): see Rusk.

4. I. e., *The Times* and (probably) the majority of London newspapers and journals: see notes 1 and 2 for example.

40. William Lloyd Garrison

Introduction

Historians debate the relevance of utilitarian faith in progress through individual pursuit of happiness, i.e., the common good of self-interest, to the intense burst of antislavery effort leading up to the American Civil War. In one view, nineteenth-century American reformers abandoned "the federal accommodation of slavery amid the widening social concerns of a new middle class of [Northern] manufacturers, merchants, entrepreneurs, and farmers" while Southern leaders' defense of slavery seemed anachronistic and corrupt.[1]

William Lloyd Garrison (1805–1879) embodied this confidence in the value of individual freedom with the added element of Calvinistic Puritanism. In late 1830, he came to Boston to launch the *Liberator* to promote immediate emancipation. On 1 January 1832, the New England Anti-Slavery Society, inspired by Garrison's ideas, held its first official meeting. In 1833, Garrison travelled to Britain to urge the wrongness of the Colonization scheme (see note 3), returning in 1840, 1846, 1867, and 1877. Fanatic, single-minded, and egocentric, Garrison had loyal followers but aroused hatred and persecution. Unable to work with others, he led colleagues to brand him a new "pope." In autumn 1859, however, he was deeply affected by John Brown's sacrifice at Harpers Ferry (cf. introduction, *"Daily News*, 24 September 1856" and *"Daily News*, 11 November 1862," note 3) and turned from "non-resistance" to the search for a political end to slavery.

Another of Garrison's beliefs—political equality for women—served the antislavery crusade well. Maria Weston

Chapman, Garrison's "lieutenant" and member of the (Garrisonian) Boston Female Anti-Slavery Society, in 1835 recruited Martineau as a member. Martineau seems to have been charmed by the handsome Mrs. Chapman and calls Garrison "the most bewitching personage I . . . met in the United States."

In "The Martyr Age of the United States of America" (*Westminster Review* 32 [December 1838]: 1–59), which helped to confirm Garrison's reputation in Britain, Martineau labels him "one of God's nobility." When she could not serve as a delegate from the Massachusetts Anti-Slavery Society to the World's Anti-Slavery Convention in London in 1840, Garrison announced he would travel to Tynemouth to see her. (He missed her in 1846, when she had left for Egypt.) In 1867, Martineau wrote to tell Garrison that seeing him would produce such "strong emotion" she feared for her life. In all her [American] antislavery writing, Martineau supports Garrison's rigid dedication to unconditional emancipation. She kept his portrait, carried home in 1836, prominently on her wall and corresponded with him up to a month before her death.[2]

Notes

1. Louis S. Gerteis, *Morality and Utility in American Antislavery Reform* (Chapel Hill: U of North Carolina P, 1987), 4.
2. See *William Lloyd Garrison: 1805–1879. The Story of His Life Told by His Children*, 4 vols. (New York: Century, 1889).

* * * *

Daily News
9 January 1866

While the American newspapers show us that good citizens feel the present Christmas and New Year the happiest they have ever known, as the first which have risen upon a nation of free men,[1] it is fitting that the world should remember those to whom these seasons must be the happiest of all. Among the newspapers brought by the last mail is *The Liberator*, which closes its existence with the year that is gone; and in it we read, "With our own hands we have put in type the unspeakably cheering announcement" of the abolition of slavery in the whole territory of the United States.[2] The man who has lived to do this is the same who with his own hands put into type, above thirty years ago, the first call upon his country and nation to put away their great sin and avoid the retribution to come. The career of WILLIAM LLOYD GARRISON is one of deep and instructive interest in itself; but it is also so implicated with the great events and influences of his time, that some understanding of it is necessary to any true appreciation of the great issue of the civil war.

Five-and-thirty years ago the main anxiety of the Southern slaveholders, anxiously kept from the knowledge of the world outside, was that the great increase of mulattoes endangered the political operations and the social condition of the Slave States. The white fathers of that race favoured their own offspring, and when the slaves on the estate became too numerous, the light-complexioned ones were emancipated instead of sold. To remedy this increase of freed people of colour, laws were passed compelling the sale of slaves and punishing their liberation. The consequence was the formation of the notorious *Colonization Society*—the hopeless device of the slaveholders for the deportation of their surplus "hands," and especially of those most troublesome from either ability or stupidity. The scheme naturally took hold of the ignorant sympathies of humane people, as well as relieved the perplexities of the more conscientious slaveholders. We need not relate the story of its failure.[3] What concerns us now is, that GARRISON was among the humane persons at first deceived, and that he was the first true man who saw through and exposed it. It was in 1829 that, while a poor student at a country college in New England, he heard of the Colonization Society, and supposed, as he was told, that a way had been found for the blacks out of slavery. With his characteristic integrity, he chose to investigate the scheme for himself; and with his characteristic sagacity, he saw through it as soon as he went to the slaveholding city of Baltimore. The inevitable consequence was that he became an abolitionist, at a time when there was no sympathy and no help to be had in a course so mischievous and so heretical. In a little while he was in gaol for having expressed in a newspaper his view of a slave-trading transaction by a New England merchant.[4] His fine for the libel was paid by an entire stranger, Mr. ARTHUR TAPPAN, of New York, who thereby showed that a second abolitionist had risen up already.[5] Presently there were four, sitting in a garret with their feet upon a wood pile, engaging with each other that slavery should be abolished in their country. Then was issued the first number of the *Liberator*, the last number of which will arrive by the next mail. GARRISON and a friend lived in a garret on bread and water, spending their earnings as printers and their spare time on this newspaper; and when it sold unusually well, they treated themselves to a bowl of milk, as the friend told us afterwards. In the first number of that newspaper was uttered the oracle which we have seen fulfilled. "I am in earnest," said GARRISON, on New Year's Day of 1831—"I will not equivocate—I will not excuse—I will not retreat a single inch— AND I WILL BE HEARD." "The apathy of the people," of which he complained, occasioned this language, and the event has justified it.

One of the most fortunate circumstances in the case has been, from first to last, that GARRISON holds the Quaker principle of non-resistance, and that this was a conspicuous feature of his conduct throughout his long conflict. It was sure to be said that he wanted to rouse the slaves to insurrection; and for many years this was said: but the slaves knew better. The Southampton massacre, which happened before his voice could reach the South, was the last negro rising in the United States.[6] Up to that time, there had been on an average one every year; but from the hour when it was known on the plantations that somebody was astir on their behalf in the Free States, there were no more insurrections, because there was no more despair. Thus was GARRISON counselling peace and patience on the part of the slaves, and securing life and property to the owners, while these latter gentry were crying out upon him as an incendiary, and setting a price upon his head. He never knew the sense of personal safety for many years from this time. Every door was closed against him, except those of comrades who were in almost equal danger; and our elder generation remembers the time when, in the autumn of 1835, he was dragged through the streets of Boston with a halter around his neck, and the tar-kettle heating at the end of the march.[7] A stout arm thrust him into the gaol, and saved him then; but nothing could save him and the few who gathered round him from the utmost contumely and injury that social rancour could inflict. As none of these things moved his noble and serene temper, and as they could not touch him in his happy home, in which poverty itself was scarcely an evil, his work prospered. By degrees his doctrine won its way, and his conscience has at length converted that of his nation. He moulded those who came near him to his own likeness, and his early coadjutors were worthy of him.

It need scarcely be pointed out that he must have failed in a political task so arduous—so apparently impossible—as that of regenerating the idolised constitution of his country, in such a matter as the institution of Slavery, if he had brought to the work no better qualifications than the "one-idea's fanaticism" which was ascribed to him, against all evidence, for thirty years.[8] In any future historical review of the case, the most striking feature of his mind and his course will probably be his political sagacity. He has been so constantly right in his anticipations, and so successful in his counsels, that few will now question that if his countrymen had had courage and conscience enough to follow his lead at an earlier time, the inevitable revolution might have been wrought without warfare and without ruin to any section of the country. Of those who had his sagacity too few had the courage or conscience to put their hand to the work in time. We now see also that some who had the courage and conscience, but had not the sagacity, have failed in the last stage of the conflict, and are now rather a hindrance than a help to the settlement of society, and the prospects of the negroes in whose rescue they have been as devoted as GARRISON himself[9]—the MOSES of the coloured race, to whom they looked, in reasonable trust, to bring them out of bondage.

The crowning glory of this man's career is doubtless in what some, who really are the fanatics that he never was, regard as its eclipse. His unerring sense, untouched by any self-regards, perceived the right moment for exchanging rebuke for encouragement—antagonism for fellowship—the intrepidity of the martyr for the sympathy of the comrade.[10] It was no pleasure to him to be before his nation and his time; and therefore when his nation and his time had come up with him and the right, he fell into their ranks, and thought no more of any personal distinction that belonged to him. Thus he has saved himself from being left behind, as some more ambitious men now find themselves. When slavery was at an end, he saw that Abolition Societies should come to an end. When the liberation of the negroes was effected, he saw that *The Liberator* should stop. When the Government and the people showed their willingness to do right, he saw that the need for invective, reproach, and avowed suspicion was gone by, and that the hour had come for helping the authorities, instead of rendering their great task impracticable. Because he saw this earlier than some others, he was scorned by them as a backslider; and now, when he devotes himself to the welfare of the freed people, and would bring them into harmony with their white neighbours, and unite the two races in a common citizenship and mutual interest, he is regarded as a trimmer by zealots who, if they were not a small minority, would end by driving the PRESIDENT and his government into the arms of the South, and kindling a war of races as a sequel to the civil war. The difference between the two sorts of abolitionists evidently is that the one takes a narrow view and the other a wide one. GARRISON has always looked further ahead and abroad than either his friends or his enemies; and it seems that he does so now. We need not institute any moral comparison. It is enough for us to recognise the hero and the patriot as worthy of the highest honour at the moment when he quietly becomes one with his neighbours, and when he ceases to preach simply because his preaching has wrought out its purpose, and the time for working in common has come. This great hour finds him with congenial work before him in the case of the freed negroes.[11] We may not hear much of him henceforth. He said he would be heard; he was heard effectually; and now he proposes to be silent. It is to be hoped that we shall not for such a reason forget him. History certainly will not; and if she relates that before the second American revolution the nation had so sunk that the world taunted it with having no great men, she will add that this was a mistake, for that there was one great man—the second printer's journeyman who did a great work for his country—WILLIAM LLOYD GARRISON.

Notes

1. The New York *Tribune* noted that "Nature seemed to join the general jubilee" (26 December 1865: 1, col. 1) and reviewed Civil War events in "The Year of Triumph" (1 January 1866: 1, cols. 1–6); the New York *Times* extolled "The Era of Statesmen—Mr. Seward and Mr. Stanton" (30 December 1865: 4, cols. 3–4); while the New York *Herald* reported "Santa Claus among the Soldiers and the Children" (26 December 1865: 1, col. 1). In fact, these were isolated stories.

2. Founded by Garrison and his partner, Isaac Knapp, the *Liberator* ran from 1 January 1831 to 29 December 1865. Garrison's "Valedictory" (206 [2], cols. 2–3) recounts his early connections with philanthropic newspapers, his struggle to gain a hearing for the *Liberator*, and his present happiness at being free of the martyr's role.

3. In "The Slave Trade in 1858" (see introduction, "*Daily News*, 25 November 1856"), Martineau sketches the origin and activities of the Colonization Society, formed by Southerners to send free blacks and restive slaves to Liberia. In her early *Demerara. A Tale* [*Illustrations of Political Economy. No. IV.*] (London: Charles Fox, 1832), Martineau gave a utopian view of the Colonization Society's efforts.

4. In the weekly *Genius of Universal Emancipation* (published in Baltimore from 1829 with Benjamin Lundy), Garrison attacked Francis Todd—owner of a vessel from Newburyport, Massachusetts, Garrison's home town—for carrying slaves from Baltimore to New Orleans. Garrison was jailed for libel.

5. Wealthy philanthropist Arthur Tappan (1786–1865) was also an early member of the Colonization Society; in December 1833, he and Garrison helped found the American Anti-Slavery Society.

6. The Southampton Insurrection, led by Nat Turner, took place in Virginia in 1831.

7. Martineau gives accounts of 21 October 1835—when she passed through Boston and when Garrison, mistaken for British abolitionist George Thompson, was mobbed—in *Society in America* (1: 169–76) and *Autobiography* (2: 23–25).

8. Garrison denounced the Constitution, which allowed for slavery, as "a covenant with death and an agreement with hell." After passage of the Kansas-Nebraska Act in 1854 (cf. introduction, "*Daily*

News, 15 November 1856"), Garrison publicly burned a copy of the Constitution.

    9. Garrison retired as president of the American Anti-Slavery Society in May 1865 and was succeeded by Wendell Phillips.

    10. Garrison came to accept the Republican Party, Lincoln, the Union, and the use of force in place of pacifism in abolishing slavery. Cf. John L. Thomas, *The Liberator. William Lloyd Garrison* (Boston: Little, Brown, 1963).

    11. Garrison had become active in the Freemen's Aid Society; he also continued to support the Republican radicals, who opposed President Andrew Johnson's Reconstruction policies.

Appendix

Harriet Martineau's Contributions to the London *Daily News*

MONTH/DAY		LEADER NO.	SUBJECT	FIRST WORDS
			1852	
May	10	3	Emigration to Australia	EVERY mail
	15	3	Emigration to Australia	"THERE is nothing new"
	17	3	Sport as preparation for militia	WE have spent the winter
	19	3	Burial practices	THE cholera
	21	1	Emigration to Australia	THERE must be
	31	2	Emigration to Australia	WHILE nobody
June	5	1	Emigration to Australia	WHILST Parliament
	8	2	Emigration to Australia: governesses	A VERY practical
	17	3	Right of public meeting	FOR seven years
	18	2	Public opinion and sanitary reform	LAST night
	24	1	Lord Malmesbury's sympathy with despots	[from 3rd paragraph] Whilst we have

MONTH/DAY		LEADER NO.	SUBJECT	FIRST WORDS
	28	3	Unchristian conduct of Christians—the Newman-Achilli case	THE weekly
July	1	3	Democracy in Australia	SOME years ago
	3	3	Gardens for the people	IT is within
	7	2	Imprisonment at Charleston of Pereira, a colored British seaman	THE case
	13	1	Henry Clay	THE mail
	19	1	U.S.A.	ENGLISHMEN
	20	2	Franklin Pierce	THE plot
	23	3	Agriculture	THE annual meetings
	23	[p. 3, col. 6]	THE BARONESS VON BECK. [and Birmingham] [letter signed "FAIR PLAY."]	
	24	3	Sports	A PAMPHLET
August	2	3	Cotton	ENGLAND is far
	13	[p. 4, cols. 4–5]	LETTERS FROM IRELAND—No. I. LOUGH FOYLE AND ITS ENVIRONS.	
	17	[p. 4, cols. 4–5]	LETTERS FROM IRELAND—II. WEST OF ULSTER—WEEDS—LONDON COMPANIES—TEMPLE-MOYLE AGRICULTURAL SCHOOL.	

MONTH/DAY		LEADER NO.	SUBJECT	FIRST WORDS
	19	[p. 4, cols. 4–5]	LETTERS FROM IRELAND—III. THE DERRY AND COLERAINE RAILWAY—PRODUCE AND TRAFFIC OF THE DISTRICT—BEAUTIFUL SCENERY—WHAT CAN PUBLIC WORKS DO FOR IRELAND?	
	21	[p. 4, cols. 4–5]	LETTERS FROM IRELAND—IV. THE LINEN MANUFACTURE—FLAX GROWING AND DRESSING.	
	23	[p. 4, cols. 4–5]	LETTERS FROM IRELAND—V. AGRICULTURAL IMPROVEMENT IN ULSTER.	
	25	[p. 4, cols. 4–5]	LETTERS FROM IRELAND—VI. IRELAND DYING OF TOO MUCH DOCTORING—THE "TENANT RIGHT" QUESTION.	
	27	[p. 4, cols. 4–5]	LETTERS FROM IRELAND—VII. HOW IRELAND IS TO GET BACK ITS WOODS.	
	30	[p. 4, cols. 4–5]	LETTERS FROM IRELAND—VIII. LEINSTER—IRISH INDUSTRY—RELIGIOUS FEUDS.	
	31	[p. 4, cols. 3–4]	LETTERS FROM IRELAND—IX. THE WOMEN.	
September	2	[p. 4, cols. 3–4]	LETTERS FROM IRELAND—X. [no subtitle]	
	3	[p. 4, cols. 4–5]	LETTERS FROM IRELAND—XI. [no subtitle]	
	7	[p. 4, cols. 3–4]	LETTERS FROM IRELAND—XII. CONNEMARA.	

MONTH/DAY	LEADER NO.	SUBJECT	FIRST WORDS
8	[p. 4, cols. 2–4]	LETTERS FROM IRELAND—XIII. THE PEOPLE AND THE CLERGY.	
13	[p. 4, cols. 3–4]	LETTERS FROM IRELAND—XIV. ENGLISH SETTLERS IN THE "WILDS OF THE WEST."	
14	[p. 4, cols. 3–4]	LETTERS FROM IRELAND—XV. ACHILL.	
17	[p. 4, cols. 3–4]	LETTERS FROM IRELAND—XVI. THE WILDS OF ERRIS.	
18	[p. 4, cols. 3–4]	LETTERS FROM IRELAND—XVII. [no subtitle]	
21	[p. 4, cols. 3–4]	LETTERS FROM IRELAND—XVIII. IRISH LANDLORDS AND IRISH POTATOES.	
25	[p. 4, cols. 3–4]	LETTERS FROM IRELAND—XIX. LANDLORDS, PRIESTS, AND VOTERS.	
28	[p. 4, cols. 3–5]	LETTERS FROM IRELAND—XX. THE WORKHOUSES.	
29	[p. 4, cols. 4–5]	LETTERS FROM IRELAND—XXI. KILLARNEY.	
30	[p. 4, cols. 2–3]	LETTERS FROM IRELAND—XXII. THE RIVAL CHURCHES.	

MONTH/DAY		LEADER NO.	SUBJECT	FIRST WORDS
October	2	[p. 4, cols. 3–5]	LETTERS FROM IRELAND—XXIII. [no subtitle]	
	4	[p. 4, cols. 3–5]	LETTERS FROM IRELAND—XXIV. [no subtitle]	
	8	[p. 4, cols. 3–4]	LETTERS FROM IRELAND—XXV. PRIESTS AND LANDLORDS—NEW FEATURES OF IRISH LIFE.	
	13	[p. 4, cols. 3–4]	LETTERS FROM IRELAND—XXVI. EMIGRATION AND EDUCATION.	
	14	[p. 4, cols. 3–5]	LETTERS FROM IRELAND—XXVII. THE PEOPLE AND THE TWO CHURCHES.	
	20	1	The Senate and expansionism	MONTH by month
	27	1	West Indian sugar industry	[from 2nd paragraph] While the slightest
November	1	3	Protestant vs. Catholic	WHO calls
	5	3	Self-reform of working men [Saturday half-holidays]	THE working men
	10	3	National Poor Law Association	THERE was recently
	17	[p. 4, cols. 5–6]	SLAVE-TRADING IN ENGLAND. [letter signed "A. Z."]	

MONTH/DAY		LEADER NO.	SUBJECT	FIRST WORDS
	19	1	Wellington	Our WELLINGTON
	19	3	Franklin Pierce	THE news
	20	2	National Poor Law Association	OUR remarks
	26	2	Irish land	THE House of Commons
	29	[p. 7, cols. 1–2]	MISS BERRY—A BEQUEST FROM THE LAST CENTURY. [obit.]	
December	1	[p. 4, cols. 4–5]	THE PICTURE OF PRESENT PROSPERITY. [letter signed "A. Z."]	
	11	2	Franklin Pierce	WHEN the news
	16	2	Tenant right [Ireland]	THE Tenant Right Question
	18	3	Cubans	ENGLISH travellers
	20	2	Jamaica	THE recent meeting
	21	3	Cuba	YESTERDAY the Message
	28	2	Imprisonment of Pereira at Charleston	A CASE of hardship

1853

January	3	1	Colonialism	THERE is scarcely
	5	2	Jamaica	OUR remarks

MONTH/DAY		LEADER NO.	SUBJECT	FIRST WORDS
	10	3	U. S. foreign establishment	IT is not often
	11	3	Newman-Achilli case	HILARY
	14	[p. 4, cols. 4–5]	THE CASE OF THE CONVICT KIRWAN. [letter signed "M."]	
	18	1	Agriculture	WE should be very glad
	21	3	Exclusion of free-soilers from Senate Committees	SOME American news
	22	1	Wool supply; need for agricultural statistics	IT is of consequence
	26	3	Drainage	IT is the privilege
	27	[p. 2, cols. 1–2]	LITERATURE. *Essays on Political and Social Science. Contributed chiefly to the "Edinburgh Review."* By WM. R. GREG. 2 vols. Longmans. [review]	
February	2	[p. 5, cols. 3–5]	MR. COBDEN AND THE WARS WITH FRANCE. [review of Cobden letters, "1793 & 1853."]	
	3	3	Jamaica	SINCE the meeting
	3	[p. 2, col. 1]	LITERATURE. *Villette.* By CURRER BELL. Smith, Elder, and Co. [review]	
	7	3	Agricultural labor	A LETTER
	9	2	Farmers' problems	FARMERS are among

MONTH/DAY		LEADER NO.	SUBJECT	FIRST WORDS
	14	2	Gervinus, persecution by Grand Duke of Baden	GERVINUS
	21	3	Monroe Doctrine	Mr. CASS
	22	1	Juvenile delinquents	LORD JOHN RUSSELL
March	3	2	International copyright	GOOD news
	7	3	Agricultural returns in the Irish census	WHEN the mind
	14	1	Gervinus	THE Grand Duke
	15	3	Maine Law [prohibition]	IT is very interesting
	17	2	Irish sugar	SOME recent
	21	3	President Pierce	FOR many months
	22	2	Education	THE nation is in
	24	[p. 2, cols. 1–2]	LITERATURE. *White, Red, Black Sketches of Society in the United States during the Visit of their Guest.* By FRANCIS and TERESA PULSZKY. 3 vols. [review; on Kossuth visit]	
	25	1	Divorce	THE Commissioners
	25	3	Colored seamen	[from 3rd paragraph] The facts of

MONTH/DAY		LEADER NO.	SUBJECT	FIRST WORDS
	26	3	Agricultural wages, poaching and Game Laws	THE movement
	30	2	Italy	THERE has been an illumination
April	2	3	Two requirements: improved food production and education	IT is a sign
	7	1	Education	WE must again
	11	1	Education and juvenile delinquency	WE are enabled
	13	2	Dwellings	[from 2nd paragraph] Though we cannot
	15	2	Statistical returns in agricultural	A PIECE
	22	2	Cotton; Harriet Beecher Stowe and *Dred*	MANY people
	25	2	International copyright	READERS, publishers
	28	2	Budget prospects	[from 2nd paragraph] We feel it useful
	30	3	Education	A LETTER from Mr. BAINES
May	3	1	Ireland	[from 2nd paragraph] In 1737,
	5	3	Education	IN the midst
	6	2	Weather, crops and sanitation	THE sun

MONTH/DAY		LEADER NO.	SUBJECT	FIRST WORDS
	9	1	Abolition: Harriet Beecher Stowe	[from 2nd paragraph] When the first Anti-Slavery
	12	1	Defective internal communications—India	[from 2nd paragraph] Amidst all the differences
	19	3	Defective internal communications—India	THE inhabitants of South America
	20	2	India	[from 2nd paragraph] If it be said
	24	2	Cheese	MEN always
	25	2	Education and charitable trusts	THE LORD PRESIDENT
	28	2	Agriculture	THE Royal Agricultural
June	7	2	India	LAST night's
	10	2	Conventual visitation	THERE are rumours
	11	2	Agricultural progress	THE amount
	15	1	Russian Czars: history	AT a time
	16	1	Stockport strike	YESTERDAY
	23	3	Idiocy	ON Thursday
	24	3	Endowed schools	A PUBLIC meeting
	25	2	Fish	THERE is a recent

MONTH/DAY		LEADER NO.	SUBJECT	FIRST WORDS
	28	3	Labor	EVERYTHING
	30	[p. 2, col. 1]	LITERATURE. *Memorandums made in Ireland in the Autumn of 1852.* By JOHN FORBES, M. D., F. R. S., &c. Smith, Elder, and Co. [review; from 2nd paragraph]	
July	4	2	Ragged schools	SOCIETY admires
	5	3	Irish education	THE serious question
	7	3	Southern Convention	THE issue
	13	1	Russia	[from 1st paragraph] The less disposed
	16	[p. 5, cols. 2–3]	TRANSPORTATION AND EDUCATION. [letter signed "A PRACTICAL REFORMER."]	
	18	[p. 4, cols. 4–5]	SAVINGS BANKS DEFALCATIONS. [letter signed "A FOUNDER OF A SAVINGS BANK."]	
	20	2	Russia	THE funds
	22	2	Reformatories	IT is with keen
	27	3	American railway	OUR active
	28	3	Arterial drainage	"YOU have learned"
August	2	1	Irish schools	THE danger

MONTH/DAY		LEADER NO.	SUBJECT	FIRST WORDS
	4	2	Crystal Palace at Birmingham	THE idea
	5	3	Agriculture	THE agricultural meeting
	9	2	Health legislation	ONE of the most pregnant
	10	2	Labor troubles and parliamentary reform	IF we are a nation
	11	2	Jamaica	PARLIAMENT having
	13	3	Colored seamen	THERE is a question
	17	3	Slave trade	A LETTER
	19	[p. 4, cols. 5–6]	THE SHORT HAY CROP.	
	23	2	Education	A DEPUTATION
	24	1	Slave trade	WE are now
	25	2	Honors for authors	OUR English public
	25	3	Guano supply	ONE of the last
	31	[p. 4, cols. 4–5]	THE SEWING MACHINE. [letter signed "AN ENGLISHWOMAN."]	
September	2	[p. 2, cols. 1–2]	THE LABOUR MARKET AND THE EMPLOYMENT OF CONVICTS. [letter signed "A PRACTICAL REFORMER."]	

MONTH/DAY	LEADER NO.	SUBJECT	FIRST WORDS
3	1	Fish culture	NO one can
3	[p. 5, cols. 1–2]	COAL AT SINAI.	
6	2	Fever at New Orleans	THE mail
7	2	Irish prosperity	THE QUEEN'S
7	[p. 4, cols. 5–6]	SUNDAY STEAMERS IN SCOTLAND. [letter signed "FAIR PLAY."]	
8	3	Brutality to women	ONE domestic subject
10	2	Observatory	THESE September days
13	3	U. S. A., Cuba, and end of repudiation	THE news
17	1	Administrative weaknesses in England [sanitary reform]	THE events of the day
17	2	Machines in agriculture	A LEADING topic
24	3	Cholera in Newcastle	THERE has hardly been
24	[p. 7, cols. 2–3]	LITERATURE. *Oakfield; or, Fellowship in the East.* By PUNJABEE [William Delafield Arnold]. 2 vols. Longman and Co. [review]	
26	3	Sanitation and peat charcoal	PRINCE ALBERT
27	3	Reformatories and the status of labor	The newspapers

MONTH/DAY		LEADER NO.	SUBJECT	FIRST WORDS
October	28	2	Coal trade	IT is a long time
	4	1	U. S. A.	BY the latest arrival
	8	1	Peace meeting	THE Peace Conference
	11	1	Cuba	WE gave at length
	14	1	Coal supply	SOMETHING
	20	1	Peace conferences	IT can hardly
	21	1	Strikes	FOR a good while
November	1	1	Strikes	THERE is probably
	4	3	Maurice's dismissal from King's College	THERE had been an under-current
	7	3	Economy of food	THE best
	23	3	Constitutional monarchy	IT seems
	24	[p. 2, col. 1]	A TREATISE ON THE PROPAGATION OF SALMON AND OTHER FISH. By EDWARD AND THOMAS ASHWORTH. Stockport: E. H. King. London: Simpkin and Marshall. [review]	
	25	1	French free trade	IF the Emperor
	26	3	Fog	THE London
	28	3	Railway extension and prosperity	IN the matter-of-fact

MONTH/DAY		LEADER NO.	SUBJECT	FIRST WORDS
	29	3	Cuba	THE American mail
December	1	2	Winter in England	TO-DAY we begin
	2	[p. 3, col. 1]	PARALYSING INFLUENCE OF FOREIGN LOANS. [letter signed "Z."]	
	2	[p. 3, col. 2]	THE CHINESE REVOLUTION. [letter signed "FANQUI."]	
	12	[p. 2, cols. 1–2]	DEATH OF MRS. OPIE. [obit.]	
	12	2	Water supply	THE deputations
	13	3	Agricultural statistics	THE most important
	14	3	Queen of Spain	"THE suspension of the Cortes"
	16	[p. 2, cols. 2–3]	[under NEW BOOKS.] *Essays on Agriculture*. By the late THOMAS GISBOURNE, Esq. Murray, 1854. [review]	
	17	3	Cattle	CHRISTMAS approaches
	19	1	Palmerston	THESE are trying
	20	1	President's message	THE AMERICAN PRESIDENT'S
	24	1	Christmas	CHRISTMAS-EVE
	26	[p. 4, cols. 4–5]	THE FOREIGN POLICY OF CROMWELL AND THAT OF LORD ABERDEEN. [letter signed "Z."]	

MONTH/DAY		LEADER NO.	SUBJECT	FIRST WORDS
	27	2	Temperance	YESTERDAY'S Holiday
	(29)[1]			
	30	[p. 6, col. 1]	A WORD ABOUT CHRISTMAS [letter signed "Z."]	
			1854	
January	2	2	Armaments	IN the present
	6	[p. 4, col. 6]	THE STRIKES. BIRMINGHAM AND BIRMINGHAM MEN. (FROM A SPECIAL CORRESPONDENT.)	
	13	[p. 2, cols. 1–2]	LITERATURE. *The Westminster Review.* New Series. No. IX. January, 1854. Chapman. [review]	
	13	2	The Czar and Napoleon	EVERY century
	14	[p. 4, cols. 4–5]	THE COMING REFORM BILLS. [letter signed "A REFORMER."]	
	16	3	Paper	MANY things
	18	1	The Circassians	ONE of the first
	20	3	Changed conditions of warfare	WHILST Naval
	24	1	Russian consistency in the Crimea	THE more imminent
	24	[p. 5, col. 5]	IRELAND. MORE SIGNS OF 'PROGRESS.'	

MONTH/DAY		LEADER NO.	SUBJECT	FIRST WORDS
	28	[p. 4, cols. 4–5]	IF THE CZAR FIGHTS, WHAT SHOULD BE DONE? [letter signed "ONE WHO REMEMBERS GEORGE THE THIRD."]	
	30	2	Limited liability and labor	THE discussion
	30	[p. 4, cols. 4–5]	THE FIGHTING AT KALAFAT [letter signed "A. Z."]	
February	3	2	Russian Christianity	SOME excellent
	4	[p. 4, cols. 5–6—p. 5, col. 1]	A WORD OR TWO ABOUT THE WAR [letter on prevention of disease, signed "A. Z."]	
	18	1	War	LORD JOHN RUSSELL
	20	2	Turkey	LORD GREY
	24	2	War aims	FRANCE and England
March[2]	1	2	Paper duty	THE CHANCELLOR
	2	2	The Allies	ON the opening
	4	2	Arms	THE more the Government
	6	1	Russian Christianity	[from 2nd paragraph] Thus the Czar
	8	3	Shortage of tallow	ONE inconvenience
	11	2	Preston strike	THE Preston

MONTH/DAY	LEADER NO.	SUBJECT	FIRST WORDS
14	1	Reform	[from 2nd paragraph?] The people of Great Britain[3]
17	2	Labor parliament in Manchester	THE "Labour Parliament"
21	3	American industry and labor relations	WE have already
22	2	Truck system	THE arrest
24	[p. 4, cols. 5–6]	A GLANCE AT THE BALTIC.—REVEL.—ST. PETERSBURG.—THE CZAR. [letter signed "COSMOPOLITE."]	
28	2	Telegraph	FOR many months
31	2	Strikes and war	"ENGLAND expects"
April 1	2	Arterial drainage, etc.	A BRILLIANT Spring
3	1	War	THE Russians
5	[p. 4, col. 6—p. 5, cols. 1–2]	DEATH OF PROFESSOR WILSON. [obit.]	
6	2	The Baltic	IT was at the end
8	2	Austria and Prussia	LORD DUDLEY STUART
10[4]	[p. 2, cols. 1–2]	LITERATURE. *The Westminster Review for April*. Chapman. [review]	

MONTH/DAY	LEADER NO.	SUBJECT	FIRST WORDS
10	[p. 4, cols. 4–5]	A WORD ABOUT THE CZAR'S VICTIMS IN SIBERIA. [letter signed "COSMOPOLITE".]	
14	2	Ireland and the War	WE wonder
15	2	Napoleon and Austria	IF any one wishes
18	2	Greece	THE first remark
19	1	Russian resources	ENGLISH and French troops
20	[p. 2, cols. 2–3]	[under LITERATURE.] *The West Indies, before and since Slave Emancipation.* By JOHN DAVY, M. D. F. R. S., &c., Inspector-General of Army Hospitals. Cash and Co. [review]	
21	3	Prisioners of war	THE electric telegraph
22	2	Austria	A CABINET
26	1	Fast day	THIS day
27	1	Sweden	"IN order to blockade"
28	1	Abd-el-Kader	[from 2nd paragraph] The secondary alliances
29	2	The war	BY accounts
29	[p. 4, cols. 4–6]	DEATH OF THE MARQUIS OF ANGLESEY. [obit.]	

MONTH/DAY	LEADER NO.	SUBJECT	FIRST WORDS
29	1	Denmark	[from 3rd paragraph] By the secret articles
2	2	Finns	GLIMPSES
5	1	War	WE are now told
6	2	Prussia	A TREATY of commerce
8	2	Norway	THE letter
9	2	War	IT was rather
13	2	Germany	[from 2nd inch] The German Princes or The talk about
16	2	Baltic	THE crisis
17	3	Proposal to take Archangel	WHILE everybody
20	1	The war	THE blows
23	3	Turkey	IN reading
24	3	Jews	THE pathetic
27	[p. 5, cols. 2–4]	[under LITERATURE.] *German Letters on English Education.* By Dr. L. WIESE, Professor in the Royal Foundation School at Joachimatal. Translated by W. D. ARNOLD, Lieutenant 58th Regiment B. N. I. Longmans. [review]	
29	1	Austria	[from 2nd inch] ?In all memories

MONTH/DAY		LEADER NO.	SUBJECT	FIRST WORDS
	30	1	Russia	[from 2nd paragraph] The Czar must
June	1	1	Prussia	PRUSSIA signs
	3	2	War at sea	YEARS hence,
	5	1	War	WE gave exclusively,
	6	[p. 3, col. 3]	ACCIDENTS TO WHITSUN HOLIDAY MAKERS	[letter signed "A. Z."]
	7	2	Scandinavia	EVERY letter
	8	3	Baltic	ALL the battles
	9	2	Denmark	THE letter
	12	2	Portugal	THE spectacle
	13	[p. 3, col. 5]	AGRICULTURAL STATISTICS.	
	13	3	Flogging and fagging	THE painful
	15	2	Prussia, Holland, and Belgium	COLONEL MANTEUFFEL,
	17	2	The independence of Georgia	THE war has
	22	2	Napier and Nelson	[from 2nd inch] ?It was a complaint
	24	3	Poland	MOST truly
	26	2	Turkey	THE present

MONTH/DAY		LEADER NO.	SUBJECT	FIRST WORDS
	27	2	The capture of Tornea	THE letter
	28	2	Divorce	"DIVORCE AND MATRIMONIAL CAUSES"
	29	2	Public schools	WE may well
July	3	3	Poland	PETITIONS
	4	1	Austria and the war	[from 2nd paragraph] Nothing that has occurred
	5	2	Nurses	THE revelations
	8	1	Austria	[from 2nd paragraph] "Why should the Allies"
	8	[p. 5, col. 2]	SLAVERY IN AMERICA. [letter signed "A REPUBLICAN."]	
	10	1	Spain	WE have news
	10	[p. 4, cols. 5–6—p. 5, col. 1]	THE CZAR'S BIRTHDAY. A ROYAL "FESTIVAL" IN ST. PETERSBURG.	
	11	1	Austrian alliance and Ministerial responsibility	[from 5th inch]
	12	1	War	[from 2nd paragraph] "The belief"
	13	1	American military backwardness	TO-MORROW

MONTH/DAY		LEADER NO.	SUBJECT	FIRST WORDS
	15	3	Wallachia	HOW are matters
	17	[p. 4, cols. 4–6]	A "KEY" TO AUSTRIA'S POLICY: METTERNICH.	
	18	2	Russian weakness	IT is rather surprising
	22	3	Saving rags for paper	THERE is a way
	24	[p. 2, cols. 1–2]	LITERATURE. THE NEW EDITION OF SYDNEY SMITH. *The Works of the Rev. Sydney Smith*. 3 vols. Longmans. [review]	
	25	2	Russia in Spain and U. S. A.	WHILST the news
	26	1	Egypt	ABBAS PACHA
	27	2	Fishery	THERE are young
	29	1	Nationalism	ONE of BONAPARTE'S
August	1	1	Russia and U. S. A.	IT is the custom
	3	1	War-demand for action	WHEN we went
	4	2	Sabbatarianism	WHEN attention
	8	1	War	TO the careful watcher
	10	1	Denmark	WHILST the allied fleets
	11	1	Czar and Queen Victoria	WHILST the Muscovites

MONTH/DAY		LEADER NO.	SUBJECT	FIRST WORDS
	12	1	Review of the Session	[from 2nd paragraph?] To-day a Royal Speech[5]
	12	3	Paper supply	THE CHANCELLOR of the EXCHEQUER
	14	1	War	THE letters
	14	3	Queen in Parliament	ON Saturday
	15	[p. 2, cols. 1–2]	LITERATURE. *Miscellaneous Works of the Right Hon. Sir James Mackintosh.* Three vols. Longman. [review]	
	16	1	Aland Islands	THERE is no doubt
	17	[p. 4, col. 4]	THE SATURDAY AFTERNOON QUESTION. [letter signed "A REFORMER."]	
	18	2	Russian weakness	WHILST Sir CHARLES NAPIER
	22	2	Russia and U. S. A.	NO longer ago
	23	1	Prussia	THE Aland Islands
	25	1	Russian history	EVERY day
	26	2	Russian weakness	THERE is a sentence
	28	1	War in the Crimea	WELL-INFORMED
	29	1	Break-up of the 1815 settlement	THE plot is thickening
September	1	1	War in the Crimea	A REPORT

MONTH/DAY		LEADER NO.	SUBJECT	FIRST WORDS
	4	3	Accidents	THE season
	[6][6]			
	9	2	Crystal Palace	AS the summer
	12	2	Slavery	THE foes
	13	3	Health	ONE day last week
	21	2	Spain	THE news
	23	2	The season	LONDON
	25	3	Crimea	WHILE awaiting
	27	[p. 4, cols. 3–5]	DEATH OF LORD DENMAN. [obit.]	
	28	1	Crimea	NOW that English troops
	29	1	Baltic	RUMOURS
	29	3	Czar	"NEWS from the Crimea"
	30	2	Harvest	TO-MORROW
October	2	3	Crimea	IN the midst
	3	2	Turkey	THERE is no reason
	4	2	Georgia	IT is a very natural

MONTH/DAY		LEADER NO.	SUBJECT	FIRST WORDS
	6	2	Georgia	FOR the lifetime
	7	2	Consequences of Russia's humiliation	WE have had more
	10	2	Newcastle	WE have already
	12	2	Czar	THE account
	13	2	Installation of new Lieutenant Governor of Victoria	WHEN Governors
	14	2	Crimea	THE Russians
	17	2	Polar expedition	TO-DAY the Court
	18	2	Crimea	THE more precise
	20	2	Germany	AMONG the saddest
	21	1	Patriotic Fund	EVERY incident
	28	3	Denmark	"PUT not"
	30	2	Public improvements	IN the last number
	31	3	Russia and U. S. A.	WE have published
November	1	2	Baltic fleet	THE Baltic fleet
	2	2	Soldiers and their treatment	IF there be
	4	2	Denmark	IN the midst

MONTH/DAY	LEADER NO.	SUBJECT	FIRST WORDS
7	2	Crimea	NOWHERE has more
13	2	Anglo-French cooperation	IN the midst of the pain
14	3	Austria	"BETTER late than never,"
15	2	Seed time	IT was once
16	1	Soldiering	"DEAR me!"
17	[p. 4, cols. 4–5]	ECONOMY OF PAPER. [letter signed "SCRIBLERUS."]	
18	2	Social improvement from war	WHY are crotchetty
21	2	Denmark	THE Meeting
22	2	Elevation of Lord Raglan to Field-Marshal	THE elevation of Lord RAGLAN
23	3	Peace posters in the manufacturing districts	SOMEBODY—knave or fool—
24	2	Prince Woronzoff	AN incident
27	3	The war of opinion	IT is not quite
28	3	Czar	THERE are reports
28	[p. 5, cols. 5–6]	JOHN GIBSON LOCKHART. [obit.]	

MONTH/DAY		LEADER NO.	SUBJECT	FIRST WORDS
	29	2	Crimea	ONE of the most interesting
	30	1	Queen	THERE is no doubt
December	1	2	Russia and England	ONE of the SIGHTS
	5	2	Proposal for government arms manufacture	WE are sorry
	6	2	Scandinavia	A LETTER from Christiania
	7	3	Quakers	SOME good
	12	2	Sources of English strength—science and a free press	WE were all agreed
	13	3	Victories of representative government	TIMES are changed
	14	1	Militia bill	LORD PALMERSTON'S
	19	2	Exploration—the North Pole and Africa	BEFORE we have
	22	2	Spies	NOW that the rigours
	23	2	Foreign enlistment	NOW that the
	25	1	Christmas Day	CHRISTMAS DAY
	27	2	Cobden and Bright	MR. COBDEN

MONTH/DAY		LEADER NO.	SUBJECT	FIRST WORDS
	30	3	POLITICAL AND SOCIAL PROGRESS IN 1854.	
			1855	
January	2	3		THE last mail
	3	[p. 2, cols. 1–2]	LITERATURE. *The Westminster Review.* January, 1855. (Chapman, London.) [review]	
	4	1	China	WE see
	8	2	Crimea	WHEN the British Legion
	9	2	Foreign auxiliaries	ON the 28th
	12	2	Santo Domingo	IF our readers
	15	[p. 3, cols. 1–2]	Immaculate Conception; Waldensians	
	17	3	MISS MITFORD. [obit.]	WHEN HORNE TOOKE
	20	2	Theodore Parker, Massachusetts, and Fugitive Slave Law	OUR Constantinople
	22	[p. 4, cols. 5–6]	Turkey	
	23	3	DEATH OF JOSEPH HUME. [obit.]	AT the time
			Backwardness of Army officials	

MONTH/DAY		LEADER NO.	SUBJECT	FIRST WORDS
			[Gap here presumably owing to Martineau's writing of her *Autobiography*.]7	
April	6	[p. 5, cols. 4–5]	DEATH OF CURRER BELL. [obit.]	
May	21	1	Scandinavia	THE breaking up
	24	2	Peace Party—Russian weakness	IT is to be hoped
	28	2	Aristocratic government	BY the echo
	31	2	Freedom of speech and press	AMONG the advantages
June	2	1	Florence Nightingale; drunkenness in Crimea	AMONG the exhilarating
	6	2	Crimean strategy	IT is probable
	8	2	Fugitive Slave Law	IT is nearly
	12	2	Effective preaching	ARCHDEACON
	15	1	Mismanagement in Crimea	NUMEROUS
	20	2	Functions of government	ONE of the advantages
	22	2	Crimea	THE photograph
	28	2	Effective preaching	THERE has been a good DEAL
July	3	1	Raglan and his successor	THE successor

MONTH/DAY		LEADER NO.	SUBJECT	FIRST WORDS
	4	2	Know-Nothings	THE Know-Nothings
	13	3	War aims	IN time of war
	19	2	Weakness of governments since Peel	WHEN the history
	21	2	Crimea	THE summer
	23	1	Excellent harvest prospect	WHILE we are
	26	2	Rosa Bonheur	THE short visit
	30	2	Swimming	A MIDSHIPMAN
August	6	2	The war; history unrolling	THE unrolling
	7	2	Temperance	WE are past
	11	3	Russia	THE departure
	14	3	Paper	WHEN we went
	17	2	Mormons	THE Americans
	20	2	The Bombardment of Sweaborg	ONE would like
	23	2	Peace	THE public demand
	24	1	Ireland	TWO items
	27	3	The war	AT the outset

MONTH/DAY		LEADER NO.	SUBJECT	FIRST WORDS
	30	2	Vegetarians	AS May
September	4	2	Nightingale subscription	NOTHING has been
	10	2	The Near East	NOBODY who had any
	15	1	U. S. A.	AMIDST the interest
	19	2	U. S. A. and militarism	IT has been a common
	20	2	Mexico	REVOLUTIONS
	25	2	Soyer	WHEN the war
	27	2	The war	HALF a century
	29	3	Church rates	THE Braintree
October	2	3	Sicily	NOBODY in England
	4	3	Irish in America	WHEN we look
	5	2	Baby shows; infant schools	WE observe
	9	2	Maine Law [prohibition]	THE most
	12	2	Russia	THESE are more senses
	13	[p. 2, cols. 1–2]	LITERATURE. *The Westminster Review.*—October, 1855. [review]	
	16	1	Nesselrode	IF it is true

MONTH/DAY		LEADER NO.	SUBJECT	FIRST WORDS
	19	1	U. S. A. and Russia	SOME of our
	23	2	Agricultural labor	TIMES are changed
	26	2	Agricultural statistics	JUST when we
	27	2	Molesworth	EVERY age
	30	2	American expansionism and disunion	IN December, 1814
November	1	2	American expansionism and disunion	WE are allies
	5	1	Teaching of history in schools	THE Fifth
	8	2	Railway thefts	WHILE half
	10	2	French refugees in Jersey	THE expulsion
	13	2	War aims: take away illegally gained Russian territory	IN spite of all
	15	2	Education	WE have no doubt
	17	2	Education: skills and content	THE points
	20	2	War allies; Scandinavia?	THE emperor
	22	2	Sarah Pellatt, Florence Nightingale, and temperance	THE Sierra Nevada
	26	2	Female education	THE discussion

MONTH/DAY		LEADER NO.	SUBJECT	FIRST WORDS
December	3	1	Savings banks in Crimea	THE curious fact
	4	2	War aims	IT is cheering
	6	2	Lessons of the war; kinds of armies	THE moral necessity
	7	2	Army	THE distinctive
	12	1	Know-Nothings	AN extract
	14	3	Russia	EVERY fact
	18	1	Army welfare	PUBLISHED letters
	19	2	Russian serfs	WE are sorry
	19	[p. 5, cols. 1–2]	SAMUEL ROGERS. [obit.]	
	22	1	Meat supply	THE season
	25	1	Christmas	CHRISTMAS
	27	2	Free speech in U. S. A.	THOUGH we are past
	31	2	Hunger [on keeping dogs while people are hungry]	THAT part of Phoenicia

1856

January	1	1	New Year	THOUGH everybody

MONTH/DAY		LEADER NO.	SUBJECT	FIRST WORDS
	4	2	Kansas	PRESIDENT PIERCE
	8	2	Cremation	WE see
	11	3	Capture of Kars	AS was anticipated
	12	3	Street begging	SIR R. W. CARDEN
	16	2	Persia	THE news
	19	3	Irish fisheries	IMPERFECT
	22	2	Florence Nightingale	MR. MILNES
	23	2	Dissolution of the Union	WE English
	26	1	Struggle over a speaker in U. S. A.; Kansas	THE new year
	29	3	Lunacy; value of worship services	A STATEMENT
	30	2	Russia	AN ALEXANDER
February	2	2	Britain and America	IF the clergy
	5	1	Persia	MR. ROEBUCK'S
	9	2	Peace terms	THE public opinion
	12	2	Factory Act	THERE is an affair
	14	2	U. S. A.	TO those

MONTH/DAY		LEADER NO.	SUBJECT	FIRST WORDS
	15	1	War threat from U. S. A.	THE tone
	16	2	Female labor	THE most exhilarating
	25	2	Election of speaker in U. S. A.	THE extent
	26	3	Abolitionists	THE latest arrivals
	29	2	Women	AT the annual
March	1	2	Jews in Palestine	ON the 19th
	4	3	Factory Act	ON Friday night
	7	2	Persia	PERSIA is a long way off
	8	2	Organization of a permanent international medical association	AS time passes
	10	2	Turkey	EVERYBODY is aware
	12	2	Egypt	IT is time
	14	2	Crime and scientific knowledge	"ANOTHER poisoning case!"
	18	2	Adulteration	ADULTERATION of food
	19	2	Kansas	WE must not lose
	21	2	Comet	THE astronomers
	24	2	Beggars and charity	IT is a long time

MONTH/DAY		LEADER NO.	SUBJECT	FIRST WORDS
	26	2	Status of women	WHEN Parliament
	27	3	Factory Act	THE Second Reading
	31	2	Lunacy; value of worship services	THE published
April	2	3	Status of women	IT is a curious
	3	1	U. S. A.—no war	AT the moment
	7	2	Factory Act	ABSURD
	8	2	Peace	IT is a significant
	10	2	U. S. A.	THE grave old
	15	3	Factory Acts	IT is satisfactory
	17	2	Working-class amusements in Birmingham	IT gives us pleasure
	18	1	U. S. A.	IT is scarcely
	21	1	Austria	THE attention
	22	2	Fighting and the Peace Party	THE frightful
	25	2	Russia: the new Czar's policies	THE Czar's
May	1	1	Russia: hope for economic, social changes	THERE seems to be

MONTH/DAY		LEADER NO.	SUBJECT	FIRST WORDS
	9	3	Laborers' dwellings	A GREAT public
	13	2	Circassians	WHATEVER
	15	1	Syria	OUR books
	20	2	Jews in Palestine	OUR Jewish
	22	2	West Indies; coolie labor	PRACTICE
	24	2	Concordat with Austria	NOTHING
	27	2	U. S. A.	THE way
	30	2	French agriculture, husbandry; the Universal Exhibition	NEXT week
June	2	2	Crime	A CRIME
	3	2	Factory Act; shipwrights' strike	"THE Factories Bill"
	5	1	U. S. A.	[from 2nd sentence] With the sincerest
	9	1	U. S. A.	IF you happen
	10	2	French agriculture	IF the inundations
	12	2	Sumner-Brooks episode	THE march
	13	3	Cockroaches	IN the course
	17	2	Female dress and despotism	IN a secluded

MONTH/DAY		LEADER NO.	SUBJECT	FIRST WORDS
	19	2	Sumner-Brooks episode	AS everybody
	23	3	French Regency	THE article
	23	[p. 2, cols. 2–5]	HISTORY OF THE AMERICAN COMPROMISES. A HISTORICAL RETROSPECT.	
	25	3	Kansas and Nebraska	IT is hoped
	30	1	Advance of labor	WE have the Irish
July	2	2	Bigness	THE worship
	3	3	Colonial Fibre Company	WE are glad
	8	3	Time-keeping and deficiency of watches in England	WHICH of us
	10	2	Presidential elections	INTERESTING
	17	3	Female dress	WHETHER we read
	19	[p. 2, cols. 4–6]	[under LITERATURE.] *Our Slave States.* By FRED. L. OLMSTED.—London, 1856. [review]	
	21	[p. 2, cols. 4–6]	[under LITERATURE.] SOUTH CAROLINA. [Concluded from the *Daily News* of July 19.] [review]	
	23	2	Qualities of recent presidents	THE interest
	24	1	Spain and Napoleon III	THE curse

MONTH/DAY		LEADER NO.	SUBJECT	FIRST WORDS
	28	1	Spain	JOHN BULL
	29	1	Spain	THE now indisputable
	31	1	Lynch law and violence in U. S. A.	ABOUT half
August	4	2	Evils of long credit	THE day
	5	2	Sabbath	THE election
	7	1	U. S. A.	THE aspect
	12	3	Swimming	THE annual affliction
	13	2	Slavery and cotton	NOT having
	14	1	Administrative reform	NO thoughtful
	18	2	Russia	A THOUSAND
	19	1	Leprosy	THERE is one
	23	3	Swimming	OUR readers
	26	2	Public Health	SIX months ago
	28	2	Freedom of the press in U. S. A.	SINCE the lost
	29	2	Harvest	BAD weather
September	1	2	Violence in U. S. A.	PROPRIETORS

MONTH/DAY	LEADER NO.	SUBJECT	FIRST WORDS
2	1	The bugbear of Socialism	THE mischief
8	2	U. S. A.	THE *Washington Union*
9	1	U. S. A.	WE have said
13	[p. 2, cols. 1–3]	LITERATURE. *English Traits.* By Ralph Waldo Emerson. Boston and London. 1856. [review]	[from 2nd sentence] It is observable
16	1	Kansas	IF our American
18	1	Slavery	IT becomes
22	3	Catering	THE most serious
24	2	Ignorance of *The Times* on America	IT is but a few
26	2	Kansas	IT is not enough
27	1	Kansas	
29	[p. 2, cols. 1–4]	LITERATURE. *Caravan Journeys, and Wanderings in Persia, Afghanistan, Turkistan, and Beloochistan: with Historical Notices of the Countries lying between Russia and India.* By J. P. FERRIER, formerly of the Casseurs d'Afrique, and late Adjutant-General of the Persian Army. Translated by Captain WILLIAM JESSE. Edited by H. D. Seymour, M. P. Murray. 1856 [review]	
29	3	Bull fights; French despotism	THE taste
30	2	U. S. A.	WHILE the information

MONTH/DAY		LEADER NO.	SUBJECT	FIRST WORDS
October	2	2	Agricultural improvement	[from 2nd paragraph] Everything seems
	3	2	Presidential election	EVERY week
	6	2	Temperance	IT is a public
	9	2	Preaching and clerical recruitment	IT is no doubt
	10	1	Kansas	THE proclamations
	13	3	Adult education	WHATEVER other
	16	1	Presidential elections	THE difficulty
	20	2	U. S. A.	THE first burst
	21	3	Women	A LETTER
	24	2	Presidential election	A POLITICAL crisis
	27	[p. 4, cols. 4–6]	REPORT OF THE CONGRESSIONAL COMMISSION ON KANSAS. I.	
	28	2	Irish emigration	THE accounts
	30	[p. 4, cols. 3–5]	REPORT OF THE CONGRESSIONAL COMMISSION ON KANSAS. II.	
November	3	[p. 4, cols. 3–5]	REPORT OF THE CONGRESSIONAL COMMISSION ON KANSAS. III.	

MONTH/DAY		LEADER NO.	SUBJECT	FIRST WORDS
	5	1	Guy Fawkes Day	THE unfolding
	7	[p. 4, cols. 3–5]	REPORT OF THE CONGRESSIONAL COMMISSION ON KANSAS. IV.	
	10	[p. 4, cols. 4–5]	REPORT OF THE CONGRESSIONAL COMMISSION ON KANSAS. V.	
	13	[p. 4, cols. 3–5]	REPORT OF THE CONGRESSIONAL COMMISSION ON KANSAS. VI.	
	15	2	Presidential election	OUR suspense
	19	3	Czar and Scandinavia	IT is interesting
	20	2	U.S.A.	"THE only mode"
	22	1	American election	IT is highly
	25	1	Reopening of the slave trade	THE latest news
	29	3	Education	IT is to some people
December	2	2	English watchmakers; women working	IN the midst
	4	3	Female education	A CORRESPONDENT
	5	3	Slave trade	WHEN the politicians
	11	3	Domestic service	THERE seems

MONTH/DAY		LEADER NO.	SUBJECT	FIRST WORDS
	15	[p. 2, cols. 3–4]	FATHER MATHEW. [obit.]	
	15	2	Parliamentary action on legislation dealing with women	THE recess
	16	1	U. S. A.	[from 2nd paragraph] As regards America
	19	2	Italy	OF all dreary
	22	4	Theft of holly for Christmas	WITH the opening
	23	2	International copyright	IT has been a common
	24	3	Fire	IN winter
	25	1	Christmas	"HERE'S a health"
	29	1	Panic over slave risings	THE character

<u>1857</u>

MONTH/DAY		LEADER NO.	SUBJECT	FIRST WORDS
January	5	2	Birmingham education	IN the great process
	10	1	Slave rising	OF all human
	13	3	Needlewomen; extremes in female fashions	THE Christmas

MONTH/DAY		LEADER NO.	SUBJECT	FIRST WORDS
	16	2	Protestants and the revised version of the Bible	WE observe
	19	2	Unemployed	IF the adjourned
	20	2	Agricultural wages	IT seems a strange
	26	2	Colored seamen in America	IT is a great
	27	1	An attack on Lord Normanby	THE Emperor
	30	2	Unemployment	THE interest
February	3	3	Slavery	MASSACHUSETTS
	5	3	Factory Bill	IT is to be hoped
	6	3	Agricultural wages	IN commenting
	10	2	English, Russian, and American railways	OUR Special
	12	2	Domestic service	THE old
	14	3	St. Valentine's Day	IT should be
	17	3	Arctic exploration	LADY FRANKLIN'S
	20	2	Local dues on shipping	IF the last
	24	4	Cotton supply	ON the all-important

MONTH/DAY		LEADER NO.	SUBJECT	FIRST WORDS
March	26	2	Cotton supply	AT the recent
	4	2	Pensions of widows of the Indian army	MUCH interest
	17	[p. 4, col. 5]	MANCHESTER AND THE RIGHT HON. ROBERT LOWE.—(FROM A NORTH OF ENGLAND INDEPENDENT-LIBERAL.)	
	18	3	Women	IT is one
	20	2	Buchanan	HOWEVER plain
	24	2	Buchanan	THE Inaugural
	24	3	Manchester Liberals	THE Manchester Liberals
	26	2	China	IN a despatch
	31	2	Manchester Liberals, the Peace Party, and national duty	THE high instincts
	31	3	Murrain	THERE are topics
April	3	3	Supreme Court	AMIDST the critical
	7	3	Slavery	THE letter
	9	1	Reform	THE prospect
	10	2	Murrain	OUR agricultural readers
	13	2	France	WHEN a potentate

MONTH/DAY		LEADER NO.	SUBJECT	FIRST WORDS
	14	2	Education	THE Education questions
	17	3	Education	IN our discussions
	21	1	Education	THE precise aims
	21	3	Passing tolls	[from 2nd paragraph] The ancient occasions
	22	2	Education	PUBLIC opinion
	29	2	China	WE have arrived
May	1	[p. 4, col. 6—p. 5, col. 1]	THE DUCHESS OF GLOUCESTER. [obit.]	
	5	1	Royal Academy exhibition	ALL the world
	11	2	Local dues on shipping	SYMPTOMS
	14	1	China	THE American reply
	15	1	Spread of debt and corruption	THE month of May
	18	2	Royal journeys	A TRAVELLING
	19	2	Education	IT is not very
	22	2	Education	THOUGH the British and Foreign
	26	1	Education	WE observe

MONTH/DAY		LEADER NO.	SUBJECT	FIRST WORDS
June	2	2	Education: industrial	THE main object
	3	2	Dred Scott	THERE are several
	11	2	Wrecks at sea	WE need not describe
	16	2	Slave trade	IT is not surprising
	18	[p. 2, cols. 1–4]	LITERATURE. *Essays from the Edinburgh and Quarterly Reviews, with Addresses and other Pieces.* By Sir JOHN F. W. HERSCHEL, Bart., M. A., D. L. C., &c. Longman and Co., 1857. [review]	
	18	1	Dred Scott	THE latest
	22	4	Cookery	IT appears
	23	1	Mormons	IT is a common
	26	1	Education	THE Educational Conference
	30	2	Cotton	THERE must be
July	1	2	French slave trade	ALTHOUGH the Earl
	2	2	Education	WHILE considering
	3	3	French slave trade	THIS scheme
	7	2	French slave trade	FURTHER intelligence
	8	3	Slave trade	"DOCTOR, the Thanes"

MONTH/DAY		LEADER NO.	SUBJECT	FIRST WORDS
	10	[p. 2, cols. 1–3]	LITERATURE. *Biographies of Distinguished Scientific Men*. By FRANCOIS ARAGO, Member of the Institute. Translated by Admiral W. H. SMITH, D. L. C., &c.; Rev. BADEN POWELL, M. A., F. R. S., &c.; Robt. GRANT, Esq., M. A., F. R. A. S. London: Longman and Co. 1857. [review]	DURING the present
	13	3	India: Bengal officers' fund	THE Report
	16	2	Cattle; meat supply	WHEN we referred
	18	3	India: Bengal officers' fund	THE strangest
	21	2	Slave trade	THE West India
	25	3	West Indian labor	IT has been said
	28	2	India	IT will be in the recollection[8]
	29	2	Cotton	WE make
	30	2	West Indian labor	IT is pretty
August	1	2	India	THE deputation
	4	2	Cotton	
	7	[p. 4, cols. 5–6]	DR. BLOMFIELD. [obit.]	
	10	1	India	WE may be

MONTH/DAY		LEADER NO.	SUBJECT	FIRST WORDS
	13	[p. 5, col. 6—p. 6, col. 1]	THE LATE JOHN WILSON CROKER. [obit.]	
	26	[p. 4, col. 6]	MRS. GASKELL'S MEMOIRS OF MISS BRONTE. [letter dated "Ambleside, August 24," signed "HARRIET MARTINEAU."]	
	27	2	India	WE thought
September	5	1	India	THERE could be no
	9	1	U. S. A.	IT is commonly
	12	1	India	AT a time
	24	3	Compensation scheme for doing away with slavery	WHATEVER may be
October	1	2	English gentlemen needed to go to India	WHAT a gallant sight
	6	2	Telling the people about India—relief fund for victims of the massacre	THE more we
	19	2	U. S. A.	THE natural history
	23	2	The American crash; women in America	A QUARTER
	28	2	Indian Christians as soldiers	AT such a time

MONTH/DAY		LEADER NO.	SUBJECT	FIRST WORDS
	30	2	American crash	THERE are probably
November	2	[p. 5, cols. 1–2]	OUR IGNORANCE OF INDIA. (COMMUNICATED.)	
	5	3	Englishwomen in India	WE observe
	7	2	Food supply	THE practical
	9	2	China	THERE are times
	10	2	Disunion Convention; Massachusetts politics	WHILE hundreds
	14	2	China	CASTING one's eye
	16	3	Brougham on the slave trade	IT is not often
	18	[p. 2, cols. 1–2]	LITERATURE. *Histoire de la Revolution Française.* Par M. LUIS BLANC. *History of the French Revolution.* By M. LOUIS BLANC. Ninth Volume. Paris, 1857. [review]	
	21	1	English officers' wives in India	SOME items
	23	4	Food supply	WHEREVER we go
	24	2	Relief of distress	THIS remarkable year
December	1	2	Use of unemployed for arterial drainage schemes	WE observe

MONTH/DAY	LEADER NO.	SUBJECT	FIRST WORDS
3	2	Drainage	THE reason why
11	2	Relief of distress	THE first interest
15	2	Haileybury	AS the Bishop
16	2	Relief of distress	IN the midst
[17][9]			
22	2	U. S. A.	IN painful contrast
25	1	Christmas	WE have seldom
25	3	English women in India	WE would fain
26	3	Floods	TOWARDS the close
29	2	Soldiers' wives	IN the early days
31	[p. 5, cols. 1–6—p. 6, col. 1]	REVIEW OF THE YEAR.	

1858

January 2	2	China	PREPARATIONS
4	[p. 2, cols. 1–3]	LITERATURE. *The Westminster Review.* No. XXV. Jan., 1858. Chapman. [review]	

MONTH/DAY		LEADER NO.	SUBJECT	FIRST WORDS
	5	3	American political parties	IT is not
	7	2	Drainage	THERE seems
	11	2	Buchanan and Douglas	ONE or two
	15	2	Preaching	THE movement
	19	2	China	IT is all
	21	2	U. S. A.	AN old friend
	23	3	Religious conversions	THE letter
	25	1	Marriage of the Princess Royal	IT seems
	27	3	Borneo	OUR wars
February	1	2	Understanding India	THERE is no
	4	1	Forthcoming session	IT is many
	9	3	France [Orsini plot]	THE elder
	18	2	Palmerston and the ignorance of the English on the India and Conspiracy Acts	AMONG the repetitions
	19	2	East India Company (Land)	THE MEMORANDUM
	22	3	East India Company (Taxation)	WHEN we want

MONTH/DAY		LEADER NO.	SUBJECT	FIRST WORDS
March	26	3	East India Company (Justice)	THE test
	1	4	U. S. A.	HOWEVER interesting
	3	2	East India Company (Treatment of Criminals)	ONE of the striking
	8	2	East India Company (Public Works)	TO Englishmen
	10	3	Englishmen's duty towards political persecutors: Italy	DURING the seven
	13	2	East India Company (Education)	WHEN the British
	19	1	France	OUR relations
	23	2	Truelove Case; freedom of publishers[10]	WHEN we say
	25	3	Indian communications	IT is a sure sign
	26	2	East India Company (Welfare of natives)	WHEN we are
	30	1	France	IT is so serious
April	2	1	Serfdom in Russia	GENERAL
	2	3	U. S. A.	WE hardly see

MONTH/DAY		LEADER NO.	SUBJECT	FIRST WORDS
	3	[p. 2, cols. 1–4]	LITERATURE. *The Views and Opinions of Brigadier-General John Jacob. C. B., &c., &c.* Collected and edited by CAPTAIN LEWIS PELLY. London. 1858. [review]	
	6	2	Princes and constitutional government	HEREAFTER
	9	[p. 2, cols. 1–3]	LITERATURE. *The Westminster and Foreign Quarterly Review.* April 1, 1858. [review]	
	10	2	Bishop of Jerusalem	THE Bishop
	21	4	Brooke: Borneo	THE leading
	26	2	Church rates	NO one expects
	27	3	Church rates	OUR readers
May	3	2	Church rates	IT is a serious
	7	2	Church rates	MR. LYGON
	12	3	Slavery	WHILE we are
	14	4	Political situation	WE do not wonder
	22	3	Church rates	WE observe
	25	3	Kansas	IT will not
	28	2	New laws on marriage	WE take our greatest
	31	4	Game laws in Ireland	IT is with a painful

MONTH/DAY		LEADER NO.	SUBJECT	FIRST WORDS
June	4	2	Slave trade	THIS collision
	4	[p. 4, col. 6—p. 5, col. 1]	A CONTRAST: RUSSIAN SERF-EMANCIPATION, AND AMERICAN SLAVE-POLICY: TOURGUENEFF AND EVERETT.	
	8	2	Church rates	AT noon
	10	2	Slave trade	THE greater
	11	2	Slave trade	IT appears
	15	1	Queen in Birmingham	"WE are"
	18	2	Slave trade	IT is wonderfully
	19	1	Twenty-first anniversary of the Queen's accession	WHEN the sun
	22	3	Slave trade	FROM the outbreak
	26	3	Slave trade	OF all desirable
	29	2	Slave trade	SOME recent conversations
July	3	[p. 5, cols. 2–3]	MRS. MARCET. [obit.]	
	6	2	Isthmian canal	IT is not everybody
	7	1	Isthmian canal	THE affair

MONTH/DAY		LEADER NO.	SUBJECT	FIRST WORDS
	13	2	Capt. Bayle's condemnation for carrying fugitive slaves	WHEN the Americans
	17	3	Virginia	WE are not eager
	20	1	Slave trade	GENERAL notices
	21	2	Russian serfdom	IT is of great
	24	1	East India Company	THE deed is done:
	27	1	Agriculture	IN these times
	27	2	Isthmus	WE may be excused
	29	3	French slave trade	WE have needed
August	2	1	India	LORD STANLEY
	3	1	Review of Session	THE Session
	6	3	Isthmus	THE letter
	10	4	Agriculture	EVEN in the short
	12	1	England's relations with France, U.S.A., and Italy	LET who will
	14	1	Telegraph	
	18	[p. 5, cols. 3–5]	GEORGE COMBE. [obit.]	THE readers

MONTH/DAY		LEADER NO.	SUBJECT	FIRST WORDS
	20	4	Explosion	WHEN there was
	21	3	Ireland	WE do not share
	23	3	Slave trade	IT is of the utmost
	24	[p. 5, cols. 3–4]	ENDOWED SCHOOLS OF IRELAND. No. I.	
	26	1	Isthmus	SINCE our last
	28	[p. 5, cols. 4–5]	ENDOWED SCHOOLS OF IRELAND. No. II.	
	31	[p. 4, col. 6—p. 5, col. 1]	ENDOWED SCHOOLS OF IRELAND. No. III.	
September	2	2	Slave trade	OUR COLONIAL SECRETARY
	3	[p. 4, col. 6—p. 5, col. 1]	ENDOWED SCHOOLS OF IRELAND. No. IV.	
	6	[p. 4, col. 6—p. 5, col. 1]	ENDOWED SCHOOLS OF IRELAND. No. V.	
	7	4	Negroes in Jamaica	THE *Times*

MONTH/DAY	LEADER NO.	SUBJECT	FIRST WORDS
8	[p. 2, cols. 1–2]	ENDOWED SCHOOLS OF IRELAND. No. VI.	
13	[p. 2, cols. 1–2]	ENDOWED SCHOOLS OF IRELAND. No. VII.	
14	3	Agriculture	THOSE of us
16	[p. 3, cols. 1–2]	ENDOWED SCHOOLS OF IRELAND. No. VIII.	
17	3	Slave trade	THE action
20	[p. 2, cols. 1–2]	ENDOWED SCHOOLS OF IRELAND. No. IX.	
21	2	Newton	THE statue
22	2	Slave trade	SOONER than
24	[p. 2, cols. 1–2]	ENDOWED SCHOOLS OF IRELAND. No. X.	
25	2	Slave trade	WE are glad
27	[p. 3, cols. 1–2]	ENDOWED SCHOOLS OF IRELAND. No. XI.	
28	2	Slave trade: Staten Island riots	IT was expected

MONTH/DAY		LEADER NO.	SUBJECT	FIRST WORDS
October	1	[p. 2, cols. 1–3]	ENDOWED SCHOOLS OF IRELAND. No. XII.	
	6	2	Harvest	HARVEST-HOMES
	11	3	Education for political wisdom	TO-DAY the National Association for the Promotion of Social Science
	14	2	Slave trade	THE difficulty
	15	2	Isthmus	WE make no apology
	19	2	Shrewsbury: Church-rates	SOME of our readers
	22	2	Isthmus	WE have recently
	23	2	Future of Galway	WHEN the clouds
	25	3	National Association for the Promotion of Social Science	IT ought not
	27	1	Slave trade	THE notorious
November	3	4	The princes	THE boyhood
	4	2	Isthmus	THERE are some
	6	1	Bright and U. S. A.—political apathy and corruption in U. S. A.	MR. BRIGHT'S
	12	3	Isthmus	WASHINGTON

MONTH/DAY		LEADER NO.	SUBJECT	FIRST WORDS
	13	2	Drainage	WE have been blessed
	16	2	Japan	IT is not surprising
	18	2	Ireland	IT is perhaps
	19	[p. 5, cols. 4–5]	THE LATE ROBERT OWEN. [obit.]	
	20	2	Liberia	OUR valued
	23	4	U. S. A.	BAD weather
	25	2	Isthmus	THE independence
	27	3	Brougham and associations for single women	THE last time
	29	3	Brougham and associations for single women[11]	THE Royal Ladies
December	2	1	France: the seventh anniversary of coup d'etat	THIS day
	8	2	Ballot in America	[from paragraph 2?] Even, however,
	8	3	Quakers	NOTHING is more
	14	2	Rural cottages	WHEN Free Trade
	16	2	Slave trade	NO time

MONTH/DAY		LEADER NO.	SUBJECT	FIRST WORDS
	20	2	Irish-Americans	AFTER all
	21	3	U. S. A.	THE rulers
	23	2	U. S. A.: President's Message	THE PRESIDENT'S
	25	[p. 2, cols. 1–3]	LITERATURE. *The Foster Brothers, being a History of the School and College Life of Two Young Men.* London, 1859: Hall, Virtue, and Co. [review]	
	25	1	Christmas	THE Anniversary
	30	2	Isthmus	THERE seems to be no
	31	1	[review of the year, untitled]	
			1859	
January	11	2	Prince of Wales in Italy	THE Prince of WALES
	14	2	American military services; Army hygiene	AMIDST the general
	17	3	Education in Ireland	WE published on Saturday
	18	2	British investment in European railways	IT seems[12]
	18	3	Army hygiene	IN saying
	20	[p. 2, cols. 3–4]	DEATH OF MRS. WORDSWORTH. [obit.]	

MONTH/DAY		LEADER NO.	SUBJECT	FIRST WORDS
	25	2	Robert Burns	AMONG the many
	25	[p. 4, col. 6—p. 5, col. 1]	HENRY HALLAM. [obit.]	
	26	2	Army hygiene	ONE of the questions
	28	1	Royal grandchild	QUEEN VICTORIA
	31	3	West Indian Labor	IF our readers
February	1	3	Army medical reform	WHEN the Admiralty
	3	2	Declaration of Southern Independence	IN another column
	8	2	Church rates	IT must be rather
	11	2	Army hygiene	IF we are
	16	3	Army hygiene	THE prospect
	18	1	Europe	IF the bulk of the people
	18	3	Cotton supply	IT is a matter
	24	3	Sewing machine and strikes against it at Northampton	THE introduction
	25	3	Church rates	THERE is no fear
March	2	2	Shoemakers and machinery	THE letter

MONTH/DAY		LEADER NO.	SUBJECT	FIRST WORDS
	5	2	Military health reform	THE graver
	7	3	Church rates	THERE has now
	8	2	Reform	WHEN our Lords and Gentry
	11	[p. 4, cols. 5–6]	AMERICAN NOTIONS OF ENGLISH REFORM. [letter signed "AN ENGLISH TRAVELLER IN AMERICA."]	
	14	[p. 4, cols. 5–6]	THE LATE LORD MURRAY. [obit.]	
	15	4	Winter	THE remarkable
	17	1	Reform	WHEN Queen CHRISTINA
	18	3	Italy	WHEN SILVIO PELLICO
	22	2	Publication of letters	THE publication
	25	2	House of Commons and reform	IF we had
	25	3	Women physicians: Elizabeth Blackwell	IT is quite true
April	2	3	Proposed European conference	THE funds
	2	4	Need of knowledge to make a good society	WE do not propose
	4	3	Pierce Butler's sale of his slaves	DEEP and gradual

MONTH/DAY		LEADER NO.	SUBJECT	FIRST WORDS
	7	3	India	THERE are men
	12	2	Drinking fountains	SOME quarter
	14	2	Recruiting and health	ONE of the very few
	19	3	Isthmus	WHILE Sir W.
	22	2	Reform	IT cannot be long
	23	3	Economic future of India	THE more we hear
	28	2	Diplomatic secrecy	THERE never surely
May	3	2	France and Russia	WE certainly are
	4	4	Defense	WE seem to be
	6	2	Italian war and English neutrality	IT is to be hoped
	9	[p. 2, cols. 1–3]	ALEXANDER VON HUMBOLDT. [obit.]	
	10	[p. 2, col. 6]	THE WORDSWORTH HOUSEHOLD.	
	10	3	Volunteers	CAMBRIDGE
	11	4	Minister to U. S. A.	IT is due
	21	3	Servants	AMONG the attendants
	24	2	Death of King of Naples	[from 3rd paragraph] It is fearful

MONTH/DAY		LEADER NO.	SUBJECT	FIRST WORDS
	26	2	The state of Europe	IN many quarters
June	1	2	Church rates	AMONG the wonders
	4	4	Protection of seamen	WE recently
	10	4	Romanizing practices in the Church	AMIDST all
	16	2	Prussia	IN every generation
	16	3	Lord Elgin	THE Court
	20	3	Handel	IS anybody
	21	3	Swimming	THROUGH all the changes
	27	3	Sidney Herbert and army administration	IT is rather surprising
July	4	2	Germany	DIFFICULT
	5	1	The war	WITHOUT any
	12	3	Slave trade	WHEN the time
	[14][13]			
	15	3	Recruiting and army reorganization—abolition of purchase	NO part
	21	3	Church rates	BEFORE the

MONTH/DAY		LEADER NO.	SUBJECT	FIRST WORDS
	23	2	Ballot and Norwich	IT is
	26	3	Ladies Sanitary Association	IT is satisfactory
	28	3	Irish education	IN the whole
August	2	2	American seamen	A GOOD deal
	3	1	Nine hours movement	AN attempt
	8	[p. 2, cols. 1–3]	MR. MATTHEW ARNOLD ON THE ITALIAN QUESTION. [fn.: *England and the Italian Question*. By MATTHEW ARNOLD. London, 1859.] [review]	
	8	2	Builders	THE surest
	10	1	India	IF to have
	11	1	Builders	THOSE of us
	13	1	Review of session	AT the close
	15	2	Builders	IT is difficult
	16	1	India	THE more
	18	3	Builders	THE Reply
	22	2	Builders	THE spectacle
	25	1	Builders	THE operative

MONTH/DAY		LEADER NO.	SUBJECT	FIRST WORDS
	26	3	Indian army medical service	THERE is a large
September	1	3	Builders	WHILE the workman
	2	2	India	THE more
	6	3	Builders	DAY after day
	10	3	Agricultural labor	THE complaints
	12	3	Builders	THE second
	15	2	India	MR. WILSON
	19	3	Trade union law	A CONTEMPORARY
	20	[p. 2, cols. 1–2]	SOME PHENOMENA OF REVIVALS.	[letter signed "A STUDENT OF ABNORMAL CONDITIONS."]
	26	2	Builders	THE members
	28	3	Colored seamen	OCCASION
	30	1	Friendly societies	IT is to be
October	3	3	Builders and friendly societies	THE time
	4	2	Builders and friendly societies	IT must
	8	1	India	MR. WILSON
	10	3	Builders	IT can be

MONTH/DAY		LEADER NO.	SUBJECT	FIRST WORDS
	11	3	National Association for the Promotion of Social Science	THIS day
	15	3	National Association for the Promotion of Social Science	IT is generally
	17	2	Builders	THOUGH it is
	18	3	National Association for the Promotion of Social Science	THE Social Science Meeting
	25	2	West Indian laborers	IT is not
	29	2	Agricultural drainage	THE year 1859,
November	2	1	Maryland and Harpers Ferry	IF there must be
	3	3	Italy	WHEN our young
	9	1	Prince of Wales	OUR young
	9	3	Harpers Ferry	THE further
	14	1	India	WHEN now
	17	3	Women's work	FOR a good
	18	[p. 3, col. 1]	*A Manual for the use of Friendly Societies.* By CHARLES HARDWICK, P. G. M. of the Independent Order of Oddfellows, &c. Report of the Registrar of Friendly Societies in England, 1859. [review]	

MONTH/DAY		LEADER NO.	SUBJECT	FIRST WORDS
	18	[p. 5, cols. 4–5]	AMERICAN SOCIETY IN A CRISIS. (FROM A CORRESPONDENT.)	
	23	3	Women's work	AS soon as
	25	3	Women's work	THE urgency
	29	3	Builders	HERE we are
December	7	4	Church rates	ARCHDEACON
	9	1	Reform	THE versatile
	10	[p. 4, cols. 5–6]	THOMAS DE QUINCEY. [obit.]	
	13	1	Volunteers	IT is satisfactory
	22	2	Opening of a new Congress	THE opening
	27	1	Agriculture	WE have had
	31		EIGHTEEN HUNDRED AND FIFTY-NINE. [review of the year]	
	31	[p. 5, cols. 2–4]	LORD MACAULAY. [obit.]	

1860

January	2	3	U. S. A.	THE march of events

MONTH/DAY		LEADER NO.	SUBJECT	FIRST WORDS
	3	[p. 2, cols. 1–2]	THE BURIAL OF JOHN BROWN. (FROM A CORRESPONDENT.)	
	9	2	Female unemployment	WE were not sorry
	12	2	Indian finance	AS the months
	14	2	President's message	WHEN Mr. BUCHANAN
	19	1	U. S. A.	BEFORE our own
	19	3	Smallpox	WHAT are we going
	24	1	Opening of the Session	NO English Sovereign
	24	3	Church rates	SIR JOHN TRELAWNY
February	1	1	French trade	THE opening of the new
	1	3	U. S. A.	THERE will soon be
	6	2	Hungary	THE good citizens
	10	3	U. S. A.	THE time is past
	15	[p. 4, col. 6—p. 5, cols. 1–3]	LIEUTENANT-GENERAL SIR WILLIAM NAPIER, K. C. B. [obit.]	
	20	2	India	OUR ignorance
	27	2	Colliery accidents	THERE was another

MONTH/DAY		LEADER NO.	SUBJECT	FIRST WORDS
	28	3	Church rates	WHILE great and grave
	29	2	Reform	NO Ministry could be more fortunate
March	9	2	Paper duties	IT is to be hoped
	9	3	Indian paper money	MR. WILSON'S
	13	3	Trade marks	AT a time
	15	2	Limitation of hours	ONE of the practical
	19	2	Taxation	WE publish in another column
	20	3	Church rates	THE Market Harborough
	21	[p. 3, col. 2]	THE SEASON.	
	29	[p. 2, cols. 2–3]	MRS. JAMESON. [obit.]	
	29	1	India	THOSE who have paid
	29	3	Seward	THE American newspapers
April	3	3	Game laws	THERE has been another
	6	3	West Indian labor	ONE can scarcely
	9	2	Slave trade	THE *New York Times*
	10	2	West Indian labor	THE further inquiry

MONTH/DAY		LEADER NO.	SUBJECT	FIRST WORDS
	17	3	Corruption in U. S. A.	IT is very desirable
	26	3	Reform and U. S. A.	NOTHING is more surprising
	26	4	The season	THE unusual lateness
May	2	4	English manners abroad	IT seems as if
	2	[p. 5, col. 2]	ARISTOCRATIC ROWDYISM. (FROM A CORRESPONDENT.)
	12	1	Irish emigration; fishing	THIS Irish Emigration
	14	2	U. S. A.	THE lists are
	15	2	Indian finance	THE difference of opinion
	21	2	Indian finance	THE more Sir C. TREVELYAN'S
	23	3	Indian finance	MR. WILSON'S Bills
	24	[p. 5, cols. 5–6]	LADY NOEL BYRON. [obit.]
	28	2	Destiny of the Catholic Church	IN the midst
	29	1	Naples	ONE of the most affecting
June	7	3	Agriculture in France	OUR agricultural readers
	15	3	Agriculture in France	IN the days of the Corn-laws
	16	3	Slave trade	THOUGH the subject

MONTH/DAY		LEADER NO.	SUBJECT	FIRST WORDS
	19	3	Price of meat	INSTEAD of holding up
	22	2	Sumner	WE are quite
	25	4	Nightingale fund	AN event of great importance
	28	3	Indian finance	THE month of May
July	3	4	Meat	WE observe with mingled
	5	3	U. S. A.	IT is difficult
	6	2	Religious liberty	ONE world have thought
	12	1	Syria	EUROPEAN travellers
	16	[p. 2, col. 3]	RELIGIOUS PROFESSION AND THE CENSUS BILL. [letter signed "SPECTATOR."]	
	17	3	Harvest	AT this time
	23	2	Syria	DAMASCUS
	24	2	Distress in Coventry	THE sad old story
	30	2	India	IT is impossible
August	1	3	Upper class ignorance of laws; volunteer movement	THE education which
	7	3	Turkey	IT was time

MONTH/DAY	LEADER NO.	SUBJECT	FIRST WORDS
9	3	Slave trade	IF we have been
13	2	Harvest	ONE effect
17	3	Distress in Coventry	IT has been a melancholy
21	2	Admiralty; military organization	IT seems strange
22	3	Military organization	THE bad quality
24	2	Distress in Coventry	WHILE the condition
25	3	Military organization	IT is no secret
28	1	Review of the session	A REVIEW
September 1	1	Distress in Coventry	THOUGH the Coventry
3	1	Prince of Wales' visit to Canada	IT would be hard
7	2	India	ONCE more it has
10	3	Distress in Coventry	THE well-wishers
13	3	Price of meat	AS our minds
14	1	India—death of James Wilson	IT is the way
17	2	French Canadians	THOSE of our readers
(17)[14]			

MONTH/DAY		LEADER NO.	SUBJECT	FIRST WORDS
	19	2	American filibustering	TOWARDS the close
	25	1	Syria	TIMES, such
	28	2	Cotton supply	IF by some stroke
October	2	2	Cotton supply	IT is a great
	3	1	Abd-el Kader/Syria	THE privilege
	8	2	Filibustering	THE friends and upholders
	9	3	Cotton in America	THERE is one department
	10	3	Cotton in America	THE American reports
	16	3	Asian commerce	THERE seems to be
	18	3	South	THE Manchester movement
	23	3	Lincoln	NO satisfactory
	24	4	Negroes	WE have another
November	2	3	Women's work	WE have taken
	3	4	Prince of Wales' visit to U. S. A.	THE PRINCE of WALES'
	10	2	The fate of Continental princes	IT still stirs
	15	2	Hungary	IN Hungary

MONTH/DAY		LEADER NO.	SUBJECT	FIRST WORDS
	21	3	The Queens of Europe	IT seems but a little
	22	2	Lincoln's election	THE election
	28	3	South Carolina	THE anticipation
December	3	1	Venice	[from 2nd paragraph] There was much
	5	[p. 4, cols. 5–6]	GIRLS' SCHOOLS. (FROM A CORRESPONDENT.)	
	7	2	Cotton	WHEN the new Cotton Company
	11	3	Incurables	THERE has been a good deal
	11	[p. 4, col. 6]	THE TEACHING OF COMMON THINGS. [letter signed "YOUR CORRESPONDENT ON GIRLS' SCHOOLS."]	
	12	2	Drainage	THIS day
	18	3	U. S. A.	[from 2nd paragraph] Although Congress
	22	3	Buchanan's last message	THE words of a man
	26	2	Agriculture; law of settlement	HOWEVER interesting
	27	1	U. S. A.	IT is not surprising

MONTH/DAY		LEADER NO.	SUBJECT	FIRST WORDS
	31	[p. 4, cols. 4–6—p. 5, cols. 1–4]	REVIEW OF THE YEAR.	
			1861	
January	2	3	U. S. A.	THE President
	3	[p. 4, col. 6—p. 5, cols. 1–2]	DEATH OF THE KING OF PRUSSIA. [obit.: King Frederick William IV]	
	8	3	Arterial drainage	SINCE the meeting
	9	2	Sidney Herbert; military reorganization	MR. SIDNEY HERBERT'S
	10	3	U. S. A.	SOUTH Carolina
	15	2	U. S. A. cotton	AS every ship
	18	2	Laborers' homes	WE have waited
	21	1	U. S. A.	WHILE some of our public
	24	3	Resources of the South	WE should not ourselves
	26	3	Poverty	NOW that we hear
	28	2	Education	THE Conference

MONTH/DAY		LEADER NO.	SUBJECT	FIRST WORDS
	29	1	Anarchy in the South	THE American revolution
	29	3	Cotton supply	SIMPLE people
February	8	1	India	SUPPOSE we know
	8	3	South	THE correspondent who
	16	2	U. S. A.	IN a month
	19	[p. 2, col. 3]	SIR G. LEWIS AND THE ROCHDALE OATH. [letter signed "H. M."]	
	21	1	Sir Arthur Cotton	THE thought
	23	1	U. S. A.	THERE is no promise
	28	3	Agricultural labor	AT present
March	2	2	Bakers	IT is to be hoped
	4	3	Inauguration of Lincoln; reform	THIS day
	14	2	U. S. A. census	THE results
	18	[p. 5, cols. 1–3]	THE DUCHESS OF KENT. [obit.]	
	20	1	Indian famine	WE are apt
	23	2	Agricultural statistics	THE best friends
	25	2	Lincoln's inaugural speech	ANY complaint

MONTH/DAY		LEADER NO.	SUBJECT	FIRST WORDS
	30	2	Indian currency	WE may hope
April	1	2	U. S. A. census	THERE is naturally
	5	2	Confederate constitution	[from 3rd paragraph] At present the Confederacy
	6	2	Confederate constitution	THE first three
	8	2	Census (U. K.)	IT is only once
	12	3	Cotton supply	THE Indian government
	16	3	American ambassadors	WHILE awaiting
	19	2	Indian education; hoarding	THE GOVERNOR-GENERAL
	23	2	U. S. A.	WHILE the American public
	23	3	Santo Domingo	WHAT does Spain
	27	3	Development of waterways in India: cotton	OUR readers
May	4	3	Windmills and watermills	THE march of civilization
	9	3	Santo Domingo	THE demonstration
	9	[p. 5, cols. 4–5]	THE CONFLICT IN AMERICA.	
	10	3	U. S. A.	IN hastening southwards

MONTH/DAY		LEADER NO.	SUBJECT	FIRST WORDS
	15	2	U. S. A.	IT is not at all
	16	1	U. S. A.	WHEN our elder
	20	2	Literary pensions	THE interests of Literature
	21	2	Cobden Treaty	THERE is more than one
	29	2	U. S. A.	IT is a very proper
June	5	[p. 5, cols. 1–2]	DUTCH AND BRITISH RULE IN THE EAST. I. [review]	
	7	[p. 4, cols. 5–6]	DUTCH AND BRITISH RULE IN THE EAST. II.	
	11	[p. 4, col. 6—p. 5, cols. 1–2]	BRITISH AND DUTCH RULE IN THE EAST. III.	
	13	[p. 4, cols. 4–6]	BRITISH AND DUTCH RULE IN THE EAST. IV. [review of *Java; or, How to manage a Colony.* By J. W. B. Money (Hurst and Blackett)]	
	19	2	Death of Douglas	ONCE more the world
	24	[p. 5, cols. 4–5]	LORD CAMPBELL. [obit.]	
	25	2	U. S. A.	NOBODY who has ever read
July	2	1	Cotton	BEFORE us

MONTH/DAY		LEADER NO.	SUBJECT	FIRST WORDS
	4	2	Fourth of July	THIS Fourth
	8	2	Soldiers' recreation halls and barracks	NOT long ago
	10	2	Indian irrigation	LORD SHAFTESBURY
	12	3	Santo Domingo	WITHIN a few days
	20	3	Future of American blacks	A POINT is now
	29	1	U. S. tariff	THE most intelligent
August	6	3	Builders' strike	WE have been in no haste
	6	[p. 4, cols. 4–6—p. 5, col. 1]	LORD HERBERT OF LEA. [obit.]	
	8	1	Lord Elgin	IT is one
	9	3	Builders	THERE can be no approach
	12	1	Builders	A CAREFUL study
	13	1	U. S. A.	WE had the satisfaction
	14	2	Indian irrigation	SOME weeks ago
	20	2	Syria	SOME "Confidential Papers"
	22	2	Santo Domingo	THE world must not

MONTH/DAY		LEADER NO.	SUBJECT	FIRST WORDS
	27	2	Cotton	IT will be a pity
	29	2	Wendell Phillips	WE often hear
	30	2	Use of fugitive slaves as soldiers—virtual emancipation	IT ought to be
September	3	2	Post Office thefts	IT may seem a great marvel
	5	3	American press	IN addition to the pain
	12	3	Morrill Tariff	FROM certain indications
	18	2	Domestic service	THE time has come
	24	3	Revised Code in education	THE present excitement
	26	2	Southern agriculture and trade	THE Circular
October	1	1	Cobden Treaty	THIS 1st of October
	3	1	The end of slavery	THE most superficial
	8	3	Progress of the laboring classes	NOTICES of bread riots
	11	1	Slavery as cause of the Civil War	THE Fast-day
	15	[p. 2, cols. 2–3]	A REAL SOCIAL EVIL. [crinolines]	
	15	3	Revised Code	AFTER a short period

MONTH/DAY		LEADER NO.	SUBJECT	FIRST WORDS
	21	1	U. S. A.	CAPTAIN JERVIS
	26	1	U. S. A.	THE time has evidently
	29	3	Indian cotton	WE are advancing
November	4	2	Blacks	THOSE of our fellow-citizens
	9	2	Prince of Wales	YET another year
	12	2	U. S. A.	THE Circular of Messrs. Neill
	14	2	Lancashire strike	IT seems almost incredible
	19	1	Indian cotton	SOME of our Colonies
	27	3	Cotton	SINCE we offered
December	2	2	Sidney Herbert	IT would seem impossible
	5	2	Commander Wilkes [*Trent* affair]	THE New York papers
	6	3	Arterial drainage	AT the beginning
	13	3	India	THERE was a time
	18	3	Blacks	THE impression left
	20	1	Prince Albert	IN an hour of affliction
	21	3	Blacks	PRESIDENT LINCOLN

MONTH/DAY		LEADER NO.	SUBJECT	FIRST WORDS
	26	3	Canada and U. S. A.	FEW things
	31	[p. 4, cols. 1–6]	REVIEW OF THE YEAR.	
			1862	
January	1	3	Capt. Maury on the Confederacy	OUR fathers
	9	3	Grattan's pamphlet supporting the Confederacy	IT is a permanent
	11	2	Grattan's pamphlet supporting the Confederacy	ONE of the few
	14	3	Mason and Slidell	AN incident
	20	2	Slavery	IT is exceedingly
	21	3	Indian cotton	MR. LAING'S
	28	[p. 2, cols. 1–4]	THE ENGLISH VIEW OF THE AMERICAN QUESTION. (MR. SPENCE'S BOOK ON "THE AMERICAN UNION.") [review]	
	28	2	Slave trade	MR. YANCEY
	31	[p. 2, cols. 1–4]	THE ENGLISH VIEW OF THE AMERICAN QUESTION. (MR. SPENCE'S BOOK ON "THE AMERICAN UNION.") [Concluded from the "Daily News" of Tuesday, January 28.] [review]	
February	3	2	The South	NOTHING can be

MONTH/DAY		LEADER NO.	SUBJECT	FIRST WORDS
	4	3	The South	THE idea that
	13	2	India	AT the time
	21	3	Indian paper currency	THESE are days
	27	2	U. S. A.	IT is a natural
	28	3	Indian cotton tariff	THE Government will have
March	1	2	Lincoln and emancipation	THERE can be no doubt
	13	1	Indian cotton	THE news sent home
	14	1	Prospects of the South	IT has been an amusement
	20	1	India	WE are accustomed
	25	3	Gradual emancipation	THE House of Representatives
	26	2	Sheffield outrages	THE peculiar reproach
	28	2	Commitment to emancipation	IF it is true
April	3	[p. 5, col. 6—p. 6, cols. 1–2]	CARL SCHURZ'S SPEECH AT NEW YORK. (FROM A CORRESPONDENT.)	
	4	3	Income tax	THE Income Tax Repeal
	9	[p. 3, col. 1]	THE WEATHER AND THE CROPS.	

MONTH/DAY		LEADER NO.	SUBJECT	FIRST WORDS
	11	3	Improved spirit of the North	THE American mails
	15	2	Indian cotton tariff	IT can be no surprise
	23	2	Indian education	NOW that the development
	24	3	Morals in the Army	IT is not surprising
	26	2	Morals in the Army	IT is no longer
May	2	3	Morals in the Army	AFTER the Crimean War
	3	2	Recreation of soldiers	THE Report
	7	2	Abolition of slavery in the District of Columbia	NEITHER Englishmen
	9	2	Indian cotton	WE are only just
	16	2	Indian cotton	IN order to ascertain
	21	3	American cotton	IT is to be hoped
	23	1	Indian finance	THERE are probably
	27	2	Drainage	TIME was
	28	3	Steps to emancipation	THE rapidity
	29	2	European activity of the Confederacy	TO people at home
June	3	4	Protection of birds	WHAT can be done

MONTH/DAY		LEADER NO.	SUBJECT	FIRST WORDS
	5	3	Union sentiment in the South	IT is quite true
	11	[p. 4, cols. 5–6—p. 5, col. 1]	PROFESSOR CAIRNES'S PRACTICAL VIEW OF THE AMERICAN CASE. [fn.: *The Slave Power; its Character, Career, and probable Designs; being an Attempt to explain the real issues Involved in the American Contest.* By J. E. Cairnes, M. A., Professor of Jurisprudence and Political Economy in Queen's College, Galway.] [review]	
	13	2	Arterial drainage	WHILE there is no difference
	14	[p. 5, cols. 1–3]	PROFESSOR CAIRNES'S PRACTICAL VIEW OF THE AMERICAN CASE. II. [etc.]	
	17	[p. 4, col. 6—p. 5, cols. 1–2]	PROFESSOR CAIRNES'S PRACTICAL VIEW OF THE AMERICAN CASE. III. [no fn.]	
	20	3	Europe's position vis-à-vis America	WHILE the steamer
	21	2	Answer to a Confederate defender	IN the letter of our correspondent
	25	3	Blacks	IT is not often
	27	1	Indian cotton and irrigation [attack on Sir C. Wood at the India Office]	IF any one
July	1	1	Marriage of Princess Alice	IF, when our
	4	3	Lancashire	IT may be not only

MONTH/DAY		LEADER NO.	SUBJECT	FIRST WORDS
	7	1	Thames embankment; Duke of Buccleuch	IF the House
	8	2	Cotton	IT seems very strange
	14	1	Cotton famine	THE one topic
	15	2	Cotton supply	WE ought to need
	15	3	American tariff	THE newly-proposed
	17	3	Cotton famine	THE third great
	21	2	Lancashire	IT is a curious
	22	3	Indian finance	THE chief public
	26	1	Fourth of July	THERE is nothing
	29	1	U.S.A.	ON such an occasion
	31	3	U.S. threat to Canada	WHEN some journalists
August	6	[p. 5, cols. 4–6]	MR. O'SULLIVAN'S POLITIC HINTS OR INSTRUCTIONS ON "UNION, DIS-UNION, AND RE-UNION." [review]	
	7	4	American tariff	"AN Englishman,"
	7	[p. 5, cols. 5–6—p. 6, col. 1]	MR. O'SULLIVAN'S POLITIC HINTS OR INSTRUCTIONS ON "UNION, DIS-UNION, AND RE-UNION." II.	

MONTH/DAY		LEADER NO.	SUBJECT	FIRST WORDS
	9	3	Cotton	WE are certainly
	12	3	Cotton	IT is deplorable
	13	1	Slavery	IT is not at all
	16	1	Blacks	THERE is something
	20	3	Manners and morals in the South	MR. ROEBUCK
	22	2	Cotton	THE two meetings
	23	2	Haitian cotton	AT the recent
	27	1	Blacks	THE immediate duty
	29	3	Cotton	SINCE the alarm
	30	3	*The Times* on U. S. A.	IT should be a strong reason
September	2	2	Lincoln's policy on blacks	WHILE we take due note
	3	1	Engagement of Prince of Wales	IT was a common remark,
	9	3	Emigration of female operatives	OF all the reports
	12	1	Spirit of America	THE letter from Baltimore
	13	2	Lancashire relief measures	THE demand for counsel
	16	3	Cotton supply	IT is not necessary

MONTH/DAY		LEADER NO.	SUBJECT	FIRST WORDS
	16	[p. 4, col. 6 —p. 5, col. 1]	THE AMERICAN WAR. (FROM A CORRESPONDENT.)	
	19	2	Lancashire relief: sewing and cooking schools	AS the distress
	22	[p. 4, cols. 3–5]	TRADE AND FINANCE. [cotton]	
	23	2	India: sale of public lands	MR. LAING
	24	1	Lincoln's policy on blacks	THE scheme
	29	[p. 4, cols. 3–5]	TRADE AND FINANCE. [cotton]	
	30	2	India	FOR those who
October	2	1	Confederacy	THE Confederate generals
	3	3	Slaves	THE question
	6	1	Confederacy	THERE is nothing
	6	[p. 4, cols. 3–6]	TRADE AND FINANCE. [cotton]	
	10	1	Emancipation Proclamation	WHAT vile imaginations
	10	3	Cooking [Lancashire relief]	THE discussion

MONTH/DAY		LEADER NO.	SUBJECT	FIRST WORDS
	11	1	Confederacy	THE longer the American war
	15	2	Post-emancipation policy	NOW that Mr. LINCOLN
	17	3	The South	THE partisans
	21	2	Lancashire relief	OUR readers
	21	3	Emancipation	IT is a rather odd
	23	1	U. S. A.	[from 2nd paragraph] All the correspondence
	24	2	Africa	THE West African Company
	28	3	Lancashire relief	IT is understood
	29	1	Emancipation	THERE is something ridiculous
November	1	[p. 4, cols. 5–6—p. 5, col. 1]	LIFE IN THE CONFEDERATE STATES. "Thirteen Months in the Rebel Camp." By an Impressed New Yorker. 1862. [review]	
	4	3	Lancashire relief: food	IT is evident
	6	[p. 4, cols. 5–6—p. 5, col. 1]	LIFE IN THE CONFEDERATE STATES. No. II. (Concluded from the Daily News of Saturday, Nov. 1.) [Thirteen Months in the Rebel Camp. By an Impressed New Yorker. London: Sampson Low, Son and Co. 1862.]	
	8	1	Prince of Wales	WHEN, to-morrow,

MONTH/DAY		LEADER NO.	SUBJECT	FIRST WORDS
	11	3	Emerson on Emancipation	ONE thing has been certain
	12	2	Lancashire: emigration	WE cannot attend
	14	3	Napoleon III's proposal to mediate in America	[from 2nd paragraph] The proposal is made
	20	1	Democratic Party	THERE is some art,
	22	1	Relief for Skye	THE great holiday
	27	2	Forster and America	MR. FORSTER'S
	28	1	Democratic Party	OF all the perverse
December	4	1	U. S. A.	THOSE of our readers
	11	2	The South	THERE is a good deal
	13	3	India	WHILE there is gloom
	15	1	Prince Consort	WITH the removal
	20	2	President's Message	NEITHER the PRESIDENT'S
	23	3	Lancashire	ALL England,
	26	1	Lancashire	IT is very natural
	26	2	The South	THERE can be no difference

MONTH/DAY		LEADER NO.	SUBJECT	FIRST WORDS
			1863	
January	31	[p. 4, cols. 1–5]	[review of the year]	
	1	2	Cooperative settlement in Queensland	GOLD-DIGGING
	7	3	Soldiers' homes	IT is very satisfactory
	20	1	Comment on a letter on America by Archbishop Whately	IF the Americans
	22	3	Emigration and relief in Lancashire	IT is a great
	24	1	Egypt	A GREAT many
	27	3	Female education in Egypt and India	IN a book
February	2	[p. 5, cols. 1–2]	THE MARQUIS OF LANSDOWNE. [obit.]	
	3	1	Indian lands	THERE has always been
	13	2	Infanticide	IF we may trust
	16	1	Indian cotton	THE country seems
	25	2	Indian lands	THE last Indian mail
	26	3	Lancashire	IT really appears
March	7	1	Princess Alexandra	THE young Lady

MONTH/DAY		LEADER NO.	SUBJECT	FIRST WORDS
	10	1	Wedding of Prince of Wales	SURELY this
	18	[p. 5, col. 2]	THE QUEEN'S HOSPITALITY. [letter signed "A."]	
	21	2	Army: soldiers' homes	DURING the debates
	31	3	Emigration	THE need seems
April	3	1	India	THE Address
	16	1	Lancashire and emigration	SOME of our readers
	17	3	Secretary of State for War	AFTER the first emotions
	30	2	The season	IT is a great pleasure
	30	3	Army	THE appointment
May	4	[p. 2, cols. 1–3]	THE CONDITION OF IRELAND. [fn.: "Report of the supposed Progressive Decline of Irish Prosperity." By W. Neilson Hancock, L. L. D. Dublin, 1863.] [review]	
	14	1	Egypt	WE return
	16	1	India	LORD STANLEY'S
	21	3	Source of Nile	THE discovery
	29	2	River system	THERE is a national
June	6	2	Russia and Poland	WHEN ALEXANDER II.

MONTH/DAY		LEADER NO.	SUBJECT	FIRST WORDS
	9	2	India	SIR C. TREVELYAN'S
	11	2	Lancashire	IT is a satisfaction
	18	2	Prussia	ALL the world
	26	2	Milliners	JUST twenty years
July	9	2	Indian cotton	THE time spent
	9	3	Women	IT is encouraging
	16	2	Indian Sanitary Report	AT last
	22	1	Prussia	SO long a time
	22	2	Indian Sanitary Report	NOTHING is more
	27	3	Mortality in India	CHEERFULNESS
	28	2	India	THE material
	30	3	Indian sanitation	AFTER such
August	4	1	Factory Act	THE task
	11	2	Factory Act	TO those who
	20	3	Harvest	IT is a much
	21	1	India	IN our impression

MONTH/DAY		LEADER NO.	SUBJECT	FIRST WORDS
	27	2	Gold and Hudson's Bay	NO items
September	1	3	Sabbath	IT might be a good deed
	2	2	Cotton supply	THOSE who, like
	9	3	Italian cotton	WHEN the alarm
	14	2	Ottawa Canal	MANY English
	21	2	Irish agriculture	WHEN the harvest
	25	3	Lancashire	QUESTIONS were sure
	29	2	Sumner's speech on British neutrality	MR. SUMNER'S Speech,[15]
	30	3	Infanticide	IT may be hoped
October	6	3	Rural cottages	WRITERS and speakers
	9	2	Santo Domingo	AS the insurrection
	10	[p. 5, cols. 5–6—p. 6, col. 1]	ARCHBISHOP WHATELY. [obit.]	
	12	1	Rams seized	THERE is now[16]
	13	[p. 4, cols. 5–6]	LORD LYNDHURST. [obit.]	
	14	2	Lancashire	THE lively

MONTH/DAY		LEADER NO.	SUBJECT	FIRST WORDS
	24	1	Indian wealth	FOR some time past
	24	2	Domestic service; rural cottages	THERE are times
	29	3	Tea	THERE are few
November	3	1	India: cultivator-landlord relations	IF the prosperity
	4	2	Agricultural steam engine inspection	THE SUFFOLK
	6	3	India	IF a man
	11	2	Lancashire relief	DURING the recent
	19	2	Egypt	THE ordinary life
	21	2	Santo Domingo	WHILE the fate
	21	3	Lancashire relief	IT is not surprising
December	1	2	Irish emigration	THE rapid
	3	2	Hoof-and-mouth disease	IT is time
	4	2	Lancashire	THE complaints
	12	[p. 5, cols. 4–6—p. 6, col. 1]	THE EARL OF ELGIN. [obit.]	
	14	1	Prince of Wales	A SECOND year

MONTH/DAY		LEADER NO.	SUBJECT	FIRST WORDS
	19	2	Lancashire	THE Central Executive
	26	2	Amnesty and pardon in U. S. A.	PRESIDENT LINCOLN'S Message[17]
	28	2	Shakespeare Tercentenary	THOUGH we are
	30	2	Land	RECENT circumstances
	31	[p. 4, cols. 2–6]	REVIEW OF THE YEAR.	
			1864	
January	8	3	Drainage	ONE reason why
	25	2	Shakespeare Tercentenary	A WEEK
	29	3	Irish education	WE hear a good deal
	30	1	Prussia	IN the early part
February	18	2	Needlewomen; training for women	THE time has arrived
	20	2	Hindoo peasants	CAN the Hindoo
	25	3	Animal-food [protein] diets; malt for cattle	A GOOD prospect
March	5	3	Benefit societies; government assurance [insurance]	A MEETING

MONTH/DAY		LEADER NO.	SUBJECT	FIRST WORDS
April	10	1	Royal christening	WE have witnessed
	26	[p. 2, col. 4]	SPRING.	MR. GLADSTONE
	5	2	Benefit societies; Government Annuities Bill	SOME of the recent
	6	1	Indian sanitation	THE part of Mr. GLADSTONE'S
	15	1	Eliminating poverty	IF a sound education,
	15	2	Education	THERE is matter
	21	2	Burials in India	ON this day,
	23	3	Shakespeare	THERE will be
	29	2	Factory acts	WHEN the case
May	5	3	Needlewomen	THERE are incidents
	10	3	Health and welfare of soldiers	SIR CHARLES TREVELYAN'S
	17	3	Indian finance	WHEN the fact
	18	3	Results of the cotton famine	HOWEVER engrossing
June	3	3	Indian army welfare	ACCORDING
	9	2	Tunis	NOBODY can wonder
	9	3	Long credits	

MONTH/DAY		LEADER NO.	SUBJECT	FIRST WORDS
July	17	2	Health of the Indian army	AT a time
	25	2	Middle-class education	A CERTAIN Middle-class
	2	2	Contagious Diseases Bill	IT is an awkward
	8	2	Workshops for soldiers	THE British soldier,
	9	2	New Reformation	SOME people,
	26	1	Indian finance	THE figures
	28	3	Foundlings	THE proceedings
	30	1	The Session	THE Session
August	4	2	Working Women's Colleges	ONE of the most
	5	2	Water supply	THE present season
	10	2	Social economy in the working classes	OUR readers
	11	3	Sport: tigers	WHAT different
	16	2	Catherine Sinclair; female beneficence	THE death
	18	1	Bhootan	EVERYBODY seems
	19	2	Duke of Bedford	THE statue
	23	1	Spain	IT is impossible

MONTH/DAY		LEADER NO.	SUBJECT	FIRST WORDS
	24	1	Water supply	A MEMORIAL
	27	3	Cotton supply	THE season
September	2	2	Indian law	IT is to be hoped
	2	3	The drought	AFTER we have said
	7	1	Middle-class education	FROM this time
	9	3	Irish flax	BEFORE the late
	10	2	Gardens	WE seem
	13	2	Indian currency	ANY one
	16	1	Russia	OF all the consequences
	16	3	Fish	AMIDST the puzzling
	17	3	Milk	IT is fearful
	22	3	Criminals	WHEN we read,
	27	1	Middle-class education	IF Lord BROUGHAM'S
	27	[p. 4, cols. 4–5]	WALTER SAVAGE LANDOR. [obit.]	
	29	2	Egypt	WHILE political excitement
October	4	3	Strikes	EVERYBODY is glad

MONTH/DAY		LEADER NO.	SUBJECT	FIRST WORDS
	5	3	Dwellings for agricultural laborers	OUR agricultural labourers
	6	1	Greece	WHILE the "fear"
	14	3	Meat supply	HERE and there,
	18	2	Colliers' strike	A LETTER appeared
	18	3	Indian army Commander-in-Chief	IT cannot be surprising
	19	[p. 4, cols. 5–6]	DEATH OF THE DUKE OF NEWCASTLE. [obit.]	
	26	3	Merchants	WHO that is not
November	11	2	Education of agricultural laborers	EVERY two or three
	19	3	Agriculture	AT recent meetings
	26	2	Accidental deaths	WHAT amount
December	1	[p. 5, cols. 4–5]	DAVID ROBERTS. [obit.]	
	2	2	Indian army health	THE country seems
	2	3	Relief of distress	PEOPLE who can live
	6	[p. 5, cols. 4–6]	DEATH OF THE EARL OF CARLISLE. [obit.]	
	7	2	Middle-class education	AT every turn

MONTH/DAY	LEADER NO.	SUBJECT	FIRST WORDS
8	2	Cooperatives	THAT modern body
13	3	Meat supply	WE hear a good deal
15	2	Ireland	WHENEVER there is
20	1	Spain	IF the accounts
31	[p. 4, cols. 1–5]	1864 [review of the year]	

1865

MONTH/DAY	LEADER NO.	SUBJECT	FIRST WORDS
January 3	1	Bhootan	IT is a great
5	1	Poverty	THE emotion
11	3	Indian finance	FOR some months
12	1	Passages to the Pacific	CHRISTOPHER COLUMBUS
14	4	Dr. Baikie	WHEN, at the end
18	3	Cooperatives	FEW days pass
19	2	Dressmaking	WE are now
20	[p. 2, cols. 1–2]	BRITISH RULE AND NATIVE STATES IN INDIA. I. *"The Mysore Reversion,* 'an *Exceptional Case.'"* By Major Evans Bell, Madras Staff Corps. 1865. [review]	
23	[p. 3, cols. 1–3]	BRITISH RULE AND NATIVE STATES IN INDIA. II.	

MONTH/DAY		LEADER NO.	SUBJECT	FIRST WORDS
	23	2	Middle-class education	THE Commissioners
	26	1	Bhootan	IF we do not know
	26	3	Sanitation of coast towns	SEVERAL of the most
February	3	2	Indian agriculture	THE news
	7	1	Opening of session	THERE is an unusual
	13	2	Dressmaking	IT must have been
	23	2	Nurses	THERE are two
	25	3	Ireland	AT a time when
	28	2	Spring	THE first spring
March	11	3	Czar	HOWEVER interesting
	15	2	Machinery and strikes	IT seems strange
	16	3	Beef	THE experiments
	23	3	Bhootan	IT seems scarcely
	30	3	Middle-class education	THE Schools Inquiry
	31	3	Bhootan	IT is not at all
April	4	2	Thames; drainage	THE act

MONTH/DAY		LEADER NO.	SUBJECT	FIRST WORDS
	11	1	Indian finance	INDIAN finance
	15	3	Druggists	THE Bills
	(17)[18]			
	18	3	Beef	AS we were
	19	4	Ottawa Canal	AT the present time,
	20	2	Agricultural education	A CONTROVERSY
	25	4	Hospitals	IT may be
	26	2	Irish, English cattle	AS long as
May	6	3	Encouraging sanitation	IN the "Seventh"
	10	3	Dublin Exhibition	THE opening
	19	2	Dogs	IT is said
	20	2	Women in agriculture	TWO and twenty
June	3	1	Suez	THERE is said
	3	3	Fire brigades	TWO centuries ago
	9	[p. 5, cols. 5–6]	DEATH OF SIR JOHN RICHARDSON. [obit.]	
	13	2	Drinking fountains, dogs	HOW long

MONTH/DAY		LEADER NO.	SUBJECT	FIRST WORDS
	19	2	Small birds	THE authors
	20	3	Labor and capital	IT is no new
	21	3	House of Commons and India	AMONG the constituencies
	27	3	Swimming	IT appears
	29	3	Domestic service	WE are still
July	12	3	Supporting Jonathan Pim as candidate for Dublin	IF the citizens of Dublin
	25	3	Meat	THE uneasiness
	26	3	Tea culture in India	AFTER all the pain
	28	3	Milk	THE Circular of the Privy Council
	29	3	Rural cottages	COUNTRY gentlemen
August	2	2	Harvest	ONCE more we are in
	8	1	Founding hospitals and infanticide	IT is not surprising
	12	3	Juvenile criminals	THE Report
	19	1	Indian land	IT is no easy matter
	22	1	Ireland	AGRICULTURAL societies

MONTH/DAY	LEADER NO.	SUBJECT	FIRST WORDS
23	1	Agricultural statistics; Russian agriculture	LAST April, Mr. FISHER,
24	3	Indian land	THOUGH the judgment
26	1	Meat in diet	POLITICAL economists
29	2	Irish seamen	IT seems a very desirable thing
30	3	Treatment of women	AN inquest
September 2	1	Queen's retirement	THE duty
6	3	Meat	PUBLIC attention
8	2	Infanticide	OUR readers
9	1	Murrain	IT is not surprising
11	1	Murrain	THE first practical point
12	1	Prussia	THE German newspapers
18	2	Cholera	AS the apprehension
19	3	Working-class diet	AMIDST the general
21	2	Bhootan	WHILE we "gentlemen"
25	1	Defectiveness of health acts	CONSIDERING that care
27	3	Sidney Herbert	SOME who were present

MONTH/DAY		LEADER NO.	SUBJECT	FIRST WORDS
	30	2	Cholera	AT a time
	30	3	Girls' education	IN a recently
October	4	3	Animal food	FOR some time
	10	2	Murrain	THE use,
	11	2	Harvest	THE time has arrived
	14	2	Indian sanitation	WHEN the Sanitary Commission
	19	4	Infanticide	THERE has been enough
	19	[p. 5, cols. 2–4]	LORD PALMERSTON. [obit.]	
	20	4	Infanticide	IN recent discussions
	21	3	Murrain	IF we look back
	28	2	Treatment of children	WE are accustomed
November	2	4	Greece	IT appears
	10	3	Murrain	THERE ought to be
	16	2	Murrain	THE first Report
	24	4	Female education	THE news
	27	2	Meat	THERE is not much use

MONTH/DAY		LEADER NO.	SUBJECT	FIRST WORDS
	30	2	Murrain; qualified practitioners	THE Cattle Plague
December	5	3	Labor in Jamaica	NOW that an attempt
	8	4	Russia	THE most care-laden man
	12	3	Development of India's resources	WHILE loan after loan
	19	1	Murrain	WHEN the Cattle Plague
	25	1	Bhootan	THE peace with Bhootan
	28	3	Treatment of unfortunates	IT is not without ample
			1866	
January	9	2	W. L. Garrison	WHILE the American
	9	3	Rural laborers	VARIOUS incidents
	15	2	Cattle supply	NOW that everybody's
	22	1	Discharged prisoners	IF every populous
	31	3	Nursing schools	THE indignation
February	1	1	Opening of the session	THIS day may be
	5	2	Indian cotton	PUBLIC attention
	17	2	Prussia	ACCORDING to the latest

MONTH/DAY		LEADER NO.	SUBJECT	FIRST WORDS
	22	1	Jamaica labor	AS our present interest
	22	2	Indian development	IN a little while
March	28	4	Beer	SIR FITZROY KELLY
April	2	2	Irish Presbyterians	IT really seems
	5	3	U. S. A.	A VERY few weeks
	11	2	Domestic service in Ireland	IN the present condition
	20	2	Prussia	THE most essential change
			1868	
May	11	[p. 5, cols. 1–3]	LORD BROUGHAM. [obit.]	
			1869	
June	8	2	Confederate ships: Motley	ALTHOUGH we are at present][19]
December	28	[p. 6, cols. 2–3]	THE CONTAGIOUS DISEASES ACTS. [letter signed "AN ENGLISHWOMAN."]	
	29	[p. 3, col. 4]	THE CONTAGIOUS DISEASES ACTS. II.	
	30	[p. 2, cols. 3–4]	THE CONTAGIOUS DISEASES ACTS. III.[20]	

MONTH/DAY		LEADER NO.	SUBJECT	FIRST WORDS
			1870	
December	26	[p. 6, cols. 4–5]	THE FUTURE EMPEROR OF GERMANY. [letter signed "H. M."]	
			1871	
May	13	[p. 5, col. 6—p. 6, cols. 1–3]	SIR JOHN FREDERICK WILLIAM HERSCHEL, BART. [obit.]	
			1872	
December	3	[p. 2, cols. 1–3]	THE LATE MRS. SOMERVILLE. [obit.]	
			1873	
October	3	[p. 5, cols. 2–3]	SIR EDWIN LANDSEER. [obit.]	
			1874	
October	7	[p. 2, cols. 1–2]	DEATH OF "BARRY CORNWALL." [obit.]	

MONTH/DAY	LEADER NO.	SUBJECT	FIRST WORDS
		²	
March 21		[letter on earthquake at Ambleside, signed "H. M."]	
n. d.		[letter to the editor of *Liverpool Mercury* from "H. M.", reprinted]	
n. d.		[appeal for material for sewing schools in Lancashire and Cheshire—during the cotton famine]	

Notes

1. Listed by Webb but not found: (29) December 1853; on Jamaica; beginning: "We see."
2. *Biographical Sketch* not found: the Marquis of Londonderry (d. 1 March 1854).
3. Webb says 1st and 2nd paragraphs not hers, but only two in all.
4. See also: *Daily News*, 10 April 1854: 3, col. 3, on a Martineau letter in the New York *Evening Post* on the Irish attitude to England.
5. Webb says 1st and 3rd paragraphs not hers, but only two in all.
6. A leader on France cited by Webb in *Harriet Martineau. A Radical Victorian* (319) but not listed and not found.
7. Listed by Webb but not found: (15) [before 21 May 1855]; on Greece; beginning: "In the tremendous."
8. Not on Webb's list but cited in *Daily News*, 4 August 1857.
9. *Biographical Sketch* not found: Rear-Admiral Sir Francis Beaufort (d. 17 December 1857).
10. Cf. MS British Library 42726, 19–20.
11. See "LADIES' HOMES," *Daily News*, 9 December 1858: 4, cols. 5–6 [letter from "PATERFAMILIAS" in response].
12. Not on Webb's list but cf. "*Daily News*, 10 February 1857."
13. In Martineau to Henry Reeve, 14 July 1859 (MS Richard Martineau), she claims to have written "Drought and Its Lessons" for the *Daily News*.

14. Listed by Webb but not found: (17) September 1860; on Coventry, beginning: "The condition."
15. Not listed by Webb; see *Harriet Martineau's Letters to Fanny Wedgwood*, 234.
16. Not listed by Webb; see *Harriet Martineau's Letters to Fanny Wedgwood*, 245.
17. Not listed by Webb; as above, see *Harriet Martineau's Letters to Fanny Wedgwood*, 245.
18. Listed by Webb but not found: 17 April 1865; leader 3, on peace in America; beginning: "Peace at last."
19. For Martineau's contribution of facts and possible writing of this leader, see Martineau to Henry Reeve, 31 May 1869 (MS Richard Martineau) or *Harriet Martineau's Letters to Fanny Wedgwood*, 303–5.
20. See also *Daily News*, 31 December 1869: THE LADIES' NATIONAL ASSOCIATION FOR THE REPEAL OF THE CONTAGIOUS ACTS. [letter from a 5-woman committee with Martineau the first of 128 signatories] [reprinted as *Contagious Diseases Acts. Memorial adopted by a Conference of Delegates from Associations and Committees formed in various towns for promoting the repeal of the Contagious Diseases Acts*. London, 1870.]

Index of Names, Topics, and Titles of Works by Harriet Martineau

Aberdeen, 4th Earl of xiv–xvi, 149–53, 167, 175, 191, 207, 213
Aberdeen 11, 16
abolitionism 12, 247–53, 263, 265, 271, 301, 304–305, 307–13 (*See also* antislavery)
accidents 32, 43, 122
Acre 173
Adelaide 7
Admiralty 169
Adrianople 144
  Treaty of 146, 157, 159
Affghan war 178
Afghanistan 182
Africa 11–12, 15–16, 264–69, 278
African slave trade (*See* slave trade)
agnostic x
agricultural machinery 43
agriculture xiv, 59, 68, 81, 101, 113–19, 130–31, 133, 135
Alabama 105
Aland Islands 169
Albert, Prince 11
alcohol 75–80
Aldershott 212
Alexander I, Czar 143, 146, 163, 274–75, 277
Alexander II, Czar 199, 277
Alexandria 242
Alexis, Czar 146

Alford, Henry 52
Alfred, Prince 244
allies 141–213 *passim*, 271, 281, 291
Alma 185
Alpine 151, 154
alum 38
Ambleside x, xii, xiii, 28, 38, 48, 57, 64, 113, 119
American Antislavery Society 314
American Sketchbook 297
Anapa 158, 159
Andover, Massachusetts 16, 158, 159
Annual Register 269
antislavery xiii–xiv, xviii, 11–16, 247–313 (*See also* abolitionism)
Apollo 178
Appleton, Frances 38
Arabian desert 179
Ararat, Mount 179
Arbuckle, Elisabeth Sanders xix, 22–23, 26
Archangel 143, 144, 170, 203, 204
Archangel Michael, monastery of the 146, 204
Arctic Sea 143
Argonauts 182
Arian 176

431

aristocratic government 154, 222
Aristotle 217
Arkhangelsk (*See* Archangel)
Armenia 179
Armenian Church 182
Armenian convent 182
Armstrong, William M. 89
army 79–80, 191–95, 200, 207–13, 300
Army Medical Service 211
Arnold, Mary 48
Arnold, Matthew 48, 130
Artemis 182
arterial drainage 114–19 *passim* (*See also* drainage)
Ashburton Treaty 270
Asia xvi, 141, 179
Asia Minor 182
Astor House 225
Atkinson, Henry x
Atlantic and Pacific Ship Canal Company 285
Atlantic Monthly 39, 301–306
Atlantic Ocean 105, 279, 285
Aulis 182
Australia x, xiv, xvii, 3–8, 14, 15, 16, 279
Austria 146, 149, 154, 160, 164–66, 196, 218, 235–38
Austrian alliance xiv
Azof 146, 180, 183
Azof, Sea of 157, 179, 189, 196

Baden 217–23
Baines, Edward 100
Balaclava 185, 188, 189, 190, 196
Balkan 144
Ballantine, James 230
ballet-dancers 36
Balmoral 28
Baltic Sea 169–74, 180–81, 188, 236
Baltimore 268, 270, 309, 313

Baltimore and Ohio railroad 83
Banks, Nathaniel Prentiss 250
banks 5
Baptist 38
Barents Sea 204
Baring Brothers 89
Bartrip, Peter W.J. 123
Bavaria 220
Bazley, Sir Thomas 14
Beard, Mary R. 20
Beaufort, Emily Anne 244
Bedford, 4th Earl of 117
Bedford, 5th Earl and 1st Duke of 119
Bedford College 48, 52
Bedford Levels 117, 119
Beecher, Charles 11
Beecher, Henry Ward 225
Beer Act of 1854 75
Belfast 76
Belize 279
Bell, Alan 73
Bell, Enid Moberly 29
Belloc, Mme. 25
Bell's and Lancaster's monitorial systems 129
Belly, Félix 279, 281–83, 285, 288–91
Benthamite 19
Bentinck, William Henry Cavendish (*See* Portland, 3rd Duke of)
Berlin 234
Berwick 136
Beyrout 243, 244
Bible 152, 177, 182, 244 (*See also* Gospel)
Bill of Rights 257
biography, comparative xvi
Birmingham 11, 94, 96, 131
"Black Charley" 174
Black Forest xv

Index

Black Sea 143, 144, 149, 155, 157, 159, 160, 169, 177–81, 189, 190, 196
blacks (*See* colored British seamen)
Blackstone 19
Blackwell, Elizabeth 27, 29
Bloomer, Amelia Jenks 29, 33
Board of Excise (Edinburgh) 230
Bolgrad 204
"Bomba," King 195
Bonaparte 110
Bonheur, Rosa 22
book reviews xiv, 57–62, 69–73
Bosnia, Gulf of 169
Bosphorus 179, 180
Bostock, Elizabeh Ann 52
Boston 24, 80, 261, 263, 266, 271, 278, 301–302, 307, 311
Boston Female Anti-Slavery Society 308
Bourbon (royal family) 110
Bradbury and Evans (printing firm) x
Bradford 76
Brattle Street Church 278
Bright, John 99, 231
Bristol 29, 57
British Association for the Advancement of Science 91, 95, 96
British Columbia 279, 284
British Minister to the United States 292
British Plenipotentiary (*See* Elgin, 8th Earl of)
British public xvi
British West Indies 99 (*See also* West Indies)
Brontë, Charlotte 28, 57
Brooks, Preston 247, 254, 277
Brougham, 1st Baron 26, 58, 69, 91, 96, 129, 130, 225

Brown, John 247, 306, 307
Browning, Elizabeth Barrett ix
Brundage, Anthony 68
Bryant, William Cullen 225, 261
Buchanan, James 255–58, 263, 283, 285, 291–92
Building Society 4
Bulgaria 177, 188
Bulwer Lytton, Sir Edward 286
Burns, Robert 225–30
Butler, Pierce 295–300

cabinet (various) 62, 104, 151, 166, 194, 207, 236, 291
cabinet ministers xii
Cadwallader, General George 298
Caffa, Straits of (*See* Kerch Strait)
California 76, 255, 279
Calmucs (*See* Kalmyks)
Calvinistic Puritanism 307
Cambridge, Duke of 213
Cambridge, England 115
Cambridge, Massachusetts 272
Cambridge, University of 47, 48, 52
Cambridge examination 48, 53
Cambridgeshire 120
Cameron, Simon 39
Canada 3, 252 (*See also* British Columbia)
Canning, George xv, 62, 146, 196, 233, 274
Canterbury, Dean of (*See* Alford, Henry)
capital xiv
Caribbean Sea 263, 269
Carlisle, 7th Earl of 11
Carlyle, Thomas xviii, 150, 303
Carolina Times 265
Carpenter, Lant 29, 57
Carpenter, Mary 23, 44
Carr, Albert Z. 285, 292

Castelbajac, Marquis de 175
Catherine I, Czarina 143–45
Catherine II, Czarina 160
Catholicism (*See* Roman Catholicism)
Caucasus 155, 159, 196
census 28
Central America xiii, xviii, 266, 279–84, 287–91 (*See also* Fourth Estate)
Chadwick, Edwin 63, 68
Chadwick, Owen 244
Channel 236
Channing, Dr. William Ellery 77
Chapman, Maria Weston xiii, 263, 307–308
Charles I 67, 117, 119, 222, 224, 260
Charles II 117
Charleston 103
Charleston Courier 278
Charleston Standard 266
Chatham 211, 213
Chersonese 178, 182, 183
Cheshire 57
Children's Employment; Factories 122
China 16, 190, 212, 269, 281
Chinese Turkestan 183
Chisholm, Caroline 3–4, 8
cholera xi, 63–67, 177, 186, 191
Christianity 16, 48, 75, 77, 127–28, 129–30, 144, 150, 152, 164, 239–43 (*See also* Baptist; Mormon; Protestant; Roman Catholicism; Unitarian)
Cicero 276
Cimmerian 179
Cimmerian Bosphorus 183
Cincinnati 257
Circassians xvi, 142, 155–59
civil service 91, 241

Civil War
 U.S. xii, xviii, xix, 233, 253, 263, 307, 313
 English 67, 260
Clarendon commission 47
Clark, George Kitson 49
Clarke, John Algernon 114
Clough, Anne Jemima 48
Coal Mines Regulation Act 127
Coalition Ministry 163
Cobden, Richard 57
Cochran, Thomas C. 89
Colchis 178, 180
college, workingwomen's 27
Colonial Office 3
colonies 3, 5, 14–15, 78, 225, 227, 260
Colonization Society 264, 276, 307, 309
colored British seamen xiii
Columbia River boundary 277
Combe, George 49
commander-in-chief xvi, 191, 208, 213
Commissioners appointed to Inquire into the State of Popular Education in England 38
Committee of Council on Education 130
common law 19, 26, 27
Common Lodging Houses Act 68
Compeche, Gulf of 284
Compromise of 1850 260
Comte x, xv, 217, 223
Concord relief fund 306
Confederacy xii, 143, 255, 266, 268
Congress (U.S.) 83, 84, 248–50, 254, 276
Congress of Vienna 237
Congressman, U.S. (*See* Representative; Senator)

Index

conservative xii, 62, 223, 247, 252, 259
conservative-whig 58, 61 (*See also* Whigs)
Conspiracy, Law of 73
Constantinople 143, 144, 169
Constitutional States 237
constitutionalism 292
constitutions (various) 105, 220, 226, 238, 258, 261, 311
Consul 241–43
Contagious Diseases Acts xvii
Cook, Sir Edward 209
coolies 266
Cooper Institute 225
Cordova, Gonsalvo de 192
Cork 78, 80
Corn Law Repeal 47
Cornhill Magazine 45
Cornwall 67
Cornwallis, Caroline Frances 26
Corporation and Test Acts 73
Corry, Rear-Admiral 174
Cortés, Hernán xvi, 192
Cossack 146, 157
Costa Rica 279, 283, 285, 288
cotton 239, 297, 298 (*See also* cotton supply)
    famine 3
    mill 57, 121
    spinners 111
    supply xii, xiv, 11–16, 99–104
Cotton Supply Association 99, 100
Cours de philosophie positive x
Court of Chancery 73
Cousin, Victor 26
Crawford, Martin 247–48
Crim Tartars 179 (*See also* Tartars)
crime (*See* murder)

Crimean War xi, xiii, xiv, xvi, xix, 28, 39, 90, 141–213, 239, 260, 271, 277, 285
crinolines xvii, 29, 31–37
Croats 160 (*See also* Slavonians)
Cromwell, Oliver xv–xvi, 113, 119, 149–53
Cronstadt 169, 171–73
Crown 67, 104
Crystal Palace at Sydenham 225
Cuba xiii, 263, 266, 267, 278, 289, 290
Cumberland, Duke of 223
Cunnington, Cecil Willett 31, 32, 37
Cunnington, Phillis 37
Cuvier 219
czar xv, 87, 141–47, 149–204 *passim*, 256, 271, 272–75 (*See also names of individual czars*)

Daily Carolina Times 269
Daily Delta 269
Daily News x, xiv, 4
Dalhousie, Marquis of (*See* Panmure, 2nd Baron)
Daly, Timothy 42
Damascus xv, 239–43
Dane (*See* Jacob)
Danube 144, 177, 190, 205
Danubian principalities 141, 146, 149, 161, 167, 195
Darby, H. C. 114, 119
Dardanelles 169
Darlington 83
Davies, Emily 52
Davis, Jefferson 83
Dead Sea 82
deafness ix, xii
death, accidental 32
Debt, Law of 73
Defoe, Daniel 99

Delaware and Hudson (canal company) 83
Democrat 255, 256, 263
Democratic Convention 260
Denmark 146, 169, 196
Derby, 15th Earl of (*See* Stanley, Edward Henry)
despotism xvii, 144, 196
Dexter, Caroline H. 37
diamond jubilee xviii
Dicey, A.V. 20
Dickens, Charles x, 11, 20, 26, 89, 97, 122
dissent 48, 57, 128, 129–30
Divorce Act 19, 20, 26, 27
Dombey and Son 89
Don River 183, 196
Dorcas 300
Douglas, Stephen A. 83, 260
drainage 63–64, 113–19
Dred: A Tale of the Great Dismal Swamp 28, 249
drunkenness 63, 75–80
Druses 239
Dublin 109
Dugdale, William 119
Dundas, Vice Admiral Sir James 180
Dundee 11
Dunne, Rev. P. 8
Dutch settlements 99

Earl, George Butler 174
Eastern European geo-politics xvi
Economist 58
Edinburgh 11, 16, 74, 225, 230, 274
Edinburgh, University of 24, 29
Edinburgh Corn Exchange 227
Edinburgh Review x, 27, 58, 61, 62, 69, 72, 73, 108, 147, 260, 263
editor xi–xii, xiv

education xi, xiv, xvii, 5, 6, 9, 27, 29, 38, 47–52, 60, 72, 80, 81, 91, 121, 122, 128, 129–35, 225 (*See also* school)
female xvii, 47–52, 72
Indian 29
Education Act of 1870 129
Education Commissioners 35
Egypt 9, 31, 156, 202, 308
Egyptian vassal 175, 182
Elbe 235
Eldon, Lord 73, 227
elections (U.S.) xiv, 149, 249, 255–60, 263
Elgin, 8th Earl of 284
Eliot, George ix, 114
Elizabeth I, Queen 116
Ely 115
Emancipation 102, 301–306, 307–313
Emancipation measure 304
emancipation of serfs 272, 274–75
Emerson, Ralph Waldo xiii, xv 261, 301–306
Emigrant Aid Company 248, 251
emigration x, xvii, 3–9, 252
Empson, William 59
English Civil War 67, 260
English Woman's Journal 27
equity law 19
Ernest Augustus (*See* Cumberland, Duke of)
Eugénie, Empress 34, 38
Euripides 182
Europe xiv, xvii (*See also* names of individual European countries)
European/American aggression xiv
Euxine (*See* Black Sea)
Everett, Edward xvi, 149, 271–78
Eyemouth 134
expansionism, western xiv
expeditionary force, British 214

Index

factory acts 20, 121–26, 136
Family Colonization Loan Society 3–4
Far East xiv
fashion xvii, 29, 31–37
Félix, Elisa (*See* "Rachel")
female (*See also* women)
    education (*see* education)
    employment 28
    physicians 20, 24–25
    prisoners 44
    property law xvii, 19–25
Female Medical College 24–25
feminist causes 47
fen 113–19 (*See also* marsh)
Feodoysiya 190
Ferdinand I of Naples 237
Ferdinand II (*See* "Bomba," King)
Fielding, K. J. 123
filibuster xiv, 265, 279–91 *passim*
Fillmore, Millard 255, 258, 278
filth xvii, 63–68, 185–89 (*See also* sanitary reform)
financial panic of the 1820s ix
Finer, S. E. 68
Finland xiv, 143, 170, 174, 199, 200, 201
Finland, Gulf of 169, 174, 175
Finmark frontier 201
Finn, James 243, 244
Finnish Laps 200–02
Finsbury 37
flatirons 32
Flemish refugees 99
flood 113–19, 171–72
Florence 234
Fonseca 284
Forester, John xi
Fourth Estate xi, 277, 287
Fox, Charles James 162
Fox, Eliza 20

France xi, 20, 23, 61, 75, 141–95 *passim*, 218, 223, 237, 240–41, 244, 274, 282–83, 288
Frankfort Diet 221
Franklin, Benjamin 260
Franz Josef 166, 238
Frederick Augustus (*See* York and Albany, Duke of)
Frederick of Baden, Grand Duke 217, 218, 220–22
Frederick IV 238
free trade xii, 250
freebooter (*See* filibuster)
Freemen's Aid Society 314
freesoil movement xiv, 254
Frémont, Colonel John Charles 255, 258–59, 263
French, Earl 16
French Huguenots 113
French Revolution 223
Friendly Societies 8
Frothingham, Paul Revere 278
Fugitive Slave Law 254, 258, 260, 265, 301
Fuller, Margaret xiii

Galileo 224
Gallipoli 169
Game Laws 73
Garrison, William Lloyd xvi, 254, 263, 271, 307–13
Geneva, New York 29
Genius of Universal Emancipation 313
Genoa 151, 154
Genoese 179
geo-politics xvi
George III 161, 162, 223
Georgia (Russia) 157, 178, 189, 183
Georgia (U.S.) xv, 295–300
Germany 100, 154, 188
Gerteis, Louis S. 308

Gervinus 217–23
Gin Act of 1736 75
gipsies (*See* gypsies)
Girton College 52
Gisbourne, Thomas 114
Glasgow 11, 12, 13, 16, 76, 109
Glasgow, University of 24
Glasgow Anti-Slavery Association 16
Gobat, Rev. Samuel 244
Godkin, Edwin Lawrence 89
Goëthe 71
gold 3, 5, 7, 14, 16, 76, 279, 280–81
Golden Horde 188
Goodrich, Carter 89
Gordon, George Hamilton (*See* Aberdeen, 4th Earl of)
Gospel 79, 151 (*See also* Bible)
Göttingen, University of xi, 220, 222, 223, 274, 278
governesses xvii, 6–8, 23, 27, 28, 47, 50, 181
Governesses' Benevolent Institution 8
Graham, Sir James 129
Granada 195
Grand Remonstrance 260
Greece 178–79, 251
Greek Church 152, 203 (*See* also Orthodox Church)
Greek professorship 275 (*See also* professor)
Greeley, Horace 295
Greg, William Rathbone 57–62
Greytown 284
Guatemala 284
Guizot, Francois 219
Gulf Stream 201
gypsies 66

Hamelin, Vice Admiral Ferdinand-Alphonse 180
Hamlin, Christopher 68
Hamlin, Hannibal 250
Hammerton, A. James 26
Haney, Lewis Henry 90
Hanover, King of (*See* Ernest Augustus)
Harpers Ferry 306, 307
Harriet Martineau: Selected Letters 20, 49
Harriet Martineau's Letters to Fanny Wedgwood 26, 28, 39, 119, 123, 302
Harris, James Howard (*See* Malmesbury, 3rd Earl of)
Harris, Jocelyn 37
Harrison, Brian 76
Hartley, David 130
Harvard University 271, 275
Hauran 241
Hautefort, Madame de 29
health xiv (*See also* invalid)
Health and Morals of Apprentices Act 121
Hebrew music 159
Heidelberg, University of 217, 221, 224
Helper, Hinton Rowan 105
Helsinki 174
Henderson, W. O. 100, 123
Henry VI 116
Henry VII 116
Henry VIII 113
Herat 178
Herbert, Sydney 207–14
Herbert of Lea, 1st Baron (*See* Herbert, Sydney)
heroes xvi, 312
Hibbert, Christopher 177, 190
High Church 154
High Treason 218, 222
Hill, Sir Rowland xiii
Hirst, F. W. 84
Hoban, Mary 8
Holborn Union 40, 45

Index

Holcombe, Lee 26
Holland 118, 120, 181
Holloway 32
Holy Alliance xv, 143
Holy Lands 31, 239 (*See also* Jerusalem)
Holy Roman Emperor (*See* Leopold I)
Home Secretary (*See* Graham, Sir James)
Honduras 288
Honduras, Bay of 284
Honduras Railway 281, 289
Honingmann, E. A. J. 154
hospital (*See also* infirmary)
  military (India) 45
  Village 43
Hospital for Women and Children 24
House of Commons 27, 59, 60, 207, 229
House of Industry 242, 244
House of Lords 59, 193
house of refuge 68
Household Words x, 8
How to Emigrate to the Gold Regions for Ten Shillings 3
Howard, Captain 243
Howarth, O. J. R. 97
Howe, Julia Ward 302
Howe, Mark A. deWolfe 302
Huguenot, French 113
human understanding xiii
Hungary 152, 158, 167, 234, 236
Hunt, Frederick Knight x–xii, xiv
Huntingdon brewer 117
Huntingdonshire 120
Huxley, Thomas Henry 155
hypnotism (*See* mesmerism)

Illinois xv, 85, 251
Illinois Central railroad 83
Illustrated London News xi

immorality xvii
India xiv, 9, 12, 14, 16–17, 39–40, 42, 63, 99–104, 166, 180, 212, 269
Indian (American) 28, 280, 293
Indian mutiny xi–xii
Indian women's education 29 (*See also* education)
Indiana 256
industrial schools 29 (*See also* education)
Industry 22, 23, 60, 99, 102, 117, 123, 135, 257
Infanta Isabella 233
infirmary 45
Inglis, Henry David 169
Inkermann 185, 186
investors, British 89, 90, 239, 282, 291
invalid ix, 63, 69 (*See also* health)
Iphigenia 178
Ireland x, xiv, 3, 75–78, 83, 85, 114, 131, 182, 225, 264
Isabella I 195
Ishmaelites 259
Isle of Serpents (*See* Serpents Island)
Isthmus of Panama xviii, 279–91
Italy 114, 151, 154, 165, 167, 181, 223, 233–37, 274

Jacob 183
Jacob's river 203
Jaffa 243
Jamaica 14–15
James 222, 260
James, Anne 3
James I 116
James II 222, 260
Jameson, Anna 28
Jane 9
Jeffrey 298
Jeffrey, Francis 58, 62, 69

Jerusalem 159, 182, 239–43
Jews 160
"John Bull" 162, 164, 166
Johnson, Andrew 314
Johnson, Samuel A. 248
Johnsonian 71
Journal of the Royal Agricultural Society 114

Kaiser 153
Kalmyks 183
Kansas xiii, 199, 247–53, 258, 267, 270, 290, 304
Kansas-Nebraska Act 255, 260, 313
Kemble, Fanny 295
Kennedy, John Pendleton 297
Kerch Strait 180
Key to Uncle Tom's Cabin, The 300
Kiddle, Margaret 8
King's College Hospital 41
King's Lynn 113, 116
Kingsley, Charles 91
Knapp, Isaac 313
Knights of the Shire 59
Knoll, The 302
Koran 154
Koss, Stephen xx
Kossuth, Louis 160, 167
Kuban River 157

labor xiv (*See also* strikes)
laborers 121–26, 132–35, 137
Ladies' New Anti-slavery Society of Glasgow 11
Lady Visitors 48
Laing, Samuel 169
Lake District xii–xiii, 57
Lambert, Andrew 170
The Land of Promise . . . South Australia 8
Laps 200–02

Law Amendment Association (*See* Society for Promoting the Amendment of the Law)
Lawrence, Amos A. 247
Lawrence, Sir John 45
Lawrence, Kansas 247
Laws Relating to the Property of Married Women (*See* married women's property law)
leaders x, xiii–xix
Lebanon 241
Leipsic 221
Leith 274
Leith road 228
Leopold I, Holy Roman Emperor 183
letters to the editor xiv, 149–53, 254, 301–302, 305, 313
Levant 240, 244
levels 117–20
Lewis, Sir G. 208
Lewis, George Cornewall 62
Lewis, R.A. 68
libel 73, 224, 310
Liberator 277, 307, 309, 310, 312
Liberia 264, 313
Liguria 54
Lincoln, Abraham xv, 254, 301, 302, 305, 314
Lincoln, W. Bruce 146, 160, 167, 175
Lincolnshire 113–19
Lind, Jenny 22
liquor 75–80
literary celebrity ix
Liverpool 11, 12–16, 45, 48, 53, 83, 91, 94, 100
Lombardy 218, 237, *passim*
London ix–xi, 29
London, Brighton and Southcoast railway line 90
London dailies xii

Index

Long Parliament 260
Longfellow, William Wadsworth 36, 261
Louis XIII 26
Louis XIV 195
Louis Napoleon (*See* Napoleon III)
Louisiana xv, 80, 103
Lowe, Robert 130, 137
Lowland Scotch 228
Lundy, Benjamin 315

Macaulay, Thomas Babington 11, 69, 260
McCrone, Kathleen E. 92, 96
McMillan, James F. 237
Macmillan's Magazine x, 17, 49
"Mad Charley" 174
Magyars 160
Mahometanism 152
Maine 76, 78, 80, 250, 251
Maine Liquor Law 76, 79
Maine Temperance Union 76
Malmesbury, 3rd Earl of 283, 291
Malta xv
Malthus, Thomas 3
management (*See* capital)
Manchester 15, 17, 99
Manchester Chamber of Commerce 14, 99, 100
Mani 182
Manichean 179
Mannheim 221, 222
manufacturing xiv, 28, 47, 99–100, 121–26, 129
Marcet, Mrs. 74
Mariendahl 193
married women's property law xvii, 19–25
Maronites 239, 244
marsh xvi, 143 (*See also* fen)
Martineau, Harriet (works)
   Autobiography xix, *passim*
   Biographical Sketches 28, 145, 175
   British Rule in India xi, 16
   "The Czar's Birthday. A Royal Festival in St. Petersburg" 145
   "Death or Life in India" 17
   Deerbrook ix, 68
   Demerara 313
   Eastern Life, Present and Past 31, 182, 239, 302
   Endowed Schools of Ireland 131
   England and Her Soldiers 39, 207
   The Factory Controversy 122
   Feats on the Fiord 169
   "Female Industry" 27
   "Florence Nightingale's Latest Charity" 45
   Harriet Martineau's Autobiography xix, *passim*
   "Health in the Camp" 39
   "Health in the Hospital" 39
   A History of the American Compromises 253, 272
   The History of England during the Thirty Years' Peace x, xiv–xvi, xix, *passim*
   The Hour and the Man 177
   Household Education 130
   Illustrations of Political Economy 108, 313
   Introduction to the History of the Peace 141, 146, 161, 166, 174, 196
   "The Last Sheffield Outrage" 108
   Letters from Ireland x, 81, 182
   letters to the editor xiv, xvii, 149–53

"Lieutenant-General Sir William Napier, K.C.B." 175
"A Manchester Strike" 108
"The Martyr Age of the United States of America" 308
"Metternich and Austria" 166
"Middle-Class Education in England: Boys" 48
"Middle-Class Education in England: Girls" 48
"A Month At Sea" 31
"The Moral of Many Fables" 108
"A New Kind of Wilful Murder" 32
"Nurses Wanted" 45
"Old and New Things for the Hindoo" 16
"On Female Education" 48
"Our Farm of Two Acres" 114
The Playfellow 130, 169
The Positive Philosophy of Auguste Comte 96, 217
Retrospect of Western Travel 31, 272, 302
The Rioters 108
"Sarah Pellat, Florence Nightingale and Temperance" 76
"Secret Organisation of Trades" 108
"The Slave Trade in 1858" 263, 313
Society in America 100, 263, 269, 313
Suggestions towards the Future Government of India xi, 6
The Tendency of Strikes and Sticks to Produce Low Wages 108
Traditions of Palestine 130
"The Training of Nurses" 45
The Turn-Out; or, Patience the Best Policy 108
Two Letters on Cow-Keeping 199
"Women's Battlefield" 45
Martineau, James 20, 57
Martineau, Rachel 48
Martínez, Tomás 285, 292
Maryland 89
Massachusetts xv, 16, 83, 247, 272, 276, 313
Massachusetts Anti-Slavery Society 301, 308
Massachusetts Legislature 24
Maule, Fox (*See* Panmure, 2nd Baron)
Maurice, F. D. 52
Mazeppa 146
Mazzini 218
Medea 182
media event xix
Mediterranean 143, 180, 182, 183, 196, 236
Mendelsohn, Jack 80
mesmerism x, 57
Metcalfe, Rev. Frederick 204–205
Metternich, Prince Klemens von 163
Mexico 102, 192, 265
Mexico City 195
middle class xi, xvii
Middle Level Commissioners 120
Middle Level Sluice 118
Middle States 252
Middlesex 75
midwife-nurses 40–41 (*See also* nursing)
Milan 223, 234

Index

military xiv, xvi, xix, 42, 87, 141–213 *passim*, 233–37, 242–43, 250–52, 255, 258, 269
military hospitals in India 45
militia 195, 207, 212
Mill, John Stuart 255
Mill on the Floss 114
Milnes, Richard Monckton 127, 131, 147, 272
Milton, John 1 50–52
Mingrelia 157, 182
Minister of State xii, 273–74, 283, 286, 287
Missouri 247, 248, 251, 253, 276, 281
Missouri Compromise 268
Mitford, Mary Russell 28
Mithridates VI 180
Mobile Register 292
Mohammedanism 155
Mohawk 243
Moldavia 146, 149, 205
Mongol Empire 190
Mongolia 190
Monroe Doctrine 288
Monteagle, 1st Baron 58
Montebello 237
Montezuma 195
Montgomery 105
Monthly Repository ix, 48
More, Hannah 28
Mormon 293
Morris, R. J. 67
Moscow 90, 181, 277
Moses 311
Moslems 239, 241–43
Mosquito Coast 279, 292
Mount Vernon (George Washington's estate) 271, 276
MP (Member of Parliament) xii, 17, 26, 99, 120, 131
Müller, Max 175

Munich 221
murder 35, 110–11, 145, 306
Murray, John Archibald 62, 69
Muscovite 180
music, Hebrew 159
Music Hall 225, 230
mutiny xi–xii

Napier, Vice Admiral Charles 149, 169, 173, 174
Napier, Lord Francis 290
Napier, Macvey 62
Naples 237
Napoleon I 23, 146, 149, 155, 163, 166, 233, 277
Napoleon III xv, xvi, 20, 38, 61, 161, 223, 237, 238, 239, 291
Napoleonic Wars xv, 279
National Association for the Promotion of Social Science xviii, 128
National Review 20, 21–22
Near East x, xiv
Nebraska territory 280
Necessarian/Positivist xviii
Nelson, Admiral 149
Nene 119
Nergaard, Bea 41
Netherlands 75
neutrality 204, 233, 282, 288
neutrality laws 277, 292
Neva 143, 171, 173
New Caledonia 279, 280
New England 6, 89, 248, 250, 253, 263, 275, 301, 309, 310
New England Anti-Slavery Society 307
New England Female Medical College 24
New Orleans 105, 290, 315
New Orleans *Daily Delta* 266, 267
New South Wales 8

New Testament 177 (*See also* Bible; Gospel)
New York 24, 29, 76, 81, 84, 85, 268, 270, 279, 283, 285, 288, 289, 293, 296, 298, 310
New York–Cincinnati railway route 89
New York *Daily Tribune* 89, 280, 284, 295
New York *Evening Post* 277, 278
New York Herald 313
New York Infirmary for Women and Children 29
New York Times 89, 105, 270, 313
New York Tribune 105, 296, 313
Newburyport 313
Newcastle, Duke of 213
Newcastle 63–68, 91, 136
Newcastle commission 130
Newham College 48
newspapers (U.S.) xii, 263–77
Newtonian 218
Nicaragua 265, 279, 281–83, 288–91 (*See also* Mosquito Coast)
Nicaragua, Lake 284
Nicaraguan ship canal 281
Nice 154
Nicholas, Czar xvi, 141–204 *passim,* 260, 271, 274–75, 277
Niebuhr x
Niger expedition 12
Nightingale, Florence ix, xvii, 23, 35, 39–44, 76, 91, 207–213
Nightingale Fund 28, 39, 43
Nightingale School of Nursing 39, 45
Nile xv, 16, 32
non-conformist ix
Norfolk 113–19
Norris, Rev. J.P. 137
North xii–xiii, *passim*
North America, British 3
North American politics 84

North British Review 58, 61
North Carolina 102, 269
North Sea 119
North Shields 66
Northamptonshire 120
Northern Convention (Russia, Sweden, Denmark, and Prussia) 146
Northwest 277, 284, 293
Norway 169, 196, 200, 201–03, 237
Norwegian Laps 200
Norwich ix, 57, 113
Notes on Nursing 35, 38, 39
nursing 25, 27, 28, 38 39–45, 208

obituaries xiv
Odessa 169
Ohio 85, 297
Olmsted, Frederick Law 105, 265, 269
Omar Pacha 196
Once a Week x, 17, 32, 45, 108, 114, 177
Ordnance 67
Oregon 281
Oriental despotism xvi, 144, 196
Orthodox Church 141, 154, 167, 182, 244
Oscar I, King 200, 202–204, 238
Otis, F. N. 284
Ottoman 285
Ouse 113, 119
Ouseley, Sir William Gore 290
overpopulation 3 (*See also* census)
Owen, Robert 129
Oxford, Bishop of 213
Oxford, University of 47

Pacha 196, 239, 241, 242
Pacific Islands 16
Pacific Ocean 273, 279, 284

Index

Pacific railway 86, 89, 281
Paine, Thomas 239
Palatinate 193
Palestine 141, 146, 177, 240–41
Palmerston, 3rd Viscount xv, 92, 213, 214
Palmyra 244
Panama Railroad 279, 281, 284–85
Panic of the 1820s ix
Panmure, 2nd Baron 210, 211
Paris 25, 29, 38, 163, 179, 193, 223, 274, 275
Paris, peace of 274
Paris, Treaty of 199, 205
Parkes, Bessie Raynor 25
Parliament xvii, 19, 20, 22, 26, 27, 47, 59–60, 75, 79, 81, 83, 87, 91, 104, 117, 119, 121–22, 129–30, 163, 165, 167, 191, 210, 214, 225, 238, 241, 260, 270, 280, 284, 286
Parliamentary reform 225–30
Patmore, Coventry 26
patriarchate 147
Paul I, Czar 143, 145, 256
Pearson, Hesketh 70
peasants, Siloam 242
Pedro V, King 238
Peel, General Jonathan 211, 213
Peelites 149
Pellat, Sarah (*See* Martineau, Harriet [works])
Pennsylvania 85, 256
penny post xiii, 71
Perceval, Spencer 163
"Peregrinus" 8
Persia 157, 180, 182, 183, 199
Personal Laws Committee 26
Peter the Great xvi, 143–45, 174, 179–81, 195
Peterborough 115
Petra (Jordan) xv

Phi Beta Kappa oration 302
Philadelphia 36, 268, 295, 298
Phillips, Wendell 314
Pichanick, Valerie Kossew xix, 131
Pictorial Times xi
Piedmont 154, 237
Pierce, Franklin 254
Pimlico 154
Pisa 224
Pitt, William 162–63, 227
Pius IX, Pope 196, 223
planter 13–14, 17, 101, 104, 264, 269, 297, 299
Plumridge, Rear-Admiral 174
Plutarchian xvi, 149
Poland 146, 157, 160, 183
  boys 157, 175
  military cadets 159, 175
  nobles 175
Polar Sea 174
political economy ix, 73
politics (North American) 84
Pollard, Sydney 108, 111
Pontus (*See* Mithridates VI)
poor law 45
poorhouse (*See* workhouse)
Pope 152, 153, 154, 195, 196, 223, 236, 237
popular sovereignty 255
population (*See* census; overpopulation)
Porte 143, 165
Porter, G. E. 83
Portland, 3rd Duke of 163
Portland (Maine) 76
Portobello xi
Portugal 99, 193, 196, 233, 235, 270
  allies 193
  navigator 279
Positivism 217
postmistress 28

Pottawatomie Creek 247
pottery 122, 124–26, 127
Practical School of Medicine 24
President (U.S.) 250, 251, 255–60, 263–64, 276, 282, 290–91, 292, 312
presidential elections xiv, 255–60
Prest, John 209
Priestley, Joseph 130
Prince Imperial of France 34
principalities 190
professor 24, 28, 49, 220, 224, 275
Professor of Greek Literature 278
progress xi, xiii, xv, xviii, *passim*
pro-hostilities xi
Prometheus 178
property of married women 19–25
proslavery 247–48, 253, 254, 255, 285 (*See also* slave trade; slavery)
Protector 151, 153
Protestant 77, 150, 152, 153, 244
Prussia xiv, 146, 149, 164, 167, 196, 236, 237, 244
Public Health Act of 1848 63, 67
publishing, Victorian x
Puritanism, Calvinistic 75, 81, 264, 307

Quaker 11, 310
Quarterly Review x, 39, 59, 62, 115, 183
Queen's College 52
Quincy 83
Quincy, Josiah 253, 254
Quinn, Vincent 209
Qur'an (*See* Koran)

"Rachel" 22
Radical 217
Raglan, 1st Baron xvi, 177, 190, 191–95

railroads (railways) 8, 83–88, 100, 104, 135, 238, 279, 281, 284, 285, 289
Rathbone, William 45
reactionism xv
reading xi
Reconstruction 314
Red Sea xv
Reeve, Henry 62, 183
reform x, xiv, xvii, xix, *passim*
Reform Bill 59–61, 231
refugee 99
Regency 121
Regina Coeli 263
Reid, Elisabeth Jesser 48
religion (*See* agnostic; Christianity; *and names of individual religions*)
Report of the Children's Employment commissioners 124 (*See also Children's Employment; Factories*)
Report of the Congressional Commission on Kansas 254
Report of the General Board of Health of the Administration of the Public Health Act 68
Report on the Personal Laws Committee . . . on the Laws Relating to the Property of Married Women 26
Reports of the Select Committee of the House of Commons on Public Petitions 27
Representative (U.S. Congress) 247, 272
Representative Government xvi, 144, 223
Republic xviii
Republican 61, 250, 254, 255, 261, 263–64, 292, 306, 314
Restoration 119
Revelation 182

Index

Revised Code 130, 134, 137
Rhine 235
rice 13, 103, 297, 298
Richardson, Samuel 37
Robinson, Henry Crabb 58, 131, 302
Robinson, Sir John xii
Rocky Mountains 284
Roman Catholicism 73, 141, 152, 154, 182, 244, 258
Romania 146, 201, 205
Rome 113, 159, 177, 218, 223
"Rosa-Matilda" 71
Royal Agricultural Society 113
Royal commission 53, 107, 122, 214
Royal commission of 1850 47
Royalists 117
rural laborers (*See* laborers)
Rusk, Ralph L. 302, 306
Ruskin, John 91
Russell, Francis (*See* Bedford, 4th Earl of)
Russell, Lord John 11, 9l, 244, 276
Russell, William Howard xiii, 191
Russia xvi, 28, 86–87, 88, 141–213 *passim*, 208, 240, 271–75, 277, 302
Russian ladies 180
Russian Legation 272
Russian Minister 274

Saardam 181
Saba, Santa 182
Sabaites 179
St. Barnabas 152
St. Bartholomew's Hospital 29
St. Louis 89
St. Petersburg xvi, 90, 145, 146, 169–73, 175, 179, 183, 273, 274, 277
St. Thomas Hospital 39, 40, 44, 45

Sale, George 154
Samsun 156
San Juan del Norte (*See* Greytown)
San Juan River 284
Sanders, Valerie 20, 108–109
Sandgate 64
Sanitary Commissions in India 42
sanitary reform xiv, 39, 63–67, 91, 207–208, 210–12 (*See also* filth)
sanitation 4, 185–87
Saratoga 80
Sardinia 151, 153, 154, 195, 237, 282, 283, 288
Savannah 295–300
savings banks 5
Savoy, Duke of 150
Savoy 154
Saxony 220
Scandinavia 169–74, 196, 199–205 (*See also* Denmark; Finland; Norway; Sweden)
Schamyl xv, 155–56
school
  industrial 29
  Union 45
school inspector 130, 135
Schools Inquiry Commission 47, 49
science ix, 25, 76, 91, 93–94, 96, 113, 117, 118–19, 135, 211, 217, 218–20, 221, 222
Sclavonian (*See* Slavonians)
Scotland xi, 11, 28, 67, 75, 77, 78, 83, 225–30
Scott, John (*See* Eldon, Lord)
Scott, John A. 295, 300
Scott, Sir Walter xviii, 62
Scroggs, William Oscar 285, 291, 292
Scutari 28, 39, 169, 212, 214

Scythian 189
sea serpent 264
seaboard states 265
Seat, William R., Jr. 272
Sebastopol 177, 179, 180, 183, 185–89, 191, 193–94, 207, 214
secession of Southern states xviii, 247, 252, 261
secessionist journals 305
Second Reform Act 225
secret diplomacy 154, 287
Secretary at War (England) 207, 213
Secretary of State
(India) 104
(U.S.) 126, 271, 276, 292
Secretary of State for War (England) 207, 213
Secretary of War (U.S.) 39, 84, 214, 292
Senate (U.S.) 89, 247, 248, 254, 271, 276, 304
Senator (U.S. Congress) 247, 254, 300
Senior, Nassau William 58
Serbo-Croations (*See* Croats; Slavonians)
serf-emancipation 272, 274–75
Serpents Island 205
Seven Churches 179
Seward, William Henry 313
"S.G.O." 133, 136
Shaftesbury, 7th Earl of 4, 11, 91, 92, 131
Shanley, Mary Lyndon 26
Sheffield 31, 107–10
Shields (*See* North Shields)
shipping 146
Short Parliament 260
Shropshire 137
Siberia 175
Sicily 197, 234 (*See also* Two Sicilies)

Sidney, Samuel 8
Siloam peasants 242
Silver, Arthur W. 100
Simferopol 187
Simon, Brian 49, 129, 131
Simpheropol (*See* Simferopol)
Simpson, General James 191
Sinai xv, 179
Sinope 149, 156
Sir Charles Grandison 33
Skagerö 204
Slater, Joseph 302
slave trade xiv, 15, 73, 102–105, 166, 254, 257, 263–69, 295–300, 313
slavery xiii–xiv, xvii, 11, 12–13, 16, 25, 84, 90, 100, 102–105, 109, 155, 247–313 *passim* (*See also* abolitionism; antislavery; proslavery)
Slavonians 154 (*See also* Croats)
Smith, Anne 123
Smith, Barbara Leigh 19
Smith, Francis Barrymore 29, 45, 231
Smith, Sydney 58, 69–73
Snake River 284
Society for the Improvement of the Dwellings of the Labouring Classes 68
Society for Promoting the Amendment of the Law 19, 26
Society for Promoting the Employment of Women 27
Solomon 244
Somerset, Lord Fitzroy (*See* Raglan, 1st Baron)
Somerville, Mrs. 74
South xiii, *passim*
South Carolina 102–104, 247, 258, 265, 298, 300
South Lincolnshire 114

Index 449

South Wales 120
Southampton Insurrection 310
Southampton massacre (*See* Southampton Insurrection)
Southern Commercial Convention 102
Southern Convention (*See* Southern Commercial Convention)
Southern elections 249
Southern Emigration Society 292
Southern ports xiii
Southern States xviii, 100, 104, 264–66, 268, 277, 297
Spain 99, 192, 193, 195, 233, 270, 278, 279, 292
Spanish allies 193
special reports xiv
spirits (liquor) 75–80
Spring-Rice, Thomas (*See* Monteagle, 1st Baron)
Spurgeon, Charles Haddon 34
Squier, Ephraim George 281, 292
Staffordshire 122, 124–26
stamp duty on newspapers xii
Stanley, A.P. 52
Stanley, Edward Henry 101
Stanton, Edwin McMasters
state bonds 69
statistics 68, 114, 211, 266
Staves, Susan 26
Stein (*See* Russian Minister)
Stephen, Barbara 52
Stephen, Leslie 248
Stephenson, Robert 83
Stirling, James 105
Stockholm 170
Stockmar, Baron C.F. von 175
Stockton 83
Stowe, Calvin Ellis 11–15
Stowe, Charles Edward 12
Stowe, Harriet Beecher 11–15, 22, 248, 253, 298

Strangford, Viscountess (*See* Beaufort, Emily Anne)
strikes (labor) 5, 107–08, 136
Stuart (royal family) 227
Sturge, Joseph 11
"Subalpinus" 154
Suffolk 120
sugar 13, 15, 103, 269
Sultan (*See* Turkish Sultan)
Sumner, Charles 247, 254, 276–77, 304
Sunderland 63
Sunny Memories of Foreign Lands 16
Superior, Lake 281
Sutherland, Duchess of 11
swamp (*See* fen; marsh)
Sweden 146, 169, 183, 196, 199–203, 235
Sweetman, John 214
Switzerland 154
Sydney 5
Sylvester, D. W. 1 37
Syria 156, 175, 239–43

Tadmor 241, 244
Tallyrand 163
Tanais River (*See* Don)
Tappan, Arthur 310
Tartar Khan 188
Tartars 160, 179–80, 188
Tatars (*See* Tartars)
Taunton commission 47, 53
Tauric Chersonese 182
Taurica Chersonesus 183
Tauris 180
Taylor, Zachary 260
Tehuantepec, Gulf of 284
temperance 75–80
Temple of the Sun 244
Texas 102, 265, 269
Thailand 37
Theodosia (*See* Feodoysiya)

Thomas, John L. 314
Thomas, Maurice Walton 123
Thompson, George 313
The Times xii–xiii, 247–53, *passim*
tobacco 13
Todd, Francis 313
Tory 62, 161, 166, 223, 227, 230, 233
Training School for Midwife-Nurses 41
treason 218, 222
Tuke, Margaret J. 49
tumor 10
Turgenev, Nikolai Ivanovitch xvi, 271–77
Turkey 156, 201
Turkish Sultan 141, 146, 175
Turner, Nat 313
Tuscany 237
Two Sicilies 197, 237 (*See also* Sicily)
Tynemouth 63, 308

Uncle Tom's Cabin 11, 300
Union Schools 45
Unitarian ix
United Kingdom Alliance 76
United States ix, xii–xiv, xviii, 3, 11–16, 24–25, 36, 39, 69, 73, 75–79, 83–88, 99–104, 109, 159, 247–313 *passim* (*See also* Middle States; New England; seaboard states; Southern States; *and names of individual states*)
utilitarian xiv, 307

Valdes, Pierre 154
Van Why, Joseph S. 16
Venetia xv, 179, 237
Vicinus, Martha 41
Victor Emmanuel, King 237

Victoria, Queen xvi, 28, 36, 38, 149, 163, 200, 204, 230, 231, 244
Victorian publishing x
villains xvi
Virginia 85

Wakefield 32
Wales, Prince of 230
Wales 28
Walker, Thomas xii
Walker, William 265, 282, 289–90
war minister 39
War-office at Washington 39
War-Office Regulations 39
war of opinion xvi–xvii, 233–38
war tension xii
Wardroper, Mrs. E. S. 40
Washington, George xvi, 192–93, 271, 276
Washington, D. C. xiii, 271
Weir, William xi–xii
Wellington, Duke of xvi, 192–95
"W. E. R." 136
West Indies 14, 88, 99
Western Africa 16
western expansionism xiv
Westminster, Dean of (*See* Stanley, A.P.)
Westminster Review x, 20, 21, *passim*
Westminster School 37
Whigs 149, 255 (*See also* conservative-whig)
Whitbread, Charles 136
White, Hayden xviii
White, Rev. Henry 136
William Lloyd Garrison: 1805–1879 . . . His Life Told by His Children 308
Windsor Castle 28

Index

women xiv, xvii, 3–52, 307 (*See also* Russian female; feminist causes)
   Victorian ix
Women's Petition 19–20, 22
Woolwich 212
workhouse 5, 7, 45
working class xi
workingwomen's colleges 27

World's Anti-Slavery Convention 308
World's Temperance Convention 76

York 44
York and Albany, Duke of 209
Young, George Malcolm 49

"Z." 153